S0-ARD-067

THE NICKELODEON
THE GREAT TRAIN ROBBERY
D. W. GRIFFITH
CHARLIE CHAPLIN
THE CABINET OF DR. CALIGARI
THE TALKIES
HOLLYWOOD'S GOLDEN AGE
THE ITALIAN NEO-REALISTS
THE FRENCH NEW WAVE
THE CHALLENGE OF TELEVISION
THE BLACKLIST
THE AUTEUR THEORY
"THE YOUNG TURKS" OF MOVIELAND
THE NEW FILM SCHOOLS
are all part of—

THE LIVELIEST ART

A Panoramic History of the Movies

ARTHUR KNIGHT has been a faculty member of City College of New York, Columbia University, Hunter College, and the New School for Social Research, and is now professor in the cinema department at the University of Southern California. He has long been an active film reviewer, and in addition to his classic, *The Liveliest Art*, he has authored *The Hollywood Style* and *History of Sex in the Movies* (with Hollis Alpert). He lives in Malibu, California.

THE LIVELIEST ART
A Panoramic History of the Movies

REVISED EDITION

by

Arthur Knight

A MENTOR BOOK

NEW AMERICAN LIBRARY

NEW YORK AND SCARBOROUGH, ONTARIO

To Mary Ann

 MENTOR TRADEMARK REG. U.S. PAT. OFF. AND FOREIGN COUNTRIES
REGISTERED TRADEMARK—MARCA REGISTRADA
HECHO EN CHICAGO, U.S.A.

SIGNET, SIGNET CLASSIC, MENTOR, ONYX, PLUME, MERIDIAN AND NAL BOOKS are published *in the United States* by
NAL PENGUIN INC.,
1633 Broadway, New York, New York 10019,
in Canada by The New American Library of Canada Limited,
81 Mack Avenue, Scarborough, Ontario M1L 1M8

First Mentor Printing, July, 1959

First Mentor Printing Revised Edition, March, 1979

18 19 20 21 22 23 24 25 26

PRINTED IN THE UNITED STATES OF AMERICA

sales and training purposes—not to mention the innumerable films created specifically for television—represent rather derivative forms of film making, forms whose techniques were discovered first in fiction or documentary films and eventually were adopted or modified for service in those other fields. Another book may be in order for their *history*; but their *art*, I like to think, has already been recorded in these pages.

While trying to lay out as clearly as possible the main lines in the development of an art that is also an industry, I have also attempted to give some suggestion of the perspectives that lie before us—the inventions and innovations that keep "the liveliest art" lively. In a medium as volatile as this, it isn't easy—and twenty years from now, when there is another new, revised edition, I may well find myself apologizing for a whole new congeries of possibilities that this volume has overlooked. Until then, I can only say that I have enjoyed all of the experiences that have gone into the writing of this book (except perhaps for the writing itself), and trust that at least some of that enjoyment is apparent to the reader—as well as the reasons for it.

Malibu, Calif.,
September, 1978

✦ 1 ✦

An Art Is Born
(1895-1920)

For more than half a century, people all over the world have been going to the movies, drawn by the mysterious fascination of lifelike images appearing on a screen in a darkened room. They go to relax, to enjoy themselves, just as they read books or listen to music. But while books and music are often discussed as art, movies for the most part remain just movies. There is something so casual about seeing a film. Somehow it is too entertaining, too popular to be identified with the arts. And so it has taken root not because of its occasional masterpieces, but because its way of telling a story, of showing life, stirs both the heart and the imagination of the viewer. It is this abiding affection of audiences everywhere for movies as movies which has provided the stimulus to directors, producers and inventors to push forward from the first crude, flickering images to the technical virtuosity and emotional power of the film today. Through eighty years of trial and error, of box-office hits and box-office failures, the novelty of 1895 has slowly been transformed into the art of the 20th century.

The present moment in film history, with its competing cartridges, cassettes and discs and movies by cable, curiously parallels the birth of the motion picture itself. In 1895 a variety of cameras and projectors was introduced almost simultaneously in the United States, in England, France and Germany. They bore such fanciful names as the Kinetoscope, the Vitascope, the Bioscope or Cinématographe, but all produced the same marvelous effects—the black-and-white image of living people who moved and walked in a recognizably real world. In 1929, when talking pictures swept the film industry, again there was a multitude of independent inventions—the Vitaphone, the Movietone, the Cinephone, the Photophone and, in Europe, the Klangfilm. Again, however, they all were working toward an identical goal, this time to reproduce not only the image but the sounds of the world around us.

Throughout the whole history of the motion picture, one finds these mounting waves of technological change that burst over the medium, altering its form and setting new problems for its artists. Indeed, the history of the film is largely an account of directors the world over who, experimenting with the machinery of the inventors, found ways to create entertaining, stimulating pictures for their audiences. Some accepted the medium as they found it, and used it effectively. Some added skill and imagination to make it a more expressive, more affecting art. And some few, the geniuses, perceived within the mechanics of film original ways of handling the camera, fresh methods of combining their shots, new functions for the actor, the settings, the sound track—perceptions that altered the entire course of film creation.

Curiously enough, in their endless pursuit of realism the film makers and the film inventors parallel each other. Sound, color, 3-D, wide screens—indeed, the very invention of the motion picture itself—resulted from the efforts of technicians to enhance the sense of actuality transmitted by the camera. The artists, working with whatever apparatus the inventors had prepared for them at the various stages of the film's development, sought always the reality that lay behind the surface. They discovered first the physical limitations of their medium and then worked out the techniques to go beyond them. Sound was bitterly resented during the first years of its existence precisely because the directors of the silent era had created a rich, subtle and immensely expressive body of techniques that quite overcame the enforced silence. When, in the fifties, we were suddenly presented with a bewildering variety of 'scopes and wide screens, there was the suspicion that the potentialities of the ordinary "postage stamp" screen were far from exhausted.

The artist, however, has no control over the inventor, nor over the technological advances that come into his medium. Often the inventors work alone, outside the industry. Their discoveries are incorporated into the film by the businessmen, the "front office" that must, of necessity, worry less about artistic achievements than financial stability. These executives are well aware that the greatest directorial triumphs are meaningless unless someone comes to see them. They know too that there are times when the industry's stock phrase, "There's nothing wrong with the movies that good pictures can't cure," just does not apply. When the box office began to sag during the mid-twenties, the producers turned frantically to sound. When the depression hit the movies, early in the thirties, color was added (and also double features). When threatened with television, the producers embraced first 3-D, then the wide screens in the theater to eclipse the small screen in the living room.

These, then, are the three points in the triangle of film creation—the inventor, the artist and the businessman. One could scarcely function without the others. But none of them could function without that vast, motley, disorganized throng which, assembled in neat rows in orchestra, mezzanine and balcony, becomes momentarily "the audience." More than in any other art, the artist in film must take his cue from his public, for it is the public that endows the film companies with the hundreds of thousands or even millions of dollars they must spend on each production. He must make pictures that are meaningful and entertaining to vast numbers of people, comprehensible in both theme and technique—popular in the most literal sense of that word. But there is a vast difference between finding a popular response and catering to a least common denominator. It may be going too far to say, with Adolph Zukor, "The public is never wrong"; but the public has been right on so many occasions in the development of the motion picture—recognizing the advances in the art created by D. W. Griffith, discovering star personalities, rejecting the spuriously "arty"—that it is impossible not to recognize the audience's contribution to the dynamics of this development. It was the audience's overwhelming enthusiasm for sound that, in 1929, put a period to the silent film. The reception of Cinerama and CinemaScope in the early fifties forever altered the size and shape of the screen. And the film makers began anew to fill that form with pictures and stories that move us by their power and subtle skill.

The Machine for Seeing Better

Certainly, it was the enthusiasm of the audiences back in 1895, when Edison in America, Lumière in France and Paul in England first threw a moving picture onto a white sheet, that made their novelty something more than an eight-day wonder. To the inventors, the movies were a scientific toy, just one in a long series of devices exploiting the scientific discoveries of the 19th century. To the public, they were a revelation. It was not merely the fact that movement and the shadow of the real world were captured by these machines—that had been done before—but now everything could be seen as large as life and, curiously, even more real. The first audiences sat entranced by such commonplace views as waves dashing to the shore, fire engines racing through the streets, trains drawing into a station, military parades or even people out walking in the sun. But they moved! And they were real! As far as the inventors were concerned, the movies might have remained at that stage—brief one-minute views of the world around us that exploited the novelty of movement. It was the showmen who transformed the novelty into a form of entertainment; and the directors, cameramen and actors, drawn to the medium from all walks of life and all over the world, who transformed it even further from a simple entertainment into an art.

But if the motion picture has by this time come to be accepted into the sisterhood of the established arts, there is no denying that it was always the child of science. Some of its biographers have insisted on tracing its paternity all the way back to the Greeks' discovery of electricity in amber, back to Leonardo's *camera obscura* and Athanasius Kircher's *magia cystera*, and investigating all the remoter branches of its family tree prior to the 19th century. Once Peter Mark Roget (of *Thesaurus* fame) enunciated his theory of "The Persistence of Vision with Regard to Moving Objects" in 1824, however, the advance toward motion pictures and motion-picture projection was rapid and direct. Almost immediately, scientists throughout Europe began putting his theory to the test. Their devices may have resembled children's toys—whirling discs, twirling coins, booklets of pictures flipped with the thumb—but they quickly established the basic truth of Roget's contention that through some peculiarity of the eye an image is retained for a fraction of a second longer than it actually appears.

On this peculiarity rests the fortune of the entire motion-picture industry. Essentially, the motion picture is simply a series of still pictures printed on a long ribbon of celluloid—generally either 8, 16, 35 or 70 millimeters (written "mm") wide. Each picture, halted momentarily, is projected on a white screen, then removed in a flash and another picture substituted. Whether run at sixteen frames per second, as in silent days, or at twenty-four frames per second as required for sound films, enough phases of an action appear on the screen for the eye to make the connection between one picture and the next, and to create the illusion of continuous motion.

Roget announced his theory in London in 1824; and at the very same time in France, Joseph Nicéphore Niepce was groping toward the fundamentals of photography. In 1822 he had succeeded in producing a crude but permanent photograph. Soon after, the famous Louis Daguerre joined him, and the two men continued to experiment until, in 1839, they were able to outline and demonstrate a complete, practical photographic process. Their method was slow and painstaking, necessitating either still life or, if their subject was alive, the metal headclamp and a rigid, motionless pose held for minutes on end. The subsequent introduction, however, first of the wet collodion process and then the gelatin emulsions both speeded up and enormously simplified the taking of pictures—so much so that by 1888 George Eastman was prepared to market his Kodak camera ("You press the button, we do the rest"), bringing photography within the reach of everyone.

Long before there was celluloid for film, however, before photography had developed to the point where it could be used for animation, the parlors of well-to-do Americans and Europeans were adorned with practical demonstrations of Roget's fascinating principle. Perhaps most popular was the Zoëtrope, a slotted revolving drum. As one watched through the slits, hand-drawn clowns or acrobats, horses or dogs seemed to leap through their paces on the strips of paper fitted inside the drum. A simpler device using a similar technique was the Stroboscope, with the figures drawn upon a slotted disc. The image was seen by revolving the disc in front of a mirror and again peeping through the slits. More elaborate was the Praxinoscope of Emil Reynaud. In its center was a ring of little mirrors; a band of images was placed opposite them against the shell of the drum. As the drum revolved, the movement almost flowed from one mirror to the next to create a particularly charming effect. Reynaud was constantly improving his invention. Soon he added a frame and tiny settings, converting the device into a parlor theater. By combining it with the magic lantern, he achieved a form of home projection. By 1889 he was able to enlarge his pictures sufficiently to present them theatrically, and he increased the number of pictures in his bands, mounting them on reels of seven hundred or more separate hand-drawn images. He was to continue with his little Praxinoscope Theater until driven out of business by the rival movies early in the next century.

In all of these devices, of course, the pictures with their tiny phases of movement were drawn by hand. They are, in fact, the precursors of today's animated films, of *Mickey Mouse* and *The Flintstones*. No sooner had photography become practicable, however, than it was applied to animation. How much simpler to capture motion with the camera! Although at first each photograph had to be made separately in a sequence of specially posed shots, when such pictures were mounted in their proper order the effect of movement was quite satisfactory. As early as 1861 Coleman Sellers, of Philadelphia, patented a Kinematoscope in which a series of six such photographs were mounted on a paddlewheel and rotated before the individual viewer to create the illusion of movement. Less then ten years later, Henry R. Heyl was projecting similar photographs onto a screen in Philadelphia's Academy of Music for an audience of 1,600 people. He called his device the Phantasmatrope. And in 1877 Eadweard Muybridge and John D. Isaacs used a battery of twenty-four cameras in sequence to photograph Leland Stanford's race horse in motion. In Paris, Meissonier, the great painter of horses, arranged for a projection of these pictures on yet another device, the Zoöpraxinoscope.

With photography and projection already linked together, the next great problem was to create a camera that would take pictures faster than the ordinary still cameras. Perhaps the first successful step in this direction came in France in 1882 when Dr. E. J. Marey, a physician and physiologist studying the nature of movement, developed a sort of "photographic gun"—a rifle that shot a series of pictures upon a revolving drum set into its chamber. Out of this experiment he evolved during the next decade a series of clumsy but original and practical cameras. Other men, scientists and inventors alike, were challenged by the problem of the camera. In England there was the strange, controversial William Friese-Green, hero of the film *The Magic Box* (1952), who according to some single-handedly solved the problems both of photographing and of projecting motion-picture film. There was the mysterious Frenchman, Louis Leprince, who disappeared from the Dijon-Paris Express in 1890, taking with him the designs for a camera that used strips of perforated celluloid as film.

But the most telling contributions to the development of a motion-picture camera unquestionably came from Thomas Edison and his talented assistant, William Kennedy Laurie Dickson. In 1888, after more than a decade of experiment, Edison produced the phonograph, an instrument for recording and playing back sound on wax cylinders. He had already seen the motion photographs of Muybridge, and the idea of combining moving pictures with sound seems to have been in his mind even before the perfected phonograph was offered to the public. In fact, his first efforts in this direction consisted of a strip of small photographs wrapped spirally about just such a cylinder. "Everything should come out of one hole," Edison maintained. When this failed, Edison turned the project over to Dickson—and with it a new film base developed by George Eastman, thin strips of clear, supple, strong celluloid coated with a photographic emulsion. The film began arriving in August of 1889. It was Dickson who solved the mechanical problem of moving it through the camera, devising the sprocket system that is still standard on 35mm film today. Indeed, this ingenious man even managed to link up the pictures with the phonograph, demonstrating the Kinetoscope to his employer on October 6, 1889, with a brief film in which Dickson both appeared and spoke. What was in all probability the first actual presentation of a motion-picture film also marked the debut of the talkies!

Edison's earliest efforts, however, were not directed toward movie projection. He had had considerable success with his penny-in-the-slot phonographs, and it was his opinion that a similar device, offering a brief picture at a penny a look, would ensure a steady profit for his invention. The Kinetoscope was a peep show in which ran a continuous loop of film about 50 feet long. For the moment the sound aspects were ignored as Edison and his crew concentrated on supplying little one-minute subjects for these machines—photographed in the "Black Maria," the world's first film studio, which he built near his West Orange laboratories in 1893. By the fall of 1894, peep-show parlors had sprouted all over the United States and soon appeared in Europe as well. Curiously enough, the inventor seems to have had little confidence in the long-range possibilities of his machine. When in 1891 he took out patents on his battery-driven camera and Kinetoscope, he neglected to pay the additional $150 that would have secured him an international copyright. Within the next few years he was to regret this oversight. In England, Robert W. Paul copied the Edison Kinetoscope and also produced a hand-cranked portable camera. (Edison's first camera had the general shape and weight of a small upright piano.) In France the Lumière brothers, Louis and Auguste, saw the Kinetoscope and promptly invented their own Cinématographe, a machine that not only took pictures but could also print and project them as well. In Berlin, Max and Emil Skladanowsky, also inspired by the Edison novelty, produced their Bioskop. These machines were soon to become a serious threat to Edison's market within the United States.

Thus, within fifty years of Roget's presentation of his theory, the theory had not only been recognized but its principle had been incorporated into various forms of entertainment. Animation, photography, projection—each was an indispensable step toward the final emergence of the movies. Significantly, none of these steps was taken in any single country. Roget read his paper before the Royal Society in London. Faraday in England, von Stampfer in Austria, Plateau in Belgium all experimented with the idea, producing the various toys and devices that incorporated its principle. Uchatius, who first projected painted pictures, was a Viennese; Désvignes, inventor of the popular toy Zoëtrope, lived in Paris. Both Sellers and Heyl were Americans. Photography, developed in France, was carried forward by Talbot in England and, immeasurably, by George Eastman in this country. There were no secrets, and everything was pointing in one direction—the projection of moving pictures upon a large screen. It should come as no surprise, then, to discover that the movies were actually invented almost simultaneously in

France, England, Germany and the United States. The only wonder is that film historians so often seek to establish priority for the inventors of their own countries, resorting to such dubious phrases as "first accredited showing," "first scientific demonstration" or "first public presentation" to bolster their claims. How much better to recognize the indisputable fact that from the very outset the movies were international, that within a single year films were being projected in New York, London, Berlin, Brussels and Paris.

Once the Europeans had grasped the principles behind Edison's Kinetoscope, they moved directly toward projecting their pictures on a large screen. In the United States too, other inventors—Eugene Lauste, the Lathams, Jean Le Roy, Thomas Armat and F. Charles Jenkins—were also building machines that would project the Edison Kinetoscope reels. Throughout 1895 there were demonstrations of their equipment in New York, Boston, Chicago, Norfolk and Atlanta. Only Edison held back. When, somewhat belatedly, he finally turned to the problems of projection, he borrowed freely (as bitter law suits subsequently revealed) from the discoveries of Le Roy and Latham, and joined forces with Armat, whose Vitascope incorporated the essential Maltese Cross movement to hold the film strip momentarily at rest in the aperture of the projector. Even so, not until April 23, 1896, was Edison prepared to present his projecting Kinetoscope to the public. The presentation took place during the vaudeville program at Koster & Bial's Music Hall, 34th Street and Broadway, the present site of the Macy store. A few months later the American Biograph, Edison's keenest rival, made its debut at Hammerstein's Olympia Music Hall. Within the year, movies were being seen in virtually every large city throughout the United States and Europe.

There is an odd and at the same time important observation to be made about the first films from the two continents. In Europe, Lumière, Pathé, Gaumont and the others delighted primarily in movement for its own sake. Anything that moved was grist for their photographic mills—a laborer felling a wall, workers leaving a factory, baby eating breakfast in the garden. As their cameramen wandered ever farther afield, they took views of ordinary street scenes, of native dances and military parades wherever they happened to be. The early European film catalogues are crowded with *actualités* and brief *documentaires*, none of them running over a minute in length, which reflected this intense interest in the world around them. In America, on the other hand, the actualities were apt to be of a more sensational sort—the Empire or Black Diamond Express rounding a bend and pounding down the track toward the camera, prize fights, cockfights, Professor Sandow flexing his muscles or Annie Oakley shooting clay pigeons. Even greater emphasis was placed on bits of staged business—vaudeville and circus turns, glimpses from plays, novelty acts by dancers, jugglers and acrobats. Much of the shooting was actually done in studios such as the "Black Maria," or on the improvised stages that had begun to sprout on rooftops all over New York. In America, at least, the film was firmly linked to a theatrical tradition from the very outset.

The Theater Sets the Stage

The importance of this theatrical tradition has too often been ignored in tracing the pre-screen history of the film. As Nicholas Vardac has emphasized in his book *Stage to Screen*, the theater of the 19th century, both in this country and in England, did much to create what might be termed a "climate of acceptance" for the movies when they finally did appear. Both in choice of themes and in manner of staging—an emphasis on melodrama, a leaning toward realism—the theater was preparing its audiences for precisely the sort of thing that movies could do better.

The 19th century, in literature, poetry, music and the drama, was an age of unbridled romanticism of spirit combined with a passionate insistence on realism of detail. Perhaps in the theater more than anywhere else this strange and unlikely coupling was most clearly visible. Playwrights might fly to the past, producers might devise elaborate and fanciful pantomimes laid in distant or imaginary lands, but for these to be successful on the stage the scenic designer had to create a palpable, realistic setting. The conventions of an earlier day were simply no longer adequate. The bosky dell painted on a canvas backdrop and framed by flats or cutouts at the wings, the truncated triangle that served for interiors, gradually gave way to heavier pieces—papier-mâché mountains and trees, elaborately designed box sets for interiors and increased emphasis on such purely mechanical devices as trap doors, elevator lifts and treadmills. The movement toward pictorial realism in the theater, begun in the late 18th century by David Garrick, was projected into the new century by such actor-managers as John Philip Kemble, Charles Macready, Edmund Kean and Edwin Forrest. It reached its apogee in the spectacles and melodramas that crowded the boards during the last half of the 19th century—in the productions of Henry Irving and the Bancrofts in England, and more especially in the work of Steele MacKaye, Augustin Daly and David Belasco in this country. MacKaye, both as dramatist and producer, thought solely in terms of strongly realistic, eye-filling spectacle. One of his plays had as its climax a fight on a drawbridge swung high over the heads of the audience. In another, an entire mining town was swept away by a cyclone. His theater provided a true preview of today's multi-million-dollar movie. Belasco produced a gigantic *Passion Play* with a cast including 400 men, women and children, 200 singers and "a flock of real sheep."

This passion for realism, this urge toward size characterized the theater of the late 19th century. *Uncle Tom's Cabin*, the melodramas of Dion Boucicault, adaptations of the novels of Dickens and Victor Hugo were not only extremely popular, but also owed no small part of their popularity to the lavish effects incorporated into their staging. And, to maintain that popularity, the scenery grew heavier and heavier as productions grew more and more elaborate. Treadmills, tanks, trap doors, moving platforms became part of the equipment essential to any well appointed theater.

Although this was all very well for the big cities, where productions were mounted on huge stages fully equipped to handle such spectacular effects, the theater of that period was not confined to a few fortunate centers as it is today. It spread throughout the country; and the road companies of a successful play could spend years traveling from city to city, from town to village. For a really big hit, there might be as many as half a dozen companies working out of New York, Chicago, New Orleans and San Francisco. One night they would appear at a civic center, another evening at a small-town opera house and perhaps the next night in a school auditorium thirty or forty miles away. Naturally, few of these stages had the facilities to fly a heavy show—and even if they did few companies could afford to carry along all the props, scenery and paraphernalia that marked the original big-city production. Not infrequently, a road-company Eliza crossed the ice against a painted river backdrop framed by flies suggesting a palace interior. In short, simplified, makeshift productions had to be worked out for the tours, versions that would fit readily into the limited facilities of most small-town theaters. It meant a reversion to an earlier style of theater, a reversion to scenery that was obviously paint, cutouts instead of solid set pieces, papier-mâché props.

And the inevitable happened. Once audiences had seen a proper production of a Steele MacKaye spectacle, they were no longer satisfied with the road-company facsimiles. Once they had traveled to the big cities and seen *Ben Hur* with three horses to each chariot, they could scarcely be content with the one-horse versions that turned up at their local opera houses. And the ones who didn't get to the big cities, those who remained at home and listened while their friends described the wonders they had seen—they were probably even more dissatisfied. Their imaginations created a richness of detail that no stage could ever hope to match. Thus, throughout the 19th century the theater was unwittingly preparing the public for movies in two important ways: by emphasizing realism and spectacle, and by underlining the inadequacy of most houses to supply them.

At this point the movies made their bow, achieving so readily, so naturally the kind of effects that theater managers could only dream of. Obviously, this did not mean the end of the theater. Indeed, we find in the early years of the 20th century that the producers in the big cities began to outdo themselves, trying to cram even more spectacle and greater realism onto the stage than ever before. Such plays as *Ben Hur, The Light That Failed, Ramona* and *Judith of Bethulia* were all huge, heavily mounted, prodigally populated pageants, filled with theatrical devices intended to thrill their audiences. Appearing only a few years after the introduction of the film, however, the very illusion of reality that they sought most ingeniously to create on the stage was what the critics attacked most vehemently. Singling out the chariot race from *Ben Hur* as an example, one critic wrote in 1899, "The only way to secure the exact sense of action for this incident in a theater is to represent it by Mr. Edison's invention."

Gradually, the producers began to forsake spectacular spectacles for a somewhat less vast and more detailed realism in their dramas, melodramas and comedies. Belasco reproduced a section of a Childs Restaurant for a scene in his production of *The Governor's Lady*. For the second act of *Brewster's Millions* the entire midships of a yacht was created on the stage, complete with mast, flapping sails and steam whistle; or, for another production, a butcher shop right down to fresh, bleeding carcasses of beef. Even so, audiences that patronized the theater primarily for its visual effects contined to desert to the new medium—and especially in the smaller cities. By the twenties the theater had bowed to the inevitable, turning to expressionism or impressionism to reinforce the mood of the play. In the field of realism, the upstart movies had won hands down.

Even the crudest, most rudimentary early pictures reflect this superiority. *Mary Stuart*, a popular stage drama of the 1880's, reached its climax, naturally enough, as the headsman lowered his ax on Mary's neck. Out of consideration for the actress playing Mary, the curtain was customarily lowered somewhat faster. One of Edison's first Kinetoscope subjects was *The Execution of Mary, Queen of Scots* (1893). This little film, running just under a minute, begins as Mary approaches the chopping block. She kneels, the headsman swings his ax—and the audience is rewarded with the edifying spectacle of Mary's head rolling in the dust! At the crucial moment, of course, the film was stopped in the camera and a dummy substituted for Mary; but the gruesome bit of action continues on the screen without interruption. When the great Joseph Jefferson consented to do scenes from his stage success *Rip Van Winkle* for the Biograph camera in 1896, his theater performance was photographed in a real forest. This difference between stage and screen is perhaps best pointed up in the popular *May Irwin-John C. Rice Kiss* (1896), a scene from the play *The Widow Jones*. Its few moments of magnified osculation resulted in the first scandalized attempt at film censorship. The "kiss" may have been harmless enough in the theater, but seen in full close-up it suddenly became so much more "real."

It was this element of reality that captured for film its first audiences, the novelty of seeing real things in motion. And there is no doubting that they accepted the flat, flickering images as reality. When locomotives thundered down the track, when waves rolled toward the camera, people in the front rows ran screaming for the exits. Soon, however—all too soon—the novelty began to wear thin. The incessant parades, the street scenes, the acrobats, the butterfly dancers and the onrushing trains lost their appeal. The film could make things move, but then what? By the turn of the century, Mr. Edison's invention—along with the Bioscope, the Cinématographe and the Vitascope—had been relegated to the position of "chaser" on the vaudeville bills, the act that would clear out the theater for the next show. They became the last stop in the tour of the wax museums and the penny-arcades. Other means had to be found to interest audiences. One showman thought he could solve the problem in a purely mechanical way, installing his projector at the far end of a rocking railway coach and presenting scenic views taken from a moving train. These *Hale's Tours* became a craze, somewhat like miniature golf, and made a fortune for their entrepreneur—but they lasted only a few years. Other movie makers, like J. Stuart Blackton and Albert Smith of the enterprising Vitagraph Corporation, suspected that headline news might bolster interest in the movies. The Boer and the Spanish-American wars afforded Smith a splendid opportunity to test this theory; and an event that he couldn't cover as an eyewitness reporter, like the sinking of the *Maine*, he staged in a bathtub! Still the public's enthusiasm for pictures continued to wane.

Dawn of the Narrative Film: Méliès and Porter

What finally saved the movies was the introduction of narrative. In France, Georges Méliès, a professional magician who early became intrigued with the movie camera, was soon combining his magic tricks with pantomimed stories. His *Cinderella* (1900), *Red Riding Hood* (1901) and *Bluebeard* (1901), and above all his celebrated *A Trip to the Moon* (1902), antedated our own *The Great Train Robbery* (1903) in demonstrating the narrative powers of the new medium. In September of 1899 he filmed an extended account of *L'Affaire Dreyfus*, following it with such serious works as *Jeanne d'Arc* (1900), *The Eruption of Mont-Pelé* (1902) and *The Coronation of Edward VII* (1902), all of them created in his fabulous glass-enclosed little studio on the outskirts of Paris. In these and hundreds of others Méliès, always the magician at heart, exploited not only the narrative but also the trick possibilities of the motion-picture camera. He quickly learned how to stop it in the middle of a scene and create miraculous appearances, disappearances and transformations. He mastered the techniques of double exposure and superimposition, producing truly extraordinary effects. A painter as well, he often designed settings that were triumphs of ingenuity, suggesting through forced perspective great vistas despite his tiny stage. He was without question the movies' first creative artist.

But Méliès, like so many of his contemporaries, remained chained to the traditions of the theater. In his hands the camera was made to perform wonderful tricks, but they were tricks ingeniously prepared for it on his specially equipped stage. In *A Trip to the Moon,* for example, to create the effect of the rocket ship en route, Méliès hauled a papier-mâché model of the moon up an elaborately constructed ramp toward the camera, instead of moving his camera toward the object, as would be done today. It was as if the camera were the sole spectator at an elaborate pageant or play, occupying the choicest seat in the house but never budging from that seat. Everything happens in his films just about as it would on the stage. The actors come on the scene either from the rear or from the wings. Action is arranged horizontally across the stage. Even his trick of merging one scene into the next Méliès adapted from existing stage techniques, making each scene appear to grow out of the last by cranking the film back a few feet and shooting the start of the new scene over the ending of the old. This device, known as the "dissolve," was quickly accepted by audiences as a movie convention, one that persists to this day.

The films of George Méliès—witty, inventive, filled with exuberant activity and fantastic imagination—were widely seen in this country through the first decade of the new century, and played an important part in convincing American producers that pictures could and should be longer than the conventional fifty feet (about one minute on the screen). Unfortunately, such showings were rarely to Méliès's financial advantage. In those days films were not rented but sold outright by the foot. Anyone with a print, of course, could strike off a new negative for a few dollars and sell "dupe" prints at far less than the original producer could afford. This practice, known as "pirating," persisted until authorized film rental exchanges were set up—but by that time Méliès had been driven out of business. He was found, years later, tend-

ing a news-stand in the Paris Métro, and died in 1938 in a
home for destitute actors.

The sharp business practices of the era, however, were not
the sole cause of Méliès failure. In 1903 a film appeared that
was to revolutionize all movie making, breaking decisively
with stage forms and stage techniques and pointing toward a
genuinely filmic style. *The Great Train Robbery* by Edwin S.
Porter, one of America's pioneer director-photographers, revealed for the first time the function and the power of the cut
in telling a story on the screen. Closely related to the chases
and gun fights of the touring "Wild West" shows at the turn
of the century, it tells of a mail train holdup by armed des-
perados, the formation of a posse and the pursuit and anni-
hilation of the gunmen—all in about eight minutes of film.
Each scene, taken from a single camera position, is complete
in itself and advances the action one step further. Once a
scene has been completed, however, Porter makes a flat cut
to the next shot without titles, without dissolves or anything
but the logic of the story to bridge the gap. Nor does the sequence of his scenes necessarily follow in strict chronological
progression, as it had in all films up to that time. We see the
robbers enter the station, bind and gag the telepragh operator, then steal aboard the train, all in the proper sequence. But
after they have held up the train and made their getaway,
Porter switches back to the unfortunate operator just as he is
discovered by his little daughter at the station. The two lines
of action are taking place simultaneously—the robbers escaping, their crime discovered. Porter, boldly juggling with
time, here demonstrated the possibilities of parallel editing,
the concept that D. W. Griffith was to develop so dramatically a few years later. At another point, the action seems to
leapfrog, jumping from the holdup on the train to the formation of the posse and then back to the gang making its escape. Again the scenes are given meaning and coherence by
the editing process, the cutting that brings them together and
relates them one to the other. In short, the technique that
Porter had hit upon in assembling this unpretentious little
Western provided the key to the whole art of film editing, the
joining together of bits of film shot in different places and at
different times to form a single, unified narrative—a principle
that Méliès, with his theater background, was never able to
grasp.

No less important to the success of *The Great Train Robbery* was its freshness of camera placement. Perhaps one reason for this was its preponderance of outdoor scenes. All of its interiors—the opening scene in the telegraph operator's office, the robbery in the mail car, the "Western" high jinks in the dance hall—were filmed as if they were scenes from a play, with the camera once more the well-placed observer. But as soon as Porter moved his camera away from the studio stage, where all the action could be controlled, he was forced to use set-ups that cut into the scene at an angle, that brought the camera closer to the actors, that required the actors to enter from behind the camera or exit toward it. To keep his horsemen on the screen, he had to swing or "pan" the camera at times. At one point, when the robbers are scrambing down a wooded slope, he tilts the camera downward to follow them. As a final fillip, Porter had a huge close-up of one of the cowboys firing his pistol directly at the camera. "The resulting excitement is great," announced the Edison catalogue of 1904. "This scene can be used to begin or end the picture."

Apparently Porter himself only dimly understood at first the full implications of *The Great Train Robbery*. Soon after, in bringing *Uncle Tom's Cabin* (1903) to the screen, he reverted to the theatrical style of animated tableaux set against painted, two-dimensional settings. It suggests how forcibly the director had been carried along by the logic of his story in *The Great Train Robbery*—and by the fact that he was working out of doors. But the success of this film was too overwhelming to be long ignored. It established the single reel as the standard length for American films (between eight and twelve minutes of film). It set both the fashion and the pattern for Western films. And it inspired other directors to join Porter in exploring the implications of his disjunctive style of editing, his free juggling of time and space. They increased the number of scenes in their little dramas. Their cameras were no longer confined to the studio: scenes taken on location were combined with shots staged against painted sets. And all were assembled and given their final form at the cutting bench, generally by the director himself. As these little stories began to reach the screen, interest in the movies revived throughout the world. In this country, nickelodeons and store shows sprang up in almost every neighborhood. Overnight the movies became the poor man's theater.

Toward an International Film

The demand for these new entertainments was tremendous. To fill it, the movie theaters found it necessary to change their bills every day—and sometimes even twice a day. In their rapidly expanding market, the original pioneer companies soon found themselves competing with dozens of fly-by-night producers with bootleg cameras and evanescent studios. The competition stiffened even further as the leading European producers—Méliès, Pathé, Gaumont from France, England's aggressive Urban Trading Company, the Scandinavian Great Northern, the Italian Itala and Ambrosio—all opened American offices to market their own films. There was no question of showing foreign movies in an "art house" in those days. The titles were simply translated into English (there rarely were subtitles), and they went into the common hopper, turning up on nickelodeon screens cheek by jowl with native productions. Thus, new developments in one country were soon seen and absorbed by the film makers here; while our own pictures, sent abroad in precisely the same way, unquestionably influenced profoundly the European producers. It is not presumptuous to assume that because of this intensive international trade at the dawn of motion-picture techniques an American movie today can be enjoyed in Japan, a Russian film in France and an Italian picture in Scandinavia. Whatever their difference in national temperament, they all spring from a common root of shared discovery and invention. Because the cinematic shorthand of the movies—the way in which a film is put together—remains just about the same all over the world, even a talking picture can provide a purely visual excitement although character relationships and motivations may be obscure.

That this interchange of styles and techniques was neither mystic nor unconscious is readily evidenced by a study of the films of the first decade of this century. Plagiarism of film ideas was rampant. No sooner had a producer released a successful picture, one that proved popular with the audiences, than half a dozen other versions of the same novelty were likely to appear from as many different studios. There can be no doubt that the directors had seen the original version of the films they copied, for not infrequently the special effect or trick that had distinguished the original turned up in the copies as well. Thus, the trick films of George Méliès were being imitated by G. A. Smith in England as early as September of 1898, followed by a long series of trick films by Robert Paul beginning in 1899 or early 1900. The popularity of these pictures inevitably produced a school of imitators in this country—led by no less a figure than Edwin S. Porter. In films like *How Jones Lost His Roll* (1905) and *The Dream of a Rarebit Fiend* (1906), he skillfully combined the tricks suggested by the Europeans with home-grown comedy situations. Similarly, the startling financial success of *The Great Train Robbery* caused others to study Porter's own techniques. By 1905 we find them already absorbed, and used proficiently, in such English pictures as Cecil Hepworth's *Rescued by Rover* as well as in most contemporary American films. In effect, it was the audience that dictated which themes, which forms, which techniques the film makers might most profitably follow up.

In France it was the early chase films and trick films that proved most popular. As pictures grew longer—stretching from one minute to ten—these merged into the mad, completely Gallic little farces of men like Ferdinand Zecca, Emile Cohl and Jean Durand. Their construction could not be simpler. Some incident—pumpkins rolling off a wagon, or merely a pretty girl walking down a street—gets a chase under way and then, with incredible inventiveness, complication is piled on complication, camera trick on camera trick, gag on gag until, with a final flourish, everything is righted again and life goes on as unruffled as before. The progress of such films as Zecca's *Slippery Jim* (c.1906) or Cohl's *The Pumpkin Race* (1907) is completely straightforward, adding incident to incident without recourse to Porter's more elaborate (and essentially more cinematic) construction. But, shot generally on the streets of Paris, they possessed a superb momentum of their own—and an inspired experimentation with the camera itself. All its resources were explored—fast motion, slow motion, stop motion, reversing the film, superimpositions and ghost effects, comic appearances and disappearnces—and always with a lively disregard for the laws of nature and man. It was these comedies that made such an impression on the youthful Mack Sennett and, as he has frankly stated, provided the inspiration for much of his own work as Master of the Revels at Keystone.

By 1910 the international trade in motion pictures had become firmly established, with the Europeans selling in direct competition with the American producers at the going rate of twelve cents per foot (extra if colored—by hand!). Denmark sent a number of somber, starkly lit dramas that impressed, among others, D. W. Griffith. Italy began to contribute its early one-reel spectacle films—rather tacky as spectacles, one finds on re-examination, but drawn from such respectable sources as history or the Bible and filled with crowd scenes and wildly gesticulating actors. A German film industry was still several years away, but Oskar Messter's slightly porno-graphic comedies were already being imported into the United States. It was, however, the French film that domi-nated the screens of the world during the first ten years of the new century, a domination secured through Méliès's delight-ful fantasies, through the comic trick and chase films, through elaborate and dramatic historical reconstructions and, after 1907, the Film d'Art.

. . The First Film d'Art

There have always been those who have sought, whether rightly or wrongly, to combine entertainment with uplift. In France in 1907 a company known as Film d'Art was formed for the express purpose of introducing to lowly cinema audi-ences the greatest artists of the French national theater in a repertory of great plays. Undoubtedly these people were well meaning. They certainly never stinted in their efforts to ob-tain the best. They brought before the camera Sarah Bernhardt, Mme. Réjane, Max Dearly and virtually the entire company of the Comédie Française. Ballet was also part of their plan, and dances were filmed with Regina Badet, Trouhanova and La Belle Otero. Stories were drawn from the works of Sardou, Anatole France, Victor Hugo and Edmond Rostand and eventually came to include such standard rep-ertory pieces as *Phèdre, The Red Robe, Tosca* and even *Werther*. The music to accompany their first film, *The Assassination of the Duc de Guise* (1908), was by no less a composer than Camille Saint-Saëns. Unfortunately, these high ideals never produced a real movie. The actors mouthed their lines even though the films were silent. Their accompanying gestures were those they used on the stage, unmodified for the more intimate camera. The scenery, far richer and more elaborate than that customarily found in any movie studio at the time, was still exposed by the camera for precisely what it was—lath and canvas. Most telling of all, the directors of the Film d'Art, Charles Le Bargy and André Calmettes, had also been imported from the theater. They neither sensed nor cared that their pictures, like those of Méliès, were already out of date. They were bringing culture to the masses—and they expected the masses to be both respectful and grateful for this largesse.

In one respect the sponsors of Film d'Art had an unanticipated success. The masses, suspicious of the whole thing, stayed away in droves; but people who would never have dreamed of going to the nickelodeons to see a cowboy picture, a tear-stained melodrama or a slapstick comedy, somehow felt that movies must be all right if they showed you the classics. For the first time the "right people" began to venture gingerly into the dark, grubby little theaters to see these new, "artistic" films. And, inevitably, the film makers in America, Italy, Germany and England began to follow this new lead. American producers were soon filming Shakespeare in vast quantities—the whole of *Hamlet* in a hectic ten minutes! The Italians intensified their already pronounced predilection for pageant-like pictures based on their historic past. German actors became interested in the disreputable movie business and began to appear in suitably artistic productions. The English turned to both Shakespeare and Dickens for inspiration. Such pictures may have had far less to do with the true art of the film than the primitive *Great Train Robbery;* but they did raise the question of whether melodrama and low comedy were the only materials proper to the motion-picture screen. They conferred a certain begrudging, even misguided, prestige upon the movies. And, perhaps most important of all in the long run, they preserved for us a first-hand document of the theater at the turn of the century.

One further effect of these ambitious Film d'Art productions was to help push the motion picture in this country beyond its single-reel length. In 1912 the great Sarah Bernhardt made a film version of her play *Queen Elizabeth* for Film d'Art in four reels. In Italy at the same time *Quo Vadis?* was being readied in eight reels—almost two hours on the screen. In America, on the other hand, film lengths had been arbitrarily frozen at one reel. It was the Motion Picture Patents Company that decided no audience would sit through a movie running longer than about ten minutes, and thus established the single reel as the length for all its films. Composed of the largest producers and distributors in the United States, it sought to control through its pooling of patents every phase of the infant industry. And between 1909 and 1912 its word was law. A Trust in the full Rooseveltian sense, it licensed both cameras and projectors—the cameras solely to its own members, the projectors to those theater men who would agree to purchase only films produced by the member companies. In addition to limiting the length of its movies, the Patents Company also blocked the identification of actors appearing in their films, fearing that they might demand more money if they became well known. Firm believers in the *status quo*, the members of the Trust waged a constant, and frequently bloody, battle with the independents who kept turning up with foreign cameras and fresh ideas.

One of these independents was Adolph Zukor, a young man who, scarcely a decade earlier, had quit the fur business for the penny arcades. He had purchased the American rights to *Queen Elizabeth*, feeling that the time was ripe for longer pictures. Zukor waited long weeks to speak to the Trust officials, to persuade them that Sarah Bernhardt in *Queen Elizabeth* was an attraction most audiences would gladly watch through four full reels. He never got past the gates. Blocked from authorized distribution, Zukor looked outside the normal channels, away from the nickelodeons and store shows. Instead, he convinced one of the leading impresarios of the New York theater, Daniel Frohman, that even on celluloid Sarah Bernhardt deserved a legitimate showcase; and on July 12, 1912, at the Lyceum Theatre, Americans saw their first feature-length film—and paid the unprecedented sum of $1.00 a ticket. No one seemed unduly upset by the fact that the divine Sarah could only be seen, and not heard. The presentation proved an enormous success throughout the country, and led directly to Zukor's formation of "Famous Players in Famous Plays," the ancestor of the present-day Paramount Pictures. As for Sarah Bernhardt, "This is my one chance of immortality," she said when invited, at 65, to film *Camille* and *Elizabeth*.

The Father of Film Technique: D. W. Griffith

A few years before Bernhardt sought immortality on celluloid, a young stage actor reluctantly consented to appear before the camera—and then only out of direst necessity. "Lawrence" Griffith had spent a decade barnstorming through the United States, more often than not with shows that folded on the road. He had tried his hand at playwriting, at poetry and, when all else failed, had sold subscriptions to magazines, picked hops in the fields, worked on ships and construction jobs. Christened David Wark, the fifth child of an impoverished Confederate colonel, Griffith chose to preserve his real name for the success he felt certain would one day come to him. It was as "Lawrence" that he approached Edwin S. Porter at the Edison Studio in the Bronx with his screen adaptation of Sardou's *Tosca*. Porter rejected the script, but offered Griffith the leading role in a film he was just about to start, *Rescued from an Eagle's Nest* (1907). This was an era in which actors from the legitimate stage viewed the movies with the utmost scorn, and felt that to perform in them was degrading. But Griffith, newly married, needed the money badly. He consented to play in it, at $5 a day. A few months later, armed with more scripts he turned up at the Biograph Studio at 11 East 14th Street, New York City. He not only sold a few, but again was invited to act. Again, presumably, necessity forced his hand; but within a few months Griffith had become a fixture at Biograph and his wife, Linda Arvidson, had also joined the little company. Griffith, however, was still "Lawrence."

What happened within the next few years is probably without parallel in the emergence of any art form. Between 1908 and 1912 Griffith took the raw elements of movie making as they had evolved up to that time and, singlehanded, wrought from them a medium more intimate than theater, more vivid than literature, more affecting than poetry. He created the art of the film, its language, its syntax. It has often been said that Griffith "invented" the close-up, that he "invented" cutting, the camera angle, or even the last-minute rescue. This, of course, is nonsense. What he did was far more important. He refined these elements, already present in motion pictures, mastered them and made them serve his purpose. He discovered ways to use his camera functionally, developed editing from the crude assembly of unrelated shots into a conscious, artistic device. Apparently to Griffith each new film was a challenge, a chance to experiment, to try out new effects. Certainly, Biograph gave him every opportunity. In his first year there he turned out well over a hundred pictures—more than two a week!

One of his first moves was to break the standard distance maintained between audience and actor by changing the camera's position in mid-scene. There is no need, he argued, to photograph an entire sequence from a single setup when, by simply shifting to a new vantage point, we can always keep the most significant action in screen center. Pursuing the same line of reasoning, he continued to push the camera ever closer to his players to emphasize a gesture or a reaction. "The public will never buy only half an actor," his employers protested. But the public saw, and understood.

Grasping instinctively the fact that the movies are in reality a form quite apart from theater, Griffith went further still. Why go through all the tedious business of having an actor open a door, step into a room, close the door, then walk to the center of the stage before the significant action begins? He started his scenes instead directly upon the action itself, and halted them as soon as the action was completed. Again the audiences understood. He became interested in the composition and lighting of his scenes. He discovered that by placing the camera at an angle to the action he could create a greater dynamism than was possible in the conventional head-on shot, that deep shadows and key highlights—"Rembrandt lighting," he called it—would intensify the mood and heighten the visual impact of his scenes. He edited his own pictures and found that the length of time a shot remained on the screen could create very real psychological tensions in an audience: the shorter the shot, the greater the excitement. As early as 1909 he introduced this principle to build a climax of suspense in *The Lonely Villa*. A trio of thugs is forcing its way into the house. The father has learned by telephone that his wife and children are in danger, and drives frantically to the rescue. The burglars batter on the doors. The mother stands guard over her little brood. By cutting back and forth from one to the other, making each shot shorter than the last, Griffith heightened the excitement of the situation. It was a device he was to use again and again, a device in which time and space were shuffled freely at the will of the director.

Griffith felt his way gradually, ever more sure of himself, ever widening the gap between film technique and stage methods. He worked his actors to and from the camera, devising groupings and compositions which, while meaningless on the three-dimensional stage, proved highly effective on the two-dimensional screen. As he moved his camera closer to the players, he perceived that the theater's eloquent gestures and overemphatic facial expressions became awkward and artificial. He trained his performers in a quieter, more intimate acting style, and developed a host of young people, preferably without previous stage experience, to work in his films. The Griffith "stock company" at Biograph came to include such future luminaries as Mary Pickford, Lillian and Dorothy Gish, Mae Marsh, Mabel Normand, Robert Harron, Owen Moore, Blanche Sweet, Mack Sennett, Arthur Johnson, H. B. Walthall and Lionel Barrymore. Actors who could not follow his direction, actors who persisted in the melodramatic style of gaslit melodrama, either left Biograph or worked with other directors there.

Perhaps even more important than Griffith's discovery of how to make film actors act was his realization that in the movies objects could become actors as well. By use of the extreme close-up, a knife, a whisky bottle, a letter, a telephone, a revolver could be made to occupy the entire screen, emphasizing its importance in the developing story. In *The Lonedale Operator* (1911), Blanche Sweet holds a pair of desperadoes at bay with a monkey wrench. We are shown in close-up that it is only a wrench. But the thugs think it is a pistol—and in the long-shots that is what it looks like to us too. It was the close-up that let us in on the secret, when the director was ready to reveal it. Griffith discovered that one basic function of the close-up was to emphasize the inanimate, to make *things* a dynamic part of the world through which the actors move.

But the close-up does more than merely emphasize what is important in a scene: it eliminates everything else. It forces the audience to see what the director wants it to see—and only that. It concentrates attention on the significant detail, whether it be an object, an actor or a portion of an actor. Griffith discovered that the close-up of a hand, an arm, the eyes or lips could often be far more expressive on the screen than the most highly trained actor projecting an emotion in theatrical terms. All the tension of the courtroom scene in *Intolerance* (1916) is compressed into the huge close-up of Mae Marsh's hands, the fingers nervously twisting together as the young wife awaits the judge's sentence of life or death for her unfortunate husband. "Visible hieroglyphs," Horace M.

Kallen once called such material, "the visible hieroglyphs of the unseen dynamics of human relations." It was Griffith's unique ability to reveal filmically the inmost thoughts and emotions of his characters, to reveal them clearly and intimately to his audiences. Knowing nothing about Griffith, "hieroglyphs" or film techniques, people everywhere responded directly to the bittersweet sufferings of Little Mary, to the harassed wife of a drunken husband, to courageous Blanche Sweet or terrified Lillian Gish. They found Griffith's pictures more realistic, more convincing, more human than anything shown upon the screen at that time, and they looked forward to each new Biograph release with greater enthusiasm than to the films of any other studio.

It is instructive to compare Griffith's films with the French and Italian spectacles that were imported in great quantities after 1912 by the distributor George Kleine. As early as May, 1911, Griffith had rebelled against the Trust's arbitrary single-reel restriction. When he made *Enoch Arden* in two reels, Biograph, which was one of the leading members of the Trust, insisted on releasing each reel separately. However, in response to audience demand, theater managers were soon showing the two parts together. And by 1912 the two-reeler had become accepted as the standard length for a serious story film. Now, spurred by rumors of the longer films being made abroad, Griffith sought to push further. Working secretly in California, he completed in four reels an opulent version of the biblical story *Judith of Bethulia* (1913). His employers were furious. They shelved the film and declared that henceforth Griffith would supervise production instead of directing. Griffith promptly left the studio, taking with him many of his "stock company" adherents—the Gish sisters, Mae Marsh, Blanche Sweet, Robert Harron, H. B. Walthall and, above all, his trusted and ingenious cameraman, G. W. ("Billy") Bitzer.

Judith of Bethulia was not released by Biograph until late in 1914. Although it appeared a whole year after *Quo Vadis?* had received its Broadway première, and in the midst of a veritable flood of similar European spectacles, the Griffith film reasserted the importance of his discoveries. The Italian and French pictures were longer, had vaster crowds and huger sets, but they were essentially static. They were like watching a tremendous pageant upon a distant stage. One felt no sense of personal involvement. *Judith of Bethulia*, on the other hand, with the most daring close-ups that Griffith had yet attempted, had the power to move audiences, to make them aware of the ancient drama in warm and human terms. Far from the best of his earlier work, it towered over its European contemporaries.

Leaving Biograph, Griffith—now at last David Wark Griffith—joined the Mutual Company and supervised for them a number of five-reel features, potboilers that, for the most part, reveal all too clearly Griffith's essential lack of interest. For during this period Griffith was gathering together his resources to tackle a subject so great, so ambitious and daring as to astonish the imagination. He had read Thomas Dixon's novel *The Clansman*, a story of the Civil War and the Reconstruction period that followed, a story of the rise of the Ku Klux Klan. Being a Southerner, the son of a Confederate officer, Griffith was drawn instinctively to its theme. But his film sense responded even more strongly to the sweep and melodramatic power of the novel—a little family ruined by the war, then fighting to preserve its integrity amidst carpetbaggers and renegade blacks. He flung himself into the production, poured into it all his own finances and those of his friends. Working without a scenario, he devised new, unheard-of effects—battle scenes photographed in extreme long-shot and reminiscent of the Brady Civil War photographs, action shots taken in extreme close-up, the climactic ride of the Clans photographed with the camera mounted low on the back of a moving truck. He drew on all the known resources of the camera and invented still more—the iris, the mask, the vignette, split-screen and triple split-screen shots. He worked out every action, every gesture for the principals in his huge cast. He mustered all his knowledge of editing to impart fluency and mounting tension to the scenes that poured from Bitzer's camera. The result was a film of extraordinary eloquence and power, *The Birth of a Nation*.

Released early in 1915, *The Birth of a Nation* took its audiences by storm. Twelve reels long (almost three hours), with a special score performed by a full symphony orchestra, it swept along with a cumulative force that a present-day viewing of the film can only partially suggest. There simply had never been a picture like this before; "like history written in lightning," Woodrow Wilson described it. The passions it aroused, the tensions it created lasted beyond the theater. They overflowed into the streets, and race riots and mob action followed in the wake of its presentation in many cities. But whether loved or hated, *The Birth of a Nation* established once for all that the film was an art in its own right—and Griffith was its master.

Even today, after more than sixty years, the strengths of this remarkable film are still apparent—the characterization through vivid symbol, the epic swelling of its first act from scenes of warm intimacy to the broad panorama of battle, then closing quietly on the Little Colonel's return to his ravaged home; the fevered melodrama of its second half dominated by the sweeping ride of the Clans. Individual scenes reveal still more clearly Griffith's sure instinct for the perfect film image. Incomparable is his portrayal of Sherman's vengeful march to the sea. Beginning with a tight iris shot of weeping women and children huddled together high on a hill, as the iris opens out to fill the screen the camera pans to the right, to an extreme long-shot of Sherman's army far below spreading destruction through the countryside. Individual shots depict the pillage, the burning, the slaughter. The sequence ends with a closing iris glimpse of the tearful women on the hill. The ruthless devastation of war is made poignant by relating it to the innocents who suffer. Again, in a scene that still seems breathtakingly daring, Griffith intercuts shots of the old people at home on their knees in prayer with cold, pitiless glimpses of trenches piled high with corpses frozen in the agony of death. The realism of the scene in the Union hospital, the painstaking authenticity of the reconstruction of Lincoln's assassination, the heart-warming moment of the homecoming, the virtuoso cutting from the wild ride of the Clansmen to the besieged family in a squalid cabin—these are passages of pure film that rank among the greatest in all motion-picture history.

What makes *The Birth of a Nation* difficult to view today is precisely what touched off the controversy that raged about the film in 1915—its use of Negro stereotypes and its sympathetic account of the rise of the Klan. Griffith seems to have been genuinely shocked at the charges of anti-Negro bias leveled against him on all sides when the film appeared, and not without reason. One has only to read *The Clansman*, on which it was based, to become aware of the pains that Griffith had taken to eliminate from his version the rabid hatred that seethes through Thomas Dixon's book. But Griffith was a Southerner, brought up in an embittered, impoverished household. His father had been a colonel in the Confederacy, and Griffith grew up hearing tales of the good old days before the war. He balanced his renegade blacks and vengeful mulattoes with happy, faithful "darkies," and thought he was being fair. He could never comprehend that to many one stereotype was as repugnant as the other. Set against this, such minor blemishes as Griffith's eternally twittering young girls and a painfully poetic epilogue depicting the arrival of universal brotherhood pale into insignificance. But perhaps the true measure of this film is to be found in the very depth of the passions it aroused. Certainly, not for another ten years was there to be a movie capable of affecting its audiences so profoundly.

It might be a kindness to leave D. W. Griffith at this point, for at 39 he had reached the very pinnacle of his career. With *The Birth of a Nation* he had made all his major contributions to the medium, had transformed the film from a halting, stumbling imitation of theater into a vigorous, eloquent, independent art. There were still years of greatness ahead of him—the daring of *Intolerance* (1916), with its four separate stories from four different eras interlocked by a single unifying theme; the haunting poignancy of *Broken Blossoms* (1919), a small, somber vignette told with great delicacy and refinement; his enormously popular version of *Way Down East* (1920), a gaslight melodrama that Griffith vigorously and resourcefully adapted to the screen; the extraordinary realism of the German-made *Isn't Life Wonderful?* (1924). But along with these films came the potboilers, more and more of them. As an independent, he had to meet the payroll and overhead of his Mamaroneck studio, the expenses of his big productions. When finally the creditors took over, he became just another staff director at Famous Players-Lasky. The end of Griffith's story is not a happy one. It is never pleasant to see greatness humbled or genius left behind. Far better to remember the tireless experimenter, the instinctive artist in an untried art, the man who trained and inspired an entire generation of directors, actors and technicians—the Griffith who declared at the height of his career, paraphrasing Joseph Conrad. "The task I'm trying to achieve is above all to make you see."

The Creative Producer: Thomas H. Ince

Soon after Griffith left Biograph for Mutual, he found himself in tandem with two other prominent producer-directors, Mack Sennett and Thomas H. Ince. Each had his own studio, his own autonomy to produce what he liked as he liked; together they contributed the three points to the Triangle Company's offerings—comedies, program features and, from Griffith, the "specials." Of the three, Ince is probably the least known today. At one time, however, his name was as familiar and respected as Griffith's. In France, in fact, the films of "T-H Ince" were generally held to be better than Griffiths', although this can partially be explained by recalling that many—but by no means all—of Ince's pictures were Westerns. The French were attracted by the exotic settings and characters of the Ince films, and especially by "Rio Jim," as they affectionately nicknamed William S. Hart, Ince's top cowboy star. Ince kept his Santa Monica studio and ranch well stocked with cattle, horses, buffalo and genuine Sioux Indians, and he had a positive genius for finding suitably atmospheric locales for his tales of the American frontier. But no less important is the fact that his pictures were quite devoid of the cloying sentimentality that marred so many of Griffith's films. Working with Hart, Ince created a frontier that was truly primitive, hard and rugged. Here was no romantic compromise, as in the Westerns of Tom Mix, Buck Jones and Hoot Gibson. As for the singing cowboys who populated the Westerns of a later era, Hart would probably have shot them dead on sight. And in the many films that Ince produced without Hart—Westerns and city-based dramas alike—that same unwillingness to compromise is still present. At his best, Ince was a stern realist, a realist with an extraordinary story sense and an ability to remake a picture in the cutting room that has probably never been equaled.

Ince, like Griffith, came to the movies from the theater. Although he had been an actor, he began directing for Biograph in 1910, moving quickly to Carl Laemmle's Imp Company and then to Mutual. By 1914 he was already a major force in the industry, heading his own palatial studio, Inceville, on the shores of Santa Monica. Gradually Ince found himself devoting far more time to the organization and supervision of his studio than to actual direction, a development that was to prove of considerable importance in the history of film making. It was Ince who introduced the concept of the creative producer to Hollywood—the man who knows so much about pictures that he can plan, organize and supervise the work of others. With himself as the over-all chief, he set up a number of producing units on his lot, each headed by a production manager. This manager, responsible directly to Ince, worked with him and the writer throughout the preparation of a script. When completed, the script was rubber-stamped with the explicit instruction, "Shoot as written." A shooting schedule was then drawn up, indicating what was to be shot where and when. This was equally inviolate. It was a system created for economic production and—at least in Ince's hands—it also resulted in many excellent pictures. His powers of visualization were so strong that, it was said, he could see from the printed page of a script exactly how each completed shot could and should fit with another. In any case, he did much of the final editing of his pictures himself. The system that Ince introduced into his studio between 1915 and 1920 is one that Hollywood continued to follow over three decades, throughout the era of large-scale mass production of pictures. The extraordinary thing about Ince's films was the fact that, no matter who directed them, they were all stamped unmistakably with their producer's personality. Few of Hollywood's subsequent producers have had quite that degree of creative vigor.

Even though Ince turned out pictures at top speed and invariably had several productions working at once, surprisingly few of his films have survived the years. We have far less opportunity to see again an Ince film than a contemporary Griffith or Sennett. Perhaps his premature death in 1924, before there was any considerable literature on the art of the motion picture, has also contributed to the relative obscurity of this gifted pioneer. But while it is difficult today to find a "vintage" Ince—a film produced between 1914 and 1920—those that do turn up are invariably admirable in editing, construction and story. Lean, tight, cut to the bone, the plot advances quickly and tersely, rarely straying from the main line of action for atmospheric, comic or romantic interludes. The characters are solid and three-dimensional, the settings uncluttered and painstakingly realistic. There is a refreshing, unsentimental naturalness about his pictures, whether a hard-hitting, two-reel action story like *The Gangsters and the Girl* (1914), social comment as in *The Italian* (1915) or a small-town comedy romance like *The Clodhopper* (1917). Of the pictures of this period, only the overly ambitious, pseudo-Griffith, semi-pacifist *Civilization* (1916) seems to waver in its point of view or to contain people who are anything less than flesh and blood.

Although Ince continued to make films through the early twenties, they became less and less exciting, more and more routine. It was as if Ince himself had been exhausted by a decade of intense creativity, as if the magnitude of the business operation now drained his energies, leaving little over for his films. Meanwhile, however, both the production techniques that he had devised and the host of directors that he had trained—Frank Borzage, Lambert Hillyer, Henry King, Rowland V. Lee, Fred Niblo, Victor Schertzinger—were spreading throughout the Hollywood studios. Like Griffith, he had made his contribution.

Sennett, the Keystone of American Comedy

Opposite Ince in the Triangle Company—Griffith, of course, was its apex—stood Mark Sennett, king of the slap-stick clowns at Keystone. When Sennett, a huge, gangling, would-be opera singer, arrived at Biograph in January of 1909, he had already steered a hazardous course through circuses, burlesque, vaudeville and walk-ons in the legitimate theater. Like most actors of the period, he was lured into films less by the potentialities of the cinema as an art form than by the $5 daily take-home pay. But Sennett was also possessed by a consuming ambition: he wanted to play a comic policeman. He thought that cops were funny long before he got the opportunity to prove it, frequently arguing this point with D. W. Griffith as the two men rambled together about the streets of New York. Griffith, however, refused to be convinced, and continued casting him in straight roles. Sennett can often be discerned shifting about in the background of the Biograph dramas dressed as a butler, a rube or a tramp "heavy"—but never a comic cop.

From Mary Pickford, Sennett learned that Biograph paid $25 for story ideas, so he promptly became an author. He claims that his first scenario was lifted from something by O. Henry—although not quite far enough to make a sale. In any case, before long he was augmenting his actor's income fairly regularly with acceptable script material, including *The Lonely Villa*. At the same time he was learning to direct—and from Griffith himself. In his autobiography, *King of Comedy*, Sennett pays a warm and heartfelt tribute to his mentor: "He was my day school, my adult education program, my university." Before long, Sennett too had become a director—at a princely $65 a week.

Sennett's years at Biograph were not altogether happy ones. He worked hard, turning out an average of two pictures a week between 1910 and 1912, acting in his own films and occasionally in Griffith's as well. But Sennett had developed some fairly definite ideas about film comedy—and not merely in regard to cops as figures of fun. He remembered the grotesques from circus and burlesque. He was fascinated by the mechanical gags and tricks he saw in the French chase comedies that had been arriving here in great quantities since about 1907, and by the agile comedies of the dapper Frenchman Max Linder (whose style was also at the time being studied by the young Charles Chaplin). Sennett felt that these elements of gag, chase, trick and character could be fused into an American comedy form. Biograph, however, had been prospering under the sober influence of D. W. Griffith. It had gained in prestige and importance. Wallace ("Pop") McCutcheon, the boss of the little studio, enjoyed his new respectability and saw no reason to encourage Sennett's slapstick notions. For Biograph, Sennett turned out a rather routine succession of rube comedies, livened occasionally by the sparkling presence of Mabel Normand.

Sennett's account of the origin of his famous Keystone studio is probably apocryphal—and hardly flattering to his associates in the business, Adam Kessel and Charles Bauman. As he tells the story, Kessel and Bauman were a pair of small-time bookies. Sennett had guessed wrong on too many horse races and owed them a hundred dollars that he didn't have. When finally cornered, Sennett declares he waxed so eloquent about the fortunes to be made in the movies that his creditors not only forgave him his hundred but put up an additional $2,500 to get into the business themselves. The name, he says, was inspired by the insigne of the Pennsylvania Railroad. Just how much of this Runyonesque tale is true, Sennett alone can tell. But in January, 1912—just three years after coming to work as an extra at Biograph—he alighted from a train in Los Angeles and began making pictures at his own studio, the Keystone. And his new bosses, back in New York, were the Messrs. Kessel and Bauman.

At first Sennett was Keystone's director, star, idea man, and sometimes he even helped out on the camera. Stories were improvised on the spot. He might hear of a parade or of a motorcar race, of a lake being drained or a captive balloon released. Sennett and his crew would arrive pell-mell, dreaming up a situation on the way. The key scenes, the scenes involving the incident, would be caught almost on the fly. Then back to the little studio in Edendale to shoot more material that would lead up to it and explain it. The explanation might not be too logical, but Sennett quickly learned to take care of that. "It's got to *move*," he would say, knowing that in a plethora of slam-bang action audiences would find little time to ask embarrassing questions. His favorite axiom for comedy was that a gag should be planted, developed and pointed all within a hundred feet of film (about a minute and a half on the screen).

Now at last he could indulge his fancy for comic policemen, and the Keystone Kops came tumbling into his pictures in their motley, outsized uniforms and collapsible tin lizzies. Now at last he could try out the dizzying camera tricks he had admired in the French chases. Now he could develop his own corps of characters and clowns, of gargoyles and grotesques. Ford Sterling, Mabel Normand, Pathé Lehrman and Fred Mace had made the trip west with him. Soon they were joined by such exuberant types as "Fatty" Arbuckle, Hank Mann, Chester Conklin, "Slim" Summerville, Edgar Kennedy, Charlie Murray, Ben Turpin, Charley Chase, Mack Swain and, of course, Charlie Chaplin. Within the first year of operation, Sennett reports, Keystone had turned out over 140 comedies.

Before long Sennett, like Ince, was forced to withdraw from direct participation in his comedies and became a producer, presiding over the destinies of his studio from a huge bathtub installed in the watchtower office where he held his staff conferences; and no less important, from a creaky rocking chair in the projection room where he viewed every last foot of film his zany crews had photographed. It proved an ideal arrangement. As an actor, Sennett scarcely invites comparison with any of the talented clowns he had gathered around him. His heavy grimaces, his raw-boned, shuffling gait were utterly lacking in precision, finesse or, when you come right down to it, humor. What he did have, born of his years of prentice work at Biograph, was an uncanny instinct for timing and editing his shots. His staff could tell from the squeaks of the rocking chair whether they were pleasing "the Old Man" or not. If not, Sennett could generally tell how to recut a scene to make it play better.

Most of the ideas for the Keystone comedies originated with Sennett himself; nothing was ever purchased from outside. With his writers, he would lay out the basic plot or situation as if planning a straight film. Characters and characterizations were discussed and tailored to fit the personalities on the lot. Only after a proper story line had been hammered out was it forwarded to the "gag room," to the men who would add the humorous scenes and situations. One of Frank Capra's first movie jobs was in the Keystone gag department. Another graduate from this asylum for inspired maniacs was Raymond Griffith, the popular "silk-hatted comedian" of the twenties. Shooting was generally a weird combination of improvisation and script, the natural high spirits and prankishness of the performers often leading to bits of business that even Sennett's accomplished gagsters would have hesitated to devise. Thus Mabel Normand splurched the first custard pie full into the gloriously cockeyed features of Ben Turpin to liven up a faltering scene. Sad-eyed Hank Mann invariably infuriated his Keystone confreres with his scene-stealing acrobatics. But if they pleased Sennett, they stayed. Sennett always thought of himself as the average audience: if he liked a scene, so would the public. He was rarely wrong.

Inevitably, with this incessant flow of ordered insanity, all the comedies were not the masterpieces that the historians, writing with an understandable nostalgia, would suggest. Some of Sennett's satires—*His Bitter Pill* (1916), *A Small Town Idol* (1912), *The Shriek of Araby* (1923)—were perfect gems of parody, generally built around the themes of successful serious dramas. His purely mechanical gags—as in *Dizzy Heights and Daring Hearts* (1916) and *The Clever Dummy* (1917)—were more than merely ingenious: they laughed irreverently at America's increasing worship of the machine. Whole series were built around the leading comics on the lot—Chaplin, Mack Swain ("Ambrose"), "Fatty" Arbuckle, the pixyish Mabel Normand and blustery Ford Sterling. The success of these films rested, of course, upon the antic gifts and graces of their stars. But intermingled with these were great quantities of wholly routine and completely uninspired situation comedies obviously borrowed from vaudeville and burlesque. And a surprising number prove to be rube comedies, all too reminiscent of the pictures Sennett had ground out for Biograph.

By the late twenties, when most of his top clowns and directors had left him for more profitable feature-film jobs, the Sennett pictures had become routine indeed, pale effigies of the speedy knockabout farces that characterized his best production. The props—the cars that fall apart, the crockery that flies into a thousand pieces, the breakaway walls and doors and trees, the pies that sail miraculously on invisible wires—all were still present; but not the great comic gusto that once transformed them into dizzy, devastating parodies of life itself.

Sennett's name today is probably irretrievably wedded to slapstick and the custard pie. While the connection is perfectly true, its connotations do him an injustice. In his hands slapstick became suddenly, indigenously filmic. He used the camera to exploit the absurd, the impossible, the fantastic. Reason was blurred by the speed of his action and editing. He reduced the real world—or at least something that perilously resembled the real world—to a shambles, and held it up to mockery as a wry joke of a place where little men were married to stern, overpowering women, where lechery abounded, where officialdom was invariably inept, and a swift kick in the pants could settle the most abstruse problems. There was philosophy in the Sennett films, and art as well, although "the Old Man" always expressed polite astonishment whenever anyone found it there. "We played it by ear as we went along," he liked to say.

Perhaps so, but his ear was good and his instincts were sound. Certainly, he discovered and developed a whole generation of top comedians—not only Chaplin and the Keystone Kops but actresses like Gloria Swanson, Phyllis Haver, Bebe Daniels, Marie Prevost, Carole Lombard, Alberta Vaughn, Louise Fazenda and Polly Moran. Marie Dressler, Harry Langdon, Harold Lloyd, Wallace Beery, W. C. Fields and Bing Crosby were all on the Sennett lot at one time or another. Perhaps even more important is the training he gave an entire school of directors—men like Frank Capra, Mal St.

Clair, Roy Del Ruth, Ray Enright, Eddie Cline, George Stevens and George Marshall. He taught them timing and the need for physical movement on the screen. And he stressed the importance of editing to tighten and sharpen a scene.

Sound and the arrival of the double feature wrote the final chapter to Sennett's story. Perhaps his methods could have prevailed only when the industry was young, enthusiastic and wildly disorganized. His free-wheeling, boldly improvisational techniques were already being toned down during the twenties when Sennett moved to Paramount. In the interest of economy, his films were more carefully planned and budgeted step by step. Sound changed shooting techniques even further, throwing emphasis completely on the written script; and double features virtually eliminated the two-reel comedy from theater bills in favor of the single-reel cartoon or band short. In 1935 Sennett finally withdrew from active production. He, too, had made his contribution.

Chaplin and the Rise of the Star System

Of the many illustrious alumni of the Sennett school, Charlie Chaplin still shines above all the rest. After all the years of Chaplin's embittered semi-retirement far from the scenes of his early triumphs and even farther out of contact with the heart and temper of the common man whose image he had created on the screen, it is somewhat difficult to imagine just how popular he once was. Within two years of his first screen appearance, his name had become a household word. There were Chaplin dolls, Chaplin toys, Chaplin contests. People danced "The Chaplin Walk"; children used his name in their counting-out rhymes. There were Chaplin imitators—even in the films—and Chaplin cartoons both in the newspapers and on the screen. "I am here today"—this simple announcement printed over a cutout of Chaplin tipping his hat was all that a theater manager needed to lure the customers into his house. No one bothered to ask either title or story.

Some measure of the whirlwind velocity of Chaplin's career, some estimate of the tremendous popularity of his pictures may be gained from a simple financial statement. He joined Keystone in December, 1913, at a salary of $150 a week—a sizable sum for a young man whose biggest job up to that time had been touring the American vaudeville circuits with an English music-hall act at $50 a week. Just one year later, in January, 1915, Chaplin was signed by Essanay at $1,250 a week. In the following year he joined Mutual at $10,000 a week—plus a bonus of $150,000 simply for putting his name to the contract. And in 1917, at the age of 27, Chaplin signed with First National for a million dollars to deliver eight films in eighteen months—this time with a bonus of $15,000. What makes this sum even more impressive is the fact that all of his pictures had been brief one- or two-reelers. The Chaplin shorts were more prized than any features except those of Mary Pickford. At the time, Mary was earning just under a million dollars a year.

Both Chaplin and Pickford were reaping the benefits of a significant development in the motion-picture industry. Prior to 1910 the identity of the players in movies was completely unknown to the general public. Gradually, as audiences began to recognize their favorites, they would refer to them by the names that were used in the pictures. Thus, the tiny, golden-locked Gladys Smith was known as "Little Mary" long before she acquired the screen name of Mary Pickford; while burly G. M. Anderson, the screen's first cowboy star, was simply "Broncho Billy." Others were known by their studio—"The Biograph Girl," "The Vitagraph Girl," "The Imp Girl." The producers, and particularly those who were members of the Patents Company, sought to maintain this anonymity. They firmly refused to acknowledge the increasingly persistent "who" letters, for if the public learned the names of their players, they reasoned, then the actors might demand more money. It remained for one of the independents, Carl Laemmle, to break this pattern. Florence Lawrence, the popular "Biograph Girl," was lured from that studio by Laemmle's promise not only to pay her more money but to feature her under her own name. Laemmle, always a great believer in advertising, publicized his coup well. A star was born. And with the star, the star system.

Laemmle quickly learned that, while he had to pay more for his actress, he could also charge more rental for her pictures. The devotees, the "fans" of Florence Lawrence could be depended upon to turn up in sufficient numbers at the box office to warrant the increased price. Soon talent raids were taking place throughout the industry. Laemmle swooped down on Biograph again to carry off Mary Pickford and her husband, Owen Moore. Vitagraph, the first of the Patents companies to break the ban, made stars of handsome Maurice Costello and its own "Vitagraph Girl," Florence Turner. Rotund John Bunny was probably the first movie comedian that the public knew by name; Arthur Johnson, the movies' first "matinee idol." By 1911 there was even a dog star—Jean, "the Vitagraph Dog." These early stars came from the ranks of the regular movie players. But after Sarah Bernhardt's success in *Queen Elizabeth*, theater people began to lose some of their traditional antipathy toward the movies and Zukor's idea of "Famous Players in Famous Plays" soon acquired a host of imitators. Between 1912 and 1915 the screen featured such illustrious stage personalities as Nat C. Goodwin, James O'Neill, James Hackett, Minnie Maddern Fiske and Lily Langtry. Naturally, there was never the slightest question about revealing *these* names.

As the studios vied with each other for stars, actors and actresses found their dollar-and-cents value to the studios spiraling upward at a dizzying rate—from $5 to $15 a day before 1910, to from $250 to $2,000 a week in 1914. The true movie stars proved worth their weight even in this much gold; but producers soon learned to their sorrow that a great name in the theater did not automatically assure great popularity on the screen, and that the public often preferred to discover its own stars rather than have them delivered ready-made. Many a top Broadway performer returned to the footlights considerably chastened by his brush with the movies; while many an unknown, yielding to the lure of good money and steady employment in the studios, quickly found himself swept to undreamed-of heights of acclaim and affection. Chaplin was one of the latter.

Few men have ever succeeded in becoming a legend in their own lifetime—especially men who have lived so long and so intensely in the public eye as Charles Spencer Chaplin. Yet Chaplin from the very start met all the requirements for legend-making. His origins are obscure, his parentage, even his name. It is known that he suffered extreme poverty in his youth, including two miserable years in a London orphanage. Coming from a theatrical family, he had learned dancing and miming almost as soon as he learned to walk. He was earning his own living by the time he was seven, dancing in a music-hall act called *The Eight Lancashire Lads;* but this was followed by another period of great hardship when his mother was placed in a mental institution and Chaplin roamed the streets, unwanted and alone. From the time he was ten, however, he began to find fairly regular employment in the theater, first as a child actor (notably in the London company of *Sherlock Holmes*), later in various vaudeville turns. In 1906, with the help of his older brother Sidney, he joined the Karno Comedy Company, an organization that boasted a large and varied repertory of skits, pantomimes, acrobatics, comedy songs and dances. Chaplin was to remain with Karno until the movies tapped him for fame and fortune in 1913.

Mack Sennett has written that when he was in New York in 1912, he and Mabel Normand caught the Karno act *A Night in an English Music Hall*. Later, when Keystone's top comedian, Ford Sterling, was bitten by the then prevalent "star fever," Sennett thought it judicious to have a substitute handy. Remembering Chaplin (although not his name), he urged his New York partners to find him and sign him. Adam Kessel handled the arrangements; but although Chaplin signed the contract in May of 1913, he was so filled with doubts and misgivings about his future in films that he refused to leave the Karno troupe until the end of its American tour. When he arrived in Hollywood in December of that year, he was just twenty-four years old.

In Chaplin's first film, a knockabout comedy called *Making a Living* (1914), there is scant suggestion of the beloved tramp to come. Outfitted as a fiercely English dandy, with top hat, monocle, frock coat and long, drooping mustaches, Chaplin played a reporter who took mean advantage of every good turn showed him by others. It was amusing enough at the time, but seen today it seems like the work of a stranger—a deft and hard-working comedian caught up in a series of frantic but meaningless gags. Yet Charlie the tramp was to appear in his very next film. Word had been received on the Keystone lot that there was to be a children's auto race at Venice, the Los Angeles version of Coney Island. Sennett told Chaplin to get himself a funny costume and keep floundering in the way of a camerman photographing the festivities. The costume proved to be one of those rare combinations of luck and genius. Sharing a dressing room with Arbuckle and Mack Swain, Chaplin borrowed "Fatty's" outsized trousers and, from Swain, a prop mustache. The floppy shoes came from Ford Sterling. The derby, the cane, the too tight coat—all were unerringly chosen in one short afternoon. During the shooting of *The Kid Auto Races at Venice*, Chaplin instinctively fell into the sore-footed shuffle that was also to remain part of the character—the remembered gait of an old peddler he had observed during his days on the London streets.

But if the costume came quickly, and with it the mannerisms that made the little tramp so irresistibly funny—the angular walk, the skidding turn, the inimitable byplay with cane and derby—the full meaning of the character emerged far more slowly. From the outset, Chaplin felt uneasy in the Sennet brand of comedy. The gags flew too swiftly, the pace was too frantic for the kind of pantomime he had mastered in the English music halls. He chafed under the direction of Sennett and Pathé Lehrman. The success of his character, however, was so immediately apparent that within three months Sennett concluded it might be just as well to let the little Englishman have things a bit more his own way. After acting in only a dozen pictures, Chaplin became his own director—a role he never relinquished.

Even so, the demands of the Keystone schedule—almost two films a week—were too great to permit Chaplin to explore and develop the tramp character to any real extent. Here he originated many of the comic bits he was to use again with greater effectiveness in later years, the brash stratagems by which the underdog discomfits his larger or wealthier rival, the visual surprises and transformations by which, in his hands, a doughnut becomes a bracelet or a lamp an object of love. Although the tramp costume remained basic to the character, Chaplin appeared in the Keystone films in a wide variety of garbs, each suggestive of comedy situations—a baker, a waiter, a dentist's assistant, a woman or a squiffy English man-about-town. His flow of comic invention was miraculous. Each of the films is fast and funny. But the gags themselves were often tasteless and vulgar, practical jokes filled with pointless cruelty and brazen dishonesty. Revealing their hasty origins, they were all too frequently laughs for their own sake, unrelated to either character or plot. One of the inducements that Essanay held out to Chaplin to sign with them was the promise of more time for each picture and his own head in production. He accepted gladly.

It was at Essanay that Chaplin began to discover the implications of the little tramp figure he had achieved. Pathos, irony, satire and, above all, a more conscious identification of the character with "the little fellow" everywhere—all of these emerged during his year at Essanay. Here too Chaplin began to build the working team that was to remain with him through the years—cameraman Roland Totheroh, leading lady Edna Purviance, character comics Leo White, John Rand and Billy Armstrong. As his own producer, he paid increasing attention not only to plot incident and story but to the use of the camera itself. Where Sennett's films were swift, choppy and filled with frantic movement, Chaplin evolved a quieter, more intimate style. His camera is more thoughtfully placed, and remains in one position for a longer period of time. Not a technique for flashy, spectacular effects, it is nevertheless wholly functional and, for Chaplin's purposes, admirably economic. Such films of this period as *The Tramp* and *The Bank* reveal a sure instinct for framing, for establishing a dynamic relationship between camera and performer that includes all the essentials and rigorously frames out any extraneous detail. The same economy Chaplin applied to his set dressings. Any property that appears in a scene is there to be used. If the president's office in *The Bank* at first seems a veritable jungle of desks, wastebaskets, telephones, electric fans and scrap paper, within a few moments Chaplin, the bank's handyman, has brought every one of them into play, tangling with them, upsetting them, tripping over them. The electric fan, finally turned on to cool the perspiring Charlie after his arduous clean-up campaign, promptly blows the papers all over the room again. Only when the gag possibilities of the last prop have been exhausted does Chaplin cut to another scene and begin the whole wonderful business all over again.

Not only was Chaplin's cinematic feeling approaching maturity during his year at Essanay, he was also developing the physical capabilities of "the little fellow," as he often called his screen character. "A technique as unfaltering as Réjane," wrote Mrs. Fiske admiringly in 1915. His agility, his precision of gesture, the sudden revelation of character in moments of seemingly unpremeditated byplay (as the delicious bit in which he prudishly slips a lampshade over a nude statuette, then naughtily lifts the skirt for a peek)—all provoked the admiration of professionals and the open adulation of movie audiences everywhere. But these audiences, it should be emphasized, consisted primarily of children and working-class adults. Contrary to the general impression, Chaplin's pictures did not become a cult with the sophisticates until the early twenties. They were too crude, too slapstick—and too popular. Perhaps it was just as well. Chaplin had the common touch, and the enthusiasm of the literati came along too late to sway him from his course.

From *The Tramp* (1915) through *Easy Street* (1917), *Shoulder Arms* (1918), *The Kid* (1921), *The Pilgrim* (1923), *The Gold Rush* (1925), *City Lights* (1931) and *Modern Times* (1936) one observes not a change but a constant deepening and development of the tramp character. Even the costume, assembled by chance and inspiration on a rainy afternoon, began to acquire its own significance— shabby gentility, the wealthy seen from the perspective of the poor, a courageous refusal to admit the stern realities of poverty and contempt. Charlie became the embodiment of the little fellow everywhere, and the marvelous transformation of objects, the sight gags that sparkle through the earlier pictures, Chaplin used increasingly to substantiate the character itself. Thus, in *The Kid* when Charlie removes his fingerless gloves and fastidiously selects a half-smoked butt from a sardine-can cigarette case, he makes this thoughtless, habitual gesture seem an act of rare extravagance. In *City Lights* the business with the swallowed whistle that emits little "peeps" at an elegant cocktail party or the paper streamers that become tangled in Chaplin's spaghetti at a nightclub, both wonderfully funny in themselves, also tell us how desperately Charlie wants to conform, to be accepted along with the millionaires and debutantes and the smartly dressed people who surround him. But Chaplin knew that his little fellow could never conform, that he was destined always to stand just outside the circle of the bright lights, waiting, hoping—and always with the inner strength to shrug off disappointment and disaster and go on down the road to his next adventure.

Perhaps there is some special significance in the fact that Chaplin finally abandoned his tramp character in a period of increased conformism. Perhaps he had himself lost faith in "the little fellow" and his abilities to withstand the pressures of society. Or perhaps Chaplin felt that the urgency of his own message to the world required a direct, verbal statement, that the spirit of independence, self-reliance and infinite tenderness always implicit in the tramp character was no longer adequate. As early as *The Great Dictator* (1940) Charlie stepped completely out of character to utter his heartfelt words of hope and courage to all those crushed or cringing under the yoke of the totalitarians. In Chaplin's next film, *Monsieur Verdoux* (1947), the tramp character had disappeared altogether. Probably the most non-conformist picture ever made, *Verdoux* was a mordant satire in which a debonaire and presumably humane mass-murderer defends himself by insisting that his crime was merely one of scale: "One murder makes a villain—millions sanctify," he says, pointing a finger at the munitions makers and the military leaders. In *Verdoux* Chaplin brazenly attempted to shock and outrage virtually every organized section of every American community with his pragmatic, unconventional morality. He succeeded all too well. Veteran and religious groups picketed and protested the film so vigorously that theaters were afraid to play it; within the year it was withdrawn from distribution completely.

But this only partially explains its failure in the United States. Chaplin films had been banned and boycotted before—notably his audacious *The Pilgrim* and, after his sensational divorce from Lita Grey, *The Gold Rush*. In the twenties, though, whatever audiences thought about Chaplin the man, they still wanted to see Charlie the comedian. By the time of *Verdoux*, few cared strongly enough either for the man or for the character to protest the suppression of his picture. Although *Limelight* (1952) was not only brilliant but in many ways Chaplin's most profound work, a summing up of his personal and artistic credo, it was greeted in this country by a mild indifference. The melancholy Calvero was no substitute for the dauntless, infinitely resourceful Charlie. By contrast, *The King in New York* (1957) proved a sad mishmash of stale jokes and ill-tempered humor, with barely a hint of the sweetness, the optimism that once characterized his work, while *A Countess from Hong Kong* (1967)—in which Chaplin made a brief appearance as a ship's steward—revealed that he was also sadly out of touch as a director of light comedy. Chaplin had created one immortal screen figure, and in so doing he had refined the art of projecting character upon the screen far beyond any of his contemporaries. His Charlie still lives—sad, funny, pathetic, heroic. The early comedies, many of them now in public domain, are constantly being revived and re-enjoyed; while Chaplin himself lived out his life in exile in Switzerland, a world away from Charlie and "the little fellow." Belatedly awarded an

Academy Oscar in 1972 and knighted by the British Queen in 1975, he died in Switzerland in December, 1977.

Movies Become Big Business

By the end of World War I, profound changes had taken place in the American film industry. Up to 1914 it had shared the world market with England, France, Italy, Denmark, Sweden and Germany. After 1914 those countries directly engaged in the war drastically curtailed their film production: celluloid and high explosives are made from the same ingredients. The Italian, French and English studios suffered a subsequent decline that was to last a generation or more. In Germany, where production was subsidized by the government for morale and propaganda purposes, the motion picture continued to flourish, but the films were created solely for home consumption. Sweden and Denmark, outside the conflict, enjoyed a brief flowering of their industries, particularly in the sober, saga-like dramas of Victor Seastrom (Sjöström) and Mauritz Stiller in Sweden and the early works of Denmark's Carl Dreyer. But it was to the United States that most of the world looked for its movies during those troubled years, to the comedies of Charlie Chaplin and Douglas Fairbanks, to the colorful Westerns of William S. Hart and Tom Mix, to the romances and adventures, the dramas and melodramas that poured from the American studios. And a new word appeared in the world's vocabulary—Hollywood!

During the early years of Hollywood's development as a production center American movies changed their complexion, acquiring for the first time the plush and polish, the glamour that has everywhere become synonymous with the name. But Hollywood itself was merely a sleepy little suburb of Los Angeles until the movie people found it and put it on the map. As early as 1910 some of the Eastern companies began junketing to California during the winter months to take advantage of its superb climate and inexhaustible sunshine. Hollywood proved an ideal center for their location work— close to mountains and the sea, desert and farm land. As the Patents war increased in intensity in New York, many of the independents came to settle permanently in Hollywood. Since of necessity they were working with bootleg cameras, it was often convenient to have the Mexican border also close by.

By 1915, although the larger companies continued to maintain studios in New York or Chicago, the tide had already turned in favor of California. Taxes in the East drove out more of the companies; the United States' entry into the war, with the drastic rationing of coal and electricity during the hard winter of 1917–1918, proved to be the final blow. Fort Lee, the studio center just across the Hudson from New York, was reduced to a ghost town. California's sunlight—and California's generous inducements in the form of labor laws and lower taxes—soon made Hollywood the capital of American film production. And with the United States clearly dominating world production after 1918, Hollywood became—as it has remained—the world's movie capital as well.

It was a change that permeated every aspect of the industry—production, distribution, exhibition, story content, even the audiences themselves. After 1912 the restrictive Motion Picture Patents Company was virtually eclipsed by the vigorous independents; and the company itself was dissolved as a trust by the Supreme Court in 1917. Meanwhile, its members limped along, clinging to the old ways and the old lengths until finally the competition they had sought to smother drove them from the scene. Almost all of today's major studios trace back to those independents who between 1910 and 1914 cheerfully flouted all the rules of the Patents Company. They lured away their more talented directors and most popular performers. They thrived on the star system. They increased the length of their pictures from two to three and, after 1914, to five reels (with occasional "specials" of seven reels or more). They discovered the value of publicity in popularizing their films and their stars. They established their own exchanges for the more efficient marketing of their product. And, after 1915, they began a race for theater ownership that was to reach fantastic proportions by the twenties.

Up to 1912 the familiar nickelodeon and store show, often furnished with hard chairs or benches rented from a nearby catering or funeral establishment, had been adequate for the working-class audiences who came to the movies for an hour's relaxation. From 1912 on, however, tiny neighborhood houses began to pop up all over the country—"The Idle Hour," "The Gem," "The Bijou Dream," "The Bluebird." Not infrequently they proved to be jerry-built firetraps, but they were far more inviting and far more comfortable than anything hitherto available. And admission prices advanced from a nickel to a dime, or even fifteen cents. Longer films, particularly the "specials" imported from Europe, were generally shown in legitimate theaters rented for the occasion, and at greatly advanced prices. Still the public came.

As more and more features began to appear from Hollywood, it occurred to at least one enterprising showman, Mitchell Mark, that a considerable public could be lured into a theater that was not only clean and comfortable but even elegant. When in April of 1914 he opened his Strand Theatre on Broadway, he inaugurated a whole new era in theater construction—and a new style as well. With gilt and marble and deep pile rugs, crystal chandeliers hanging from the ceiling and original art works on the walls, with luxurious lounges and comfortable chairs, a thirty-piece symphony orchestra to accompany the feature and a mighty Wurlitzer to play for the shorts, the Strand established new standards of luxury for motion-picture audiences—and at only twenty-five cents a ticket! It was an immediate success. The Rialto, formerly Hammerstein's Music Hall, and the Rivoli followed in short order, similarly appointed, similarly equipped. At the Rialto, manager S. L. Rothafel ("Roxy") introduced stage shows to precede the feature film, often bringing in stars of the Metropolitan Opera and the concert stage to emphasize the high plane of his presentations. Most of the other legitimate houses located on Broadway—the Astor, the old Criterion, the New York Theater—also converted permanently to the showing of first-run films. Out in the neighborhoods, only slightly less elaborate theaters were going up. And what was happening in New York was soon being duplicated in every big city across the country. The movies were at last becoming respectable. They were moving into homes of their own. And frequently these were better appointed, better staffed and more comfortable than anything the legitimate theater had to offer.

For their part, the film producers soon learned the value of these first-run houses as a suitably impressive showcase for their wares. Film costs had advanced tremendously in just a few years, from $500 to $1,000 for a two-reel subject in 1912 to between $12,000 and $20,000 for a five-reel feature in 1915. The longer "specials" or films with an expensive star cost still more to make. From the new, large houses the producers could not only obtain a higher rental for their pictures, but the advertising and publicity surrounding these presentations created a stronger demand for them in the subsequent runs. The owners of neighborhood houses would pay more for them, hold them longer and play them at the most favorable time of the week because they knew that their patrons had been pre-sold by the downtown ads, publicity and, with growing frequency, by the newspaper reviews. In fact, producers who were unable to book their pictures into the main-street palaces soon found that they had great difficulty in earning back their investments.

To ensure first-run outlets for their films, the larger companies began to buy into strategic locations, particularly into the downtown theaters of the larger cities. As the competition grew keener, some—notably Fox and Paramount—began to build their own theaters. In consequence, many of the independent theater owners, both frightened by this new competition and outraged by the gouging rentals that the studios had begun to demand, determined to finance their own productions. Organized under the banner of First National in 1917, they won Mary Pickford away from Zukor at Paramount and gave Chaplin his million-dollar contract. Although the original plan called for each star to produce his own pictures, First National soon found it expedient to establish its own studio as well. By 1920 the ties between the producers and the theaters had grown so strong that theater-owner Marcus Loew, in order to maintain a flow of films to his vast chain of movie houses, found it necessary to purchase his own studio, Metro, the forerunner of the formidable Metro-Goldwyn-Mayer company.

Another feature of the Hollywood companies' operations that infuriated the theater owners was the practice of block booking. As the studios grew in power—and especially in star power—they discovered that they could sell an entire year's output in advance of actual production by tying their pictures together in groups or blocks. The theater owner who hoped to play a Mary Pickford picture, a Fairbanks or Wallace Reid or Charles Ray would have to contract for the dozen or more pictures sold in the block with the few he really wanted. For the studios this made perfect sense. Knowing what their sales would be, they could proceed to budget for their entire year's production. But in consequence the theater men found themselves saddled with many undesirable and sometimes even unplayable titles, all tied in with a possible box-office attraction or two in the form of a star feature still unmade. Despite the anguished cries of the exhibitors, however, the studios with their stars, their own exchanges and their own growing chains of key theaters felt no need to conciliate. Quite the opposite. Notoriously obstreperous theater owners were either bought out or forced out of business if they refused to fall into line. The numerous small, independent studios that owned neither exchanges nor theaters by 1920 found themselves with their backs to the wall. Some few were absorbed into the larger companies; the others quietly expired.

It is difficult to determine at this point whether these fundamental changes in the structure of the industry reflected a change in the composition of the movie audiences or vice versa. Unquestionably, up to 1912 the movies were primarily a working-class entertainment. Representative titles of that year would include *One Is Business, the Other Crime, Man's Lust for Gold, Root of Evil, Loan Shark, A Corner in Wheat,* themes reflecting working-class indignation at favoritism in the courts, usury and big business in general. But as small, comfortable houses—the "Bijou Dreams"—began to appear in neighborhoods all over the country, these audiences became tinctured with the middle classes; while the appeal of such large houses as the Strand and the Rialto was definitely directed toward the middle class. By 1915 the film companies themselves had become oriented toward this audience, drawing their themes now from such popular novels as *David Harum* or *Graustark,* from literary or dramatic classics like *Vanity Fair* and *Peer Gynt,* even from operas. Mary Pickford played Cio-Cio-San in *Madame Butterfly.* Both Geraldine Farrar and Theda Bara starred in productions of *Carmen,* while Chaplin burlesqued both the opera and these two films in still a third version of *Carmen* that same year. In 1912 few recognized actors would dream of appearing in the movies; in 1915 the movies virtually swept the New York theater of its first-string talents, bringing before the cameras such stars as De Wolf Hopper, Fritzi Scheff, Mrs. Leslie Carter, Sir Herbert Beerbohm Tree, Billie Burke, Weber and Fields, Frank Keenan, Blanche Ring and Willard Mack. As early as 1913 the first fan magazine had made its appearance as a house organ of the Vitagraph Company. Within the next few years three independent fan magazines were busily selling Americans on the glamour and romance of the movies.

Laughter, love and make-believe—that was what the world wanted while war raged in Europe, and that was what the new Hollywood concentrated on. Romance, adventure, comedy, glamour—the studios took these basic elements and, in the years between 1915 and 1920, transformed them into a multi-million-dollar industry.

♦ 2 ♦

The Growth of an Art
(1920-1930)

In all the arts, one discovers in various countries and at different times that happy combination of social, cultural and economic forces which provides creative artists with just the right stimulus to produce their best work. In painting, one thinks of the Italian Renaissance, the Flemish realists, the English portraitists, the French impressionists. In music, there are the composers of the Italian baroque, the Austrian symphonists, the German romanticists and, again, the French impressionists at the dawn of this century. The same process can also be discerned in the motion picture, with the sole difference that the creative history of this art has been crammed into considerably less than a century. Yet even within that narrow space of time one can glimpse eras in which the films of one country or another clearly dominated world production and made their most important contributions to the artistic growth of the medium. Thus, the French chase and trick films between 1900 and 1907, the Film d'Art of 1907 to 1912, the Italian spectacles between 1910 and 1914 and the Swedish film of 1918 to 1923 can all be regarded as definite "schools," each with its own characteristics and each influencing the work of film makers in other nations. Since World War II we have seen the same process at work in the emergence of the documentary-style British feature film, in the vigorous, neo-realistic Italian school and, more recently, in the exquisite mixture of ancient art and modern themes in the films from Japan. During the twenties, two schools dominated the artistic development of the film and its techniques. The first was in Germany; the second, in the Soviet Union.

Germany's Golden Era

Germany's "Golden Era" lasted only a brief six or seven years, roughly from 1919 through 1925. Yet what an era it was! In other lands other directors had already developed the techniques of film. It remained for the Germans to take this vocabulary and extend it, deepening and enriching the entire medium, turning to themes, emotions and relationships never before essayed on the screen. And to treat these new subjects, the German artists evolved additional techniques that are still impressive for their boldness and originality. They discovered the importance of costume and décor and lighting, the nuances of acting for the camera and, perhaps most important of all, they treated the camera itself as a creative rather than simply a recording instrument.

The sources of this extraordinary development of the film in Germany are twofold. During the First World War, although Germany was cut off from contact with all the Allied powers, she was still seeing films from Sweden and Denmark. These pictures, many of them set in the past, were essentially character studies of great power and penetration, handsomely mounted and making dramatic use of natural backgrounds. Their themes were somber, their tone sober, dignified and compassionate. After 1912 the opportunities for film making in Germany encouraged a whole colony of Danish artists to begin working in Berlin—Asta Nielsen and her husband, the designer-director Urban Gad; the directors Carl Dreyer, Stellan Rye and Svend Gade. They formed one nucleus of the German film. Meanwhile, leaders in the German theater—directors like Max Reinhardt and Leopold Jessner, actors like Emil Jannings, Conrad Veidt, Fritz Kortner and Werner Krauss—began to take a genuine interest in the new medium and had none of the prejudice that theater people in France and America had shown toward it. From the very outset they regarded the motion picture as a serious art with its own problems and potentialities. Encouraged by generous subsidies from the government, which in 1917 grouped together most of the leading German studios into the all-embracing Universum-Film-Aktiengesellschaft (better known as Ufa), they began the incredible series of pictures that was soon to establish the German film as the most exciting in the world.

There would seem to be three main types of German productions during this period, all more or less concurrent. First, and probably most popular, were the great costume spectacles—films like *Passion* (1919), *Anne Boleyn* (1920) and *Danton* (1921). At the outset these dealt with less than savory incidents from the history of Germany's recent enemies; but they did so with great flair, with a tremendous feeling for the sweep of history in the mob scenes and an absorbing intimacy and irreverence in their treatment of the great ones of the past. Indeed, Ernst Lubitsch, who made his reputation directing many of these films, was dubbed by one writer, "The great humanizer of history." When eventually these pictures began to reach England, France and the United States—often thinly veiled as Danish or Scandinavian productions—they were promptly hailed as triumphs of picture making, and their more tendentious aspects overlooked.

The German government had originally subsidized film production for morale and propaganda purposes, to stimulate national pride and patriotism. It continued to do so because pictures soon proved a valuable export commodity. Now the tales, the lore and myths of old German times were revived. Fritz Lang's *Destiny* (1921) achieved a truly medieval folktale quality with its story of a young girl who bargains with Death for the life of her lover. The medieval element turns up again and again in the films of this period—in Paul Wegener's *Golem* (1920), in von Gerlach's *The Chronicle of the Grieschaus* (1923), in Paul Leni's *Waxworks* (1924) and in Pabst's *The Treasure* (1924). The *Nibelungenlied,* that symbol of the heroic life of ancient Germany, was conjured up in two films by Fritz Lang, *Siegfried* and *Kriemhild's Revenge* (1924). Massive, architectural and static, they were based more closely on the original legend than upon the Wagner operas, despite their rather operatic flavor.

Possibly such themes afforded an escape from the uncertainties of the Weimar Republic and the miseries of postwar Germany. Possibly they were a calculated appeal to the wounded pride and shattered morale of a defeated people. Certainly, the hardships that the Germans themselves were suffering at the time never turned up on the screen in these elaborately mounted visions of an earlier greatness. Working in the huge new Ufa studios at Neubabelsberg—the largest and best equipped studios in the world—the directors had the facilities to fling up whole towns, whole forests, whole mountains. As Siegfried Kracauer has pointed out in his superb study of the German film, *From Caligari to Hitler*, they rarely ventured outside the studio, preferring to create their settings from the ground up, to control every aspect of their productions. As a result, one is at all times intensely aware of the artistry in each of these pictures, of the skill and planning and technical mastery that went into their making.

The Shadow of Caligari

Accompanying, and frequently shading into these historical romances is a group of films without parallel in the work of any other nation, films of macabre and fantastic imagination that were far more than mere horror stories. Paul Wegener's early *Student of Prague* (1913), at once their forerunner and prototype, provides the clue to their strange fascination. Concerned with the problem of identity, it told a Hoffmannesque story of a student whose mirror image is claimed by the devil—and eventually his soul as well. The devil and the supernatural creatures of evil became the motivating forces in these films, exerting their demonic power over weak, will-less, helpless, tormented men. It was the Faustian legend extended into a world of nightmare terrors.

Perhaps the most famous picture in this group—in fact one of the most famous films of all times—is Robert Wiene's *The Cabinet of Dr. Caligari* (1919). It is a story told by a madman (although his madness is not revealed until the end of the picture). Shortly after a strange doctor has displayed his somnambulist at a fair in a small German town, the community is plagued by a series of weird, inexplicable murders. When the hero's best friend is found dead, the young man begins to suspect Dr. Caligari and the somnambulist Cesare. He reports his suspicions to the authorities, but without avail. Beside the wily doctor's powers, the efforts of the police prove childishly ineffectual. The hero persists, however, and discovers that Caligari had gained his power over Cesare through his mastery of medieval witchcraft and had commanded him to commit the murders. Thus, Caligari is presented as evil incarnate, a man who kills solely for the pleasure of killing. But the final scene reveals that Caligari is actually the head of the mental institution in which the young man is confined.

Two things distinguished *Caligari* as a film: the daring of this story-within-a-story and the startling originality of its décor. To suggest that what we see are the ravings of a madman, Wiene deliberately adopted stylized settings—great angular shadows painted a deep black, streets and walls and sky all starkly white. Even the furnishings are unrealistic. When the young man reports his friend's murder to the town constable, he finds that official perched high on a six-foot stool writing in a tremendous ledger—an eerie symbol of authority. The actors too were made to further this sense of irreality—the stark white of Lil Dagover's face emphasized by her huge dark eyes and framed by raven-black hair, the dead white of Cesare's skeletal face contrasted with the black of his skin-tight leotard, the streaks of gray and white on Caligari's face and hair, making him at once more and less than human. And with Werner Krauss as Caligari and Conrad Veidt as the somnambulist, the stylization of make-up and settings was echoed in the performances as well. Veidt clings to wall and tree like a ghastly, attenuated shadow, gliding through each scene like a dark specter of death; while Krauss, peering nearsightedly through his tiny spectacles, stumping stiffly about on bowlegs, bowing and scraping with mock-genial politeness, creates a figure of such sinister malignance as has rarely been equaled on the screen.

Postwar artists and intellectuals, looking upon the movies for the first time as something more than a mere entertainment for the masses, found in *Caligari* a film they could safely admire. Its unconventional story, its Freudian overtones and, above all, its obviously "artistic" settings (related both to the stage work of the Expressionists and to the experiments of the Cubist painters) won for it an acclaim that was actually somewhat in excess of its contributions to the growing art. For many, however, it was the introduction, the doorway into film. *Caligari* stands alone, a unique picture. Neither its story pattern nor its style of setting has ever been attempted again, but its influence was inestimable. It foreshadowed the vampires, golems and monsters, the personifications of evil that dominated the German screens in the early twenties—*The Golem* (1920), *Destiny* (1921), *Nosferatu* (1922), Fritz Lang's demoniacal *Dr. Mabuse* (1922), the unholy trio in *Waxworks* (1924), right through to the robot girl of Lang's *Metropolis* (1927). As Dr. Kracauer has shown, the shadow of *Caligari* hung over all German films right down to the advent of Adolf Hitler.

The Street Films:
Murnau and the Moving Camera

Less popular than either the costume dramas or the macabre fantasies, but infinitely more important to the art itself, was the extensive series of films dealing realistically with the life of the common man in those depression-ridden years. Dr. Kracauer has aptly called them the "street films" because city streets play such an important role in them. The titles alone are suggestive: *The Street* (1923), *The Joyless Street* (1925), *Tragedy of the Street* (1927), *Asphalt* (1929). Early in the twenties German art in general, and the German film in particular, became tinged with *die neue Sachlichkeit*— "the new realism with a socialistic flavor." The "street films" lent themselves admirably to these expressions of sympathy for the common man in all his misery. Typical is the plot of one of the first in the group, *The Street*. Eugen Klöpfer plays a middle-aged man bored and fretful in the comfort and security of his own home. Venturing out into the lawless, uncontrollable city, he meets with a series of sordid and terrifying adventures, then returns to his wife, sadder, wiser and grateful for the ordered routine that means peace.

Kracauer, studying these films, found their themes symptomatic of a deep-seated German predisposition toward conformity and authoritarianism. But whatever significance they hold for the sociologist and psychologist, for the film makers their greatest interest will always be the new techniques that came from these ingenious attempts to create both the appearance and the feeling of reality within the studio. Reality has always presented the greatest challenge for the film director. The camera's capacity for distortion, for altering reality, may stimulate the imagination and ingenuity of the artist; but it is this same propensity for distortion that the director must control and use to produce his own version of reality upon the screen. To build a city in a studio—even in a studio as vast and splendidly appointed as Neubabelsberg—is not enough. It has to feel like a city. It needs not only a realism of detail—shop windows, electric signs, automobiles—but also the psychic sensations of rushing crowds or loneliness, of opulent good cheer or claustrophobic squalor. To bring the principles of *die neue Sachlichkeit* to the screen, the German directors had to break through the surface reality to the emotions that lay beneath, to the reactions and sensations of the people caught up in this milieu. And to achieve this penetration, directors like F. W. Murnau, E. A. Dupont and G. W. Pabst used their cameras in ways never before attempted or even dreamed of.

It was Murnau's *The Last Laugh* (1924) that brought on this revolution. Throughout the film his camera was constantly on the prowl, roaming freely through city streets, crowded flats and long hotel corridors. But the camera's movement of itself was not the revolution, any more than the close-up was revolutionary in D. W. Griffith's films. There had been close-ups before Griffith; there were moving cameras before Murnau. What was revolutionary in both instances was the creative, interpretative use each man made of these devices. In Griffith's hands the moving camera suggested sweep and spectacle, the excitement of the chase. There was, however, little of sweep, spectacle or excitement about *The Last Laugh*. Another of the "street films," it tells of an aging doorman at a big hotel, proud of his commanding position, proud of his fine uniform, but past his prime: he can no longer lift down the heavy trunks and suitcases from the top of the Berlin taxicabs. The hotel manager, not without a certain malice, gives him a new job more commensurate with his strength and capabilities—and a new uniform: the white jacket of a washroom attendant. Except for a wittingly improbable finale tacked on by screenwriter Carl Mayer as a parody of the Hollywood happy endings, that is just about all the story there is to *The Last Laugh*. Within this framework, however, the film thoroughly explores the relationships between the *déclassé* doorman and his family, his friends and his neighbors. And it explores them, for the most part, through the use of what might best be described as a subjective camera.

Theoretically, the camera is an objective instrument, photographing coldly and impassively everything set before it. In point of fact, however, the camera is invariably placed in some special relationship to the material it is photographing, a position determined either by the director or by the cameraman. The very act of choosing a camera position—

close or remote, gazing down on the scene from on high or looking up from below—is the product of the director's perception of his subject, his awareness of the emotional reactions he hopes to create in his audience. The camera's "objectivity" is still further delimited by the lens itself. Only in Cinerama does the camera begin to approach the entire field of human vision; the ordinary 35mm camera takes in only a narrow wedge from that field, a 30° to 45° segment of the scene before it. It is the director who determines just what portion of that scene his camera will reveal, what will be included, what will be framed out. The objectivity of the camera is actually nothing more than a mechanism for conveying the director's artistic decision.

When Murnau and his brilliant script writer Carl Mayer set to work on *The Last Laugh*, it occurred to them that the camera might be used not merely to show the objective world of external details but, like a secret eye, to record the inner emotions and reactions of their central character. They wanted to use their camera "subjectively" to reveal the old man's feelings about his degradation, his fear of the people who laughed behind his back, his gratitude to the little night watchman who alone offered him friendship. Mayer, who also wrote *The Cabinet of Dr. Caligari*, had already begun to approach the problem of an objective-subjective camera in that film. The angular settings, the artificial shadows, the accentuated whites and blacks were Mayer's idea: they reflected the distorted image of the world in the mind of the young man telling the story.

While writing *The Last Laugh*, Mayer consulted with Karl Freund, its photographer, to discover the physical limitations of shooting long passages with a camera that moved about continually. When Freund assured him it could be done, Mayer tore up all he had written and began afresh. In his new conception of the film, the camera moved with the old doorman through the courtyard of the apartment building in which he lived, receiving with him the salutations of his neighbors and friends, feeling with him their derisive laughter after he had lost his lofty position. It groped with him down a dark hotel corridor to steal from a cupboard the splendid uniform that had been his cloak of authority. It even, at one point, got riotously drunk for the old man, whirling dizzily around the room until the audience comes to share his vertigo. Through the ingenuity of Mayer and Murnau—and

Karl Freund—the camera did as much to create the identity of the old doorman as the actor who played the role, Emil Jannings. It was the first appearance of the camera as actor.

The Last Laugh was far more than a tour de force. It was an innovation—and one that could have been brought off only with the facilities and technicians of the Neubabelsberg studios. The very opening shot strikes the key for all that is to come, a vast long-shot of the lobby of the Hotel Atlantic taken from a descending elevator. The gates open and the camera rushes across the entire lobby up to the revolving door and the proud old doorman. While behind him is a broad city street filled with cars and buses and pedestrians hurrying to get out of the rain! Frequently the walls of the sets were suspended on coasters from the beams overhead, rolling aside to admit the camera as it passed. Special elevators carried the camera aloft. It was wheeled on dollies through corridors and streets. It was strapped to the cameraman's chest as he spun about in a chair during the drinking scene, or suspended by wires and swung in a basket to and fro to suggest visually the sounds of a street band boozily heard. The story is told, as it were, completely in the first person, subjectively, the way the old doorman saw it and felt it. So fully does the camera convey his emotions that not a single dialogue title is needed throughout the entire length of the film.

For Murnau correctly perceived that the camera could be made to shift its point of view in an instant, that it could be the doorman looking up at the supercilious hotel manager at one moment, the manager looking down at the pitiable old man at the next, and a detached bystander looking impersonally at the two of them a moment later. He found that even while the camera was showing the doorman it could still reflect his mood or suggest his emotional state. There is one astonishing scene as Emil Jannings leaves the hotel after his demotion, the precious uniform clutched to his bosom. He dashes across the street, then pauses breathlessly to look back. As he looks, the walls of the hotel heave and sway as if threatening to fall in upon him. Is this objectivity or subjectivity? Are we seeing what the doorman actually saw? Or is the camera telling us how he felt? Or is it perhaps a little of both?

By these constant shifts of personality, of point of view, the film remains constantly vivid and affecting, the psychology of its characters clearly understood. And although *The Last Laugh* employs the moving camera extensively, it by no means exploits it. The use is always logical, motivated and sensitive to every nuance of the script—the more so because Murnau realized that its effectiveness could best be heightened by moments of utter immobility, by scenes in which the camera remains completely at rest. Mention should also be made of the settings by Robert Herlth and Walter Roehrig, so consistent with the tone of the entire picture. The bold gray planes of the hotel façade pierced by great slashes of light, the working-class apartments drably uniform with their dark, square windows all sustain the subjectivity of the camera: this is the way the doorman sees his world.

The Last Laugh made a tremendous impression in America, not only on film people in Hollywood, which one might have expected, but on the general public as well. The absence of subtitles, although not unique in German films, proved an exciting novelty in this country; while the smoothness of the camera movement and the obvious artistry of Jannings's performance won favorable comment everywhere. American producers consciously began shooting their pictures "in the German manner." But the film that completed the revolution, at least as far as Hollywood was concerned, was Jannings's next picture *Variety* (1925), directed by E. A. Dupont and brilliantly photographed by Karl Freund, the cameraman of *The Last Laugh*. Like the earlier film, its story was simplicity itself. A trapeze artist, played by Jannings, discovers that his wife is deceiving him with his handsome partner. He kills him, then goes to prison. Like the earlier film, it was told with a camera that seemed to be everywhere, entering and externalizing the consciousness of each member of its central triangle, building up the atmosphere of seedy side-show life and the glamour of Berlin's Wintergarten through an infinitude of sharply observed and closely integrated details. Unlike *The Last Laugh*, however, it is impossible to escape the impression that all of this camera movement—darting up to an ear listening at a door, flying through the air with the acrobats, plummeting down from the heights into the very faces of the terror-stricken audience as an aerialist falls to his death—has been created for the effect alone. The discretion, the utter functionalism of Murnau's work is dissipated in a virtuoso show of camera angles and movements, scenes superbly lit and masterfully joined together, but all adding up to an impressive tour de force based on melodrama rather than on the revelation of true characters in a crucial situation.

Nevertheless, the success of *Variety*, when presented to American audiences early in 1926, hastened the already apparent Germanization of Hollywood's studios. Dupont, Freund, Jannings and the female star of *Variety*, Lya de Putti, were all brought to America; and German themes, German acting styles and, above all, German production techniques were incorporated into the most ordinary studio films—a domination that was to continue until sound once again immobilized the camera and sent many of the German artists back to their native land.

Pabst and the Freudian Influence

Perhaps of all the "street films" the most famous is G. W. Pabst's *The Joyless Street* (1925)—if only for the adventitious reason that it featured the young Greta Garbo (along with Asta Nielsen, the ubiquitous Werner Krauss and Einar Hanson). A harshly realistic story of inflation-ridden Vienna, it reflected the economic chaos and ruptured moral values of the day through the interlocking lives of the inhabitants of a single street—an impoverished professor and his daughter, an American Red Cross field worker, an oily procuress and the brutal, profiteering butcher who dominates them all. To convey the psychological truth—and horror—of these characters, Pabst began to explore and develop yet another power of the camera, the expressiveness of viewpoint and angle.

As every still photographer knows, the same scene can be photographed from a virtual infinitude of positions to produce an infinity of visual impressions. But always there is one angle, one position that is most revealing. Only after the photographer has decided upon the emotional tone of his scene, the story that it is to convey and his own reaction to it, can he proceed to locate the exact position for his camera. He is helped, of course, by the basic elements of all pictorial composition—the knowledge that predominating horizontals produce a feeling of repose, while strong verticals suggest action and unrest. And there are psychological elements too in the relation of the camera to its subject—close or far, at a strong angle or a non-committal eye level, above it or shooting from below. By his choice of the camera's position, the director creates for the audience an unconscious predisposition toward the scene, the characters and the action.

Pabst applied his own awareness of this technique to his use of the camera throughout *The Joyless Street*. The butcher, always with a huge white hound by his side, is invariably photographed from below, suggesting his domination over the people of the street. The professor in his bare apartment (much of his furniture has been pawned for food) is generally seen from afar—emphasizing the bleakness of his surroundings—and with the camera slightly above eye level. Scenes in the black-market nightclub are taken sensually close, and often at waist level. If the cutting in *The Joyless Street* seems jumpy and disturbingly obvious, it should be emphasized that few have ever seen the film precisely as Pabst planned it; it has been subject to censorship and the whims of its distributors in every country where it has been shown. Even so, the power and penetration of Pabst's later style are already abundantly apparent in this remarkable film.

Pabst did his next work under the supervision of two disciples of Sigmund Freud, Dr. Hanns Sachs and Dr. Karl Abraham. Essentially, *The Secrets of a Soul* (1926) is a case history translated into vivid screen images. An elderly man (Werner Krauss again), alarmed at his impotency and by disturbing dreams in which he pictures himself killing his young wife with a knife, turns to a psychiatrist for help. A few more dreams, a few meetings with the psychiatrist, and the cure is completed. Naïve as this may seem today, it marked the first serious treatment of psychiatry on the screen. More important, it emphasized the camera's proclivities toward the use of symbolism. Griffith always had an affection for symbols, but his were almost literary in their connotations. A closeup of Lillian Gish or Mae Marsh followed by a shot of a bird inevitably suggested a childlike innocence; Barthelmess dreamily holding a flower in *Broken Blossoms* bespoke a wistful longing for beauty. In *Secrets of a Soul* Pabst's use of the symbol went beyond this into the more affecting, more revealing—and essentially more cinematic—world of the dream image, of objects charged with a subconscious emotional power.

The knives and doors, the stairs and ladders which, in double and triple exposure, disturbed the slumber of Werner Krauss in *Secrets of a Soul* were to reappear on another, more realistic plane in such subsequent Pabst films as *The Love of Jeanne Ney* (1927) and *Pandora's Box* (1929).

Here they exist simply as objects, part of the atmosphere, part of the settings surrounding the characters until the camera moves in to isolate them and underline their significance. Thus, in the opening scene of *Jeanne Ney* the camera sets off on a wordless exploration of Fritz Rasp's sordid, cluttered room—dirty clothes flung about, overflowing ashtrays, erotic pictures and statuettes. We know the character well before laying eyes on him. A shattered mirror in an elegant frame, a spiked iron fence separating two lovers, a knife in the hand of Jack-the-Ripper—all are ordinary objects, but charged by Pabst with emotional overtones as vivid and evocative as dream symbols. Even action is at times deliberately staged for its symbolic effect, as when Rasp preparing to rape Jeanne Ney slowly pulls open his tie.

Above all a director's director, Pabst developed a technique of shooting and editing that was to influence film makers everywhere, and perhaps most especially in Hollywood. In order to maintain the balance between his characters and the objects that surrounded them, he increased the fragmentation of his scenes. The camera leaps incessantly from place to place, from position to position, always discovering the best vantage point to reveal an actor's gesture, action or expression—or to permit the background to make its own eloquent comment upon the action. In one brief section from *The Love of Jeanne Ney*, a scene running less than three minutes on the screen, there are forty separate shots, the longest about twenty seconds in length. But the actual movement from one camera position to the next is barely preceptible. Pabst consciously sought to eliminate from his films any feeling of jerkiness between shots while still allowing his camera the utmost freedom. He soon found that by focusing the audience's attention upon some physical movement, he could effectively disguise such breaks. By having an actor begin a gesture in one shot and carry it through to completion in the next, he created a visual bridge. The eye, following the flow of the action, ignored the cut itself. This technique of editing on movement, which Pabst discovered and polished with incredible finesse, was to become fundamental after the introduction of sound.

Pabst's most important work was done during the years that marked the decline of the German film. Lest this seem curious, it should be remembered that his pictures never enjoyed the wide popularity that greeted the work of Lubitsch,

Murnau, Fritz Lang and E. A. Dupont. While his art was essentially cinematic—in some ways superior to the technique of any of his contemporaries—his stories were frequently so melodramatic as to alienate all but the most discerning critics, or so flagrantly erotic as to invite censorial emasculation. And yet no director of the silent era is more highly esteemed as a craftsman than Pabst. He had a passion for realism; and no one excelled him in concretizing that reality. Whether filming an actual flower market in Paris or a misty London street built in a studio, he sifted each scene for the details that would be at once most revealing and most evocative, using his camera like a probing surgical instrument to lay bare in fragmentary glimpses those secret meanings that lie beneath the surface. He worked with a sensuous intellectuality, suggesting the emotional and psychological drives of his characters through vivid, affecting and often grotesque screen images. There is a tremendous compression in his films, a richness of detail that holds layer on layer of meaning. To see one is a haunting experience, like peering down a darkened corridor at a bright and shadowed world. Long after the story is done, the images linger and mingle and grow in the realms of the subconscious, in the phantasms of our dreams.

If the "Golden Era" of the German film was brief, its twilight was relatively long. Throughout the late twenties the German pictures excelled in sheer physical beauty, in the size and richness of their mountings, in the artistry of both performances and direction. Instead of being virtues, however, these very qualities soon turned into defects. Such major Ufa productions as *Faust* (1925), *Tartuffe* (1926) and *Metropolis* (1927) were altogether too self-consciously "artistic" for their own good—handsome, impressive, but dreadfully slow and ponderous, lacking the creative vitality that had characterized most German films only a few years earlier. The reasons for this gradual decline are by no means obscure. By the dawn of the twenties, Hollywood had entered into its own "Golden Era" of giant studios and virtually unlimited financing. Whatever Hollywood could not produce itself, it bought. And as the German pictures began to create a furor in this country, negotiations were soon under way to import the talents that had made them—stars, directors, producers, cameramen, set designers. The first star to arrive was Pola Negri, whose immense popularity with American audiences paved the way for actors like Emil Jannings, Lya de Putti and Conrad Veidt. Ernst Lubitsch was the first important German director to come to Hollywood. His success inspired the wholesale importation of others—Ludwig Berger, Michael Curtiz, William Dieterle, E. A. Dupont, Paul Leni, F. W. Murnau. Even Pabst had a brief, unhappy fling in the Hollywood studios. Top cinematographers like Karl Freund, Karl Struss, Kurt Courant and Theodor Sparkuhl brought German camera techniques to the American films. And finally, in 1927, Erich Pommer himself, the astute production head of Ufa, the man directly responsible for most of the great successes of the "Golden Era," was lured to Hollywood by Paramount. Thus throughout the late twenties, the German studios were being persistently drained of their best talents.

At the same time the Germans who remained at home were increasingly tailoring their films for the American market, hoping to repeat the box-office success of *Variety*—and hoping, many of them, to receive their own invitations to cross the Atlantic. Their pictures began to shed those specific qualities that had first won attention for the German film; they became vaguely international in tone, following formulas rather than creating styles. This process was hastened when, in 1925, both Paramount and M-G-M negotiated a pact with Ufa to co-produce on the Continent, using mixed casts and technicians. American stars were sent abroad to appear in these films and guarantee their success on both sides of the water. As a result, the already serious drainage of Germany's best creative talent was accompanied by a steady dilution of those creative energies that remained. Dr. Kracauer has described such films of the late twenties as *Homecoming* (1928), *Asphalt* (1929) and *The Wonderful Lie of Nina Petrovna* (1929) as "a synthesis of Hollywood and Neubabelsberg." The marvelous German craftsmanship persisted, but the magic fire of the early twenties was being slowly extinguished.

New Beginnings in Russia

At the very time that the German industry was slipping into a decline, the Western world began to be aware of a vigorous film movement stirring in the Soviet Union. The Revolution of 1917 had virtually severed Russia from the rest of Europe both economically and culturally; but throughout the

early twenties travelers were bringing back reports of daring
experiments in the arts. Music had become determinedly
atonal, imitating cement mixers and riveting drills. In the theater, classic plays were being staged with acrobats and trapeze artists. Films too were sharing in this upheaval. Not
until 1925, however, were any of these circulated in western
Europe, and the few that did appear were by no means representative. Non-political subjects, they included *Polikushka*
(1922), from a story by Tolstoi; Pushkin's *The Stationmaster*
(1925) and *The Marriage of the Bear* (1925) by Lunachar-
sky. Seen mainly by critics and film enthusiasts in the numerous film societies and *ciné-clubs* that had begun to spring up
in England and on the Continent, this handful of pictures
gave barely a hint of the great cycle of Russian films that was
to appear between 1925 and 1930. Beginning almost simultaneously with *Potemkin* (1925) and *Mother* (1925), it included such masterworks as *End of St. Petersburg* (1927),
Ten Days That Shook the World (1928), *Storm over Asia*
(1928), *Arsenal* (1929), *Fragment of an Empire* (1929),
Old and New (1929) and *Earth* (1930). They were films of
extraordinary visual impact, revolutionary both in theme and
in style. In them, for the first time, the motion-picture
medium was treated not only as an art but as a science as
well—a science that developed out of the scarcity of film
stock and camera equipment that plagued the Russian film
makers for almost a decade after the Revolution. Compared
to the Germans the Russians were creating films out of thin
air.

At the end of the Revolution, the new Soviet Union found
itself with the merest shell of a film industry. Its beginnings
had been tentative, its roots shallow. Not until 1907 was
there a native Russian studio. Up to that time, the only films
made there had been shot by itinerant cameramen sent out by
the French firms of Gaumont, Lumière and Pathé. Other
small studios followed, some of German, some of French and
a few of Russian origin. In all of Russia on the eve of the
Revolution, there were only 1,045 theaters with 364,000
seats.

Feature production, which began in 1914, was necessarily
on a very limited scale, and reflected the producers' determination to woo the middle classes. The great stage director
Vsevolod Meyerhold put three of his plays on film, while the
most ambitious picture of the period was an adaptation of

Tolstoi's *Father Sergius* (1917), directed by Feodor Protazanov. It remains a highly dramatic and impressive film, distinguished particularly by handsome Ivan Mozhukhin's extraordinary performance as the licentious young officer who, after a multitude of sins, becomes a shaggy, tormented old man roaming the countryside in search of redemption. Much of it was actually shot in the sumptuous clubs and marbled palaces described in the novel. Although the film was immediately suppressed by the czarist government for its revelations of corrupt court life, the ban was soon lifted by the Kerensky régime that followed. Not until after the Revolution, however, did the Russian film makers begin to concentrate on the literature, the culture and the life of their own country. But by that time the personnel of the industry and the composition of the audience had undergone a drastic change.

Once the Revolution broke, whatever industry there was promptly disintegrated. The Europeans withdrew and the White Russians hastily followed after, seizing in their flight any bits of film and camera equipment they could lay their hands on. Thus it was almost an empty gesture when, in August of 1919, the Russians nationalized their motion-picture industry and placed it under the People's Commissariat of Propaganda and Education. Considering the wrecked studios, the meager equipment and the pitiful supplies of raw stock available at the time, Lenin displayed incredibly shrewd foresight in declaring that "Of all the arts, the cinema is the most important for us."

The Editing Principle: Vertov and Kuleshov

It is scarcely surprising to find that during the years of civil war and counter-revolution following the Bolsheviks' accession to power, the Russian film makers were concerned almost exclusively with what would today be called the documentary film. Virtually all available equipment and raw stock were used to record the progress of the Red armies on the various fighting fronts and the changes being effected by the new government. And as the negatives come in from all corners of the Soviet Union, they were shaped and edited by a youthful poet and film enthusiast, Dziga Vertov. Released first in newsreel form, the material was finally assembled into one thirteen-reel film (almost three hours) as *The Anniver-*

sary of the October Revolution (1918). It was the Soviet's first feature. From this experience Vertov developed a theory of film making which he called "The Kino Eye." In a series of bold manifestoes, he argued that the only proper film form for the new Russia was the factual film and that the only true function of film was to bring the facts of the new society to the people who were helping to build it. In 1922 he launched *Kino-Pravda* (*Film-Truth*), a weekly newsreel, but a newsreel specially edited to give not only facts but some background for an understanding of these facts—and, not infrequently, an emotional tone coloring the spectator's acceptance of them. Titles punctuated the reel, lettered poster-fashion, bearing propagandist slogans and exultant statistics. From the very outset the Soviet film makers were aware of the importance of editing in their work.

Vertov was to grow increasingly dogmatic in his manifestoes. He compared the motion picture to a living organism, its eye being the eye of the cameraman, its hands the editor who assembles the images, its brain the author-supervisor, Vertov. But Vertov's manifestoes were soon being countered by others. This was an era of manifestoes. As money became more available, new equipment and additional film stock were purchased from abroad and placed at the disposal of artists who promptly enunciated *their* theories on the nature of the film. With the government actively encouraging experiment in every field, technological, scientific and artistic, it was only natural that the motion picture should share in this intellectual ferment. Everything was tried, from straight story-telling pictures (with propagandist overtones) to classic plays featuring the Moscow Art Theatre. One group, calling itself FEX—The Factory of the Eccentric Actor—even sought to apply slapstick, vaudeville and circus techniques to serious themes, using tumblers and acrobats as actors. In such films as *The Adventures of an October Child* (1924) and *The Cloak* (1926), the founder-directors of FEX, Grigori Kozintzev and Leonid Trauberg, achieved a curious form of expressionism based on exaggeration of gesture by the actor and distortion of angles by the camera, both producing an impressive if artifical heightening of the emotional content of the scenes.

Interesting and even audacious as these experiments were, the most fruitful experimentation was to come from the workshop of Lev Kuleshov, one of the few pre-Revolutionary film makers to remain in Russia after the mass exodus of 1917. Kuleshov, like Vertov, insisted on the importance of editing; but where Vertov became increasingly mechanical—even mathematical—in the development of his editing principles, Kuleshov was concerned with the emotional and psychological potentialities inherent in joining one image to the next. And in order to understand fully the fine art of cutting, he began to study and experiment. With raw film still precious and scarce, Kuleshov and his disciples—including Vsevolod I. Pudovkin—set forth upon an intensive investigation of films that had already been made, outstanding among them being D. W. Griffith's *Intolerance*. According to Pudovkin, in his still valuable handbook *Film Technique*, these films were screened over and over again, the mechanics of their construction dissected, analyzed and discussed. The films were physically torn apart and the shots rearranged, the sequences edited in different ways; and each time the new effects were studied to see whether they improved upon or altered the intent of the original.

Perhaps the most famous of Kuleshov's experiments—also recorded by Pudovkin—was one involving an old film with the actor Mozhukhin. From it Kuleshov obtained a close-up in which Mozhukhin appeared perfectly expressionless. This same shot he inserted at various points into another film—once in juxtaposition to a plate of soup, once next to a child playing contentedly with a teddy bear, and again next to a shot of an old woman lying dead in her coffin. Audiences shown the experimental reel praised Mozhukhin's performance—his look of hunger at the bowl of soup, his delight on seeing the child, his grief over the dead woman. For Kuleshov, however, it was a conclusive demonstration of his theory—based on what Griffith had already achieved instinctively—that it is not merely the image alone, but the juxtaposition of images that creates the emotional tone of a sequence. In his film *By the Law* (1926), based on Jack London's taut study of three people snowbound in a cabin for an entire winter, Kuleshov utilized his mastery of the medium to the full. Within a single setting, with only three actors, he created a film in which the emotional tensions, the frictions, the fraying nerves and incipient madness of the characters are experienced almost too intensely by the audience. From Griffith, Kuleshov had learned the kinetic values of longer

and shorter shots, the ability to heighten or release emotion
by editing. Through his own researches into the relationship
of shot to shot, through his calculated assembly of the most
revealing movements of an arm, a leg, a hand, his technique
of adding detail on detail, he achieved an intensity of emotional identification, of empathy, such as Griffith never attained.

Pudovkin and the Personal Epic

Vsevolod I. Pudovkin, the outstanding director to come
from the Kuleshov workshop, built upon his teacher's discoveries. For Pudovkin the cut was still fundamental to film
technique, but he gave increased attention to the emotional
content of his separate shots, broadening Kuleshov's approach
to embrace the entire range of human feeling. Because the
film is essentially a visual medium, Pudovkin maintained that
it was necessary to discover visual means to convey not only
story elements but character traits as well. "Plastic material,"
he called this, the visible manifestations of personality, of attitude, of an inner emotional state. In his book *Film Technique* he cites a crude but unmistakably clear example from
an American film by Henry King, *Tol'able David* (1921). To
characterize Ernest Torrence as a cruel, heartless, sadistic
brute, King introduced him through a brief sequence of shots
in which the man, about to enter a house, spies a kitten sleeping in the sun. His eyes glittering with malice, Torrence seizes
a rock and prepares to fling it at the tiny creature. This wanton bit of cruelty might, at least in those pre-sound days,
have been dispensed with altogether and a title substituted:
"The Tramp—a cruel, heartless, sadistic brute . . . Ernest
Torrence." But how much more effective to introduce the
character visually, through use of this "plastic material"! Pudovkin's films are filled with such shots. In *Mother* the young
hero awaits his impending release from jail. His thoughts are
of the world outside; and Pudovkin cuts from his smiling face
to shots of a thawing mountain stream, of sparkling waters
liberated from their wintry prison.

In *Storm over Asia*, Pudovkin refined and polished this
technique to an astonishing degree, achieving a precision of
plastic expression that has never been excelled. One sequence
of great complexity, for example, is played completely without titles, yet every turn of the action, every nuance of mood

and motivation is crystal clear. A British soldier has been instructed to take a captured Mongol out to the sand pits beyond the city and shoot him. Clearly reluctant to carry out this command, the soldier carefully finishes binding on his puttees, slowly taps out his pipe and shoulders his rifle. Outside the barracks the Mongol awaits him, not knowing what to expect. Gruffly, the Englishman shoves him forward. They come to a large, muddy puddle in the middle of the road. The soldier makes a wide detour around it; the Mongol splashes straight on through. When they arrive at the sand pits, the scene of the execution, the soldier tries to delay the distasteful business for a moment. He lights his pipe, then offers a cigarette to the Mongol. Smiling, the Mongol refuses. The soldier motions him forward, toward the edge of the pits. Still smiling, the Mongol obeys. In a sudden frenzy, the Englishman tries to unsling his rifle while the Mongol's back is turned. The Mongol sees him and, only half comprehending, is shot down. On the way back to the barracks, his rifle dragging, one of his puttees untied, the soldier sloshes without knowing, without caring, through the puddle he had so fastidiously avoided only a few moments earlier. Each shot has its own significance, carrying us deeper and deeper into an understanding of the characters and their emotions. "Brick by brick," Pudovkin described his method of building a film—brick by brick, solidly, the way a good mason constructs a wall.

When one thinks of Pudovkin, it is invariably in terms of the marvelous moments of character revelation with which his films abound. He knew how to make one feel with them their joy, their pain, their victories, their defeats. From his collaboration with Pavlov on the purely expositional film *Mechanics of the Brain* (1926) he learned, perhaps better than any other film maker, the nature of reflexes and reactions. Certainly, in his pictures one is always tactilely aware of the world in which his characters move—the mud of a road, the steel and stone of a prison, the rough planks and plaster of a peasant hovel; conscious, too, of the impact of a blow or a bullet, of breathless flight or impassioned resistance. Like Pabst, Pudovkin had a keen awareness of the emotional power of carefully chosen and closely observed details. Both men were primarily concerned with revealing the inner impulses that motivated their characters. Both had absorbed much from science—Pudovkin from Pavlov, Pabst

from Freud. Quite independently, they had evolved techniques that were strikingly similar: a carefully composed realism of settings and milieu, an abundance of close-ups both of
objects and of people, brief shots seen from constantly shifting points of view, and adroit cutting on movement to make
all flow together smoothly. For Pabst, however, the interest
was always on the individual, on the instincts and passions
behind an act of violence, eroticism or death. Pudovkin, on
the other hand, portrayed the individual as a social being,
and sought to create in his films the dynamic relationship between a man and his background, the impact of ideas and
events upon his character.

Pudovkin's films may properly be described as epic. In
each of them—*Mother* (1925), *End of St. Petersburg*
(1927), *Storm over Asia* (1928), right through his first
sound picture, *Deserter* (1933)—the hero is in fact the personification of the masses, an ideal, perhaps even an idealized
figure, caught up in the turbulent stream of living history. In
this respect Pudovkin's work stands in sharpest contrast to his
brilliant contemporary, Sergei Eisenstein. For Eisenstein, the
masses themselves were the hero; and at least in *Potemkin*
(1925) and *Ten Days That Shook the World* (1928) Eisenstein was able to create a film form in which character and
characterization were subordinate to the sweep and turmoil
of broad, revolutionary movements. While frequently in bitter
opposition to each other during their lifetimes, the names of
Eisenstein and Pudovkin will always be linked in film history;
they were at once Russia's greatest film makers and most
searching theoreticians. "Pudovkin's films resemble a song,"
wrote the French film historian Léon Moussinac, "Eisenstein's, a shout."

Eisenstein and the Mass Epic

Sergei M. Eisenstein, the son of a wealthy shipbuilder, had
been trained in architecture and engineering. Drawn to the
arts during the period of upheaval just after the Revolution,
he worked in the theaters of Foregger and Meyerhold as a
designer, then joined the Proletcult Theatre as director. Always he tried to infuse into the theater his own changing,
evolving concepts of what he referred to as "Soviet realism."
Indeed, his last play before moving into films, *Gas Masks*
(1923), was so very realistic that it was not staged in a the-

ater at all. Instead, it was performed against the background of an actual gasworks, the action shifting from place to place within the building itself. One can imagine the audience bustling about after it. In any case, it was this experience that led Eisentein to suspect that the motion picture might provide a happier solution to his artistic problems. He saw quite clearly that the real settings in *Gas Masks* had made the play itself seem quite false. *Strike* (1924), his first full-length film, seems to have come as the logical result of his experience with this play. "The cart fell to pieces and the driver dropped into the cinema," he once wrote. The drop was not without preparation. Eisenstein observed the Kuleshov workshop in production and discussed editing with Dziga Vertov, then engaged the support of the Proletcult collective to produce his film and appear in it. Describing the incidents leading up to an all-out strike in a metalworks during czarist days, the film is at once exuberantly youthful and enormously creative. Its climax, with its scenes of strikers being murdered intercut with shots of cattle being slaughtered in an abattoir, was already pointing toward the editing techniques made famous in *Potemkin*.

In recognition of his accomplishments on *Strike,* the Russian government commissioned Eisenstein to make a film commemorating the abortive revolution of 1905. Pudovkin, similarly commissioned, chose Gorki's *Mother* for his theme, but Eisenstein preferred to work without any prepared narrative. He intended to recreate on film key incidents in the nation-wide uprisings and the brutal czarist repression that followed. He had already done some initial shooting in Leningrad before going south to Odessa to take a few brief scenes depicting the famous mutiny of the sailors aboard the battleship *Potemkin*. When he saw the great flight of stairs leading down from the center of Odessa to the waterfront, however, the steps on which Cossacks had methodically shot down hundreds of citizens sympathizing with the rebel sailors, Eisenstein was convinced that here was the heart of his entire picture, the perfect symbol for the whole 1905 uprising. In this one incident he found reproduced in miniature the alignment of social forces that had boiled over throughout Russia in that year—the sharpening lines of class against class, the increasing hatred of the czarist régime and the emergence of a militant revolutionary leadership. The slaughter on the steps epitomized the savage reprisals that followed the uprisings everywhere, one more instance of the czarist government's shocking contempt for the people of Russia. In addition, for dramatic purposes, there was even the indication of a "happy ending." When the *Potemkin* approached the massed ships of the Imperial Navy, the sailors on the other vessels refused to fire upon their comrades, permitting them to escape unchallenged—a symbol of the solidarity of the Russian people and of the eventual victory over their czarist oppressors. In view of all this, Eisenstein dropped his former plans for the 1905 film and expanded the few scenes originally allotted to the Odessa mutiny into a full six-reel feature, which he titled *Potemkin*.

Seen today, *Potemkin* remains as striking and original as when it first appeared in 1925. In no other film has a historic event been reconstructed as the microcosmic symbol of an entire society, nor made so immediate and affecting without an individual hero or personalized story. Its visual excitement, the power of its images and the brilliance of its editing, have retained all their ability to startle and impress. From its opening sequence of increasingly turbulent waters dashing against a quay to its final shot in which the entire ship, seen from below, glides triumphantly across the screen, Eisenstein conceived his film as a series of images assembled in a completely new, revolutionary manner. For him, everything rested on what could be done with the separate shots on the editing table; every shot was made with a view to its position in the completed film. But the theory underlying their assembly was Eisenstein's own, one that he described as "shock attraction."

Eisenstein formulated his theory of editing from his studies of Japanese hieroglyphic writing. The Japanese word picture for crying, he noted, combined the pictures for "eye" and for "water"; sorrow was represented by the hieroglyphics for "knife" and "heart"; and singing joined together their word pictures for "mouth" and "bird." This juxtaposition, Eisenstein felt, did more than simply add one idea to the other: it "exploded" them into a totally new concept—weeping, sorrow or song. Because motion-picture editing is essentially the art of bringing together similarly independent images into new relationships, Eisenstein argued that this same technique applied to cinematic construction. Indeed, he insisted that it was basic to any dynamic film technique because it involved the active participation of the audience in comprehending and completing the artist's intentions.

For all the apparent rigidity of his theoretical formulations, Eisenstein on film was a good deal less dogmatic than Eisenstein on paper. While *Potemkin* abounds in marvelous examples of the "shock attraction" technique, the editing is by no means limited to this one method. In fact, it would probably be impossible to base an entire picture on "shock attractions" alone. Out of the hundreds of shots that make up any feature film, only the briefest cluster can be held together in this fashion, unified by a single idea and making a single statement. Yet when Eisenstein did use the "shock" method, as in the incredible "steps sequence" from *Potemkin*, he filled the screen with images of overwhelming power, a power drawn from the audience's own instinctive association of the content of one shot with what is seen in the next. A Cossack in close-up slashes with his saber in one shot; the next shows us a close-up of a woman with her glasses smashed and her face bloody. A line of Cossacks fires and we see a young mother clutching at her vitals, the blood streaming out over her hands. Her baby carriage starts bounding wildly down the steps, and we watch its progress through the horrified eyes of a student crouching down below, his head slowly turning as he follows the descent. Actually, of course, what we are shown is simply a series of independently photographed shots—one of rifles firing, another of a young woman simulating agony, another of a carriage rolling down a flight of stairs, and another of a young man turning his head. It is the editing that establishes their connection for us, the "shock attraction" that binds them together and makes us share with the student his sense of helpless horror. And each shot was arranged and photographed with a precise knowledge of how it would relate to all the others; just as, at the close of the sequence, shots of three stone lions—one lying, one crouching, one rearing up—have been edited together to create the illusion of a single beast suddenly startled and roaring in rage.

In *Potemkin* one finds equally brilliant examples of other editorial techniques—techniques that Eisenstein himself was to develop further in *Ten Days That Shook the World* and in *Old and New*. Tonal cutting, in which continuity is provided by the gradual lightening or darkening of the shots in a sequence; directional cutting, in which the flow of movement from one shot to the next establishes the continuity; and cutting on form—the curve of an arm giving way to the arc of a parasol, followed by the bend of an arch—all of these Eisenstein experimented with in *Potemkin* (and all of them have found particular application since that time in the field of documentary film making).

But perhaps Eisenstein's greatest editorial discovery was the discrepancy between screen time and real time. Through editing, he found, he could destroy real time altogether. Why pay as much attention, he asked, to one's most insignificant gesture as is given to the most crucial moments in one's life? Psychologists have long been aware of the relativity of time. An agonized moment can seem like an eternity; a happy hour flies by in an instant. Griffith had already shown how to eliminate the inessentials, to concentrate the significant into a single dramatic close-up. Now Eisenstein proceeded to *expand* time, to accentuate the moments of peak significance.

Early in *Potemkin* a young sailor, beaten by his petty officer, half starved on the miserable rations served to the crew, is washing the dishes in the officers' mess. He comes upon a platter on which is inscribed, "Give Us This Day Our Daily Bread." His indignation suddenly wells over and he sends the dish crashing to the floor. To break a dish—to lift it up and throw it down—is the action of only a moment. But this was a moment of tremendous importance, both to the boy and to the development of the entire film, the first external manifestation of the spirit of revolt that was sweeping through the crew of the battleship. Rather than photograph it in a single shot from a single position, which would merely reproduce the action in its ordinary time value, Eisenstein took the same action from a number of angles, then cut the shots together in a slightly overlapping progression. The result was to emphasize the action by the abrupt hail of shots, and to prolong it through the overlaps.

Eisenstein repeated this technique at each crucial moment in *Potemkin*. In the sequence on the quarter-deck, the Marines' growing determination not to fire on their comrades is suggested in a series of shots of clenching fists, flinching eyes and wavering rifles that delay the moment of action long after the officers have given their command. At the climax of the film, as the victorious crew of the ship tensely wait to discover whether the fleet will fire upon them or not, the tension is prolonged through shots of the men waiting motionless, the engines racing and the cannon slowly mounting to the ready position.

This cinematic expansion of time reaches its fullest, most complex expression in the scenes of the massacre on the Odessa steps. The people of Odessa have assembled on the steps to see—and many of them to cheer—the sailors who have thrown off their hated officers. Suddenly, from behind, comes a fusillade of bullets. The Cossacks have been ordered to put an end to this demonstration, to clear the steps. They march slowly, deliberately downward, firing as they go. The crowd immediately breaks in panic, leaping, running, jumping to the foot of the stairs and safety. Now as one look at the steps would show, any reasonably able-bodied citizen could run down the entire flight in a minute or two—particularly if his life depended on it. But Eisenstein realized that for the people trapped on the steps these would be the most terrifying (and for many, the final) moments of their lives. Obviously the scene should not be simply recorded, newsreel fashion, reproducing the atrocity exactly as it happened in time and in incident. To provide a proper psychological expansion and dramatic weight, Eisenstein broke up the mass into its component parts: the Cossacks moving ruthlessly downward and the crowd fleeing in terror before them provide the main motifs. Against them, he set a group that crawls up the steps cringing, begging for mercy; another that huddles together in prayer; and a woman whose child has been shot, defiantly carrying the bleeding body in her arms back to the very barrels of the Cossack rifles. Others are picked out as individuals: a legless cripple who scrambles down the embankment on his hands, the mother with the baby carriage, the horrified student. Each character, each incident provides not only an interruption but a counter-rhythm to the steady, measured tread of the Cossacks. Each action extends the scene upon the steps just a little bit longer until, ultimately, each of these knots of resistance has been broken. The final moments of the sequence capture the sense of headlong flight, of panic and disaster in a rapidly accelerating series of shots of the baby carriage, the student, a praying woman and—in an incredible shot just four frames long—the frenzied face of a Cossack slashing with his saber, cutting off the retreat at the foot of the stairs.

In this one, brilliant sequence of film making, Eisenstein created virtually an editor's handbook, a truly virtuoso display of all the basic cutting principles—parallel editing, rhythmic, tonal, directional and "shock." When later Eisenstein wrote and lectured on his theories, he used the French word for editing, *montage,* which means literally "mounting," or "putting together." But as first *Potemkin,* then *Ten Days* swept through the Western world taking film makers and critics by storm, the word *montage* came to identify not cutting in general, but specifically the rapid, shock cutting that Eisenstein employed in his films. Its use survives to this day in the specially created "montage sequences" inserted into Hollywood films to suggest, in a blur of double exposures, the rise to fame of an opera singer or, in brief model shots, the destruction of an airplane, a city or a planet. It is scarcely necessary to add that this is a far cry from Eisenstein's original conception of the word.

In *Ten Days That Shook the World,* Eisenstein further developed many of the editing techniques he had introduced in *Potemkin.* Time is again extended in the justly famous sequence of the opening of the bridges during a workers' demonstration in St. Petersburg. To cut off the workers from their quarters, the police have been ordered to raise the drawbridges around the center of the city. On one of the bridges is a dead woman, shot by the police. Her long hair lies sprawled across the crevice formed by the two sections of the bridge. As the center begins to rise, the instant of its opening is prolonged in a marvelous series of shots of the hair falling, falling, falling into the abyss. The bridge continues to rise, and the steepness of its ascent is accentuated by a horse hanging over the ledge. The camera rides up with the rising bridge to the very summit, trained on the carriage being held at the tip of the roadway by the weight of the horse. At the last moment the traces part, and a quick succession of shots catches the carriage rolling down the incline on one side, and on the other, the horse plummeting into the water far below. Here not only has time been extended, but the finality of the act, the completeness of the separation between the two parts of the city has been emphasized visually, symbolically.

It was the symbol, the filmic metaphor, that seems to have attracted Eisenstein most strongly during the making of *Ten Days.* Commissioned in celebration of the tenth anniversary of the 1917 Revolution, the film covered the stirring events between Lenin's secret return from exile and the Bolsheviks' seizure of power. As conceived by Eisenstein, it was to embrace activity on many fronts—in the councils of the Kerensky government, in the hectic sessions of the Bolsheviks, at the front and in the workers' quarters, all culminating in the final, decisive attack upon the Winter Palace. Once again he had a broader theme than could be developed through any conventional narrative devices. And even more than in *Potemkin,* he was faced with the necessity of characterizing in sharp, swift visuals all the many elements involved in the history of an era.

Eisenstein found his solution in an elaborate—perhaps even over-elaborate—series of filmic symbols. Thus, the dictatorship of Kerensky is wryly satirized in a sequence showing Kerensky gravely mounting the stairs of the Winter Palace. At each landing he is bowed to by assorted generals and flunkies and saluted with ever more grandiose titles. His Napoleonic ambitions are implied when he carefully assembles the four quarters of a crystal decanter and meticulously places upon them their crown, or gazes upward at an ornate marble statue that extends a wreath of laurel over his head. The ceremony of the Old Guard is suggested by richly paneled doors slowly closing; the bustle of the Bolsheviks by the constant banging open and shut of the battered door to their central headquarters. The symbol, the part for the whole, is used repeatedly to epitomize events. The Army is with the Bolsheviks—a mass of rifles waves in the air. The Kerensky government has lost control of the situation—bureaucrats click vainly on their telephones. The revolutionary forces have won—a young boy sits upon the Romanov throne gaily kicking his legs. The camera—operated by Edouard Tisse, who was to Eisenstein what Bitzer had been to Griffith—adds further emphasis to these meaningful vignettes. Men and women drag a small cannon into position—the camera is tilted to emphasize the difficulty of the operation. A faded woman, a soldier in Kerensky's Battalion of Death, gazes longingly at a statue of young love—the camera observes her mistily, through soft focus lenses. A gross, mannish woman in the same Battalion is photographed sharply and from below, emphasizing all her corpulence and brawn.

During his making of *Ten Days,* Eisenstein encountered his first difficulties with the Soviet authorities. While the picture was still in production, Stalin and Trotzky had clashed; Trotzky, one of the leading tacticians of the Revolution, fled the country into exile, and Eisenstein suddenly found himself faced with the necessity of removing from his film one of its main protagonists. The subsequent re-editing delayed its release for over a year; but one has only to compare *Ten Days* with Romm's *Lenin in October*, produced in 1937 to mark the twentieth anniversary of the Revolution, to realize how dynamic—and, in spirit, how much more authentic—was Eisenstein's version of the Revolution. In Romm's film as the troops charged through the Winter Palace, someone sings out, "Be careful, those are works of art!" Their leader's first action on breaking into the inner council of the Provisional Government is to comb his hair. Romm's was a self-consciously neat Revolution. In *Ten Days*, the troops charge like troops, smashing as they go; and their leader, a ratty, intense little man in a floppy black hat, plants a revolver on the table the moment he gains the inner chamber, sweeps aside the clutter of books and papers, and declares that the Bolsheviks have taken over. Only at one point does Eisenstein seem to go out of his way to glorify Lenin, introducing a brief but embarrassingly obvious lap-dissolve penetrating Lenin's disguise on his return to Russia to lead the Revolution. It seems almost an afterthought.

Eisenstein's clashes with his government were to continue throughout the remainder of his career—a career, incidentally, in which there were to be only four more completed films, *Old and New* (1929), *Alexander Nevsky* (1938) and Part I of *Ivan the Terrible* (1944). (Part II of *Ivan*, although finished in 1946, was not released until 1958, and then only outside of the Soviet Union in a less complete version than Einstein had envisaged.) Perhaps he would have clashed with authority under any system of government, such was his temperament, such was his genius. When in 1930 he came to the United States to work for a time at Paramount, he arrogantly submitted his brilliant adaptation of Theodore Dreiser's mammoth *An American Tragedy* with a note that read in part: "Here it is, the miracle completed—*An American Tragedy* in 14 reels . . . And 'Honi soit qui mal y pense.' " The script was rejected, as were all the other projects he originated at Paramount. Later in Mexico, directing *Que Viva Mexico* on funds raised by Upton Sinclair, Eisenstein's relations with his benefactor became so acrimonious that the film was never completed. After he returned to Russia, his film on the Soviets' peasant policy, *Bezhin Meadow*, was scrapped on charges of being "too formalistic." Bureaucrats prevented the realization of other projects—a comedy, a film on Spain, another on the organization of the Red Army in 1917. Work on the first part of *Ivan the Terrible* was delayed repeatedly while Party ideologists tried to decide whether Ivan was a wicked old czar or a national hero who had helped to unify the country. Meanwhile, Eisenstein lectured, taught and directed plays and operas, often creating for them his own scenic and costume designs. He died in 1948, at the age of 49, still planning the completion of the third and final section of his *Ivan* film.

Poetic Symbolism: Dovzhenko

Toward the end of the twenties, one more highly original talent emerged in the Russian film to take a place beside Eisenstein and Pudovkin, the Ukrainian Alexander Dovzhenko. Dovzhenko, it must be admitted, has never shared the popularity abroad of either of his great contemporaries, largely because the symbolism that suffuses his pictures makes them seem strange and difficult to follow. Indeed, many of the symbols in such early works as *Zvenigora* (1927) and *Arsenal* (1929) are so very special as to be quite unfamiliar outside the Ukraine itself. Even so, few pictures are so rewarding to see again and again. With each new viewing their meaning grows clearer, their surface difficulties providing fascinating clues that lead to the rich and complex core of his films. Dovzhenko seems to stand between Eisenstein and Pudovkin. Like Eisenstein, he created bold new film forms, cutting freely to pursue a broad theme rather than a story line. Like Pudovkin, he personalizes his themes, choosing heroes who typify or personify the masses; but where Pudovkin insisted on the reality, the actuality of his central character, Dovzhenko's heroes remain allegorical figures. The protagonists in Pudovkin's *End of St. Petersburg* and Dovzhenko's *Arsenal*, for example, are remarkably similar—simple men who attain maturity through their contact with the forces of the Revolution. Pudovkin's hero dies in combat. When the hero of *Arsenal*, however, is captured by the counter-revolutionaries and led before a firing squad he stands impervious to their bullets. The embodiment of Ukrainian resistance, he is Dovzhenko's symbol of final victory.

For Dovzhenko, as for Eisenstein, the symbol proved the

most natural form of filmic expression. In all his major works from *Arsenal* to *Frontier*, the subject itself—the arsenal, the collective farm in *Earth*, the Dneprostroi Dam in *Ivan*, the new air city in *Frontier*—seems to stand as one gigantic symbol for a new phase in the advancing Soviet economy. Around this central symbol, to build and re-enforce it, Dovzhenko supplies a wealth of additional details, scenes that are themselves filled with symbolic imagery. As a result, his pictures have the kind of compression, the intensity that one associates more often with great poetry. They unfold slowly, revealing new layers of meaning, new levels of perception. And, as in poetry, the more one brings to them, the more one is able to carry away. Dovzhenko's films are odes to life, to the land and to a better world expressed in terms at once highly personal and deeply affecting.

Perhaps with Dovzhenko more than with any other director, one remembers separate images rather than sequences or stories. There is a vividness in his shots that is tremendously exciting, even though its meaning may be obscure. In *Arsenal*, for instance, audiences never fail to be startled by the scene in which a framed portrait of a Ukrainian national hero suddenly comes to life and spits upon the ikon lamp burning before it. Although few may recognize the portrait, no one can miss the contempt implicit in the action. Dovzhenko's fascination with horses often produced equally startling images. One remembers the revolutionaries in *Arsenal* carrying a dead comrade home in a sleigh with the horses "singing" as they gallop across the snow; when the soldier himself, a rope biting into his frozen mouth, is dumped at the feet of his mother, the horses cry, "Such is our revolutionary life and death, Mother!" One also recalls the faces of the bourgeoisie poised, straining to hear the sounds of the approaching Revolution, or the little stationmaster disappearing into nothingness—the end of an era—when he learns that the Communists have commandeered the trains; or the stillness just before the Revolution uncannily captured in a single longshot of a legless man slowly pushing himself across a darkened street.

The kind of juxtapositions that other directors generally achieve through cutting, Dovzhenko is very likely to encompass within a single shot, finding the perfect visual image through which to transform or alter a meaning with maximum intensity. The very opening shot of *Arsenal*, for example, shows a quiet, peaceful field. Suddenly an explosion bursts the field asunder, and we are carried directly into the war. In *Earth* there is a long moment of ineffable, almost unearthly beauty as its hero walks along a dusty country road, the golden harvest shimmering in the twilight on ·either side of him. Unable to contain his delight, he breaks into a gay, twirling peasant dance which is rendered by the camera in slow motion. As the dancing figure nears the top of the screen, this vision of pure contentment is shattered by a shot fired by a half-mad boy who fears the approaching collectivization of the land.

It is this same compression, this uncanny ability to bring together within a single shot the few stark details that most sharply characterize a person or a situation, that makes Dovzhenko's images linger in the mind long after the film has passed. In *Arsenal*, the war's depletion of a village is implied in one almost motionless scene: a tired woman stands in the doorway of a peasant hovel while in the center of the floor sits a legless cripple wearing a war medal. The realism of such shots, however, did not deter Dovzhenko from combining them into highly unrealistic, poetic patterns, broadening their implications, deepening their meaning. During the sequence in the peasant village in *Arsenal*, he shows a one-armed man plowing a field with a bony old horse. In a sudden frenzy, the man seizes the reins in his teeth and flogs the beast with a stick. The horse says, "It isn't me that you're angry with, old man"; and Dovzhenko cuts to Czar Nicholas sitting before his open diary as if gazing on the distant scene. "Today I shot a crow," writes the czar. And the old man collapses in the field. Or, in the same film, a Ukrainian soldier returns from the front to find his wife holding a baby. "Whose?" he asks. Whereupon Dovzhenko cuts immediately to identical scenes being enacted in the homes of French and German soldiers. From Dovzhenko these references and associations come less as intellectual effects than as outbursts of passion—or compassion—inspired by the material itself.

Dovzhenko, more than any of his Russian contemporaries, infused his films with a deep vein of 19th century humanism. The villains of his pictures—the old kulak of *Earth*, the simple trapper of *Frontier*—are not essentially evil. He never caricatures them or makes them hateful. In his view, they are villains only in their inability to understand the new ways, the new life in the Soviet Union. The most moving scene in all

Dovzhenko's work is the death of the old trapper in *Frontier*. The man has sabotaged the air city; he must die. His friend, a partisan of the new order, leads him up into the mountains where for decades the two had roamed free of governments, of cities, of progress. For one long moment the old man's cry of remembrance echoes from mountain to mountain. Then a shot rings out. Progress has won—but there is no delight in the victory.

Not until Akira Kurasawa's *Rashomon*—not even in the later films of Dovzhenko himself—were we to see again such bold stylization, such intensity of visual image, such freedom in cutting, although Dovzhenko's work has had a profound influence upon many of the documentary film makers both in the United States and in England. After 1934, however, film making in the Soviet Union became increasingly art by ukase, with themes dictated to fit national policy and styles altered for ready assimilation by a mass audience. There are still moments of intensity in *Shors* (1939), the story of a popular Red Army commander; some beautifully lyric passages in *Life in Bloom* (1946), the story of the Russian botanist Michurin. But both exude the uncomfortable feeling of having been made to order. They lack the sustained, exalted power of his earlier works. Unfortunately, at the present writing the only Dovzhenko films still available in this country are the early *Arsenal, Earth, Shors,* and *Life in Bloom*. Each of them, however, gives splendid evidence of his powerful and original filmic intelligence, while *Earth* remains one of the true masterworks of the silent screen.

Around these three towering figures in the Russian film of the late twenties are clustered a number of lesser, though far from insignificant, talents—Friedrich Ermler, Abram Room, Kozintzev and Trauberg, V.I. Gardin, Ilya Trauberg, Fedor Ozep, as well as the women directors Olga Preobrashenskaya and Esther Shub. Lev Kuleshov continued to train new talents and to direct an occasional film. Dziga Vertov, who first had drawn the attention of Russian film makers to the importance of editing, produced an increasingly mechanical and trick-filled series of experiments in *Man with a Movie Camera* (1928), *Enthusiasm* (1931) and *Three Songs About Lenin* (1934). Victor Turin's *Turksib* (1929), a dramatic, factual account of the construction of the Trans-Siberian railroad, proved an early milestone in the development of the documentary film. And Grigori Alexandrov, Eisenstein's assistant on *Potemkin* and *Ten Days,* made the impressionistic *Romance Sentimentale* (1930), while on holiday in Paris, then returned to become Russia's leading director of comedies.

The arrival of sound brought to a close the "Golden Era" of Russian films, a period of tremendous creative vigor and extraordinary artistic accomplishments. One fact stands out clearly in a re-examination of their greatest works, however. With notably few exceptions—Room's *Bed and Sofa* (1926), Ermler's *Fragment of an Empire* (1929), Eisenstein's *Old and New* (1929)—they were concerned primarily with the past, with the hardships of life under the czars or with the revolutionary events leading up to 1917. It is astonishing that in a land where films were produced not for profit but for enlightenment, the pictures reflected so little of the contemporary scene. Or was it perhaps a case of the policy makers, the Party ideologists, deciding that the "inglorious" past of Russia under the czars was safer matter than the shortages, the famines and the work quotas of Russia under the commissars? Whatever the cause, the Russian film makers developed a technique for recreating the past that produced some of the most exciting and original pictures of the silent era. They helped increase the feelings of national pride within the Soviet Union, and generated considerable prestige for Russia among those who saw the films abroad. As Lenin had predicted, for the Communists the cinema had indeed become "the most important of the arts."

Postwar Decline in England and Italy

In western Europe, recovering slowly from the effects of World War I, films were dominated almost entirely by imports from America. The history of the British film during the twenties is fairly typical of what was happening in most small countries with a restricted home market for their own motion pictures. Native producers could not afford to compete with Hollywood either in scale or in stars. The general public flocked to the American films, and governments found it necessary to assist the home industry either by legislating restrictions upon the American product or through outright cash bounties. In England, for example, the government in 1927 introduced a "quota law" designed to encourage British production. Singularly ill advised both in plan and in execution, it granted to British studios the right to distribute American-made films provided that they produced a certain number of films themselves. To acquire these profitable rights, most of the British firms stuck to the letter of the law. They made pictures cheaply and quickly—"quota quickies," they came to be called—in which they had no real interest.

Despite the unpropitious times, a number of the figures who were later to carry forward the standards of British film making had already entered the industry. Michael Balcon began his long career as a producer as early as 1922. Alfred Hitchcock, whose first work in films was as a designer of title cards for Paramount's British studio in 1920, had graduated to directing by 1923. His version of Mrs. Belloc Lowndes's *The Lodger* (1926) was one of the few significant British features of the twenties. Until the arrival of sound, Hitchcock, like Anthony Asquith, Herbert Wilcox and other first-rate directorial talents, had to be content with marking time in the production of "quota quickies." In one last effort to compete with the international success of the German films, a group of British financiers invited E. A. Dupont, the director of Germany's biggest box-office hit, *Variety,* to work in England. But the films that resulted, *Piccadilly* (1929) and *Atlantic* (1929), proved to be simply costly hybrids that won neither critical esteem nor popular favor. The English studios entered the sound era with little prestige and meager financial resources.

Italian production throughout the twenties was, if anything, at lower ebb than the British. Cut off from the rest of the world by fascism, the techniques of Italian film making remained at a virtual standstill as producers returned again and again to such scenes of former triumph as *The Last Days of Pompeii, Cabiria, Theodora* and, inevitably, *Quo Vadis?* It was *Quo Vadis?* that had first won international acclaim for the Italian industry back in 1912, the biggest and longest film of its time. In 1924, in an effort to win back some measure of their former prestige, the Italians planned another, more sumptuous version of Henryk Sienkiewicz's hardy perennial. To gain entry into a broader market, Emil Jannings was imported from Germany to play Nero, along with Georg Jacoby to direct and Kurt Courant to photograph—while Gabrielle d'Annunzio's name was added as co-director. Spectacular the film certainly was, filled with crowds, lions, pagan debaucheries and sensational sadism on the grand scale. Unfortunately, the film was also spectacularly dull, combining the worst features of the deliberately-paced German dramas and the remote, pageant-like Italian spectacles. Its reception throughout the world failed to justify the vast sums that had been poured into its production, with the immediate result that the Italians' enthusiasm for the motion picture as a source of either prestige or profit was considerably dampened.

With capital hard to come by, production fell off drastically. By the middle of the twenties, barely 6 per cent of Italian screen time went to Italian pictures; American features claimed almost 70 per cent. Then for a time it looked as if Hollywood might come to the aid of the enfeebled industry. Henry King brought a company to Italy headed by Lillian Gish and Ronald Colman to film *The White Sister* (1923) and *Romola* (1924), giving employment to many Italian technicians and even more mob extras. Soon it was announced that M-G-M would film *Ben Hur* in Italy as well, promising to out-spectacle the native product. Many Italians felt certain that the influx from Hollywood would set their industry on its feet again, but they were in for a sad surprise. M-G-M changed its corporate mind midway in production, and the Americans sailed for home to reshoot in Hollywood most of the scenes that had already been made abroad. Although *Ben Hur* (1926) was one of the biggest box-office hits of its day, the double shooting made it one of the most expensive pictures of the twenties. Because of this, American producers continued to regard production in Italy as an unnecessary extravagance and shunned Italian overtures to make pictures in their country for the next two decades. An effort by Italians to make on their own yet another version of *The Last Days of Pompeii* in 1926 only demonstrated again how out of date their techniques and values had become. Indeed, as far as the Italians themselves were concerned, the most popular pictures of this era were the dozens of films featuring the genial giant Maciste (Ernesto Pagani), a sort of home-grown Tarzan. Significantly, Maciste had made his bow in Giovanni Pastrone's spectacular *Cabiria* (1913), when the Italian industry was at the very pinnacle of its success. The sustained popularity of both the character and the star who played him underscores the Italians' reluctance to leave the past.

As in England, the government itself finally began to take an interest in the all but moribund industry. In 1925 the Mussolini government organized LUCE, an agency for the production of educational and propaganda films, and then a central office to supervise all film production. In Rome a Centro Sperimentale was set up to train and encourage new talent to enter the industry. On the verge of the sound era, the Italians were just beginning to catch up with their fellow film makers in other parts of the world, just beginning to absorb influences from the Americans, from Germany and from the Russian films. Few of their efforts, however, received distribution outside Italy itself. For most of the world, the Italian industry had simply ceased to exist until its sudden, dramatic re-emergence at the end of World War II.

Eclipse of the Scandinavian Film

Similarly, the Scandinavian film, which had flowered so intensely during and immediately after World War I, fell into a gradual decline and eventual obscurity as American movies dominated more and more of the world market, and one after another of its major talents departed to studios in Neubabelsberg and Hollywood. But during its own brief "Golden Era" the Scandinavian film made an important impression on film makers in America, Germany and France. The Danish film, though remembered primarily for the work of Carl Theodor Dreyer, proves on the basis of the limited re-examination possible today to have been not only extremely active but richly creative as well. One finds in the early Danish trick and chase films elements derived from popular French and American efforts; but one also finds, as early as 1910, a style of acting already as intimate and expressive as anything that Griffith was doing at the time, an attention to décor and costume equaled only by the French Film d'Art, a photography that clearly foreshadows the Germans of a decade later and, by 1913, a mastery of cutting that not only rivaled Griffith's but was strikingly similar to the style of the Thomas Ince thrillers. It is difficult to say just how much Griffith and Ince were themselves influenced by these remarkable films from Denmark that so closely paralleled their own work. Certainly, after 1908 Danish pictures were shown here in great numbers and were highly popular. It is hard to imagine that men like

Griffith and Ince would not seek out such films for study and emulation.

In the case of the Danish influence on German production, the evidence is far clearer. As already noted, even before the First World War Berlin had attracted an entire colony of Danish film makers, working there either for Paul Davidson's Projection A.G. Union or the German branch of Nordisk. When, late in 1917, the German High Command moved to form the gigantic Ufa combine, both firms were incorporated into it. At first, Danish stars and technicians moved freely back and forth across the border. As Ufa continued to prosper, however, more and more of the Danish nationals came to settle in Germany, working exclusively for the German studios. One has only to look at a few frames of *Toward the Light* (1918), Asta Nielsen's last film in Denmark, to recognize in its photography—dark backgrounds, with the faces and hands of the actors picked out in harsh white light—a style that a few years later was to be identified as peculiarly Germanic. Nielsen's acting technique, with its sparing use of gesture, its suggestion of inner tensions through the innuendo of a glance, was universally admired; but it was the introverted German film of the twenties that could best utilize and copy it. Gradually the Germans robbed Denmark of its best talents—just as a few years later Hollywood was to empty the German studios.

Film making had begun in Denmark as early as 1896, and Nordisk, the major Danish studio, was established ten years later. Not until 1909, however, was there any production at all in Sweden; and not until 1912 did the two men most responsible for the character and development of the Swedish film, Victor Seastrom and Mauritz Stiller, enter the industry. Rather than proving a handicap, this tardy beginning had the real advantage of eliminating from the very outset the theatrical methods of the French and Italian studios. Swedish directors chose as their examples the works of D. W. Griffith and Thomas Ince—especially, it would seem, Ince's Westerns—setting their dramas against the snowy peaks, the rolling meadows and towering forests of their own country. For their themes, they turned ambitiously to their national legends, history and literature—including practically everything by the prolific Selma Lagerlöf. Her vast, saga-like novels provided the basis for most of the outstanding Swedish productions of the period.

Because of their literary origins, and the overwhelming seriousness of purpose with which these works were filmed, the characters emerged with a depth and dimension unprecedented and unparalleled in films anywhere at the time. By the end of World War I, the Swedish film had achieved both critical respect and international popularity. For many intellectuals, particularly on the Continent, such pictures as Seastrom's *The Outlaw and His Wife* (1917) and *The Phantom Chariot* (1920) or Stiller's *Sir Arne's Treasure* (1919) became the first intimation that the motion picture might be taken seriously as an art. Matching the dignity of the material, the acting was notably restrained and the photography often hauntingly beautiful—not merely picturesque, but penetrating into the rough-hewn settings and natural beauties of background to create an almost tactile impression of the world in which the characters moved.

But, as in Denmark, and, later in Germany, the Swedish film paid the price of success. Its best artists were lured away to work in larger, more prosperous studios elsewhere—the technicians, for the most part, in the German studios, Seastrom and Stiller to Hollywood. Before leaving, Stiller made one final grand-scale feature, at once a summary and a swan song of the Swedish film, *The Story of Gösta Berling* (1924). Based on another of the Selma Lagerlöf novels, the story is set in Sweden just after the Napoleonic Wars. Gösta Berling, a wild, defrocked priest, joins the roistering pensioners at Ekeby, a mansion presided over by a wealthy but strange woman. To the house comes a lovely Italian girl, betrothed to an elderly aristocrat. When Berling and the girl fall in love, the curse that hangs over Ekeby threatens to engulf them, but true love saves the day. Conventional narrative, however, was not Stiller's primary object in *Gösta Berling*. Most of Sweden knew the story already (it had won a Nobel prize for its author); what Stiller wanted was to bring alive its host of characters. The extent to which he succeeded can be estimated in the prints of the film presently circulated in this country by the Museum of Modern Art Film Library, a two-hour version of a picture that originally ran twice as long. Whenever the narrative thread becomes lost—which is frequently—the strength of the characterizations, the emotional tone that surrounds them and the perfectly sustained period flavor of the entire film still compel admiration. As one Swedish critic wrote at the time, "No masterpiece . . . it is, of course, one of the really great movies." It was the last great movie to come from Sweden for many a year. On the strength of it, Stiller was invited to Hollywood. He left early in 1925, taking with him the "Italian girl" of his cast—Greta Garbo.

While Hollywood would seem to be the villain of the piece in this steady deflowering of the European cinema throughout the twenties, the fact is that the American studios were simply profiting from the drastic change in film economics that followed World War I. Prior to that time, pictures could be made on a relatively low budget—low enough for a studio in a small country to show a profit through distribution in the home market alone. But as production costs rose, as films became longer, the machinery of film making more complex and skilled stars, directors and technicians more expensive, the home market proved increasingly inadequate. To show a profit, studios had to be able to sell their productions abroad. Only in the United States were producers able to make back their costs in the home market. With this advantage, the larger American studios boldly budgeted their films so that the profit margin depended on the market abroad. They had stars of international popularity, and the money to wage a ceaseless battle for screen time in theaters everywhere. They could afford to gamble on the foreign market. The Europeans, on the other hand—excluding Germany and Russia— were hard pressed to hold even their domestic markets. If they tried to keep production costs down, they lost their best stars and technicians to Hollywood; if they tried to make films of international appeal, they ran the risk of losing the specific national characteristics that had made their pictures interesting in the first place—and bankrupting themselves into the bargain. It was a disastrous dilemma, as the gradual eclipse of the national cinema in one country after another testifies.

French Renaissance: Delluc, Clair, Feyder

Only in France was there an industry with sufficient vigor to survive the twenties without governmental assistance. This was due in part to the tremendous interest that French postwar intellectuals took in the medium, in part to a sharply different mode of production than obtained elsewhere. Instead of half a dozen or so large studios grinding out a year's supply of pictures for their affiliated theaters, most of the studios were small, their facilities rented by production firms often set up specifically to make a single picture. A special enthusiasm sparked each new venture, and most films were made primarily because their directors wanted to make them. True, the French pictures of this period are scarcely comparable numerically to production in Germany, Russia or even England (much less the United States); but an extraordinary number of them turned out to be first-rate works.

One man was responsible for the resuscitation of the French film after World War I. Louis Delluc, an author and editor, had become attracted to the motion picture as an art form during the war years. He was impressed particularly by the work of the Swedes and by the American directors Ince, Griffith and Chaplin, and wrote tirelessly about the need for establishing a French cinema. He pleaded for films that would be truly French and also truly cinematic, arguing at once against the re-establishment of the stagy Film d'Art and the imitation of the production of other nations. Around him he gathered a small but influential group of film makers— Germaine Dulac, Abel Gance, Marcel L'Herbier and Jean Epstein—who came to share his views. Together they initiated a series of pictures that set the style of the first few years of the period. Impressionistic in technique, intimate in form, rather literary in flavor, they were for the most part highly romanticized studies of French low life. Perhaps such films as Delluc's own *Fièvre* (1921) or L'Herbier's *El Dorado* (1921) were too intellectual, too self-consciously artistic to be acceptable today as first-rate examples of film art. Nevertheless, they revealed a new direction for French film makers in the subtlety of their expression, in their feeling for those muted, inchoate passions too tenuous for speech, and in their accenting of atmosphere and milieu. Typical is the gloomy water-front den in Delluc's *Fièvre* with its hard-faced barmaid, its swaggering sailor-hero and his half-caste wife who crouches dumbly at his feet gazing longingly at a single flower on the bar. "Photogenic" was Delluc's term for such material.

Such films as these continued to recruit new talents, many of them with backgrounds in the older arts. Jean Renoir, youngest son of the famous painter, made his first picture in 1923. Alberto Cavalcanti turned from architecture to set designing, then finally in 1925 to directing. René Clair had been a novelist before coming to films, Jean Epstein a poet

and essayist, Dimitri Kirsanov a musician. Each was attracted
to the film as a new art form; and each, as artist, brought to
the medium a sense of style, of personality. One sees reflected
in their works the temperaments of the men themselves—the
volatile, impishly witty Clair, the ponderous but sensitive and
poetic Renoir, the sharply observant, caustic Jacques Feyder.
And the mode of production in France fostered just this kind
of individuality.

Of all the French directors of this era, none was more talented or original, or had a greater instinctive feeling for the
medium itself, than René Clair. His very first film, *The Crazy
Ray (Paris Qui Dort,* 1923), made on a shoestring, reveals
his sharp eye for the absurd and his enormous appreciation
of the comic possibilities inherent in the motion-picture
camera. A group of travelers alight from their plane; atop the
Eiffel Tower they discover that all Paris is in the grip of a
mysterious paralyzing ray. They alone, being above the ray,
have escaped its effects. As they pass through the city, they
discover its inhabitants frozen into the most delightfully grotesque positions—a pickpocket caught in the act, two sand-
wich-men bending over to pick up the same franc, a
nursemaid with pram kissing a gendarme. Later, they come
upon the source of the ray in the home of a mad inventor
and prevail upon him to throw the switch that will start life
moving again. He does so but, in a manner very reminiscent
of the early French trick films, everything goes out of gear,
first too fast, then too slow. For all its crudities, *The Crazy
Ray* is still fresh and tremendously funny.

The next few years found Clair feeling his way—the brilliant and hilarious Dadaist comedy *Entr'acte* (1924), more
fantasy in *Le Fantôme du Moulin Rouge* (1924) and *Le
Voyage Imaginaire* (1925); an adventure film, *La Proie du
Vent* (1925). Each contributed to the fine art of comedy that
burst forth so joyously in his next picture, *The Italian Straw
Hat* (1927). Drawn from a popular 19th century farce
comedy by Eugène Labiche, it betrays little of its theater
origins. As adapted by Clair, it is completely movie, with the
camera mobilized in a fashion clearly derived from the post-
Murnau German film, its cutting as swift and precise as the
best American productions, and all sparked by a crackling
Gallic wit and exquisite sense of the ridiculous. In Labiche's
story, a young man on his way to his wedding is so unfortunate as to have his horse eat the hat of a respectable married

lady while she is embracing her lover, a fierce, mustachioed officer. Since the lady can not return home without her hat, the officer forces the apologetic bridegroom to search for its twin throughout his nuptial day.

Quite apart from making full use of Labiche's highly serviceable plot, Clair kept his picture moving swiftly forward through a veritable cataract of marvelous sight gags. First, there are the characters themselves, the members of the wedding, each endowed with his own comic quality—the bride's father whose new shoes are too tight, her deaf uncle with a wad of paper lodged in his ear trumpet, a very proper cousin who has misplaced one of his white gloves, an elderly gentleman whose tie keeps slipping down. Then there are the incidents—the mayor's florid speech after the ceremony (punctuated by glimpses of the little man with the slipping tie, so intent on every word that he fails to catch his wife's frantic signals which the mayor comes to interpret as being meant for himself), the frequent and abrupt disappearances of the groom from the midst of the wedding festivities, the delightful bit of theater pantomime through which he outlines his version of his predicament to the suspicious husband. And finally there is Clair's virtuoso use of the camera itself, photographing in dreamlike slow motion the officer's wanton destruction of the young man's apartment, in nightmarish fast motion the bridegroom's enforced participation in the dancing after the wedding banquet when he would rather be out searching for the all-important hat—each shot impeccably placed and perfectly timed. *The Italian Straw Hat*, using a minimum of titles, suggests the full fluency of the silent film by one of the most imaginative directors of comedy the medium has yet produced.

The name of Jacques Feyder was frequently linked with René Clair's during the twenties. Like Clair, Feyder worked primarily in comedy. But whereas Clair specialized in the fantastic and satiric, Feyder was an ironic humanist. In such films as *Crainquebille* (1923), a modern rendering of the Anatole France story; in Zola's *Thérèse Raquin* (1928) and *Les Nouveaux Messieurs* (1928), he delivered sharp, cutting criticisms of French justice, French morals and French politics. Indeed, so devastating were his comments on dishonest politicians and parliamentary chicanery in *Les Nouveaux Messieurs*—including a roguish dream sequence in which the benches of Parliament are occupied by charming ballerinas, the mistresses of the politicos—that the film was banned outright by the French censors. Although later the ban was removed, Feyder had already left for Hollywood in disgust—the first of the French directors to be invited to this country.

Les Nouveaux Messieurs, with its sophisticated boulevard wit, reveals only one aspect of Feyder's tremendous versatility. Less inventive, less spontaneous than Clair, he also had a greater feeling for people and the stresses of ordinary living. It was this quality that enabled him to direct such a variety of pictures well. "A setting, an atmosphere, and a popular plot with a little melodrama in it"—these Feyder once stated were all he needed to make a film. Certainly, he was a master in the art of creating and sustaining an atmosphere, and doing it unobtrusively. *Crainquebille* was praised in its day for the tricky courtroom scene in which Féraudy, the old pushcart vendor, stands tiny between the policemen in front of the looming bench of justice. But its real merits are seen today to lie in such authentically colorful scenes as the old man's heated argument with the gendarme while all the traffic in Paris piles up around them, such closely and wryly observed sequences as the vendor in his prison cell, and such warm and happy moments as his welcome in the newsboy's little room after his return from jail. These vignettes of daily life hold a pathos that makes this film a human comedy, intimate, quiet and often quite poignant. Even in *Thérèse Raquin* there is a certain poignance about the weak and sensual characters of Zola's story. Thérèse seems pitiable though she is a murderess. Feyder asks merely that we understand her, not hate her. Like Zola, he was interested in the human condition in all its manifestations, and excelled in bringing it to the screen with an air of unforced reality. Skilled in realism, comedy, pathos and melodrama, Feyder remained among the most popular French directors of the decade.

Jean Renoir's early work is even less known in this country than Feyder's. After several unsuccessful and imitative efforts, he emerged suddenly as a major talent with his adaptation of Zola's *Nana* (1926), which he both directed and financed. His wife, Catherine Hessling, played the title role, supported by Werner Krauss and Valeska Gert from the German studios. Both a popular and a critical success, *Nana* has been described by the French historian Georges Sadoul as "one of the best French films of the later twenties . . . rich in its combination of the pictorial inheritance of impressionism and the realism of Zola's naturalist tradition, and drawing its inspiration also in part from the films of von Stroheim and the German school." In all, an impressive combination. Despite its great success, however, the profits went to the distributors, not to Renoir. As a result, aside from his *La Petite Marchande d'Allumettes* (1927), a gloomy and sentimental version of the Andersen fairy tale, Renoir had to work for other producers, turning out commercial films like *Tire au Flanc* (1928) and *Tournoi dans la Cité* (1928), a medieval melodrama. Nevertheless, his handling of the camera in these pictures reveals his characteristic sensitivity to mood and atmosphere, a quality of carefully suffused light and soft-focus photography that creates scenes of slow, shimmering beauty. Like his famous father, Renoir painted with light.

Two other members of Delluc's impressionist group whose work during the twenties deserves mention here are Jean Epstein and Abel Gance. Epstein's early efforts, created under the influence of the avant-garde experiments of the time, include the nervous, rhythmic, technically masterful *Le Cœur Fidèle* (1923) and a version of *The Fall of the House of Usher* (1928), self-consciously full of moving cameras, double exposures, symbols, Germanic "effects"—and moments of haunting imagery. Inspired by the Soviet films that began to appear in Paris around 1927, Epstein abruptly turned his back on such art-for-art's-sake experiments. His very next film, *Finis Terrae* (1928), was a raw, semi-documentary study of the kelp gatherers on one of the barren islands off the coast of Brittany. In it Epstein revealed anew the camera's ability to present remote patterns of life in human and affecting terms. Though frequently appallingly clumsy both in cutting and in construction, it built its story of primitive hardships and rude heroism with dignity and integrity. Meanwhile, Abel Gance, who had won his title as "the Griffith of France" with the anti-war film *J'Accuse* (1919), continued to produce grandiose, ponderous spectacles in *La Roue* (1922), and *Napoléon* (1926). It was Gance who, in *Napoléon*, introduced the huge triple screen, a precursor of today's CinemaScope. Vastly admired, vastly praised in their own land and time, his pictures seem distressingly empty and sentimental today.

The Summing Up: Carl Dreyer

If any single film can be said to characterize and summarize the entire era of production in the twenties, that picture would be Carl Dreyer's *Passion of Joan of Arc* (1928). Though made in France, its cast and crew were extremely international. Its director was a Dane and its star, Falconetti, an Italian. Its gifted cameraman, Rudolph Maté, came from Poland, while its set designer, Hermann Warm, had created the décor for many of the outstanding German films. Inspired by Dreyer, the company worked together with an almost mystic fervor. "It was a film made on the knees," one of Dreyer's assistants has said. Falconetti, who played The Maid, was never able to make another picture, as if drained by the demands made upon her by this extraordinary experience; while Dreyer himself has never again equaled the sustained intensity of his *Joan*. Into it went the distillation of almost a decade of creative film making on the Continent.

The film is centered upon the last day of the trial of Joan and her execution, concentrating within that brief time span a mass of documentation on the trial that had come to light in 1924 and had only just been made generally available. From this material Dreyer drew his portrait of Joan as a simple peasant girl mystically inspired in her heresy. Also from the trial records he established the motives of her tormentors—the compassion of Bishop Cauchon, the sadism of de Courcelles, the prosecutor; and in the case of the British Earl of Warwick, the desire for military revenge. But Dreyer's method for recreating the past was far different from the ordinary historical pageant. To capture a sense of living history, he built his film in a series of huge, revealing close-ups of faces, hands, books, weapons, instruments of torture and symbols of religion. The camera searches constantly for the look, the gesture, the detail that will reveal most tellingly Joan's tragic story, her anguish, her fears and her steadfast convictions. From the very first image—an extended traveling shot across the faces of the priestly jurors—one is startled by the intimacy of these historic figures. Within a moment the spectator has forgotten completely that these are actors; it is less their acting than their eyes, the lines about the mouth, their very gait and carriage that serve as the index to their characters. None of them wore make-up; and Maté's harsh, penetrating photography throws emphasis constantly on the textures of skin and hair, the smooth jowls of a fat priest, the pale eyes of another, the heavy brow of Warwick, the dirt-rimmed fingernails of Joan herself—details that assert the reality of the characters. Similarly, one is always tactilely aware of the cold stone floors, the wooden benches, the rough plaster of the walls, the rude settings of this fierce struggle for the soul of an anguished girl. Even though Dreyer had built a complete town square for the exteriors, the scenic details shown on the screen are the sketchiest—a distant bell tower, the corner of a battlement, a cross against the sky, with the sky always dead white to serve as a neutral background for the earthly drama. The film literally has no long-shots—at least, no long-shots without a huge face in the foreground. By keeping the camera this close to his principals and their surroundings, Dreyer magnified them beyond human dimension, suggesting the monumentality first of his characters and, ultimately, of the trial itself. As the inquisition grows in intensity, tighter and tighter become the shots until, in a final hail of questioning, the camera swoops up to huge mouths that fill the screen, and glimpses of Joan cowering under each new barrage, her hands over her ears, her great eyes flowing with tears.

It is in this sequence that one becomes most disturbingly aware of the limitations of the silent film. The images, for all their power, for all their expressiveness, do not tell all. The subtitles are still necessary; but even when cut to a minimum they are intrusive. They break the rhythm of the visuals, the emotional continuity of the scene. Dreyer seems to have pushed the silent cinema to the very edge of its limitations. It could go no further in baring the soul of its characters; already it was straining toward the added fluency of sound, the added levels of self-revelation possible in speech. Nor was Dreyer himself unaware of this. Sound had already arrived in France as he began work on *Joan of Arc,* and he would have preferred to make it as a talking picture. The financing was not available, however; and what might have been the first masterpiece of the sound era became instead a summing up of all the virtues of silence—the last great work of the French silent film.

The European Avant-Garde

Before returning to the American film, it is important to consider one other aspect of Continental production during the twenties, the work of the avant-garde, the experimentalists. Both individually as artists and collectively as a movement they made a valuable contribution to the development of the art of the film, and especially in France. Officially, however, the movement began in Germany. Two abstract artists, Hans Richter and Viking Eggeling, were wrestling with the problems of developing a visual theme in paint the way a musical theme evolves in the symphony or the sonata. They found a compromise solution in an adaptation of Chinese scroll painting, the gradual unfolding of the scrolls providing movement in time as well as in space. Unfortunately, they discovered, this device provided little control over the pace of the development and afforded no flexibility in surface area. Attracted to the motion-picture medium like so many other young artists of the postwar era, they tried out their ideas in two brief animated films, Richter in his *Rhythmus 21*, Eggeling in *Symphonie Diagonale*, both made in 1921. Richter remained closely identified with the avant-garde movement until his death in 1976. Eggeling, his friend and colleague, died in 1925.

Using masks, cutouts, stop-motion animation and an interesting variety of double exposures, Richter went on to create a whole series of films in which he experimented directly with the camera itself. The tricks, devices, rhythms and effects that he produced were possible only with the motion-picture camera. It became, in effect, the brush of the artist—and he felt it was the proper function of the artist to increase the range and expressiveness of the camera in ways inconceivable in the ordinary, story-telling film. The "absolute film," Richter called his kind of picture, meaning that it had nothing to do with narrative, studio settings or actors. Instead, his films are abstract paintings in motion, a world away from both the intent and the content of the studio film. They explore the changing relationships of shapes moving in space, the effects of varying tonalities of gray, superimpositions of unexpected objects, the distortions made possible by lenses and prisms. Richter was concerned with texture and light, with movement drawn from inanimate things, with rhythms created by cutting.

If any one common purpose motivated all avant-garde efforts of the twenties, it was this desire to break with the increasingly conventional story patterns and forms of the films made for theatrical exhibition, to discover new worlds for the camera to explore. Other artists soon joined Richter in trying their hand at similar abstract, non-objective films. In Germany, Walter Ruttmann worked out a stop-motion technique of improvisation with abstract forms, moving them frame by frame to create fluid, impressionistic designs. It was Ruttmann who created the terrifying dream sequence of the black hawks in Fritz Lang's *Kriemhild's Revenge.* Another prominent artist who contributed films to this movement was Ladislaus Moholy-Nagy, one of the members of the Bauhaus, who made several *Lichtspiele* (light plays) in which forms and textures of specially constructed objects were transformed by shifting lights and shadows. At about the same time, in 1928, Oskar Fischinger began his long series of animated abstractions, using a cartoon technique to create visual accompaniments to standard orchestral works.

By this time the impulse toward filmic experiment had also seized artists in France, with the result that all the main art movements of the twenties—impressionism, cubism, Dadaism, surrealism—were soon to be represented on celluloid. The impressionists had already found their leader in Louis Delluc, who maintained that the story film was itself an art form. His followers looked on movies as a popular entertainment that could be made more artistic by using the camera to capture their own special concepts of mood and atmosphere. In *The Smiling Madame Beudet* (1922), for example, Germaine Dulac chose a fairly conventional little story—an incident involving a romantic middle-aged woman and her stolid, insensitive husband. It was treated almost as an inner monologue on the part of the woman, the camera capturing in shimmering soft-focus photography her mood as she plays Debussy on the piano. In slow motion we see her daydreams of handsome young men stepping out of the pages of a magazine into her arms; in fast motion and with distorting lenses, her vision of her husband angrily banging on the piano, eating his soup or—his favorite prank—threatening to blow out his brains with a revolver. The film conveys, through this mesh of visual fantasy, a full sense of the woman's neurasthenia. By her impressionistic use of the camera, Mme. Dulac proved Delluc's basic contention that a film could be both artistic and entertaining. In Dimitri Kirsanov's poetic, tragic *Ménilmontant* (1925), the subject again was scarcely unique. Two orphaned girls came to Paris where they are both betrayed by the same young man. Kirsanov's nervous, impressionistic camera style, a thing of fleeting glimpses and staccato editing, endowed this drab and sordid story with an intensity that is even today profoundly affecting.

The anarchistic art of Dada, an energetic movement that thumbed its nose at every bourgeois convention during the early twenties, found its first filmic expression in Man Ray's *Le Retour à la Raison (The Return to Reason,* 1923). As Man Ray, an American photographer working in Paris at the time, recalls the incident, he made the film overnight for a Dadaist function—a mélange of Dadaist poetry screamed at the top of the lungs, literary works read in pure gibberish and music featuring primarily sirens and bells. His picture was scheduled to close the program. Never having made a film before, he used a technique he had originated in still photography, stretching strips of raw stock upon his work table and sprinkling them with objects lying about the studio—nails, tacks, collar buttons, even the photograph of a nude. As their outlines appeared on the emulsion, he developed the strips and pasted them together as best he could. The effect of this kind of "return to reason," coming at the close of such a session—and heightened by frequent partings of his homemade splices—was to provoke a riot that all but wrecked the hall. It was considered a very successful Dadaist evening.

One true masterpiece of Dada exists, however, in René Clair's incredible *Entr'acte* (1924), with its mock funeral procession patterned after the old French chase films. Commissioned by Rolf de Maré as an interlude for his Ballet Suédois, its cast includes the *premier danseur* of the company, Jan Börlin, as well as such prominent representatives of the arts as Erik Satie, Darius Milhaud, Marcel Duchamp, Francis Picabia, Man Ray and Maré himself. Early in the film, amidst the imagery of Paris in miniature and a game of chess played on a rooftop ledge, Börlin is killed by a shot aimed at an amusement park target. The funeral begins with the hearse drawn by a camel, the mourners setting out in majestic slow motion after it. But somehow the hearse breaks loose from its moorings, and soon the entire procession is racing in hot pursuit through the streets of Paris. The leaves blur overhead. Clair cuts in a ride on a roller coaster to heighten the sense of speed, or mounts his camera on the front of a car as it races down a curving mountain road. Suddenly the hearse stops, the coffin falls out, and up pops Börlin smiling and unharmed. Clair punctuated his film with typically Dadaist bits of business. There are repeated shots, photographed from below, of a graceful ballerina whose skirt opens and falls like a lovely flower as she dances—until a final slowly rising shot reveals her to be a heavily bearded gentleman with a pince-nez. A seemingly legless cripple who has been pushing himself along in a cart all during the procession suddenly leaps up and starts running with the rest when the pace grows too fast. Clair's agile filmic imagination responded with characteristic wit to the Dadaists' basic demands for the absurd and the unexpected.

Fernand Léger, one of the first of the cubist painters, turned to film in 1924 with the wholly abstract *Ballet Mécanique*. "To create the rhythm of common objects in space and time, to present them in their plastic beauty, this seemed to me worthwhile," he wrote. "This was the origin of my *Ballet Mécanique*." As its title implies, the film is a dance created out of the movement of levers, gears, pendulums, egg beaters, pots and pans—and incidentally, people whose movements are also mechanized. A girl swinging lazily to and from the camera becomes as automatic as a moving pendulum, an eye opening and closing as mechanical as a piston. Most astonishing of all is a sequence in which a stout washerwoman plods heavily up a steep flight of stairs. Just as she reaches the top, holding out her hand to grasp the rail for the final step, Léger cuts back to the beginning and starts the poor woman again on her weary climb. Twenty-four times he does this, using the same shot over and over and over again at various points in the film until the spectator develops an almost overwhelming desire to hold out his own hand and haul her up the final step himself.

The curious thing is that in this film the machines and other objects set up similar strong physiological reflexes in the audience. Léger forces the eye to work. Shadows move swiftly across the screen from right to left, from left to right, and the eye follows. A straw hat cuts directly to a ballet slipper, and the eye merges them into a single distending shape. A gleaming pendulum swung directly into the camera lens causes the pupil to dilate and contract, dilate and contract until the rhythm of its movement is felt in every nerve and muscle. Words and numbers are stripped of all their connotations, reduced to meaningless symbols. Circles, triangles and squares, cut rapidly together, create a visual punctuation. Just as Gertrude Stein played with words to find new cadences in the combinations of their sounds, Léger disregarded the function of machinery and the utility of objects to display the abundant vitality of their operation and the intrinsic beauty of their design. Both Richter in *Filmstudie* (1926) and Man Ray in *Emak Bakia* (1927) were to continue this abstract exploration of the object.

An outgrowth of Dadaism, the surrealist movement appeared on the Continent in the mid-twenties. But where Dada was pure anarchy, surrealism had a purpose, a program and a political edge that was sharply Left. One of the most notorious of all surrealist films, *L'Age d'Or,* lashed capitalism and Catholicism so viciously as to provoke a riot when it was first shown in Paris in 1930. The activities of the surrealists spanned the gamut from politics to pathology. Their avowed aim was the destruction of conventional concepts in manners, morals and art, and the exploration of unexpected beauties in the world of the irrational. Through their dynamic manifestoes, through the new vistas they opened up to painters, poets and writers, and through their boundless revolutionary zeal, the surrealists began to attract artists away from all the older movements. By the end of the twenties, surrealism had become the dominant influence in modern art. Inevitably it attracted to it many of the avant-garde film makers. In 1928 alone Man Ray, Germaine Dulac and Jean Epstein added to this latest "ism" such films as *Étoile de Mer, The Seashell and the Clergyman* and *The Fall of the House of Usher*—films based on such pleasant passions as unrequited love, murder, guilt, incest, and general over-all frustration.

Perhaps what most attracted the film makers to surrealism was its heavy dependence on dream imagery. The growing popularity and familiarity of Sigmund Freud's teachings among European intellectuals during the late twenties had created a new and irresistible vocabulary for expressing the subconscious. Sex themes, sex relationships too indelicate to be treated directly on the screen could now be suggested through a kind of visual shorthand that could readily be transcribed by anyone *au courant*. Indeed, watching *The Seashell and the Clergyman* is very much like solving a cryptogram, with Freud holding the key. But such films were more than an intellectual game. They were also a rather disturbing emotional experience, with content more appropriate to the analyst's couch than to the therapy of entertainment. Audiences viewing them often had the uneasy feeling that they were peeping in on someone else's very personal inner turmoil. Because of their nightmare imagery these films could still shock, but the earlier Dadaist exuberance was gone and the atmosphere was now heavy with a referential reverence for everything Freudian.

One of the few surrealist films to avoid this over-intellectual application of Freud was *Un Chien Andalou* (1929) by Luis Buñuel and Salvador Dali. Neither inhibited nor awed by Freud, they plunged into the new subterranean world with curious glee. Like other surrealist film makers, they used dream imagery, but without trying to make it conform to some mechanical, premeditated plan. In preparing their scenario, they pointedly discarded anything which they could either explain or rationalize. Their one aim was to shock and horrify the viewer, and consciously—even self-consciously— they thumbed their noses at all conventional standards of aesthetics, decency and taste. Where others had moved each symbol reverently into place like the pieces of a shadowy jigsaw puzzle, Buñuel and Dali grabbed exuberantly at whatever appealed to them—and the more outrageous, the better.

Its very first sequence sets the tone of the entire film. A young man (Buñuel), stropping his razor, steps out upon a balcony to gaze at the night sky. A young woman is also on the balcony. As a thin sliver of cloud passes across the moon, he takes his razor and in extreme close-up slits the girl's eyeball. Horror falls quickly on horror—a traffic accident, an amputated hand, an attempted rape. As in a dream, there are strange perturbing visions that linger in the mind long after the film has passed: a cocktail shaker that simulates the ringing of a doorbell and, of course, that favorite Dali trademark, a swarm of ants crawling out of a hole in a man's hand.

It should not be imagined, however, that *Un Chien Andalou* is composed exclusively of sensational or sickening images. There are glimpses of fragile beauty which are intensified by the horror that surrounds them—moments of wistful tenderness as when the hero, "sixteen years earlier," turns toward the camera remembering what might have been or falls dying in a Corot-like wood. There are many scenes which have the unexpected order and cleanliness, the atmosphere of a Vermeer painting. These seeming inconsistencies were part of the authors' calculated plan to shock the spectator into a new awareness of beauty by laying bare the sensibilities, to create a dream that was, to use the surrealist phrase, "more real than reality."

While the surrealists delved into the imagery of dreams and nightmares, other avant-garde directors found themselves increasingly attracted to the real world that surrounded them. But it was a real world without reality, arbitrarily shaped and organized by the film makers into what they often called "city symphonies," compositions in which documentary shots of ordinary street life provided the raw materials for a semi-abstract *ballet mécanique*. Alberto Cavalcanti's *Rien que les Heures* (1926), an impressionistic study of Paris that sought to capture its characteristic color and rhythms, uses as a recurrent motif shots of a sick old woman creeping ratlike through the back alleys of the city. Contrasts between the lives of the very rich and the very poor were shown but never examined: they were simply part of the texture, part of the kaleidoscope of the city's ever-changing pattern.

At the same time in Germany, Walter Ruttmann produced *Berlin, the Symphony of a Great City* (1927), compressing into five reels a dawn-to-midnight portrait of Berlin. More mechanical, less personal than the Cavalcanti work, its opening passages of a train coming into the city and the shopkeepers raising the iron shutters on their stores beautifully capture the rhythms of a city waking up. In Holland, Joris Ivens made *Rain* (1929), a brief, hauntingly photographed impression of a passing shower in Amsterdam. But the era of the "city symphony" was passing. Stirred by the social realism of the Soviet films, Ivens turned from such pleasant, neutral poetic documentation toward a serious commentary upon society. In his documentary classic *New Earth* (1933), begun in 1929 as a record of the slow, painful reclamation of land from the Zuider Zee, he hoped to create an ode to the men whose heroic labor drove back the waters. Its unforeseen ending was tinged with the bitterest irony when in 1933 the Dutch, to protect tumbling wheat prices, dumped their first hard-worn harvest back into the sea.

In Germany, Hans Richter had also turned from abstraction to the social scene with an impressionistic study of a horse race, *The Race Symphony* (*Rennsymphonie*, 1928) and *The Stock Exchange* (*Die Börse*, 1929), which described, first through old engravings, then through documentary photography, the history and operation of the exchange. In Ernö Metzner's brief, stark, excitingly photographed *Überfall* (1929), we are back in the world of the German street films of the early twenties; but this time the streets are real, not studio constructed. And the adventures that befall its pitiable hero have none of the comforting reassurance of a happy ending. Another effort to move the camera out of the studio was the warmly observed *People on Sunday* (*Menschen am Sonntag*, 1929). Photographed in Berlin and its surrounding parks, it is a vivid and frequently poignant little story of four young workers from the lower middle class trying to have a little fun on their day off. In it appear again many of the details, the rhythmic motifs and experimental techniques of the "city symphonies," but here mobilized for the purpose of social comment rather than purely aesthetic effect.*

If the dominating philosophy of the avant-gardists through the twenties had been art-for-art's-sake, the sudden advent of the depression in 1929 soon changed all this. With panic, starvation and ruin all about them, they found it peculiarly inappropriate to be concerned solely with revolving starfish and swinging pendulums, with textures and prisms and the dream world of the subconscious. The penetrating works of Soviet realism had been seen and discussed in the numerous avant-garde ciné-clubs that spread throughout the Continent after 1925. For many they were a revelation, a proof that the problems of treating the real world could be as intriguing, as challenging—and as artistically valid—as anything they had done before. After a decade of altering reality, kidding reality, ignoring reality, they suddenly found themselves concerned with reproducing reality, substituting social purpose

---

* *People on Sunday* has an added interest because so many of its artistic participants later became prominent in the international film industry. Curt Siodmak wrote the original story; Billy Wilder wrote the screenplay (his first); and Fred Zinnemann served as camera assistant to the late Eugen Shuftan, one of the most ingenious cameramen of all time. Edgar Ulmer began the picture, but Robert Siodmak (Curt's brother) directed it, creating a new style of naturalistic film that anticipated the Italian neo-realists by more than a decade.

for aesthetic experiment. For many of the avant-garde film makers—Buñuel, Cavalcanti, Epstein, Ivens, Moholy-Nagy, Rouquier, Ruttmann—the documentary film became the next step. What John Grierson was to call "the dog biscuits of documentary" proved infinitely more attractive to them than a more profitable retreat to the conventions of the studio film they had been railing against for an entire decade.

3

Hollywood in the Twenties

By the end of World War I, as we have seen, the American film industry had come to dominate the world market. For movie makers and movie fans alike, all roads led to Hollywood. Hollywood was fame and fortune. Hollywood was "the big time." By the turn of the twenties, Hollywood had become big business as well, the newest major industry in the United States. Studio stocks began to be listed on Wall Street in 1919, handled by such respected firms as J. P. Morgan and Kuhn, Loeb. When United Artists was formed by Charles Chaplin, Mary Pickford, Douglas Fairbanks and D. W. Griffith, their combined box-office value had reached the multimillion dollar level. The new company could afford to engage as its legal counsel, at $100,000 a year, William Gibbs McAdoo, Secretary of the Treasury under Wilson, the man who had floated the wartime Liberty Loans. In the studios at the dawn of the twenties the cost of an average feature with a first-rate star had reached between $100,000 and $125,000. And this was only the beginning!

As the companies grew in size and power during the early twenties, so too did the costs of production. Star salaries continued to climb, but they soon ceased to represent the sole major item in a film's budget. Story properties, once an insignificant factor, became increasingly important as the studios acquired the rights to best-selling novels and hit plays. Expensive settings and costumes, once used over and over again in picture after picture, were now designed specifically for each new production. The physical plants themselves were expanded, the open-air or glass-enclosed stages giving way to huge concrete vaults lit by powerful Klieg lights and arcs; while acres and acres of "back lot" held entire villages, city streets, wharves and railroad stations, awaiting only the designer's touch to transform them into locales appropriate to the current production. Some of the studios even acquired ranches close to Los Angeles, vast areas incorporating many kinds of terrain and kept permanently stocked with horses, cattle, covered wagons and similar properties necessary to the production of Westerns. By the mid-twenties, fully 40 percent of a film's budget went to pay for studio overhead. Naturally, as the lords of such princely domains, the studio heads allocated to themselves correspondingly princely salaries, and men like Adolph Zukor, William Fox, Marcus Loew and Louis B. Mayer emerged as eminent figures on the scene of American high finance.

With hundreds of thousands of dollars—sometimes even millions—riding on each production, inevitably the studios sought to protect their investments as far as possible. A top-ranking star, for example, provided an almost fool-proof insurance of box-office success; and the twenties witnessed a determined effort on the part of the studios to cultivate new stars, new personalities guaranteed to please millions of fans. Whole departments were added to feed tidbits of information to the newspapers and to the increasingly important fan magazines. No stunt was too outlandish, no "angle" too improbable if it might capture a front-page headline or a magazine feature story for the studio's current darlings. Perhaps the most famous publicity man of this era was the irrepressible Harry Reichenbach. It was Reichenbach who, during a temporary lull in Rudolph Valentino's astonishing career, put the Latin lover back on the front page by persuading him to grow a trick beard, kept him there by reporting the protests of women and barbers all over the nation, and capped the climax—months later—with a great public "debearding" performed by representatives of the Master Barbers of America. Such a campaign was typical of the studios' efforts to build or maintain the box-office value of the players they kept under contract. Whole careers were built on what Reichenbach himself referred to as "phantom fame."

And the public responded to this determined star-making. Not only the success but even the approximate box-office "take" could be confidently predicted when films featured such top players as John Barrymore, Rudolph Valentino, Norma or Constance Talmadge, Richard Barthelmess, Milton Sills, Pola Negri or Gloria Swanson. Dozens of other stars, by virtue of some special cuteness or appeal—Clara Bow, Madge Bellamy, Lila Lee, Thomas Meighan, Bebe Daniels, Evelyn Brent, Jackie Coogan—made any picture they appeared in a reasonably safe investment. The studios, selling their productions on the strength of star names, zealously built up their rosters of reliable box-office performers until, late in the twenties, M-G-M was proud to be identified as "The Home of the Stars." With a contract list that included Greta Garbo, John Gilbert, Norma Shearer, Lon Chaney, Ramon Novarro, Lillian Gish, Marion Davies, Buster Keaton and Joan Crawford, it was by all odds the most profitable, the "safest" studio in the world. The star system, so bitterly opposed by the producers in 1910, proved within ten short years to be the studios' strongest single asset.

Stories, too, provided an important element of control, although inevitably less gilt-edged than star security. Early in the twenties the works of such popular novelists as Blasco Ibáñez, Rafael Sabatini, Joseph Hergesheimer, Booth Tarkington and Elinor Glyn began to appear on the screen with increasing frequency. And the studios watched and charted the public's response to each new offering. When the income at the box office revealed an unexpected interest in some new theme, the studios immediately threw into production whole series of films on the same subject. In short, movies began to run in cycles. The popularity of Cecil B. De Mille's provocative sex comedies just after the war inspired a wave of sophisticated bedroom farces—and incidentally accomplished something of a revolution in screen morality. After the success of Metro's *Prisoner of Zenda* (1922), Graustarkian romances blossomed on every eucalyptus tree. When *The Big Parade* (1925) proved a tremendous hit despite all authoritative insistence that war stories were box-office poison, every studio head immediately ordered a war story.

It was this same desire to give the public what it wanted—or at any rate, what the producers thought the public wanted—that led to the wholesale importation of European talents during the twenties. The public was raving about Pola Negri in *Passion*? Get Negri—and for good measure, her director as well! The Swedes were making great pictures? Get Seastrom! Get Stiller! (For good measure, they got Garbo as well.) *Variety* broke all box-office records for foreign importations? Get Jannings! And Murnau, and Dupont, and Pommer, and Freund, and Leni, and Jacques Feyder, and Lars Hanson and Einar Hanson, and Lya de Putti. The movement reached avalanche proportions in 1926 and 1927, until the arrival of sound brought it all to a panic-stricken halt in 1928.

Throughout the twenties Hollywood acquired more and more of the earmarks of a major industry. The roistering, carefree ways that characterized the first two decades of film history became outmoded. A Mack Sennett could no longer arrive in Los Angeles with a camera and a few comedians and consider himself in business. A D. W. Griffith could no longer borrow several thousand dollars from friends and turn out a *Birth of a Nation*. With the acquisition of huge, costly plants in which to make the movies, and vast networks of theaters in which to show them, production had entered a new era—an era of cost accounting, of profit-and-loss statements, of cautious budgeting and cut-throat competition. There was still a virtue in flinging money around. It made good copy. It added to the glamour. It helped to sell tickets. But the money had to be flung with a certain accuracy. It had to get more money. So Hollywood went on paying weekly kings' ransoms to its top stars, paid small fortunes for popular novels and plays, ransacked the European studios for talents guaranteed to please the audiences throughout the United States. Hollywood had become big business—and its first dictum of business was, "The customer is always right."

Sin, Scandal and the Hays Office

When the movies first went West, around 1910, Los Angeles boarding-house keepers were advertising, "Rooms for rent—No dogs or actors allowed." By 1919, mollified by the $20,000,000 the studios were spending annually in salaries and the $12,000,000 for raw materials, this attitude had changed considerably. The natives were now pointing with civic pride to the new Chaplin studio on La Brea Avenue, to Carl Laemmle's Universal City just beyond Cahuenga Pass, to the way Paramount had expanded from a barn to whole blocks of stages in the very heart of Hollywood. They welcomed the tourists who came to gape at these new wonders of the Western world, and turned their fretful attention to the problem of the thousands of teen-age girls who were pouring into town from all over the country. The vast salaries of the stars, the well-publicized glamour of their lives, led many a small-town belle or beauty-contest winner to head for Hollywood convinced—or at least hoping—that she was the next Mary Pickford or Mabel Normand. Shady "talent schools" added to the influx. Most of these eager young hopefuls were doomed to the cruelest disappointment—or worse. Accounts of vice in Hollywood began to crop up in the newspapers and magazines of America.

Through the early years of the twenties these stories gained substance. The pattern was obvious. Too many people had got too rich too quickly. Unprepared for sudden wealth, unaccustomed to open adulation, many of them began to react like children in a room full of bright new toys—only, their toys included high-powered cars, bootleg whisky, expensive women and drugs. They believed their own publicity. They were kings and queens who could do no wrong. But the very glamour that the publicists had gone to such lengths to concoct proved to be their undoing. The eyes of America were focused upon Hollywood. Newspapers assigned reporters to cover the Hollywood beat, reporters who were not content merely to reprint the studio handouts. They pointed to the rising incidence of prostitution, of studio "call girls," casting couches and orgiastic parties. By 1922 Hollywood had gained the reputation of being not only the most glamorous but also the most corrupt city in the United States.

Part of this can, of course, be explained by the general relaxation of morals following World War I. Hollywood, its publicists argued, was just like any other big city in America, but with the spotlights turned on—and everything magnified by the sudden eminence, the sudden wealth. At the same time, Hollywood in its films was reflecting the change in moral standards. Sophisticated sex had suddenly become big box office, whether in comedies or played straight. Drinking scenes abounded in pictures, despite the recent adoption of Prohibition. Divorce, seduction, the use of drugs were presented in film after film as symbols of the fashionable life. America was launched upon an era of high living, and Hollywood was pointing the way. But in towns and hamlets across the nation, the new morality had not taken hold. Many who went to the movies were genuinely shocked by what they saw there—and concluded that what they saw was representative of Hollywood alone.

Their suspicions seemed fully confirmed late in 1922 when, within the space of a few short months, there came in quick succession the sordid "Fatty" Arbuckle rape case, the mysterious and still unsolved murder of director William Desmond Taylor (implicating both Mary Miles Minter and Mabel Normand, two top box-office stars of the time), and the shocking revelation of handsome Wallace Reid's addiction to drugs. Public indignation swelled to alarming proportions. Although their outrage was directed against individuals (Arbuckle and Miss Minter never appeared in films again; Mabel Normand's career was permanently damaged), the protests rapidly assumed the form of a threatened national censorship of all movies. Official and unofficial busybodies suddenly found all sorts of sinister, obscene or salacious material within even the most innocuous pictures, while organizations with their own special axes to grind (such as the temperance societies) lent their voices to the outcry. Everything was condemned, the good with the bad.

Faced with such an overwhelming public protest, the producers ran for cover. Though at one another's throats in the course of normal business, the major studios came together in the face of the common danger to form the Motion Picture Producers and Distributors of America, the forerunner of today's Motion Picture Association of America headed by Jack Valenti. Organized late in 1922, the M.P.P.D.A. had two immediate tasks: to fight off national censorship and to set up a policy of self-censorship and regulation of their own films that would convince the public of the producers' good faith. Members of the Association pledged themselves to abide by a set of standards mutually drawn up and agreed upon by all. And to enforce this agreement, to supervise its operation, the movie companies appointed as head of the new organization—their "Czar"—Will H. Hays, a Presbyterian elder, Chairman of the Republican National Committee and at the time Postmaster General in the Harding administration.

The choice of Hays proved a wise one. His prominence made him an impressive buffer against outraged citizen groups. Through him the motion-picture producers bought a measure of both political and religious protection. Certainly, they averted national censorship by the federal government. On the other hand, state and municipal censor boards

mushroomed on all sides, groups with full local authority to
cut offensive sequences out of pictures or even to ban them
entirely. Rather than oppose these groups—which in the light
of public opinion at that time might have been foolhardy—
the Association set about codifying the most frequent censor
complaints from all over the country, and advised their member companies just how far they dared go. As the memory of
Hollywood's scandals began to fade, however, and the organized voices of protest died to a murmur, the producers became bolder again, often putting on the screen scenes of
nudity and debauchery that far exceeded what would today
be called "contemporary community standards." The
M.P.P.D.A.—"The Hays Office," as it came to be known—
"advised" its hotly competitive members whenever one of
their pictures became too rough, and spent much of its time
trying to build good will around the country by assuring civic
groups that movies had become cleaner and more moral than
ever before.

More moral they certainly were, although in a peculiarly
inappropriate sense of the word. The Hays Office promul-
gated among its producers a theory of "compensating values"
to be followed in the production of their pictures. According
to this quaintly Victorian theory, if virtue were always rewarded and sin punished, if good eventually triumphed and
the evildoer perished miserably, the laws of God, man and
the drama would be simultaneously satisfied. The studios
were quick to perceive that what this meant, in effect, was
that they could present six reels of ticket-selling sinfulness if,
in the seventh reel, all the sinners came to a bad end, and
that they could go through all the motions of vice if, at the
last moment, virtue triumphed. Censors around the country
might continue their snipping of occasional scenes, but who
could object to movies in which "morality" was so eagerly
espoused?

With such a mechanical yardstick as a guide to "jazz age"
modes of conduct, there was an inevitable duality, a conflict
between thought and deed that made most pictures of the era
seem basically dishonest. Thus Clara Bow might invade a
bachelor's apartment, dance suggestively in front of him,
drink his cocktails and leap provocatively into his bedroom.
But when the bachelor made the proper responses, she
promptly ran home to mother. Or if a young couple snatched
some seemingly illicit hours of love-making, a last-minute

"switch" would show that they had been secretly married all the while. Drinking, petting, orgiastic parties—all of these were shown in gleeful detail, but always with a compensating cluck of disapproval to indicate how proper and moral the producers really were.

De Mille and the New Morality

The films of Cecil B. De Mille during the middle twenties reveal clearly how superficial, even hypocritical, this new morality essentially was. Apart from D. W. Griffith, De Mille was the best known and most successful director of the era; and no small part of his success lay in his shrewd ability to change with the changing times. He had realized at the very outset of his long career that the public's taste, as revealed at the box office, was the producer's surest guide, and he patterned his films accordingly. His first picture was a Western, *The Squaw Man*, made early in 1914 (and one of the first features produced in Hollywood). It proved an immediate hit, and De Mille quickly made several more movies in the same vein. When in 1915, however, the industry switched to a policy of filming stage plays with famous Broadway stars, De Mille promptly put into production a version of *Carmen* starring the noted diva Geraldine Farrar—and for added insurance, a movie favorite, Wallace Reid. Highly praised at the time for its "theatrical effects," *Carmen* established De Mille as a "name" director. Then, as the war clouds began to gather, he nimbly turned out a series of violently patriotic pictures—*Joan the Woman* (1917), *The Little American* (1917), *The Whispering Chorus* (1918).

Even before the war had ended, De Mille sensed that the demand for such films would soon be over. In casting about for a new popular subject, he released in quick succession a series of pictures in sharply different styles and noted carefully the public's reaction to each of them. The swing, he decided, was toward a more sophisticated approach to sex; and in a long series of modern comedies produced between 1919 and 1923 De Mille catered to the postwar trend toward higher living, heavier drinking and looser morals. Dwelling on both the fashions and the foibles of the fabulously rich, he opened up a whole new world for the films, a world that middle-class audiences, newly won to the movies by the luxurious theaters then springing up, very much wanted to see.

Male and Female (1919), *For Better, for Worse* (1919),
Don't Change Your Husband (1919), *Why Change Your
Wife?* (1920), *Adam's Rib* (1923)—all promised the last
word in elegance, refinement and *haute couture*. And by link-
ing fashion with fashionable undress, De Mille was able to
provide something for everyone.

William De Mille, Cecil's brother, who plowed the same
field with perhaps less box-office approbation but certainly
with greater taste, has amusingly described the elements of a
typical De Mille success of this era. In his *Hollywood Saga*
he wrote: "He made of the bathroom a delightful resort
which undoubtedly had its effect upon bathrooms of the
whole nation. The bath became a mystic shrine dedicated to
Venus, or sometimes to Apollo, and the art of bathing was
shown as a lovely ceremony rather than a merely sanitary
duty. Undressing was not just the taking off of clothes; it was
a progressive revelation of entrancing beauty; a study in
diminishing draperies. The theme was that in no stage of
dress or undress, whether in the bathroom, the kitchen, the
ballroom or the bedroom, need a woman look unlovely. To
this end underclothes became visions of translucent promise,
and nightgowns silken poems set to music." De Mille turned
out over a dozen pictures in this vein, celebrating the dawn
of the jazz age, relishing the sybaritic opulence of the world
of fashion and the new freedom from moral restraints. In all
of them he condoned the new morality, the flouting of conventions, the hedonistic scramble for wealth and pleasure at
any price. "See your favorite stars committing your favorite
sins" was the ad line for a De Mille film of this period.

And then, with a conjuror's quickness, he reversed himself.
In *The Ten Commandments* (1923) De Mille climbed the
mountain with Moses and thundered forth his "Thou shalt
not's." The reformers' chorus had reached his ears; the Hays
Office had been formed; the women's clubs throughout the
land were making known their dissatisfaction with the
amount of sex and sin they found in their theaters. The time
had come for change—of sorts. Sex would still sell tickets,
but flagrant immorality would not. De Mille solved this
dilemma in *The Ten Commandments* by simply masking the
kind of sex melodrama that was typical of the era—the very
kind that the women's clubs were protesting against most violently—behind a biblical façade. The modern part of the film
presents Rod La Rocque as a building contractor who goes to

the dogs over sultry Nita Naldi, skimping on the concrete for a cathedral he was building so that he might buy more silks and jewels for his charmer. All of this, of course, De Mille detailed with his customary relish for spicy high life. For the early reels, however, De Mille skipped back to Exodus to demonstrate, parable fashion, the moral lesson, "Thou shalt not kill," "Thou shalt not commit adultery," "Honor thy father and thy mother . . ." For all the impressiveness of such scenes as the Israelites crossing the Red Sea, their wanderings in the desert and Moses receiving the Law on Mount Sinai, none of this had much intrinsic bearing upon the modern story in the film. They were merely the cloak, the smoke screen for the sort of thing that, despite the hue and cry, De Mille felt sure would still make money. And who would dare to protest against a picture that included Moses and the Ten Commandments? Characteristically, even while Moses was receiving the Commandments on the Mount, De Mille made the most of the bacchanalian revels around the Golden Calf below.

Perhaps because De Mille has always trumpeted his moral lessons more sententiously than any other director would dare, his films have also carried more sensational sinning than anyone else's. Better than any other director of the era, he seems to have apprehended a basic duality in his audiences—on the one hand their tremendous eagerness to see what they considered sinful and taboo, and on the other, the fact that they could enjoy sin only if they were able to preserve their own sense of righteous respectability in the process. Certainly, De Mille gave them every opportunity, and his pictures won the crowds. For years *The Ten Commandments* remained among the top-grossing films; while *The King of Kings* (1927), his first all-out essay in the field of sin-cum-morals spectaculars, is still being shown. No one could have remained so completely successful for so long without a shrewd knowledge of his audience—and more than a little willingness to pander to the least common denominator of public taste.

What De Mille did with his special showmanlike flair, most of the other directors of the mid-twenties were also doing, somewhat less flamboyantly, as a matter of studio policy. The Hays Office approach to morality, combined with the mass production of entertainment in the new, huge film factories, resulted in a preponderance of formula pictures—complete with built-in happy endings and an automatic meting out of just desserts to all the "heavies." Their characters were stock and immediately identifiable: the hero was a clear-eyed, clean-profiled young man; the heroine, blond and virginal; the villain was dark, mustached and addicted to cigarettes; the "other woman" was also dark, exotic, given to low-cut gowns and long, long cigarette holders. There was, in addition, generally a middle-aged comic-relief couple. The action was as obvious and predictable as the gaslit melodramas of the late 19th century. Early in the film the hero discovers his girl friend in some terribly compromising position nastily contrived by the villain; there follows a long misunderstanding between the two, the hero's chance discovery of the truth, the punishment of the villain and the big reconciliation scene. Originality lay in dreaming up some especially salacious situation for the misunderstanding and a sufficiently gruesome fate for the "heavies." By comparison, the European films, with no such standardized patterns, with no artificially imposed moral ending, inevitably seemed far more honest and true to life.

Hollywood Imports "Art"

By the same token, when European directors were brought to Hollywood and asked to adapt their techniques to Hollywood formula stories, the results could not help seeming superficial and forced. The techniques of the Swedish, Danish and German studios had been devised to explore and create the realities of character and background; now they were being used to disguise—or at least, to make more palatable—patently false stories about improbable people. The surprising thing is that so many of the Europeans succeeded as well as they did.

F. W. Murnau, for example, in his first American film, *Sunrise* (1927), created at least one-half of a masterpiece. Based on Hermann Sudermann's *A Trip to Tilsit*, it tells of a young peasant seduced by a vamp from the big city vacationing in his village. They plan to murder his wife and run away together. But the wife becomes suspicious and frightened of her husband just as he realizes that he still loves her and can not kill her. After several clumsy, tentative efforts at a reconciliation, there is a touching scene of their spiritual remarriage as the two sit quietly together in a cathedral. The film might well have ended right there were it not for the fact that the moral code had still to be fulfilled: the husband had yet to suffer for his philandering, the vamp had still to be punished for her vamping. Consequently, the plot takes a sudden, melodramatic turn. On a trip across the lake, a squall springs up and the newly reconciled couple are separated as the wife is swept out of the boat into the storm-tossed waters. After a night of agonized search, the remorseful husband in a fury turns on his seductress, beats her and sends her packing even as the wife is discovered safe and alive. This formula finale quite destroyed the extraordinary depth of character Murnau had created in the first part of his film. These are no longer people but puppets who have been jerked into a conventional—and singularly unconvincing—moral ending that would satisfy the demands of the box office and the official custodians of the public's morals.

The same rigid formula surrounded many of the great European actors brought to this country during the late silent era. Certainly, the greatest of these was Emil Jannings, imported on the strength of the box-office success of his German films *The Last Laugh* and *Variety*. In both of them he had played tragic old men broken by Fate. It was inevitable that Hollywood should cast him again in the same type of role; what is also clear is that to capitalize on his European reputation the Paramount script writers deliberately prepared for him a series of pictures in which tragedy struck in retribution for the old man's sexual peccadilloes. In *The Way of All Flesh* (1927), *the Last Command* (1928), *The Patriot* (1928) and *Sins of the Fathers* (1929), Jannings was made to feel every sling and arrow of outrageous fortune that the Paramount script department could devise. He sinned, and he suffered—but his suffering was so arbitrarily conceived, his retribution so mechanical that not even the great Jannings could conceal the basic falseness of both the stories and their characters. For *The Way of All Flesh* and *The Last Command*, he won the first Academy Award ever given for acting; in neither of them, however, was he able to achieve the sense of truth that had made his old doorman in *The Last Laugh* or his betrayed husband in *Variety* so deeply affecting. Indeed, not until Jannings returned to Germany and made *The Blue Angel* (1930) was he again able to create a role in which tragedy was not confused with maudlin melodramatics, in which disgrace and death came as the inevitable consequence of a shattered life and not the smug punishment of a facile moral code.

Despite their obvious differences in temperament, technique and aesthetic outlook, the Hollywood studios continued to woo the European film makers in great numbers. Nor was their motive purely commercial, although the invitees were invariably the stars and directors of commercially successful pictures. But through the rising tide of film criticism, the idea was getting around that the film was a popular art—one of what Gilbert Seldes had aptly termed in 1924 the "seven lively arts." The films from Europe were being raptly hailed as "artistic." If, the producers reasoned, a European picture could be both artistic and successful at the box office, why not bring its maker to Hollywood to introduce such profitable "art" into American movies? They had no objection to their pictures being "artistic"—not if they showed a good profit as well. The trouble was that, too often, they viewed artistry in terms of camera angles, tricky lighting and specially constructed settings, a technique that was applied to a story rather than being an outgrowth of the story itself. They set their expensive importees to work on formula films, and were naïvely astonished to discover that the pictures they turned out were neither artistic nor, in many cases, commercially successful.

Nor did the native American directors escape these Continental influences. The moving camera, the low-keyed lighting, the slow, deliberate tempo and greater emphasis on pictorial composition all recommended themselves to producers seeking to make their pictures look more impressive and artistic than (too often) they really were. Once the European invasion had begun in earnest, many Americans changed their style overnight. Clarence Brown, who had made his reputation directing Will Rogers' typically American comedies, turned *Flesh and the Devil* (1927) into a full-blown imitation of the Germans, right down to a duel scene staged in picturesquely framed silhouettes. King Vidor's *La Bohème* (1926), Frank Borzage's *Seventh Heaven* (1927), Victor Schertzinger's *Forgotten Faces* (1927), Josef von Sternberg's *Underworld* (1927) and *The Last Command* (1928) all reveal the German influence at its strongest. Whole passages were frequently copied from the German originals; plot incidents were often suspiciously similar; and the increasingly daring camera angles, the extended use of dissolves, the efforts to eliminate or minimize subtitles were similarly German-inspired. Sometimes these effects clashed badly with American themes and formula plots, or with the acting styles of American players. But happily the American directors proved a resilient lot. They not only imitated the new styles; they quickly absorbed them and transformed them from tricks and mannerisms into a strong and highly fluent technique. Indeed, solely in terms of technique, the American films of the late silent era compare favorably with pictures made anywhere in the world.

The Cowboys and the Clowns

There were two major American film forms that had sufficient vitality and integrity to withstand the effects of the foreign invasion throughout the twenties—the slapstick comedy and the Western. Immensely popular all over the world, there was no need to make these more "artistic" by following the latest European fashions. At once too successful and too lowly to warrant such improvements, they were considered "just entertainment." They bore no weighty messages, inspired no cults or schools of aesthetics. But they delighted audiences, both here and abroad, because they were so purely and simply American. Unconsciously, unobtrusively, they epitomized all that was best in America without the slightest trace—or intention—of self-righteous sermonizing. It was there in the ingenuity and eternal optimism of the comics. It shone again in the cowboys' spirit of adventure as they rode the plains in search of the next frontier. To tired Europeans, to cramped city dwellers, to small boys, to people everywhere these films carried the message of the American dream. In them the humble triumphed over their powerful adversaries, the weak outwitted the strong—and always with the implicit promise of riches, freedom and happiness for all. As seen in the Westerns, the world was a simple place for men with the pioneer virtues of honesty, courage, a taste for adventure and a quick trigger finger. The world was a crazy place, said the comics, but with a little faith, a little luck, a little ingenuity—and possibly a couple of pratfalls—it was anybody's oyster.

Perhaps because they were so consistently popular on both sides of the water, perhaps because they had no counterparts abroad—whatever the reason—the Westerns and the come-

dies were permitted to go their merry ways free of foreign
entanglements. It is not surprising, therefore, to discover that
these two indigenous forms during the twenties produced not
only some of our best directors—men like Frank Capra, John
Ford, George Stevens, William Wyler and the many disciples
of Thomas H. Ince and Mack Sennett—but also all that is
most characteristic of American film style. The speed, the
tightness, the brilliant timing of action and editing, the steady
progression of story line, the clean, bright photography and,
on a somewhat more technical level, the knowing use of
camera lenses and filters came primarily from the practice
and practitioners of these two schools. A Tom Mix horse opera or a Buster Keaton two-reeler may not have seemed as
"artistic" as some of the European imports, but often it had a
lot more to do with the genuine art of the film.

Despite their basic simplicity, however, both the Westerns
and the comedies changed with the times. Early in the twenties the Westerns veered sharply away from the realistic portrait of frontier life that characterized the William S. Hart
pictures. Hart's hero had been the Good Bad Man—a hard-
drinking, hard-riding, hard-shooting he-man, often an outlaw,
often the adversary of law and order, but always true to the
moral code of the old frontier. After the First World War,
Hart's descriptions of the West, although essentially truer
than anything that has been done since, came to be dismissed
as "old-fashioned." Movie-goers—even Westerners—preferred the more romantic version of the West they found in
the films of Tom Mix, Buck Jones, Hoot Gibson and Ken
Maynard. Now the hero was a Good *Good* Man, riding the
range to protect the weak and bring the outlaws to justice.
He never drank, seldom smoked and—unlike Hart with his
blazing six-shooters—he used his pistols only when forced to.
He was quick on the draw, tall in the saddle, handy with his
rope and fists. He lived cleanly and simply, and whatever
complications beclouded his life usually came from the
machinations of greedy big-city "varmints"—nothing that
couldn't be straightened out by the final reel. This was the
Old West as city folk, country folk and the cowboys themselves idealized it, and each new Western of the period added
its embellishments to this popular myth. Their plots were formula, but their tempo was fast, their technique clean and
uncomplicated, and they quickly found their niche in the production scheme of the twenties. Although rarely playing the

big theaters in the larger cities, they had a virtually assured audience in the neighborhoods, in rural and Western towns and in theaters abroad. Consequently, every studio then (as now) produced a certain number of Westerns every year. Inexpensive to make, they were one of the few staples in the business.

It was in this spirit that Paramount in 1923 undertook to make *The Covered Wagon* from a *Saturday Evening Post* story of the cross-country trek of the Forty-niners. Impressed with its epic qualities, however, the studio decided to raise the budget and permit director James Cruze to take his cast on location to Snake Valley, Nevada. Here, against the natural splendors of butte and mesa, amidst the same hot sands and torrential rivers that had harrassed our ancestors more than a hundred years ago, Cruze produced a film of tremendous sweep and spirit. Despite the shallow romance that served as its story thread, the essential grandeur of its theme, the vigor and humor of its frontier types and—perhaps above all—the beauties of its backgrounds at a time when pictures were being made increasingly inside a studio, immediately won for *The Covered Wagon* tremendous critical acclaim and, no less important, tremendous support at the box office. By combining the stars and production values that assured big-city box-office appeal with the sure-fire small-town pull of any Western, Paramount had come up with a new kind of winner—the "big Western." For years *The Covered Wagon* remained among the top money-makers in the business. When the following year Fox produced John Ford's *The Iron Horse* (1924) which romanticized in a similar fashion the construction of the first transcontinental railroad, its resounding success proved that the "big Western" was no mere flash in the pan. It still remains the most consistently lucrative of American film forms, occasionally raising the routine horse opera to the level of a national epic, as in Henry King's *The Gunfighter* (1950), George Stevens' *Shane* (1953), or William Wyler's *The Big Country* (1958).

In the meantime the slapstick comedy was also undergoing a transformation. Two-reelers persisted right through the twenties under the aegis of such Masters of the Revels as Mack Sennett, Hal Roach and Earle W. Hammons of Educational Pictures (a singularly inappropriate soubriquet). All of them, however, were losing their top comics, their best directors, their cleverest gag men to the feature films. In the face of rising production costs and spiraling star salaries, the shorts field could no longer afford to pay its talent on a scale comparable to the big studios. One by one, the best comedians of the prewar era deserted the two-reelers for feature production. Charlie Chaplin, Harold Lloyd and Buster Keaton led the list, both in popularity and ability, closely followed by such notable clowns as Harry Langdon, Raymond Griffith, Larry Semon, Louise Fazenda and the charming, devil-may-care Mabel Normand. Happily, they carried the slapstick spirit with them.

In their feature-length comedies, each presented a precise and carefully prepared character to the public—generally, some version of the little fellow that everything happens to. But their variations were as different as the performers themselves. Chaplin's tramp had pathos; there was a deeply sentimental vein running through all his films. Keaton was straight-faced, a poignant automaton caught up in a world that was beyond his control or understanding. Lloyd's eager, bespectacled youth understood everything perfectly well but was physically unable to do anything about it—unless Fortune favored him, as she invariably did in the end. Harry Langdon was a baby-faced innocent hopelessly trying to act grown up. Only Raymond Griffith, dapper in spats and silk hat, attempted sophisticated slapstick on the screen, but even he made all the blunders and *faux pas* that harrass the average man.

As a group, these feature comedies of the twenties were far more concerned with character and comic incident than with the camera itself. They had little of the effects photography of the early French chases, few of the mechanical gags and tricks of the Sennett Keystones. Their camera work, simple and straightforward, had no room for European angles or fancy lighting; their editing, fast and clean, had no need for European theories. This does not mean, however, that their technique was in any way inferior to that of more portentous productions. To make a sight gag pay off properly required a perfect placement or movement of the camera in relation to its material. To build a laugh to its climax demanded a precision of editing, an acute sense of timing that was nothing short of prodigious.

The camera work throughout Harold Lloyd's *The Freshman* (1925), for example, is superbly functional. The film begins with an iris-shot of Harold in collegiate sweater and cap leading a rousing football cheer, then opens out to reveal that he is leading the cheers in front of his bedroom mirror. In a rash attempt to win friends at college, he offers to stand treat for ice-cream cones; a moving camera keeps pulling farther and farther back as more and more undergraduates join the merry throng en route to the ice-cream parlor. During football practice Harold lands heavily on a tackle dummy—and the camera catches him at just the right angle to imply that he has rather grotesquely broken his leg. In fact, the finest gag in the whole picture depends completely upon a skillful placement of the camera. Harold goes to a ball wearing a new tuxedo that has only been basted. His tailor accompanies him, in case of an emergency. And, inevitably, the emergency arises. Harold, bashfully talking to a girl, twists a bit of thread about his finger—and with each twist the seam of his trouser leg falls open wider. Discovering his error, he beats a hasty retreat to a ringside table where, hidden behind the portieres, the tailor awaits him. Harold sits at the table with his girl, his chin resting on his hands, his legs extending out to the tailor behind him. But the tailor is subject to sinking spells, and chooses just this moment to faint dead away across Harold's legs. The camera moves around front to show Harold sinking lower and lower at the table, still chatting, still smiling and desperately pretending that it is all the most natural thing in the world.

Complementing this unobtrusive but superbly functional use of the camera was an equally incisive editing technique. During the twenties, and primarily owing to the influence of the Chaplin films, the comedy tempo had tamed down considerably from the frantic pace of the Sennett Keystones—although still recognizably swifter than that common in drama or melodrama. A shot remained on the screen just long enough to make its statement—perhaps even less if the gag dictated an accelerating speed. The best comedy directors, aware of the importance of tempo in their films, customarily made more and shorter takes than directors in the other forms, leaping from set-up to set-up in order to provide the editors with a wide variety of angles from which to build a scene. The swift pace of the silent comedies was sustained by the swift changes of point of view, the hail of shots that made up each brief sequence.

Nor were the possibilities of building or prolonging a gag through editing overlooked. The pool game in Buster

Keaton's *Sherlock Junior* (1924) affords a brilliant example
of this technique. Each shot, each incident plants a laugh that
contributes to the cumulative effect of the scene through
adroit cutting. The villains, intent on murdering Keaton, invite him to join them at pool—with one of the balls loaded
with enough dynamite to blow him to smithereens. To make
doubly certain of his sudden demise they also hold in read-
iness a poisoned glass of wine, while over an inviting chair is
poised a mighty halberd triggered to drop the moment he sits
down. Cutting from one bit to another—Keaton almost sitting on the chair, almost drinking the wine, almost hitting the
loaded ball, the reactions of the villains, the superb innocence
of Keaton—the scene builds to a climax that invariably
reduces the audience to near hysteria.

In an equally brilliant and even more subtle way, Frank
Capra built up one of the comedy scenes in Harry Langdon's
The Strong Man (1926), prolonging it and capping its climax
with a particularly masterful bit of editing. A beautiful but
quite large blonde has fainted in Langdon's arms. The little
fellow must carry her from the street up to her apartment on
the first floor. He tries to carry her but can barely lift her off
the sidewalk, much less up an entire flight of stairs. Instead,
he places her in his lap and goes up backward step by step.
Unfortunately, a workman has placed a ladder at the head of
the stairs and Langdon, all unawares, continues to edge his
way right on up the ladder. The audience, of course, knows
that the moment Langdon and the girl reach the top of the
ladder, they both will go over, and the nervous laughter begins to build. Playing on this sense of anticipation, Capra
photographs the impending disaster from the front, then from
the side, then from the rear. By overlapping each cut just a
little, he is able to hold off the moment of climax, the moment when the anticipated will happen and the laughter will
cease. It is doubtful if Capra had even heard of Eisenstein in
1926, but he too had mastered the technique of extending
time. For comic effect.

Such achievements in editing and photography, however,
provide only one aspect, one clue to the great art of the silent
comedies. Better than any other form, they also created and
sustained a sense of character of such deep persuasiveness
that audiences literally could not imagine a smiling Buster
Keaton or Harold Lloyd without his glasses. They were characters fashioned out of a thousand richly photogenic de-

tails—Chaplin's shuffling walk, Langdon's dead-white face, Keaton's staggering physical dexterity in juxtaposition to his immobile features, the ingenuous smile lurking behind Harold Lloyd's spectacles. These men built their characters for the camera, developing mannerisms and traits that, magnified on the screen, admitted the audience into the secret places of their souls—Langdon's curious, tentative half-gestures of guileless friendship, Lloyd's nervous gulp before tackling the impossible. The scripts, the stories, the plot incidents were all devised to further this one character who reappeared in film after film. Even the world through which they moved was a fantasy of their own creation—the echo of a London slum in the Chaplin films, a world of overwhelming mechanical monsters for Keaton, a cold and insensitive place for Langdon's innocent. In their unique ability to make believable both their private worlds and their public characters lay the genius of the silent slapstick clowns.

To these comedians should be added the name of Douglas Fairbanks. Fairbanks, of course, was not a clown; but he created a true comic character in his earliest films, while his swashbuckling romances of the twenties were invariably enlivened by wonderful sight gags that made splendid use of his incredible athletic prowess. Brought to Hollywood in 1915 as one of more than sixty Broadway stars scooped up by Triangle in its effort to make the movies "legitimate," he quickly established himself as one of the few real finds in a largely unpopular package. His first pictures were directed or supervised by D. W. Griffith, who despaired of ever making a film actor out of him. Then Fairbanks had the good fortune to pass, by default, into the hands of John Emerson and Anita Loos. They sensed the brash optimism, the healthy good humor of the man, and set about creating a screen character that incorporated not only his athletic ability but his bracing personality as well. They fashioned for him a series of modern comedies, many of them directed by Emerson, that gave free rein to his natural vitality, but at the same time edged him toward the character once described by Alistair Cooke as "the popular philosopher." During the last half of the teens, Fairbanks became above all the laughing debunker of fads and false standards, the city man who longs restlessly for the West and freedom, the ardent booster of clean living and simple common sense. In most of his comedies he appeared as the "average American male," and the touchstone of his success was the flattering assumption behind all his films that "if I can do it, you can do it too."

Then, on the threshold of the twenties, Fairbanks, like De Mille, underwent a sudden change. But where De Mille had embraced the new, sophisticated pleasures of wine, women and wrong, Fairbanks the optimist, the exponent of clean living and thinking, could take no such course. His alternative was to turn away from the confusions and upheavals of the postwar world, back to a simpler time when the moral values that the Fairbanks screen character had always embodied might have a clearer justification—back to those days when all injustice and oppression stemmed not from the ways of the world but from the malevolence of some master villain, and when a healthy aristocrat with high principles and a lively sword could right all wrongs. In the place of a brisk, clean-shaven, able-bodied young American stood now a mustachioed D'Artagnan, a ringleted Robin Hood, a bronzed Thief of Bagdad. And in place of the everyday, workaday background of the early Fairbanks films appeared huge, handsome settings and elaborate mechanical and photographic effects. Through these serio-comic extravaganzas, however, Fairbanks continued to romp with his inimitable, balletic grace. His utter ease inspired not envy but admiration, and his screen character rivaled only Chaplin's in world-wide popularity.

Sophistication and Style: Chaplin and Lubitsch

The films of Fairbanks, like those of the great slapstick clowns, appealed to people everywhere because their characters were universally recognizable. Fairbanks typified the ideal lover, romantic, nimble and gallant; the others were slightly battered, slightly foolish, often pathetic creatures, but beneath their tattered vests beat the heart of Everyman. What the world recognized and loved was their essential humanity. After World War I, however, another form of film comedy began to appear with increasing frequency. It was the comedy of manners, which specialized in depicting the escapades and excesses of the very rich. Rarely hilarious, not even necessarily funny, it was a wry way of looking at the complications of leisured living. This type of comedy had long been popular in the theater; and when the middle-class audiences began flocking to the movies it soon became a popular film form too. This was the field that Cecil B. De Mille dominated so profitably from 1919 to 1923. He and his imitators turned out countless glittering comedies of high society. Soon other directors were bringing to this form the incisive style and true sophistication that De Mille himself lacked. When in 1923 Charlie Chaplin turned to the comedy of manners in *A Woman of Paris,* and when Lubitsch, soon after, produced *The Marriage Circle,* they introduced a new spice and sparkle that was both more comic and essentially more filmic than anything De Mille had done.

Chaplin seems to have produced *A Woman of Paris* partly to satisfy his own desire to direct a comedy without the tramp character, partly as a gesture to his veteran leading lady, Edna Purviance, whom he rewarded with stardom in the film's title role. (Chaplin himself appears in the picture only for a moment, disguised almost beyond recognition, as a heavily-laden porter at a French railway station.) "A drama of fate" was Chaplin's own subtitle for the film—and despite his light, sardonic treatment of its theme, he clearly regarded it as a work with deep social implications. His foreword read, "Humanity is composed not of heroes and villains, but of men and women, and all their passions, good and bad, have been given them by God. They sin only in blindness, and the ignorant condemn their mistakes, but the wise pity them." His story, in outline, might have been the scenario for a tear-jerking tragedy, but his outlook, his approach transformed its bathos into an ironic comedy. Marie St. Clair (Edna Purviance), a girl from a small French village, runs off to Paris after an unfortunate love affair. A year later, Marie has become part of the smart world of Parisian society, the mistress of a suave philanderer, played by Adolphe Menjou (who tootles a saxophone in his more debonair moments). One day, by accident, she meets her former fiancé, now a struggling artist, and commissions him to paint her portrait. Their old love revives, but in the meantime the artist has learned of her new relationship. He persuades her to leave the philanderer but, overhearing a fragment of a conversation, becomes convinced she never will. The young man commits suicide—just as Marie discovers that her fickle lover is planning to marry another. Destitute and disillusioned, she returns to her native village to live with the mother of her dead fiancé.

Chaplin took this maudlin story and by his witty, sophisticated direction turned it into a comedy that set new standards for those American directors who had until then been copying the tasteless excesses of the De Mille extravaganzas. His picture had *style*—the sly implication of an immoral or risqué situation rather than the forthright presentation of one. The nature of the relationship between Menjou and the girl, for example, is adroitly defined when he calls on her at her apartment, then casually goes to her bureau and takes from it one of his handkerchiefs. Again and again Chaplin showed his preference for a tickling innuendo of sex rather than the naked fact. A thinly clad dancer at a Parisian revel twirls out of her costume, but the unveiling is suggested by holding the camera on the man who is wrapping her garment about himself. Chaplin filled his picture with wry little incidents that delighted the moviegoers of that day, as when the girl angrily flings a diamond necklace out of the window while Menjou, amused, blows on his saxophone; then, noticing a tramp picking up the jewels in the street below, Marie promptly forgets her pique and dashes out after him to retrieve them. Especially prized was the ironic note on which the picture ended, a rarity in films of that time. Chaplin dismissed the entire little tragedy with a cool cynicism that startled his audiences. The girl, now back in the country, is riding on a haywagon while Menjou passes by, unknowing, in his high-powered car. "By the way, whatever became of Marie St. Clair?" his friend asks him. Menjou merely shrugs as cart and auto continue on their separate ways.

It is impossible to imagine how *A Woman of Paris* would look today. As a matter of strict policy, Chaplin has refused to permit this; indeed, only in recent years has Chaplin permitted any of the pictures that he controls to be re-released—and *A Woman of Paris* is not among them.* Perhaps it is just as well. All too often, films that have played an important role in the evolution of the techniques of the medium prove strangely disappointing on re-examination. The fresh-

---

* Happily, shortly before his death Chaplin sanctioned a re-issue of the film, complete with a synchronized score that he composed for it in 1976. Perhaps in *A Woman of Paris* the long arm of coincidence is stretched too far in the name of irony, and the morality has grown a bit dated, but its essential virtues remain intact. Indeed, the sophistication of Chaplin's style has, if anything, been enhanced by the passing years and his basic inventiveness is still abundantly evident.

ness, the originality, the sense of innovation that gave them their initial excitement have disappeared. Their cinematic devices have been copied in film after film. Their technique, once daring and original, has become part of the standard repertory of directorial tricks. The same might well be true of Chaplin's film. In 1923 audiences were tremendously impressed when a passing train was suggested by the reflection of its lights on Marie's face. Critics also made much of the fact that the young artist's suicide was not actually shown but implied in the close-ups of faces reacting to the sound of the shot. Today, such effects are commonplace. But it was this kind of inventiveness, this kind of awareness of the possibilities of the camera for sly, indirect statement that made *A Woman of Paris* such a revelation in its day. Several of Chaplin's assistants on the film—Monta Bell, Harry d'Abbadie d'Arrast and Eddie Sutherland—went on to become directors, working in this same genre and carrying through the same cinematic suggestiveness that Chaplin had introduced. Many others were to follow his lead, the most important of them being the erstwhile "humanizer of history" in the German studios, Ernst Lubitsch.

Lubitsch had been brought to this country in 1923 by Mary Pickford to direct her in a grand-scale costume drama, *Rosita*. It was a costly flop. Released less than a month before *A Woman of Paris*, its failure followed by the immediate success of the Chaplin film seems to have given Lubitsch his cue. He had directed comedies in Germany before producing the pageant films. Now he turned back to comedy—and specifically to the comedy of manners, which he spiced with his own highly Continental brand of humor. His first film in this style, *The Marriage Circle* (1924), reached the screen less than four months after the Chaplin film, notably similar to it both in theme and technique. Contemporary critics made the inevitable comparisons (predominantly in Lubitsch's favor), and Lubitsch was launched on a new career and a new style in which he was to remain pre-eminent until his death in 1947.

It should not be imagined, however, that Lubitsch was a mere imitator of Chaplin. In picture after picture he gave evidence of his own highly cinematic imagination—*Forbidden Paradise* (1924), *Kiss Me Again* (1925), *Lady Windermere's Fan* (1925), *So This is Paris* (1926)—until even the general public became aware of the "Lubitsch touch," that naughty twinkle of sophisticated Continental wit. He was a master of understatement, compressing in a single humorous bit of business his own shrewd insights into the ways of the world. In one of his pictures, for example, Lubitsch wanted to suggest that a man had grown bored with his wife, that their relationship had become quite matter of fact. The husband's attitude was made abundantly clear in a brief sequence showing the couple leaving their apartment for a dinner date. As they enter the elevator, he is wearing his hat. The car stops a few floors below and a pretty girl gets on. He takes off his hat. For *Lady Windermere's Fan*, Lubitsch invented a sequence at a racetrack in which all sorts of intimate relationships are implied by glances, by quickly averted eyes, knowing smiles and whispers that neither are explained by subtitles nor require explanation. Undoubtedly one reason that Lubitsch became so popular with the smart set during the twenties—and with other directors as well—was his skillful skirting of the censor problem. He implied censorable volumes, but offered precious little that anyone could actually cut out.

Lubitsch also, virtually singlehanded, accomplished a revolution in American set décors. Prior to *The Marriage Circle*, almost any decoration would do—either wholly nondescript for a routine film or, for a more elaborate production, rooms choked with bric-a-brac and overstuffed chairs set off by loudly ornamental drapes and busy wallpaper. Lubitsch cleared away the clutter, providing clean playing areas for his action. The advantages were so immediately apparent that they were incorporated into the majority of pictures from that moment on. Few directors, however, have quite his ability to use settings to their fullest advantage. To Lubitsch, a door was always more than simply a way to get into or out of a room: it was a way to end an argument, to suggest pique or coquetry or even the sexual act itself. Corridors, stairways, windows—all had a dramatic function in the Lubitsch films. With his sparkling wit and polished technique, he soon became the leading exponent of the comedy of manners, inspiring and influencing a coterie of directors that came to include such talents as Mal St. Clair, Lewis Milestone, Wesley Ruggles and Frank Tuttle. For them, style was the thing, and the "Lubitsch touch" can be found echoing through such pleasant trifles of the late twenties as *The*

Grand Duchess and the Waiter (1926), *Beware of Widows* (1927), *Two Arabian Knights* (1927) and *Gentlemen Prefer Blondes* (1928).

Typecasting the Director

During the twenties the studios developed a strong tendency to "type" their directors as thoroughly as they were typing their stars. Lubitsch and his followers were the "smart" directors, invariably assigned to situation comedies. "Gag" comedies went to men like Clarence Badger, H. C. Potter, Erle Kenton, Marshall Neilan and Charles Reisner. Frank Borzage, George Fitzmaurice, Edmund Goulding and Henry King were known for their ability to direct "women's pictures" (a term that, considering the films, women should find particularly offensive); Lambert Hillyer, J. P. McGowan, Al Rogell, Richard Thorpe and William Wyler directed Westerns; action stories were assigned to men like Jack Conway, Victor Fleming, William K. Howard, Rowland V. Lee, W. S. Van Dyke, Raoul Walsh and William Wellman. Tod Browning, who directed most of the Lon Chaney thrillers, found his special niche in tales of horror and the macabre. Rex Ingram, whose *The Four Horsemen of the Apocalypse* (1921) catapulted Rudolph Valentino to fame, became identified with colorful costume romances. Invariably, perhaps even inevitably, the studios saw to it that a director who had scored a hit with one type of film followed it up with more of the same.

As for the general public, there were few directors it either knew or cared about. The studios were selling stars, and their publicity machines were geared to glamorizing their contract players. Nobody saw a director, so why bother about him? The exceptions were men who, either as their own producers or as potent box-office draws, were able to focus some of the attention upon themselves. Perhaps the prototype for all directors, in the public's mind, was the colorful Cecil B. De Mille, who saw to it that his name made the headlines almost as often as the leading stars of the day. He gave the first interview held in an airplane, was the first director to use a megaphone on the set, the first to install a loud-speaker system to address his players. In his broad-brimmed hat, open-throated shirt, riding breeches and leather puttees, De Mille was as familiar a figure in the fan magazines as John Gilbert or Clara Bow. If, however, anyone were asked to name the greatest American director during the early part of the twenties, the answer would still have been D. W. Griffith, even though his name above the title of a picture was no longer a guarantee of box-office success. When Griffith went to work for Paramount in 1925, this order of billing was reversed. Chaplin, of course, was known primarily as an actor, but most people were aware that he also directed his own productions. Ernst Lubitsch, with his perennial cigar, had become fairly well known outside the industry by the late twenties when his ceaseless stream of hit films had elevated him to the slender ranks of the star directors.

Few contemporaries shared either the fame or the independence of these top men. Most directors were simply assigned by their studios to work on a picture, whether its theme was one that interested them or not. The studios had the power to alter their work in any way they saw fit. Few were even accorded the privilege of cutting their picture the way they thought it should be. There was a constant tug-of-war between the "front office" and the directors, who were often bitterly convinced that the studio heads knew nothing about movies and cared less; while the producers, keeping track of the mounting costs on their pictures, resented every change or retake that might send the budget up higher. Perhaps there was some truth in the directors' charge that the producers were secretly craving to be "creative" when they carved up their pictures, but it was equally true that the producers were the men closest to the public and its tastes and therefore most aware of what constituted good box office. At M-G-M during the late twenties, for example, the youthful Irving Thalberg was considered almost infallible in his knowledge of what would please the public. He had full authority to re-edit any film produced on the lot—and has been credited with saving many a picture from disaster. It was the producer's job to make a successful film, and to make it on a budget, whether this meant hurting the director's artistic sensibilities or not. It was also the producer's job to find stories that would assure big box-office receipts, whether they happened to please a director or not.

Fortunately, many of the directors of the twenties were incredibly versatile, able to change their styles to keep abreast of changing public tastes and interests. James Cruze, for example, followed up his big Western, *The Covered Wagon*, with films as diverse as the comic *Ruggles of Red Gap* (1923), the satiric *Beggar on Horseback* (1925) and the sophisticated *Waiter from the Ritz* (1926) before returning to the epic style in *Old Ironsides* (1926). King Vidor, after a number of modest, essentially realistic studies of the contemporary American scene, directed in quick order the epical *Big Parade* (1925), an operatic adaptation of *La Bohème* (1926) and a swashbuckling romance, *Bardelys the Magnificent* (1926). He then turned back to the contemporary scene with *The Crowd* (1928), a heart-warming story of the tragedies and joys of an ordinary man, a clerk in a big office. It was Vidor's masterpiece of the silent era. Herbert Brenon's directorial assignments ranged all the way from sentimental fantasies like *Peter Pan* (1925) and *A Kiss for Cinderella* (1926) to the romantic heroics of *Beau Geste* (1926). A similar versatility is to be found, on occasion, in the works of John Ford, Henry King, Marshall Neilan and many more of the top directors of the twenties.

It was this versatility, above all else, that kept them in the front ranks of the directors. Highly skilled and thoroughly trained through long years of apprenticeship under such masters as Griffith, Ince and Sennett, they had the innate ability to rise to an important theme or a dramatic story. Unfortunately, too few of the films of the period placed such demands upon them. A director was expected to keep the pot boiling with whatever kind of picture was currently in vogue. Consequently, most of them were known as craftsmen rather than as artists, as types rather than as creative personalities.

The Rebel: Von Stroheim

And yet the American producers seem to be irresistibly drawn to strong, creative personalities, to artists with a flair for using film to make a highly personal observation on life and the ways of the world. Invariably, the studios put them under contract with considerable fanfare, then proceed to force them into the mold of their own preconceptions of what constitutes good box office. Ironically, what brought them to the producers' attention in the first place was often some independent, off-beat production that was successful precisely because it lacked the conventional themes or values that producers considered "safe." Once under contract, however, a director was expected to conform. For individualists like Erich von Stroheim, Robert Flaherty and Josef von Sternberg, such conformism was difficult if not impossible. The running warfare that always existed between the "front office" and the creative personnel burst forth with added intensity upon such people. For them, there were only three alternatives: complete withdrawal, an uneasy truce or abject surrender.

For von Stroheim, throughout the twenties, it was an uneasy truce. This Austrian-born jack-of-all-trades first won attention during World War I as an actor. In film after film—including Griffith's *Hearts of the World* (1918)—he portrayed a be-monocled, sadistic, lecherous Prussian officer. When he turned to directing with *Blind Husbands* (1919), he again played in it his favorite role, "the man you love to hate"—a professional adventurer, blackmailer, and seducer. As an Austrian officer who captivates the bored wife of an American businessman, von Stroheim openly suggested that a married woman whose husband is too busy to be romantic has every right to seek love elsewhere. This attitude, one of the first statements of the new postwar morality to be made in films, shocked many and delighted more. In the ensuing hullabaloo it became one of the box-office hits of the year.

The success of *Blind Husbands* prompted Universal to grant von Stroheim greater leeway on *The Devil's Passkey* (1920) and *Foolish Wives* (1921), films that virtually repeated both the theme and the setting of his first picture. All of them were marked by their director's passion for a detailed realism of background and atmosphere. In making *Foolish Wives,* it was reported that he had installed a complete electrical wiring system for each room of a dummy hotel that appeared briefly in the film. In another picture he ordered $10,000 worth of special medals to be struck off for officers in the army of a mythical kingdom, had the royal crest embroidered on his players' underclothes, held up a costly scene for hours until the smoke from a single chimney was rising to his satisfaction. Such details, he argued, may not have added to the physical reality of his pictures, but they did enhance the feeling, the atmosphere that he was trying to create. Given an unlimited budget on *The Merry-Go-Round* (1923), von Stroheim permitted his passion to exceed his discretion and the picture was completed by another, less exacting director. Even so, his reputation was such that the newly formed Metro-Goldwyn studio promptly offered him carte blanche to make for them any picture he wanted. The story that he chose was Frank Norris's *McTeague*. And the film he made from it was *Greed* (1924), one of the greatest triumphs of American realism.

Written in 1899, at the dawn of the muckrake era of American literature, *McTeague* was a vast, sprawling novel about money and its power to corrupt. Von Stroheim, apparently, had been attracted to it soon after his arrival in America, drawn as much by the harsh realism of Norris's descriptive passages as by the theme itself. Preparing his own adaptation, he proposed to film the book scene by scene, line by line, in the very places so vividly described by the author. Accordingly, he moved his cast out of the studio and up to San Francisco, the locale of the novel. There he commandeered whole blocks of houses, even tearing out the walls to facilitate the photographing of interiors. At one point, a funeral procession had to pass a certain window at a given moment. He tied up city traffic for blocks around until he got the scene just as he wanted it. For the finale, set in Death Valley, he took his principals, Gibson Gowland and Jean Hersholt, into the Valley itself, where they worked for days under the blazing sun. Hersholt has recalled the experience as the most grueling of his long career.

The ironic—and tragic—outcome of all this heroic effort is that von Stroheim's *McTeague* never did reach the public. He had made a film 42 reels long (about ten hours) and suggested to Metro they release it in two parts. The studio refused. Von Stroheim cut it to twenty reels (or approximately the length of *Gone With the Wind*, released by the same studio just fifteen years later). Again Metro refused, this time taking the film away from him entirely and turning it over to June Mathis, a staff writer, to reduce and rearrange into a more marketable form. The result was *Greed*, in ten reels. For years von Stroheim refused even to look at it.*

Perhaps the full measure of the greatness of *Greed* is to be found only by comparing what remains with the original novel, supplemented by Herman G. Weinberg's loving re-creation of the film from existent stills and scenario excerpts (*The Complete Greed*.) So faithful was von Stroheim to the text that his intentions are clear in every scene, even though the structure of the story and the development of its charac-

---

*Despite persistent rumors to the contrary, von Stroheim's original version of this film no longer exists.

ters were destroyed in the course of re-editing his footage. Such minor characters as the swaggering, cigar-smoking charwoman, or the stooped, evil-looking old junkman, for example, seem much too strongly drawn for the insignificant roles they play in the film, unless one remembers that originally they were the principals in an important subplot, the story of a mysterious treasure to which the charwoman holds the key. Similarly, the strange, symbolic inserts of hands caressing golden cups and fingering sparkling jewels which seem so out of keeping with the rest of the picture were actually salvaged from the avaricious dreams of the old junk dealer. Occasionally in the lengthy subtitles used to supplant eliminated action, abrupt references are made to ideas and incidents for which there is no longer any visual preparation. Worst of all, the McTeagues' descent from middle-class respectability to the direst poverty and Trina's disintegration from a gentle, loving wife to a slovenly, penny-pinching shrew takes place so quickly, so baldly as to tax one's credulity. Small wonder that *Greed* remains one of Metro's most expensive flops. It confused and bewildered audiences through what it didn't show—while what it did show is mighty strong meat even for audiences today.

It is strong because von Stroheim, as he said in his foreword to the picture, refused to "truckle," refused to make the kind of picture that ordinarily charmed or amused movie audiences night after night. What he put on the screen was the truth as he saw it—the truth in Norris's characters, the truth of Norris's setting, the truth of Norris's theme. Even in its bowdlerized version, *Greed* remains one of the most uncompromising pictures ever made. Because von Stroheim built his effects primarily within his individual shots rather than through the juxtaposition of shots, the subsequent pruning and condensation could not wholly destroy his intentions. And such sequences as the wedding of Mac and Trina and the grotesque banquet that follows, as well as the scenes in which Mac abandons Trina and subsequently murders her, appear to have been lifted intact from the original version. As a result, the film still reveals his harsh power and brilliance, his consistency, his integrity, even though the final assembly was the work of another hand. Through shots of disturbing intensity, he created an overwhelming sense of the psychological reality of the slow-witted McTeague, his miserly wife and their false-hearted friend Marcus. And veri-

fying and substantiating these people at every point was a realism of background ordered and organized down to the last
minute detail. An old saloon and a butcher shop, the exterior
of a church on a Sunday morning, the meeting of Mac and
Marcus at the Cliff House with crowds strolling the boardwalk below—all of these made *Greed* appear to be a
documentary shot in San Francisco in 1900 instead of 1924.
But von Stroheim's technique extends beyond the mere appearance of authenticity. His backgrounds play an active role
in his creation of character and incident.

Just what all this means in terms of creating tension and
atmosphere in a picture is perhaps better illustrated than
described. His was not a technique that can be explained in
terms of daring editorial juxtapositions, moving cameras or
artistic lighting. It lay instead in the patient invention and addition of thousands of small, skillful, knowingly arranged
touches that gradually built up around his scenes and his
characters an indefinable aura of reality that made them palpable and alive. The clearest example of the effectiveness of
this method is to be found in an almost forgotten von Stroheim film, *Queen Kelly* (1928), which he directed for Gloria
Swanson. Shooting had proceeded at his customary leisurely,
precise and expensive pace when the advent of sound brought
the production to a halt. The producer, Joseph P. Kennedy,
felt it prudent to stop and salvage what he could. Von Stroheim was removed from the picture and another director—re-
putedly Swanson herself—brought in to add the few finishing
scenes. And one can tell at precisely what moment the new
hand took over. The cast is the same, the settings the same,
but somehow the pressure has suddenly been taken off. The
force, the emphasis, the insistence on minute detail to build
character and background alike have suddenly disappeared,
and within a moment the picture turns flat and ordinary.

In the four years between *Greed* and *Queen Kelly,* von
Stroheim produced only two more films, *The Merry Widow*
(1925) and *The Wedding March* (1928). He had become
identified as a difficult and expensive director, two unforgiv-
able traits in an industry where mass production and
economy had become the watchwords. Not only that, but
much of his work—the orgies in *The Merry Widow,* the un-
savory sex relationships in *The Wedding March* and *Queen
Kelly*—was at once too crude and too sophisticated for the
increasingly morals-conscious Hollywood. Von Stroheim sud-

denly found it impossible to get work. Hopefully he persisted in his efforts throughout the early thirties, writing original scripts and offering to direct them. Only one studio gave him a chance—and then shelved the picture, calling in another director to reshoot it. Finally, disheartened, he returned to acting, eventually moving to the Continent. His few American roles since that time—Rommel in *Five Graves to Cairo* (1943), the ex-director Max in *Sunset Boulevard* (1950)— remind us again what a talent we lost. Von Stroheim was a temperamental, tempestuous but authentic artist; Hollywood preferred a more conventional type.

The Poet: Robert Flaherty

If von Stroheim was driven out of Hollywood, Robert Flaherty voluntarily withdrew. Throughout his career a wholly individualistic film maker, Flaherty had won the attention of Hollywood with the international success of his first film, *Nanook of the North* (1922), a record of Eskimo life based on his own observations as an explorer in northern Canada. At just about the time that von Stroheim was doing *Greed* for Metro, Paramount dispatched Flaherty to the South Seas with instructions to "bring back another *Nanook.*" For Flaherty, however, all film making was an exploration. He consistently refused to work from prepared shooting scripts or preconceived stories, preferring to discover his theme, his characters, his settings with his camera. For almost two years he remained in Samoa, talking with the natives, learning their legends and superstitions, observing the daily minutiae of their lives. Only after he had become completely familiar with their ways did he begin to make his picture, shooting it, developing it and editing it himself on the primitive island of Savaii. When finally he presented his completed *Moana* (1926) to the Paramount executives, they were bitterly disappointed. They had envisioned a South Seas equivalent of *Nanook,* complete with typhoons, sharks and more than a touch of dusky romance. Instead, all they got was the loveliest idyll of the silent screen.

What Flaherty had discovered in his slow, patient way, was the astonishing fact that for the Samoans there existed no classic conflict between man and nature. The gods were kind. Food was plentiful, and the raw materials for clothing and shelter grew on every tree. He might have dramatized the influence of traders and missionaries upon a fast-disappearing culture but, as he often said, he had no interest in showing what these people had become under the demoralizing influence of the whites. As far as possible, he recaptured the past, the essence of Samoan life, and placed at the very heart of his film the agonizing ritual of the tattoo which every Samoan youth must undergo to establish his manhood. In the absence of natural hardships, Flaherty found, the Samoans had themselves invented pain to test and protect the fiber of their stock. With this sequence as his key, all the rest of the incidents fitted into place—gathering coconuts, fishing, hunting the wild boar, the women at their cooking and cloth making, the ceremonial feasts and dances. All of these Flaherty observed with a loving eye, over and over again until he had become so completely familiar with them that he could anticipate their movements with his camera, creating the same sense of time-worn smoothness that one associates both with perfect craftsmanship and with ancient ritual. Each frame from *Moana* is almost classically beautiful, with its finely modeled photography (it was the first film to use the new panchromatic stock) and soft, lush lighting. But it is no mere gallery of beautiful stills. Flaherty understood, better than many of his studio contemporaries, the function of editing and camera placement to keep his film alive, and had an uncanny instinct for the most telling detail and the most revealing angle for every shot.

Yet Paramount chose to sell this film as "the love story of a South Seas siren," and the presentation houses brought in bevies of hula-hula girls as a fitting prologue. Flaherty himself objected to these tactics, arguing that there were whole sections in every community which, while not habitual moviegoers, could certainly be brought out in support of a special feature like *Moana*. Furthermore, he proved it by personally selling his picture in six of the most difficult territories that Paramount's distribution department could designate. He organized his audiences through the schools, the Chambers of Commerce, the literary, civic and social clubs in each community. But, as the Paramount officials firmly pointed out, it was their job to sell people on the idea of coming to the movies fifty-two weeks out of the year to see *ordinary* pictures, not once in a blue moon to see a *Moana*. The "South Seas siren" campaign went on. (Parenthetically, when Sir Laurence Olivier's *King Henry V* was brought to this country in 1946, its sales campaign was handled in precisely the manner that Flaherty had prescribed twenty years earlier—and it became one of the most successful foreign films ever to be shown in the United States.)

For a time Flaherty continued in his efforts to convince the studios that pictures could be made—and sold—his way. At one point M-G-M sent him back to the South Seas, to Tahiti, to co-direct with W. S. Van Dyke an adaptation of Frederick O'Brien's *White Shadows in the South Seas*, a book that he very much admired. When it turned out that what the studio really had in mind was a sultry melodrama, Flaherty withdrew. Fox allowed him to work up a plan for a film on the Pueblo Indians, then lost enthusiasm for the project. In 1929 Flaherty joined forces with F. W. Murnau, the director of *The Last Laugh* and *Sunrise*, and again set sail for the South Seas, this time as an independent producer-director. Although a less likely team could hardly be imagined—Murnau the studio perfectionist, Flaherty the patient, poetic student of real people and real settings—the two men remained close friends even through the throes of picture making. Actually, *Tabu* (1931), the product of their joint effort, emerged as far more typical of Murnau's work than of Flaherty's. It had an abundance of Flaherty's visual magic—laughing girls sliding down a waterfall, majestic shots of trees, and seas and natives in all their innate dignity. But there are also cardboard moons and rubber sharks and a story as patently manufactured as the props. Murnau died soon after in a tragic motor accident, while Flaherty went on to England to work with the new documentary movement then forming about John Grierson. He never returned to the studios, remaining identified with documentary film making until his death in 1951.

The Compromise: Von Sternberg

Like Flaherty, Josef von Sternberg also attracted the attention of the major studios with an independently produced, low-budgeted, decidedly offbeat production, *Salvation Hunters* (1925). Essentially a mood piece, it told a simple story of three lost souls, an unemployed, ambitionless family who live on a river scow until a procurer offers them a room in exchange for the wife's services. Only when the scabrous villain mistreats their child does the husband recover his self-respect sufficiently to face up to the man. The implication is that, having taken this first step, he will lead his little family on to happiness. The film's dominant mood of hopeless, spiritual defeat was heavily underlined by long, almost static shots of the principals drooping in attitudes of picturesque despair. Over-symbolic details like the great, swinging dredge that scoops up mud from the bottom of the river into the sunlight, or the billboard reading "Here your dreams come true" behind the scene of the fight, were directorial touches that made a profound impression in their day. Although considerably less impressive when seen today, *Salvation Hunters* was hailed as an artistic achievement without peer, an American film that rivaled anything then being imported from Europe—an opinion confirmed (and perhaps influenced) by the ardent championing of the film in Hollywood by two such respected figures as Charles Chaplin and Douglas Fairbanks.

Both the film's critical reception and its low budget recommended von Sternberg to the major studios. He made one film (never released) for Chaplin, another for M-G-M, then moved to Paramount where, to everyone's astonishment, he scored an immediate box-office success with the gangster melodrama *Underworld* (1927). No small part of its popularity was due to Ben Hecht's timely script, virtually written off the headlines of the daily papers. But to this von Sternberg added his own strong pictorial sense, his knowledge of editing, and his ability to draw vivid performances from his casts. George Bancroft, the rugged star of *Underworld*, was a von Sternberg discovery; he never excelled his work as the brutal, blustering gangland chief. Von Sternberg quickly repeated his success with another hard-hitting crime picture, *The Dragnet* (1928), then turned back to the depressed mood and milieu of *Salvation Hunters* in the extraordinary *Docks of New York* (1928). Brilliantly photographed, with deep, glistening blacks and an amazing tonal range of grays and whites, it depicted the dingy bars and rooming houses of the waterfront in a series of strongly composed, superbly atmospheric scenes. Bancroft was starred again, this time as a roistering stoker off a tramp steamer who saves a despondent girl from suicide by promising to marry her, though fully intending to ship out again next day. Von Sternberg's handling of the waterfront types, his skillful use of the sordid settings and, above all, his masterful changes in mood and tempo as the story progresses reveal his artistic growth, his complete grasp of the essentials of his art. Unfortunately, *Docks of New York* did not repeat the resounding commercial success of his previous pictures. Apparently its lack of conventional romance or thrills was too much for audiences expecting another underworld thriller. Von Sternberg was faced with the age-old dilemma of whether to direct artistic failures or less artistic hits.

For a time, von Sternberg continued to waver between the two. *The Last Command* (1928), starring Emil Jannings, reaffirmed his ability to ring the bell at the box office; while *The Case of Lena Smith* (1929) revealed again his masterly ability to create atmosphere and scenes of matchless pictorial beauty—but at the expense of story values and audience interest. As his Paramount contract neared its end, he was happy to accept Emil Janning's offer to direct him in *The Blue Angel* (1930) in Germany. It proved to be one of the most creative films of the period, filled with movement and a richness of pictorial elements at a time when most movies were stagnant and flat. *The Blue Angel* was an immediate hit in Germany, and almost as successful in its American engagements where, despite the language barrier, it played in the largest theaters. When von Sternberg returned to Hollywood, it was with a new star and a new contract—to direct the films of his German discovery, Marlene Dietrich. He became her mentor, her Svengali. But as Dietrich's star rose, von Sternberg's descended. In a series of handsomely photographed, artfully composed, static films, von Sternberg grew increasingly absorbed with the beauty of his images, with Dietrich glimpsed through a clutter of nets and fans and draperies. The style, the sharpness, the originality that had distinguished his earlier, silent efforts degenerated into tricks and mannerisms. He had made the commercial compromise. John Grierson wrote his sad epitaph as early as 1932. "When a director dies," said Grierson, "he becomes a photographer."

In short, throughout the twenties, as the studios became more industrialized, more set in the commercial patterns of producing and marketing their films, they had less room for the highly gifted individual unwilling or unable to accept these patterns. A Chaplin or Fairbanks could afford to ignore them. A De Mille could thrive on them. But they smothered D. W. Griffith and Mack Sennett, drove off von Stroheim and Flaherty, sucked down von Sternberg. Nor were these men alone. Others, less prominent, faced the same alternative of making pictures that were considered commercially safe by the "front office" or not making pictures at all—at least, not in Hollywood. Either way meant an indescribable loss to an industry that is also an art. For the vitality of the film grows out of the daring, the experiments, the originality of the individual artist. Whenever purely commercial considerations are permitted to check that growth, the loss is incalculable— to the art, to the filmgoers, and to the industry itself. It is a shocking waste of the movies' greatest single natural resource, the man of talent.

The End of the Silent Era

Despite the fact that Hollywood's films dominated the screens throughout the world, despite the complex mechanisms that had been perfected to make, sell and exhibit them, the industry was experiencing a profound uneasiness during the late twenties. Attendance had fallen off. The radio and the automobile presented new and powerful competition. The era of Coolidge prosperity had expanded the income of the average family who could now afford more elegant entertainments than the movies. At the same time, some of Hollywood's most reliable, most expensive contract players were losing their box-office appeal; while the fight for theaters, carried on during the boom of real-estate values, had saddled many of the studios with properties costing far more than their actual worth. As early as 1926 one important company, Warner Brothers, found itself on the verge of bankruptcy. In desperation they invested their remaining fortune in a daring novelty—the Vitaphone. In August of 1926, they introduced a program of Vitaphone talking and singing shorts, and the feature *Don Juan* with a synchronized musical accompaniment. On October 6, 1927, they presented the first talking feature on Broadway, Al Jolson in *The Jazz Singer*. Its immediate success marked the end of an era.

In the United States the silent film died with alarming suddenness, although it lingered considerably longer abroad. Warners followed *The Jazz Singer*—essentially a silent picture with musical accompaniment and four talking or singing sequences—with a cheaply produced "quickie," *The Lights of New York*, the first full-length, all-talking picture. It was released in July, 1928. In the meantime, however, every major studio, jealous of the S.R.O. signs that appeared wherever *The Jazz Singer* was showing, began to convert to sound as rapidly as possible. Talking sequences were inserted into pictures that had gone into production as silents. Each studio rushed into production its own "all talkie." Within a single year, every important picture "talked" (although often a silent counterpart was made for showing in houses not yet wired for sound). By the middle of 1929, even this protection was no longer necessary, so swift and final was the transition to sound. At the end of 1928, of the 20,500 theaters in the United States, only 1,300 had sound installations. By the end of 1929, there were over 9,000 theaters equipped to handle the new medium. And these included, inevitably, all the key houses in the big cities around the country, all the theaters on the major circuits and the important neighborhood houses. Theaters that found the sound systems too expensive or had waited too long to put in their order for an installation, soon discovered that it was more economical simply to board up until they could show the new talkies. Overnight the public seemed to have forgotten that the silent film ever existed.

But if the silent film died swiftly, it did not pass unmourned. Critics and film lovers alike recognized that in a mere three decades the silent film had developed into a subtle, complex and highly expressive art form. They also recognized that the new emphasis on dialogue was robbing the screen of its visual impact. For the sake of a novelty, these critics argued, the discoveries of an entire generation of creative artists were blindly being ignored.

Many of the studio heads were quite willing to agree that talkies were simply a thing of the moment—but at the moment, they pointed out, it was the thing that the public wanted. Indeed, those producers who hesitated to bow to this obviously popular demand, preferring to hold off until the whole thing blew over, were soon out of business entirely. The public's enthusiasm for sound was so strong that attendance leaped from 60,000,000 paid admissions per week in 1927 to 110,000,000 in 1929. When the stock market crashed in the fall of 1929, the impetus provided by the introduction of sound proved strong enough to carry the industry safely through the first years of the depression. By 1930 the silent film was a thing of the past, Charlie Chaplin's *City Lights* (1931) and the Flaherty-Murnau *Tabu* (1931) coming as last, lovely reminders of an art that was no more. By the start of the thirties, in every film-producing nation the studios had converted to sound. It was to take them many a year, however, before they could regain the artistry and power of the best of the silent era.

4

The Movies Learn to Talk

The silent film had created a world of persuasive reality despite the absence of voices and the verifying clangor of natural sound. Indeed, much of the art of the silent film lay in the invention of means to circumvent these artificial limitations. Then, suddenly, they were all removed, and the sounds of the real world had become as much a part of the film as its sights. The audience's wholehearted acceptance of the new order, despite all the grave headshakings of industry leaders, despite the shocked protests of the film aestheticians, suggests a certain, dimly sensed inadequacy in the silent film itself. The public positively reveled in the new sensation, the opportunity to hear its favorite stars talking and singing, to hear the crack of a pistol, the roar of a motor or even the ring of a telephone. It was exactly like the first years of the movies all over again. Then, anything that moved was fascinating; now, the most commonplace noises, the most obvious dialogue acquired a marvelous quality simply by virtue of its coming from the screen. From our vantage point today, we can see clearly that the original objections of the aestheticians were based less upon the nature of the sound film than upon the crude excrescences of the first talking pictures. They just never stopped talking!

Actually, in the strictest sense, there probably never was such a thing as a completely "silent" film. From the very outset, from the time when movies were first shown as part of a vaudeville or music-hall presentation, they had some kind of sound accompanying them. Even the nickelodeon theater had its cheap, twangy, upright piano on which "the professor" banged out *Hearts and Flowers* and other tunes more or less appropriate to the emotions emanating from the screen. The large-scale "specials" that began to appear from Europe after 1912 were generally exhibited with a live orchestral accompaniment. Not to be outdone, D. W. Griffith presented *The Birth of a Nation* in its initial engagements with a symphonic score compiled by Joseph Carl Breil and arranged for an orchestra of seventy pieces. The same score was later simplified for smaller orchestras, for trios and for solo piano, to be used with showings of the film in the subsequent runs.

When the big downtown theaters began to spring up after 1914, most of them had large pit orchestras to play at least for the evening shows. Afternoon performances might be accompanied either by a smaller ensemble or by the organ. As de luxe houses extended into the neighborhoods, the standard equipment included a mighty Wurlitzer, that behemoth of mechanical sound with its banks and banks of gleaming keys and special effects. Sometimes it was even augmented by a trio of piano, violin and percussion. Whatever the form, the purpose of such accompaniment was twofold: to provide suitable mood music for the picture, and to blot out for the patrons such distractions as the whir of the projectors, the banging of chairs and (above all) the noises of other patrons. Throughout the twenties the film companies regularly provided cue sheets which suggested standard selections to be played at indicated moments during all their features. Building the musical accompaniments for silent films became something of an art in itself; and when the studios began to "can" their scores on the Vitaphone or Movietone, they turned to such master practitioners of the art as Erno Rapee or Hugo Riesenfeld. In fact, a number of the musical directors in the studios for the next three decades were men who had begun as arrangers and conductors of the pit orchestras of the silent era.

During the twenties too, the "effects" became more important as the music was wedded more and more closely to the picture. In the larger theater orchestras, the drummer was virtually a one-man sound effects department, operating with a tremendous variety of drums, whistles, Klaxons, sirens and bells. Some of these men became true virtuosi in synchronizing the sounds of footsteps, knocks, thunderclaps or pistol shots to the visuals on the screen. The range of effects incorporated into the organs was also increased. By the middle of the twenties, directors frequently included sequences in their pictures that depended for their full effect upon some special sound. They knew they could fairly well rely upon the ingenuity of organist, drummer or even pianist to supply it. The battery of drums, thunder sheets and other devices that many theaters installed to provide a realistic accompaniment to such war films as *The Big Parade* and *Wings* were often as elaborate as the effects departments of the first sound studios.

The arrival of sound made possible a far closer integration of music and visuals, a more precise synchronization of the sound effects. But more important, it gave the screen a voice to take the place of the awkward subtitle. Though readily accepted as a convention of the silent film, the subtitle was at best a makeshift arrangement, performing a function that obviously called for sound. At worst, as in Dreyer's *Passion of Joan of Arc*, it could destroy the rhythm of the visuals. Creative directors might try to say as much as possible through imagery, but even a well-made film of the period contained an astonishing number of titles. Run-of-the-mill productions, particularly those adapted from stage plays, would be little more than a succession of big heads in close-up alternating with dialogue subtitles. Many an addict of the silent movie became extraordinarily adept at lip reading, thus providing for himself some of the gratification denied him by the mechanical limitations of the medium. It also provided, from time to time, the odd realization that what the actors were saying was quite at variance with what the titles indicated. Indeed, so adept had the general public become at reading lips by the end of the silent era that when Edmund Lowe and Victor McLaglen, for example, burst out in mute but eloquent profanity in *What Price Glory?*, the studio was flooded with letters of shocked protest.

Breaking the Sound Barrier

Contrary to popular belief, sound did not burst suddenly upon a completely unprepared public in the winter of 1927. As we have already seen, Edison had conceived of movies accompanied by sound (or, more accurately, sound accompanied by pictures) as early as 1889, synchronizing his phonograph to the Kinetoscope. Quite a number of films were

actually made in this fashion in France even before 1900—
brief affairs little more than a minute long but preserving for
the world the voice of Bernhardt in *Hamlet,* of Coquelin as
Cyrano, the vaudeville turns of Little Tich and Vesta Tilley.
Until about 1912 inventors persisted in their efforts to join together sound and visuals, going so far as to run endless belts
from the projector motor through the entire length of the theater to a phonograph installed behind the screen. But they
soon discovered, as houses continued to grow larger, that the
problem was one not merely of synchronization but of ampli-
fication as well. The ordinary talking machine simply could
not produce the volume of sound required to fill an entire auditorium.

The solution lay in the silenium tube, the so-called "audion
amplifier" developed by Lee DeForest shortly before World
War I. With it, volume could be controlled, stepped up. Of
great importance in long-distance telephone and telegraph experiments, it was basic to the development of the infant radio
industry and the talking picture. De Forest sold his amplifica-
tion patents to Bell Telephone; but soon after the war he began to devote his attention to the problem of sound and films,
choosing an entirely new approach. Hitherto, the sound had
always been separated from the film strip, a phonograph
record to be played along with the picture. De Forest saw
that this presented strong disadvantages. The loss of a few
frames of film through a break or a splice would throw the
whole remaining reel out of synchronization with its accompanying sound, while a broken record could wreck an entire
show. In addition, the mechanics of obtaining and maintain-
ing synchronization between the sound and the image became
infinitely more complicated when the two were handled on
separate machines.

To circumvent this, De Forest developed a method of photographing sound directly on the film itself, recording it in
fine striations of grays and blacks along one edge of the strip.
Vibrations caught by the microphone broke the current of a
photo-electric cell; the resulting fluctuations of light and dark,
photographed on motion-picture film, gave back the original
sound impulses when passed around another photo-electric
cell in the sound head of the projector. As early as 1923 De
Forest was presenting his Phonofilm as a novelty in theaters
around the country, recording the acts of such top vaudeville
personalities as Eddie Cantor, Phil Baker and Weber and

Fields. Although his shorts were well received, they caused little stir in the industry.

Even while De Forest was demonstrating his invention, the Bell Telephone Laboratories persisted in their efforts to link movies with sound on disc. By 1926 they had developed a special turntable and 13- to 17-inch records large enough to accommodate the sound for an entire reel of film. It was this process that Warner Brothers acquired and titled the Vitaphone. At the outset, like De Forest, Warners used their process exclusively for novelty shorts, recording the performances of ensembles and stars of the concert and vaudeville stage, among them the New York Philharmonic, Giovanni Martinelli, Mischa Elman and Eddie Foy. On August 6, 1926, when Warners held their Vitaphone première for the general public, they presented a selection of these shorts, preceded by a filmed address by Will H. Hays hailing the new miracle. The feature on the program, John Barrymore in *Don Juan*, was accompanied by a specially recorded symphonic score. Audiences were interested—nothing more. The crude reproduction of a vaudeville act or a concert aria failed to create any wild excitement, and not even Will Hays's eulogy to sound was able to convince them that they were on the brink of a revolution. Indeed, the recorded musical accompaniment for the feature was something of a comedown for audiences accustomed to having large orchestras perform "live" with their pictures. Even so, Warners continued to record the scores for all their more important releases, and particularly those that made heavy demands upon the sound effects department.

Early in 1927, as more and more of the key theaters around the country wired for sound, William Fox secured the rights to the German Tri-Ergon patents, an independently developed sound-on-film system that seems to have antedated De Forest's. At the same time he paid a reputed million dollars to a former associate of De Forest, Theodore W. Case, for the patents and development of yet another sound-on-film apparatus which made its bow under the name of Fox-Case. On it Fox released a series of shorts rivaling the Vitaphone subjects and also began to add scores to his feature films. (*What Price Glory?* was the first.) In April of 1927 he launched the Fox Movietone News, the first sound newsreel. Its success was instantaneous. The June issue, devoted entirely to Charles A. Lindbergh's triumphant flight from New

York to Paris and his frenzied receptions, first at Le Bourget
and then in New York City, brought people into the theaters
just as, twenty-five years later, the Kefauver investigations
were to hold them spellbound at their television receivers.
Soon such oddly assorted personalities as Calvin Coolidge,
George Bernard Shaw and Benito Mussolini had also faced
the Movietone cameras and microphones. There was a special
fascination in seeing Coolidge in Indian feathers and hearing
him sworn in as a Great White Brother of the Sioux, in listening to Shaw as he paced the gravel path in his garden and
spoke jocularly of himself and world affairs. But these were
novelties, outside the main stream of picture making. These
were the "extra added attractions." What sound still needed
was the spark, the flame that would kindle the public's imagination and enthusiasm. And that was Al Jolson's contribution. In *The Jazz Singer* his tremendous vitality and
personality were able to break through the primitive
recording apparatus to charm audiences in a way that no
movie had ever done before. And Jolson did it, not in a Vitaphone short but in a feature-length dramatic film. The panic
was on.

The Tyranny of Sound

In 1929, after little more than a year of talkies, *Variety*
wryly reported, "Sound didn't do any more to the industry
than turn it upside down, shake the entire bag of tricks from
its pocket and advance Warner Brothers from the last place
[among the film companies] to first in the league." The films
had learned to talk, and talk was uppermost in everyone's
mind. Script writers who had trained themselves to think in
terms of pictures gave way to playwrights who thought in
terms of stage dialogue. Established directors were either replaced by directors from the New York stage or supplemented by special dialogue directors. Many a popular star—
especially the European importees—suddenly found himself unemployed; while the Broadway stage was again swept
clean to replace those actors whose foreign accents, faulty
diction or bad voices the temperamental microphone rejected. To fill the need for dialogue at all costs, plays—
good, bad and indifferent—were bought up and rushed before the cameras. It was the era satirized in George S.
Kaufman's *Once in a Lifetime,* when the Mr. Glogauers of

Hollywood were valiantly but vainly trying to understand the change that had come over their industry, when self-styled geniuses were able to make incredible blunders simply because no one else had any better idea of how the talkies should be made.

And then a new and imposing figure appeared in the studios, the sound expert. It was the sound expert who concealed the microphone in the vase of flowers or on the boudoir table, who dictated where actors must stand in order to record properly, who decided where the camera must be placed in order to keep the microphone outside its field. He was the final arbiter on what could and what could not be done, and his word was law. The camera itself, now imprisoned within a soundproof booth, was robbed of all mobility. And the experts, concerned with nothing beyond the sound quality of the pictures they worked on, continually simplified their problems by insisting that scenes be played in corners, minimizing long-shots for the more readily controllable close-up. In no time at all the techniques, the artistry that directors had acquired through years of silent films were cast aside and forgotten in the shadow of the microphone.

As a result, 1929 was for the most part the year of static, photographed stage plays, the year of "all-talking, all-singing" musicals, the year in which raw sound was exploited in every imaginable way. In Mack Sennett's first two-reel talking comedy, *The Family Picnic* (1929), audiences were regaled by the sounds of the picnickers crunching celery or munching potato chips. Warners, not content with having made the first part-talking picture, *The Jazz Singer,* and the first all-talking picture, *The Lights of New York,* soon followed these with the first *all* all-talking picture, *The Terror* (1928). In place of the normal, printed credit titles, it offered Conrad Nagel in mask and opera cape to introduce the picture and its characters. Fox countered with "the first 100% all-talking drama filmed outdoors," *In Old Arizona* (1929). Other studios presented "the first all-Negro all-talking picture," "the first 100% talking, singing college picture," the mathematically absurd "100% talking, 100% singing, 100% dancing" musicals. Warners capped the climax in *On With the Show* (1929). Not only was it "all-talking, all-singing, all-dancing"—it was "100% all-color" as well.

Color, like sound, had long challenged the film makers. Many of the early short films from France were actually colored by hand, frame by frame, producing an utterly charming—if somewhat unpredictable—effect. A practical but overly cumbersome three-color process known as Kine-macolor was introduced in England as early as 1908 (and used to photograph the Coronation in 1910). Other inventions appeared soon after in England, France, Germany and the United States. But color, whether hand painted or mechanically contrived, was merely a novelty, something added to the regular show. And its added realism was in fact at the outset so utterly unrealistic, so obviously false in values and lacking in definition that few producers thought it worth the extra expense and effort. Besides, whenever the suggestion of color was important, they could always print the black-and-white images on tinted stock—blue for night scenes, red for fires, green for fields and forests. The effect could be heightened by "toning" the lighter parts of the shot in a contrasting color—a purple sea with a pink sunset, a green meadow with a sunny yellow sky. Few producers felt any need to go beyond this.

Nevertheless, Herbert Kalmus launched his Technicolor researches in 1918, convinced that color could be reproduced photographically just as readily as shades of gray. By 1923 he was prepared to market a two-color process in which the red-orange-yellow portion of the spectrum was photographed on one negative, the green-blue-purple portion on another. When prints from the two negatives were laminated together, they produced a pleasing though still far from accurate color scale. At first the public was only mildly interested. Enthusiasm began to mount only after producers began to incorporate color sequences into their bigger productions, such as Lon Chaney's frightening appearance as the Mask of the Red Death in *The Phantom of the Opera* (1925). Technicolor scored its first major success in Douglas Fairbanks' *The Black Pirate* (1926), which used the color process throughout. Despite a palette with a strong propensity for blue-green and orange, and flesh tones that altered unpredictably from deep ochre to shrimp-pink, Technicolor definitely enhanced the romantic period flavor of this film and the audiences' enjoyment of it. Soon after, Kalmus perfected his process, eliminating the need for two prints by coating both sides of the celluloid strip with an emulsion. At the very moment that sound arrived, a practicable color process was also ready.

And with the overwhelming success of their sound experiments, the producers were now willing to try almost any novelty. In 1929 several of the major studios added to their pictures not only color but the "grandeur screen" as well, using them for the spectacular musicals that literally streamed out of Hollywood. But the public, attracted by sound, was more irritated than impressed by this additional bounty. The big screens emphasized the graininess of the prints, making them look gray and washed out; while Technicolor, faced by a sudden expansion of business, was totally unprepared to handle this new volume. There were constant laboratory delays, infuriating the producers, and the processing itself left much to be desired. Prints were fuzzy, out of register, painful to the eyes. In addition, the color values were still far from true. Within the year both color and the wide screens had virtually disappeared from the scene, awaiting an era when the public would once more be receptive to the appeal of something altogether "new."

Just as movies had appeared at virtually the same moment in the United States and Europe, so too was sound developed simultaneously in England, Germany, the Soviet Union and America. There had been many versions of the motion-picture camera and projector; now there were numerous sound mechanisms. There was sound on disc (the Vitaphone) and sound on film in half a dozen systems including the Movietone, the RCA Photophone, Cinephone, Phonofilm and, on the Continent, the Tobis Klangfilm. Russia's Dr. Shorin produced a sound-on-film system for the Soviet industry. Except for the Vitaphone, all were compatible with one another. All could be played through the same type of sound head in the theaters, thus permitting the continued worldwide dissemination of pictures. But the struggle for control was a sharp one. For almost three years Warner Brothers asserted not only the priority but the superiority of their Vitaphone system. Meanwhile, William Fox with his German Tri-Ergon patents and a battery of lawyers attempted to dominate sound films all over the world. He failed—ultimately forced out of his own business by his creditors and the combined opposition of the American Telephone Company and its Wall Street representatives. Finally, a patents pool settled matters to everyone's satisfaction (except, of course, Fox, who retired from the scene with a paltry $18,000,000); and after 1931 the sound-on-film system was accepted as standard, with Western

Electric and RCA splitting the field between them in the United States, and Tobis supreme on the Continent.

Sound gave the banks and the investment houses their first real hold upon the motion-picture industry. Every studio needed sound, and most of them also needed vast sums of new working capital to make the equipment purchases and studio alterations required to convert to sound. Both the equipment and the financing led ultimately to the same sources, to Western Electric, RCA and their affiliated banking houses. Soon their representatives were sitting on the boards of the motion-picture companies, making policy with—and sometimes in place of—the veteran showmen who had brought their studios from obscurity to world-wide prominence. They appointed the sound experts who dominated the studios through 1929 and 1930. These men knew only about acoustics and microphone characteristics. But because they had the backing of the people who were paying for it all, they often usurped the functions of both producer and director. As a result, a transition that would have been difficult in any case was made more difficult still. Producers whose main stock in trade was their knowledge of entertainment values suddenly found their hands tied. Directors who understood the necessity to keep the picture moving and alive found themselves arbitrarily over-ruled in favor of the microphone.

Liberating the Camera: Ernst Lubitsch

It is to the eternal credit of genuinely creative and courageous men like Ernst Lubitsch, Rouben Mamoulian, Lewis Milestone, King Vidor and Raoul Walsh that they had the ingenuity and vitality to circumvent the experts and lift the new medium out of the rut of dully photographed plays and vaudeville routines into which it had fallen. They had no rules to go on, no precedents to quote. They had the opposition of the sound men to contend with, and the indisputable fact that at the box offices across the nation almost any film was making money as long as it talked. But these men sensed that talk alone was not enough, and that the public would soon tire of the novelty of sound for sound's sake and demand again to see a *movie*. It was their pioneer work that brought forth the techniques to make the movies move again.

Ernst Lubitsch, by 1929 the top director at Paramount, made the important discovery that a talking picture did not have to be *all* talking, nor did the sound track have to reproduce faithfully each sound on the set. In his first talkies, *The Love Parade* (1929) and *Monte Carlo* (1930), he included many passages that were shot without dialogue or any other synchronized sound. For these, he was able to bring the camera out of its sound-proofed box and proceed in the old silent techniques, moving his camera freely, changing its position frequently. Music or effects were put in later. One of the high-points of *The Love Parade* was a running gag with Maurice Chevalier telling a risqué joke to members of the court. Each time he approaches the tag line, his voice sinks to a confidential whisper, a door closes, or the camera leaps outside to view the effect of his story through a window. Audiences of 1929 were delighted to find a new element in the talkies—silence!

Working mainly on the Maurice Chevalier—Jeanette MacDonald musicals, Lubitsch quickly established himself as one of the most inventive directors of the period. With his strong feeling for the relationship between music and visuals, he brought back some of the rhythm that had been present in the silent films. In *Monte Carlo*, for example, Lubitsch cuts together the sounds of a train getting under way. As it picks up speed, the characteristic tempo of the wheels is translated into the music of the theme song, *Beyond the Blue Horizon*. The impressive wedding ceremony in *The Smiling Lieutenant* (1931) was staged without the confining microphone, but each opening door, every step down the great flight of marble stairs, every gesture of the players was timed to the beat of a score that was dubbed in later. He was the first to be concerned with the "natural" introduction of songs into the development of a musical-comedy plot, the first to find a cinematic way to handle verbal humor in the new medium.

But Lubitsch also knew how to use the sound camera to serious purpose. In *Broken Lullaby* (1932), his one dramatic film of this period, he emphasized its anti-war theme in many brilliantly conceived shots. The sights and sounds of an Armistice Day parade are glimpsed between the crutches of a one-legged soldier. Early in the film, while a minister is praying for peace, the camera in ironic counterpoint moves slowly down the center aisle of the cathedral, past row on row of kneeling officers, their spurs gleaming, their swords stiff by their sides. By shooting such sequences silent and adding the sound later, Lubitsch obtained not only greater freedom for his camera but the kind of control of the elements in his scene essential to artistic creation. The "Lubitsch touch," that sparkling combination of wit and irony already famous in the silent film, reached its fullest expression in his early talkies.

Meanwhile, King Vidor in his first talking picture, *Hallelujah!* (1929), explored the possibilities of the sound track to evoke mood and atmosphere. It was an all-Negro picture made, for the most part, in Memphis, Tennessee, and the swamps of Arkansas. The fact that the film was done largely on location, away from rigid studio supervision, gave Vidor an enviable amount of freedom for that time. Much of it he shot silent, later creating an impressionistic sound track for all but the direct dialogue passages. The rhythmic swell of Negro spirituals, a woman's scream or a barking dog heard in the distance, the sounds of the swamp and the river supplied the dominant mood or emotional tone for many of the scenes. The whole final sequence, a frenzied pursuit through the swamps, was shot silent with beautiful, long traveling shots of pursued and pursuer. Only later, back in the studio, did Vidor add the magnified sounds of breaking branches, the screech of birds, agonized breathing and the suck of footsteps stumbling through the mire. Without the present-day equipment for reading sound, without synchronizers or multiple-channel sound mixers Vidor performed a tremendous feat. He showed that the source of a sound is less important than its quality, that sound can create an emotional aura about a scene quite independent of the words and faces of the actors. In *The Cock-Eyed World* (1929), Raoul Walsh ingeniously intercut brief silent shots with the camera in motion into static shots while his characters spoke. Lewis Milestone worked in much the same way in making his *All Quiet on the Western Front* (1930), photographing his scenes of troops on the march and in the trenches with a silent camera and adding in later the whine and crash of bombs, the clatter of small-arms fire and the shrieks and moans of the wounded and dying.

This process of adding sound later to scenes shot with silent cameras, known as post-synchronization or dubbing, played an important role in freeing directors from the early notion that everything seen must be heard or that everything heard must be seen. Once post-synchronization had been achieved, such a literal use of sound was clearly no longer necessary. We might see an ordinary street scene, but the dialogue has been post-synchronized to eliminate the irrelevent honks and screeches that would blur the words. Or a director might let us hear the crash of an automobile while showing us only the horrified faces of the onlookers. The experience of post-synchronizing such scenes in the recording studio helped directors to realize that, essentially, the sound track is a composite of many sounds—voices, music and all sorts of noises and effects—and that all of these were completely under his control. Each sound could be independently distorted, muffled, exaggerated or eliminated at will. The director could shoot his scene with a silent camera and dub in the sound for it later. He could reinforce dialogue passages with music, combine them with noises or bury them under other, post-synchronized sounds. And as the technicians provided more and better equipment to facilitate the handling of sound, these manipulative possibilities within the sound track assumed an ever greater importance. Post-synchronization became the first point of departure in the development of the new art.

The other was an improvement in the camera itself. During the first years of sound, the camera had been forced into a small sound-proofed booth to keep the whir of its mechanism from reaching the sensitive, cranky microphone. As long as it remained confined, most directors were willing to work in long, static "takes." Often, three cameras simultaneously photographed the same scene from different angles, very much as in television today. This technique vastly simplified the problems of cutting and matching the sound to its proper visual, but it also resulted in a slow, draggy tempo on the screen. The choice of camera positions was too limited and too arbitrary to produce a truly cinematic effect. During 1930, however, the cameras began to emerge from these boxes, enclosed now in sound-proofed "blimps" which, while still cumbersome, permitted a far greater freedom of movement. It then became the director's problem to force the reluctant sound experts to give that new mobility full rein, to demand from them more flexible microphone set-ups. In shooting his first film, *Applause* (1929), Rouben Mamoulian demanded two microphones on a single set, one to record the voice of Helen Morgan as she sang a lullaby to her daughter, the other to record the girl's whispered prayer in bed. The experts argued that this would necessitate the use of two separate channels, a thing unheard of at the time. "Unheard of but not impossible," Mamoulian insisted—and proved his point. Today nine channels are not unusual for a single shot, while on stereophonic epics the number may rise to as many as fifty.

Not only was the number of microphones increased, but their quality improved. They became more "directional," able to hear only in one area so that the director could manipulate other sounds in other portions of his scene. Before long, the stationary microphones were being replaced by mikes suspended on long booms that could be swung to follow the players anywhere. Thus, slowly, the sound experts of Hollywood were defeated by directors with fresh ideas about the nature of the new art—and the prestige and stamina to fight them through.

Mastering the Sound Track: René Clair

Perhaps the first director to appreciate fully the implications of sound was the Frenchman René Clair. Originally opposed to the whole idea, he insisted on the predominant importance of the visual element, declaring that the sound film need not and should not be, to use his own term, "canned theater." This opinion, almost revolutionary among film makers at the time, was brilliantly confirmed in a trio of sparkling comedies that quickly made Clair the most admired and imitated director in the world. In *Sous les Toits de Paris* (1929), *Le Million* (1931) and *A Nous la Liberté* (1931), he worked with a minimum of dialogue, using music, choruses and sound effects to counterpoint and comment upon his visuals. In this principle of asynchronous sound, sound used against rather than with the images, Clair discovered a new freedom and fluidity for the sound medium. Why show a door closing when it is enough merely to hear it slam? Or why listen to a clock's ticking just because it is shown? In *Le Million* there is a brief glimpse of a clock on a mantel shelf, a clock elaborately over-decorated with porcelain cupids blowing trumpets. Clair's sound track at that point carries a blast of trumpets. In *Sous les Toits* a fight takes place at night near a railway embankment. The fight is almost obscured by the shadows, but its force and fury are conveyed in the roar of the passing trains heard on the sound track. In *A Nous la Liberté,* Clair goes so far as to kid the whole notion of synchronous sound by showing his heroine singing away at her window while the hero admires from afar. Suddenly something goes wrong with the voice—it whines and whirs, then fades away. A moment later, while the young fellow is still looking up at the window, the girl appears in the street, the song begins again and we discover that what we have been listening to all along is a phonograph record from another apartment.

Because Clair's early sound films were both musicals and comedies, he could permit himself an impish audacity denied practitioners of the more serious forms, whose dramatic themes forced them to use more straightforward techniques. Their efforts at realism made it difficult for them to break with the conventional practices that quickly surrounded the microphone soon after it had made its appearance in the studios. Clair, on the other hand, could ignore conventional sound, omitting the characteristic noises of a street, a factory or an opera house altogether unless they served his purpose. It was *his* world, and he did with it as he wished.

And because above all he liked music and the dance, his pictures flash along like ballets. The incessant chases, the scramble after the flying bank notes in *A Nous la Liberté*, the mad party that opens and closes *Le Million*—all are set to gay, infectious tunes. Choruses sing a witty commentary upon the action as it unfolds. Whole sequences are bound together by music alone. In the opening reel of *Sous les Toits de Paris* a street singer is vending the title song of the film. While the camera wanders up and down the street, peering into the apartments and shops, one by one of the people of the neighborhood join in the song. In this way Clair quickly introduces the principal characters in his story and gaily sets the mood of the entire film. Throughout his pictures, music functions in dozens of bright and unexpected ways, playing an integral part in the development of his diverting stories.

What Clair had done, what creative directors everywhere were trying to do at the same time, was to discover how to control all the elements that went into the making of a sound film as completely as, in the simpler days of silence, one could control everything that went before the camera. He demonstrated to everyone's satisfaction that much of silent technique was still valid, that it was the image and not the word that kept the screen alive. Sound, and especially asynchronous sound, could add its own grace notes, its deeper perceptions, its enrichment of mood and atmosphere—but not independently of the visual.

Because René Clair had instinctively grasped this princple in his first three films, and turned them out with a flair and finish unmatched anywhere at the time, his pictures had a profound effect upon other directors. He had achieved what they were groping toward. He had brought back into films spontaneity, movement, rhythm. The extent of his influence is immediately revealed by a comparison of the opening reel of his *Sous les Toits* with the first sequences of Geza von Bolvary's *Zwei Herzen im Dreiviertel Takt* (1930) or the "Blue Horizon" number in Lubitsch's *Monte Carlo* (1930). But more important than imitation are the innumerable films of the early thirties that suggest his liberating spirit. In Germany Eric Charrell's *Congress Dances* (1931), in England Victor Saville's *Sunshine Susie* (1932), and in Hollywood films like Frank Tuttle's *This Is the Night* (1932), Gregory La Cava's *Half-Naked Truth* (1932), and Lewis Milestone's *Hallelujah, I'm a Bum* (1933), all reveal not only a new freedom in the use of sound but also—as in the Clair films— a rhythmic structure imparted by the sound track.

Clair's work was especially valuable to those men in the American studios who were themselves seeking to liberate the talking film from the confines of "canned theater." More daring than they dared to be, the fact that such pictures had found considerable popular as well as critical success was helpful in encouraging them to go ahead—quite apart from any technical lessons they might have learned. In this respect the early sound period was very much like the first decade or so of the silent era. The medium itself was still in a highly experimental stage, and directors looked to the box office to tell them how successful they were with the new techniques, and to the works of one another for useful hints that they could incorporate into their own efforts. In this period of search and confusion, Clair's pictures appeared as beacons to the future. And if Clair had a tendency to overstress the silent techniques in his early films, they provided a healthy counter-influence to the over-accenting of the sound track in the films made by almost everyone else.

Exploring the New Medium:
Rouben Mamoulian

Perhaps the leading director of dramatic films in this country to revolt against "canned theater" movies during the early years of sound was Rouben Mamoulian—ironically, one of the many Broadway directors brought to the studios in 1929 specifically to make "canned theater." Despite his theater background, Mamoulian sensed at once the differences between the two forms. He felt that the camera could and should move, appreciated the importance of the close-up for dramatic emphasis, fought against the prevalent notion that the source for every sound must be seen. For him, the camera was far more than a passive observer looking on while actors recited their lines—and the function of the director was more than merely helping the actors to say their lines better. He had to help the audience find what was dramatically significant in a scene, picking out what was important with his camera, making it seem fresh and illuminating through the imagination and inventiveness of his visuals.

In his first two talking pictures, *Applause* (1929) and *City Streets* (1931), Mamoulian gave repeated evidence of his desire to move away from stereotyped techniques. A particularly effective moment in *Applause* began with a close-up of Helen Morgan, the aging burlesque queen, reminiscing about her youth; as she speaks, the camera leaves her tired, dissipated face and wanders across the room to a photograph of her as a lovely young girl. At another point, a long tracking shot shows only the feet of the heroine as she leaves the theater, and the feet of the men she encounters as she walks home. The nature of each encounter is revealed as fully in the footsteps as in the fragments of conversation accompanying the scene. In *City Streets* a montage of china figurines is used symbolically over the clash of voices in one of the film's key dramatic scenes. Dialogue spoken earlier in the picture is heard again over a huge, tear-stained close-up of Sylvia Sidney as she recalls the past. Even as in Griffith's day, the producers protested that the public would never understand what was going on, that hearing a sound without seeing its source would only confuse the audience. Mamoulian stuck to his point, however; audiences did understand—and the sound "flash-back" has become a standard technique in talkies ever since.

By the time he made. *Dr. Jekyll and Mr. Hyde* (1932), Mamoulian had full control of his new medium. From start to finish, it was a virtuoso work; almost every scene revealed the director's desire to break away from a literal use of the camera and a conventional use of sound. The entire first reel was shot in the first-person technique, the camera assuming the identity of Dr. Jekyll. From that position we see his hands as he plays the organ, the shadow of his head upon the music rack. When Jekyll is ready to go out, the butler hands hat, cloak and cane directly to the camera. After a carriage ride through the streets of London, it enters the doors of a medical school and passes on into the operating theater. Here a complete 360° turn around the hall brings the camera to rest for the first time upon the face of Dr. Jekyll (Fredric March). Quite apart from its indisputable pictorial effectiveness, this use of the subjective camera built a growing suspense, a curiosity about the appearance of the man we know will turn into the monstrous Hyde. The transformations themselves were ingeniously achieved upon the screen (Mamoulian has steadfastly refused to divulge the secret of his technique), accompanied by a vivid, synthetically created sound track built from exaggerated heart beats mingled with the reverberations of gongs played backwards, bells heard through echo chambers and completely artifical sounds created by photographing light frequencies directly onto the sound track. The recordists referred to it as "Mamoulian's stew," but it was probably the screen's first experiment with purely synthetic sound.

Outstanding for its understatement both of sound and visual was Mamoulian's handling of the scene in which Hyde murders "Champagne Ivy" (Miriam Hopkins). Hyde forces the thoroughly frightened girl to sing her pathetic music hall song. Suddenly he bends over her, passing completely out of the frame. For a long moment the shot reveals only the bedpost, a highly ornamental carving of the Goddess of Love. Then the singing stops abruptly, and Hyde's triumphant face rises once more into view. We need be shown no more.

The impact of René Clair's films upon men who, like Mamoulian, were themselves concerned with the creative use of sound is perhaps most clearly revealed in Mamoulian's next picture, *Love Me Tonight* (1932). Although in the tradition

of the Jeanette MacDonald-Maurice Chevalier musicals that
Ernst Lubitsch had been making so successfully, suddenly the
form is freer, lighter, more imaginative than ever before.
Greater liberties are taken with reality, and less effort is made
to explain or excuse the obviously absurd to the audience. In
the midst of a hunt, deer bound across the screen in dreamy
waltz time; or characters march about a French château
gleefully caroling, "The son of a gun is nothing but a tailor."
Through this kind of fantasy, in which trick sound is combined with trick camera to create a world of gay illusion, the
literal techniques of the realistic dramas were jolted loose,
stirred about. The experience of making such musicals provided directors with new insights into their craft that inevitably carried over into the more serious forms. There was a
pronounced tendency toward more vivid imagery, a more
imaginative use of sound, even in stories still written mainly
in the theatrical tradition.

Mamoulian's own films after *Love Me Tonight* are again
indicative. *Song of Songs* (1933) with Marlene Dietrich,
Queen Christina (1933) with Greta Garbo, *We Live Again*
(1934) with Anna Sten had a visual beauty, a sensuous quality that often surmounted the banality of their scripts. Certain
scenes—Garbo with the grapes in *Queen Christina* or the
long tracking shot to the completely immobile close-up of
Garbo that closes the film—linger in the mind as directorial
touches that added cinematic life to stories that made their
main points through dialogue. Certainly, Mamoulian's concern for the dramatic effect of his imagery made him the
logical choice as the director of the first feature-length film
shot in the improved, full-colored Technicolor, *Becky Sharp*
(1935). His handling of the great ball before the battle of
Waterloo with its artfully designed shifting patterns of color,
its gay pastels mounting to a climax of blood-red cloaks disappearing into the darkness, reveals again his ability to work
imaginatively with the raw materials of his art. And when in
1936 he turned once more to musical comedy in the satiric
Gay Desperado, he showed that he was now able to move as
lightly and freely in a realistic world of thieves and radios
and high-powered motorcars as in the fantasy world of *Love
Me Tonight*. Always the creative director, Mamoulian best
exemplifies those talented men of the early thirties who were
consciously seeking to transform the talking picture into a
genuinely cinematic art.

New Forms, New Techniques

It was perhaps inevitable that, during the first hectic years of sound, the film cycles reappeared with renewed vigor. They seemed to chase each other across the screen, one right after the other—transcriptions of Broadway musicals, prison pictures, gangster pictures, newspaper pictures, back-stage musicals. With the entire industry unsure of itself, any outstanding success was soon followed by the simultaneous release of literally dozens of other films on the same subject from every studio in Hollywood. Curiously enough, this had a salutary effect on the films themselves. The studios did not try merely to imitate what had gone before: they tried to make their films better than their competition. They tried to polish techniques and stories until their own efforts were more attractive, more effective, more "box office." The number of films in each cycle may have driven the moviegoer of the early thirties almost out of his mind by making it seem that every new picture he went to was the one that he had seen the week before. But through these cycles the film forms were themselves able to develop characteristic styles and techniques, an increased mobility and cinematic power.

One of the first and most obvious fields for exploitation by the new sound camera was, of course, the Broadway musical. During 1929 and 1930, a great many of these made the transition to film—*The Vagabond King, The Desert Song, Rio Rita, Sunny, Golden Dawn, Gold Diggers of Broadway, Song of the Flame* . . . The list is endless. Actually, however, very little original thinking went into them. It was enough that they had popular titles, famous stars and familiar tunes. In 1930, however, Samuel Goldwyn brought to Hollywood a dance director from the New York stage, Busby Berkeley, to handle the musical numbers for *Whoopee*, starring Eddie Cantor. And things began to happen. Berkeley, one of the most original and daring of the directors in this field, saw no reason why the dances should be a mere reproduction of the stage originals. Not with a camera capable of taking scenes from any angle and any position. In *Whoopee* he carried his camera high up into the flies and shot straight down on the dance floor. In subsequent films, he photographed from below, from the sides, from above. He zoomed the camera in from afar to extreme close-ups of his dancing girls or singing stars. He devised trick shots, matte shots and kaleidoscopic lenses to obtain ever more novel effects. For one astonishing moment in "The Shadow Waltz" from *Gold Diggers of 1933*, he tilted the camera at a 90° angle to the floor and photographed the girls mirrored in a lake, pirouetting down either side of the screen. He increased the fragmentation of his dances into a series of all but motionless abstract designs. Meaningless in themselves, they acquired line and continuity when the separate shots were assembled in the editing rooms. Since such dance sequences were generally inserted into wellworn backstage stories, purists frequently pointed out that Berkeley's work was ridiculous, that his dances could never conceivably take place on any stage in the world. They were, of course, absolutely right. What they ignored was the fact that the story was merely an excuse for the production numbers, and that Berkeley was producing the purest combinations of visual and sound that had yet come from the American studios. His dance sequences were abstract, complete in themselves and, ultimately, self-defeating, an artistic cul-de-sac without links to the more common narrative forms. But, like the avant-garde works of the twenties, they were both stimulating and provocative, suggesting to others new ways of using the freedom that Berkeley had found for himself. He remains unique for his special kind of musical spectacle, although his vogue was to be gradually superseded by the growing popularity of the more intimate style of dance films introduced by Fred Astaire and Ginger Rogers during the mid-thirties.

The popular gangster films of the early thirties—*Little Caesar* (1930), *The Public Enemy* (1931), *Scarface* (1932)—and the almost concurrent cycle of newspaper melodramas also did much to return to the screen some of its former mobility and vitality. Generally written directly for the screen, they eliminated the long, fragrant speeches of the legitimate theater in favor of such pungent phrases as "We're gonna take you for a ride," "He got bumped off," and "You can dish it out but you can't take it." In keeping with the tone of this dialogue, the editing was similarly taut and to the point. In a typical scene from *Little Caesar*, the gang is discussing the fate of one of its members:

"Eddie's turned yellow. He's goin' to rat on us."
"He can't get away with that."

"I just seen Eddie goin' into the church."

"Get Eddie," says Little Caesar. And the scene cuts abruptly to a church exterior, with Eddie coming down the steps. A long black car swings ominously into view; there is a burst of machine-gun fire and Eddie lies sprawling on the steps. Followed by a flat cut to the next scene, Eddie's funeral.

There was a speed, a vigor, a sense of the contemporaneous scene, a realism of character and incident about these films that was in sharp contrast to the talky problem plays that surrounded them. They had action, racy dialogue, the sharply naturalistic performances of people like James Cagney, Edward G. Robinson, Joan Blondell, Lee Tracy, Paul Muni and George Bancroft. They boasted that their incidents were based on fact, that their stories came from the headlines. And they excited audiences in ways that the drawing-room comedies, boudoir romances and static musical comedies did not. They were like a breath of fresh air sweeping through the heavily padded studios of the early sound era, blowing away some of the conventions, some of the stiffness that had crept into the medium with the advent of the microphone.

And directors—even directors who were not working on gangster films—responded to their tonic. In *The Front Page* (1931), one of the first and fastest of the newspaper cycle, Lewis Milestone solved the problem of translating the Hecht-MacArthur play into a film by keeping the camera almost constantly in motion, by cutting frequently and by staging the dialogue at breakneck speed. King Vidor, faced with much the same problem in bringing to the screen Elmer Rice's *Street Scene* (1931), used few moving camera shots but worked out a shooting script in which every single shot was taken from a fresh angle. Josef von Sternberg, in films like *Blonde Venus* (1932) and *Shanghai Express* (1932), used long traveling shots, scenes arrestingly decorated, composed and lit, long lingering lap dissolves and sparse dialogue to sustain the visual interest of his films. By 1932, at least the opening reel of most pictures had strong pictorial values. Typical was William K. Howard's *Transatlantic* (1931), a very ordinary melodrama for the most part, but its first few minutes beautifully captured both the excitement and the mechanics of an ocean liner preparing to leave port. Once the ship got under way, unfortunately, so did the story—and it promptly fell back upon dialogue to make all its points. The film makers, however, were growing increasingly aware of the fact that their medium could not live on words alone.

Nowhere were the dislocations caused by the addition of the sound track more apparent than in the field of film comedy; and yet here too a balance was soon reached that proved of value to film makers in all fields. Prior to the introduction of sound, of course, comedy had been almost entirely a visual medium, with emphasis on character and physical humor. Subtitles—especially those subtitles that introduced the various characters—might carry an occasional wisecrack. ("He had water on the brain. In the winter it froze and everything slipped his mind.") In the sophisticated or folksy comedies of the twenties, there might even be a snappy retort. Will Rogers, for example, punctuated his silent comedies with typical Rogers-isms—but, significantly, Rogers was never as popular on the silent screen as he was after sound came in. In sound, the humor shifted abruptly from visual to verbal, and a whole new crowd of comics—largely imported from the New York stage and from vaudeville—came clamoring through the studios. The Marx Brothers, Ed Wynn, Lou Holtz, Eddie Cantor, W. C. Fields, Jimmy Durante, Frank Morgan, Bobby Clark, Charlie Ruggles and, soon after, Bob Hope were all brought west because they could handle a humorous line or witty repartee. Keaton and Lloyd, Harry Langdon and Raymond Griffith drifted into either the obscurity of studio office jobs or complete retirement. At the same time, such relatively minor comics from the silent days as Laurel and Hardy, Edward Everett Horton and Joe E. Brown were suddenly boosted to stardom. They were stage trained. They could talk.

Typical was the case of Buster Keaton. At the close of the twenties, he was M-G-M's highest paid comedian. Early in the thirties he was cast in a series of comedies with Jimmy Durante. Nominally, Keaton was the star; but whatever success the pictures scored was so clearly due to Durante that Keaton's contract was simply allowed to expire. He had established himself as a silent, frozen-faced comedian. Durante's natural style was volatile, explosive. It was Durante, not Keaton, that the talkies wanted.

Nor were all the stars of the stage completely at home on the talking screen. Ed Wynn's simple-minded funny man,

Beatrice Lillie's cool sophistication, Fanny Brice's broad dialect humor and even broader bathos found scant acceptance outside New York. Even Eddie Cantor and Jack Benny—successful in theater, radio and, later, television—were never as warmly received in the movies. Radio stars like Stoopnagle and Budd, Fred Allen and Kate Smith were notably unsuccessful when they tried the screen. The characters that had sparked the imagination of millions when heard in the living room never quite seemed to satisfy those same millions when they came to see them in the movie houses.

On the other hand, the Marx Brothers, W. C. Fields, Will Rogers, Bob Hope, Jimmy Durante and Marie Dressler—each had some special quality of voice and personality that found an immediate response in audiences around the world. Their humor was verbal, but it also had a strong visual quality. It is difficult to think of Will Rogers and Marie Dressler without recalling their shrugs and gesticulations, their special forms of mugging. Jimmy Durante is a veritable fury of activity, magnifying every emotion until it becomes a parody of itself. Bob Hope, with the smooth patina of years of vaudeville trouping, has a cock of the eye, a twist of the lip or a flip of the hand to accompany every line.

Inspired Mayhem: The Marx Brothers and W. C. Fields

It is in the films of the Marx Brothers, however, and of W. C. Fields—and in such rare, offbeat items as *Million Dollar Legs* (1932), *Six of a Kind* (1934) and the Hope-Crosby *Road* series—that one finds the real flowering of comedy in the sound films. Indeed, the Marx Brothers presented a perfect filmic combination—the fast-talking Groucho, the silent, nimble-witted pantomime of Harpo, and Chico, the saturnine fall guy (with statuesque Margaret Dumont generally around to play straight). Even though their very earliest films, *The Coconuts* (1929) and *Animal Crackers* (1930), were nothing more than crudely photographed versions of previous stage hits, the swiftness of the dialogue and Harpo's eloquent byplay all but concealed their technical deficiencies. Such a fantastic colloquy as the one from *Animal Crackers* in which Groucho and Chico discuss the mysterious disappearance of a valuable painting needs nothing beyond a sound track and a well-focused camera:

"We'll search every room in the house," says Groucho.

"What if it ain't in this house?" says Chico.

"Then we'll search the house next door."

"What if there ain't no house next door?"

"Then we'll build one," says Groucho—and the two immediately set about drawing up plans for building the house next door.

All their better pictures had similar sequences. In *Duck Soup* (1932) Groucho as the Prime Minister of Fredonia holds up a document and says to his assembled council, "Why, a four-year-old child could understand this report"; then, *sotto voce* to Chico, "Run out and find me a four-year-old child. I can't make heads or tails out of it."

Just as in the gangster films, this dialogue had a racy fascination of its own. It was talk, true; but it was also more than talk. It had, in the most literal sense, a picturesque quality—a quality that was best conveyed by a wholly passive camera. But alternating with and counter-balancing all this dialogue were sequences of frantic activity and pure pantomime—the trick with the mirror in *Duck Soup*, with all three Marxes dressed as Groucho and circling suspiciously about one another; the travesty on opera in *A Night at the Opera* when Harpo inserts "Take Me Out to the Ball Game" into the orchestra's score for *Il Trovatore* and then runs amuck in the scenery; the inspired mayhem of the operating scene from *A Day at the Races*, with Groucho calling for X-rays and Harpo and Chico rushing in with the evening papers.

As a team, the Marx Brothers achieved an almost perfect balance of sight and sound, marred only by the occasional *scènes obligatoires* of Harpo playing the harp and Chico the piano. (In one of their pictures Groucho, as if aware of the letdown in tempo, says directly to the audience, "Look, I have to stay here, but why don't you go out to the lobby for a smoke until this whole thing blows over?") Although directors invariably sought to enliven such sequences with trick shots of Chico at the keyboard, with close-ups of Harpo's unique fingering of his instrument, with zoom shots and striking angles, they were never able to force cinematic life into what remained essentially stagy performances. Apart from such moments, however, the skillful interplay of the Marx Brothers created a kind of humor that was ideally suited to the requirements of the sound camera.

If the Marxes provided perfect foils for one another, W. C. Fields was the perfect sound comedian in himself. The irascible, bumbling braggadocio that was his screen character was also, it would seem, his off-screen character as well. He was an unpredictable eccentric whose confirmed pessimism had been nourished by years of adversity. A lifetime of rigorous training as a juggler in circus and vaudeville had made his every gesture and movement a masterpiece of precise timing. The result was an incomparable blend of half-articulate howls of rage, mumbled bits of private philosophy ("No man who hates small dogs and children can be .*all* bad"), and eloquent pantomime. Many of the best sight gags in his earlier pictures were developed from his old stage routines, such as the golfing scene with the bent clubs in *You're Telling Me* (1934), his attempts to sleep on a noisy back porch in *It's a Gift* (1934) and the hilariously crooked poker game in *Mississippi* (1935).

There was always an air of improvisation about a Fields picture, as if his comedy patter and throw-away lines had been caught almost by accident by the camera. One had the feeling that the next time the picture was run, they might not even be there! It gave his films the peculiar fascination of a newsreel, of a one-time happening to a truly unique character. The pictures themselves were invariably abominably constructed, a hodgepodge of plot and gags that shot off in all directions. Indeed, his final film, *Never Give a Sucker an Even Break* (1941), almost defies description, its narrative has so many breaks and changes. But, like all the Fields films, it is full of the most inspired inanities—Fields diving out of an airplane after his whisky bottle and comparing an ordinary cigarette to the new king size as he plummets to earth, his running warfare with the formidable waitress at the local hash house ("I did *not* say this meat was tough. I just said I didn't see the horse that's usually tethered outside.") And, as in all the Fields films, there were the familiar props—the agile cane, the straw hat that constantly popped out of his hands or flew off his head, the stump of a cigar that half concealed his more scurrilous oaths.

Fields wrote most of his own pictures, using such improbable noms de plume as Otis J. Cribblecoblis or Mahatma Kane Jeeves; probably no one else could have realized quite so well the picaresque qualities inherent in the character, or dreamed

up the mass of petty harassments through which Fields
fought his way with beady eye and wide-swinging cane. Like
the Marx Brothers, like Will Rogers and Bob Hope, Fields's
humor was verbal; but what gave it character and substance
was the bulbous nose, the look of outraged dignity and lar-
cenous innocence that accompanied everything he said or did.

Integration and Style: Astaire and Hitchcock

The fact is that in the work of the best comedians of the
thirties the sound film was coming closer to striking a proper
balance between its visual and aural elements. Much of this
was instinctive, much was the result of happy accident; but
also, out of the accumulating skill and experience of directors
and technicians alike, a sure craftsmanship was emerging.
And as accident gave way to method, so too did the flamboyant trickery of the early years of sound give way to style. In
the series of Fred Astaire and Ginger Rogers musicals that
brightened the mid-thirties, for example, a camera technique
was evolved that broke sharply with the exuberant, exhibi-
tionistic patterns of the Busby Berkeley dances and permitted
the closer integration of musical and story elements. The
Astaire films were intimate, the dances coming not as inter-
ruptions but as extensions of the story. Astaire and Rogers
danced because words alone could not convey their feelings.
At first, the problem of getting into the dance was often
solved mechanically, with the awkward expedient of the song
cue—a bit of dialogue incorporating the title of the number
or explaining its presence in the picture ("Listen, dear,
they're playing our song!") Soon, however, the Astaire films
were simply letting the music steal in under the dialogue
without any attempt at explanation or excuse. The dancers
respond to it, and the number is under way. Obviously,
Berkeley's swooping cameras and picturesquely posed chorines were out of place under these circumstances. And yet,
the Astaire dances were created for the camera every bit as
knowingly as Berkeley's. Few of them could be reproduced
on a stage, but not because of angles or tricks but because
they utilized the camera's innate ability to cover great areas,
to fall back as the dancers move forward, to cut nimbly from
place to place.

In the exhilarating "Bojangles of Harlem" number from *Swing Time* (1936), there are repeated examples of this new integration of the camera into the choreography of the dance itself. At one point Astaire is working solo to the accompaniment of only guitar and drums, the camera in very close to him. Suddenly he stops and flings out his arms ecstatically, the chorus dances on from either side, and the camera moves up and back to enlarge on the scene as the orchestra swells out to full volume. This synchronization of the movement of the dance, the camera and the music creates a moment of rare gratification to both eye and ear. Within this same sequence there is an astonishing shadow play in which three silhouettes of Astaire work first in unison with him, then in tricky counter-rhythms. But though his routines were often tricky, his use of the camera itself was not. After his first few pictures, Astaire began to direct as well as to choreograph his dance sequences with notable success. He brought his camera increasingly into the play of the dance, judiciously placing it to provide a tight frame for his own solo work, pulling it back to create new dimensions for the ensembles, moving it freely to sustain at all times the line of the dance. It was an unobtrusive, discreet and beautifully functional use of the camera—and one that, for the first time, achieved the balance between camera, image and the sound track that is the true art of the sound film.

What the Astaire films reveal, with their grace and lightness and sureness of touch, is the approaching technical maturity of the American film makers. From an overemphasis of sound, many had moved to the opposite extreme, to an overemphasis of the visual element. By the middle of the thirties, a happier balance was being achieved. Directors no longer feared sound, nor did they try to conceal long dialogue passages behind a myriad of artificially created scenes. The better writers had long since discovered the difference between stage dialogue and talk on the screen while, at the top level, people like Dudley Nichols, Robert Riskin and Joseph Mankiewicz were writing with a strong awareness of the visual requirements of the medium as well. A whole corps of superbly trained cameramen—many of them, like James Wong Howe, Karl Freund and Arthur Edeson, with experience extending far back into the silent era—were fully prepared to transform their words into striking images. The sound engineers and technicians had, in a brief half-dozen years, supplied the studios with equipment that, for all its complexity, was incredibly flexible and allowed a maximum of control at every point; they stood ready to supply the director with virtually any effect he might request. As is always the case, masterpieces were few and far between. But the period of experimentation was over and the period of integration and consolidation could begin.

One of the first directors to achieve this integration in dramatic films was England's Alfred Hitchcock, whose mystery thrillers began to appear on American screens in 1935. Perhaps because the mystery form has always laid emphasis on visual shocks and surprises, the full extent of his contribution has been somewhat underestimated. Hitchcock did far more than simply bathe his stories in somber lighting and deep shadow to create in his audiences a dread of the unexpected. And also, it should be added, he did more than invent a series of brilliant, equally disquieting surprise effects on the sound track (although some, such as the woman's scream in *The 39 Steps* that merges with the shriek of a locomotive's whistle, have become classics in the field).

One has only to read through the first few pages of John Buchan's *The 39 Steps*, however, and compare the novel with Hitchcock's screen treatment of it to recognize his full stature. From Buchan's description of his hero wandering about London, looking in windows, stopping in bars, taking in a show, Hitchcock selected the one incident—scarcely more than a passing phrase—that lent itself best to dramatic screen treatment. He opens the film at a variety theater— something for the eye, something for the ear—and leads the narrative back there for the dramatic finale. Throughout the film the incidents are suggested by the novel rather than reproducing it scene for scene. Hitchcock, who has always worked on his own screenplays, prefers to invent around an idea, letting it develop in filmic terms rather than in terms of the novel or short story used as source material. His favorite device was the "magguffin," his own term to describe a visual or sound gimmick—a snatch of music, a man with a twitching eye, a ticking time bomb—that runs throughout the picture as a sinister leitmotif. In *The 39 Steps* this "magguffin" is a man with a missing finger. The key figure in the mysterious spy ring, he is wholly Hitchcock's invention: there is no counterpart for him in the original novel.

What contributed to the fascination of such vintage Hitchcocks as *The 39 Steps* (1935), *Secret Agent* (1935), *The Woman Alone* (1936), *The Girl was Young* (1937), and *The Lady Vanishes* (1938) was his deliberate underplaying of climactic scenes. A woman staggers toward the camera and then, as she collapses, we see the hilt of the dagger in her back. A boy unwittingly carries a time bomb across London; we see him mount a bus and then, in long shot, the bus blows up. We are not shown the kidnaping of the old woman in *The Lady Vanishes;* we only know that suddenly in her place in the railway carriage has appeared a dreadful grim-faced substitute wearing her clothes and claiming to be Miss Froy. In *The Woman Alone*, while Sylvia Sidney is preparing to murder her husband in the shadowy movie house, on the sound track is heard the macabre refrain from Disney's cartoon *Who Killed Cock Robin?* Indeed, what is perhaps the most perfect moment of pure cinema is to be found in Hitchcock's *North by Northwest* (1959). Cary Grant arrives in the midst of endless acres of cornfields, the only visible sign of life a distant plane making lazy circles in the sky. A man drives up, looks at the plane and says, "That's funny. That plane's dustin' crops where there ain't no crops." A moment later, when Grant is alone again, it sweeps in to gun him down. The point is that the plane was merely a background detail until it wheeled to make its assault. There was a casual urbanity about Hitchcock's most carefully prepared moments, whether visual or aural, that quickly established his supremacy not only as a director of thrillers but as a master of the sound-film medium. His pictures, eagerly awaited during the late thirties, led inevitably to a Hollywood contract. Although Hitchcock frankly admits that he is now doing what he calls "the commercial thing," few directors today can rival him in the grace and polish, the slick surface finish of his star-studded comedy melodramas.

The Script and the Stars

Unquestionably the greatest single difficulty that faced the directors of the mid-thirties was the problem of handling dialogue gracefully. The public had visibly tired of the "100% all-talkies"; the critics railed against them. With sound itself no longer a novelty, audiences grew bored and restless at movies that didn't move, at pictures that told their stories almost entirely in words. Although Lubitsch, Clair, and Mamoulian had gotten around this by minimizing their dialogue, the majority of films continued to consist solely of long, tedious conversations that came either directly from the theater or—what was just as bad—from stage-trained writers. Frequently writers and directors sought to give the screen some semblance of mobility by breaking up long dialogue passages into scene fragments. A conversation might begin in a taxi, continue in the living room and wind up in the bedroom. Too often such a device was simply distracting, drawing attention away from the words themselves while adding nothing to the cinematic feeling of the film. Obviously, another approach was needed.

Before any approach could be successful, however, there had to be a drastic revision in the dialogue itself. The script writers, whether recruited from the theater, from radio or the silent movie, had to discover a truly filmic language, a language with a lively fascination of its own. Primarily, it was a dialogue that had to approximate more closely the patterns of ordinary speech than is either necessary—or desirable—on the stage or in literature. The theater demands a richness of verbal imagery to help cloak the immobile and restrictive nature of its settings. Stage dialogue is full of descriptions of off-stage events that must be reported because they cannot be shown. It is laced through with psychological insights into character and motivation that sound highly artificial in the movies. It is, in a word, "theatrical." Only in the theater can a character say, as in *Death of a Salesman*, "Nobody dast blame this man. You don't understand; Willy was a salesman. And for a salesman, there is no rock bottom to the life. He don't put a bolt to a nut, he don't tell you the law or give you medicine. He's the man way out there in the blue riding on a smile and a shoeshine. And when they start not smiling back—that's an earthquake. And then you get yourself a couple spots on your hat, and you're finished. Nobody dast blame this man. A salesman is got to dream, boy. It comes with the territory." Such words create their own spell, their own poetry in the theater, but they disintegrate and destroy all sense of character in the more naturalistic film medium.

Nor is the language of literature, particularly as discovered in the novel, any more suitable for direct filming (although there is growing evidence that many of today's writers have

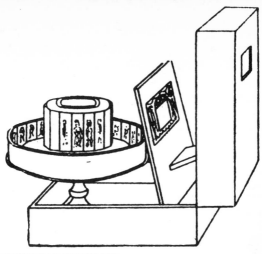

THE TOY THAT GREW UP

The Praxinoscope, a 19th-century parlor entertainment, was one of many toys designed to demonstrate persistence of vision. Its hand-drawn images, reflected in the mirrors, seemed to come alive when the drum was revolved.

The Panavision camera, shown here shooting a scene for *Roller-coaster* (1977), is used extensively for photographing today's wide-screen entertainments. Director James Goldstone stands beside it. The film also featured a stereophonic Sensurround sound track.

D. W. Griffith, the Father of Film Technique, with his trusted cameraman, G. W. ("Billy") Bitzer, preparing a scene for *The Birth of a Nation* (1915).

D. W. Griffith, Mary Pickford, Charles Chaplin and Douglas Fairbanks formed United Artists in 1919 to produce and distribute their own pictures; no studio could afford them.

D. W. Griffith enriched the art of film by heightening its sense of intimacy and reality, as in this frame from *Musketeers of Pig Alley* (1912) . . .

While in *The Birth of a Nation* (1915) and *Intolerance* (1916), he introduced the sweep and spectacle that still astonish and delight audiences today.

THE GOLDEN AGE OF GERMAN FILM

As the films grew more introspective and subjective, F. W. Murnau in *The Last Laugh* (1924) deployed a moving camera to assume the identity of Emil Jannings.

A nightmare reality surfaced in the "street films," and especially those of G. W. Pabst. The scene is from his *The Love of Jeanne Ney* (1927).

As film makers gained mastery of the camera, their basic shots became more precise and expressive, as demonstrated in this sequence from Harold Lloyd's *The Freshman* (1925).

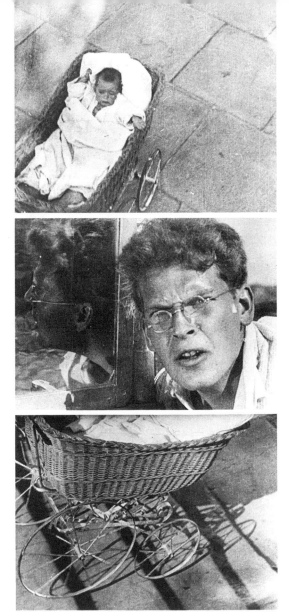

THE ART OF FILM: THE EDITING PRINCIPLE
The terror of the Odessa Steps sequence in S. M.
Eisenstein's *Potemkin* (1925) was captured through
the dynamic assemblage of hundreds of separate

shots. In these frame enlargements, the power of editing to suggest relationships between a rolling carriage, a horror-stricken student, and a Cossack waiting with saber poised is clearly illustrated.

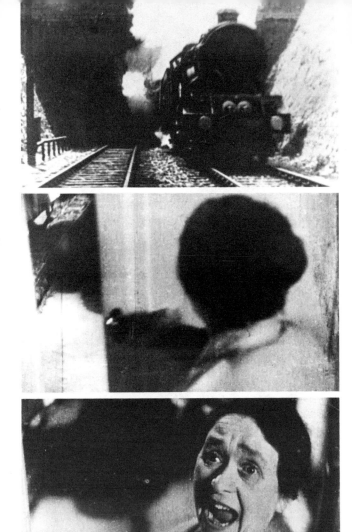

THE ART OF FILM: SOUND MONTAGE

In Alfred Hitchcock's *The 39 Steps* (1935), sound motivates the cutting. Discovering a corpse in the hero's room, the landlady screams; her scream merges with the whistle of the train on which he is fleeing.

THE COMING OF SOUND

Warner Brothers' *Don Juan* (1926) had its own Vitaphone musical score, but the silent era ended totally in 1927 when the studio released *The Jazz Singer*, the first talking picture.

As *Variety* headlined, the public's immediate acceptance of the Vitaphone revolutionized the movie industry. By 1930, the "novelty" of sound had prevailed.

To accommodate the demand for the new medium, vast new stages were built and others hastily sound-proofed. This is the Warner studio in 1929.

INTERNATIONAL TRENDS: ITALY

For most of us, the Italian film began with the post-war neo-realist movement, of which Vittorio De Sica's *The Bicycle Thief* (1949) was a shining example.

Although neo-realism was to take many turns, its root purpose—to depict "the way things are"—persists in such films as Bernardo Bertolucci's *The Conformist* (1970).

INTERNATIONAL TRENDS: FRANCE

The French sound film flowered in the late thirties through directors like Marcel Carné, René Clair, and Jean Renoir. Shown here is Jean Gabin in Renoir's *Grand Illusion* (1937).

But French films continue to charm international audiences with such wry, frank examinations of love among the sexes as Charles Tacchella's *Cousin/Cousine* (1976).

TOWARD AN INTERNATIONAL FILM

By the mid fifties, American studios were financing vast productions with international casts and technicians, such as David Lean's *The Bridge on the River Kwai* (1957).

Uniquely Japanese films like Akira Kurosawa's *Rashomon* (1950) found universal favor, but Japanese film makers' luck ran out when they tried to imitate Hollywood movies.

AMERICAN FILM GENRES

No other nation has ever approximated the verve and style of the American movie musicals. Stanley Donen's *Singin' in the Rain* (1952) remains one of the best.

The American West is more than a movie setting; it exemplifies a way of life. George Stevens' *Shane* (1953) is a Western in the classic mold.

THE INTERNATIONAL DIRECTOR

England's cherubic Alfred Hitchcock, in Hollywood since 1939, enjoys an international esteem, especially as father of the French "*Nouvelle Vague.*"

Last of the original Italian new-realist film makers, Federico Fellini exemplifies the complete "*auteur*" — the director whose personal vision dominates every frame of his movie.

"*Nouvelle Vague*" director François Truffaut (shown here with Jean-Pierre Aumont) wrote a book on Hitchcock, later imitated his style in *The Bride Wore Black* (1968).

AMERICA'S *"NOUVELLE VAGUE"*

Francis Ford Coppola, director of *The Godfather* (1972), is "godfather" to a whole new generation of American film makers who look to him for help and guidance.

Martin Scorsese, who both studied and taught film making at New York University, ultimately established his reputation with the tough, ultra-realistic *Taxi Driver* (1975).

George Lucas (shown below with Alec Guinness during production of *Star Wars,* 1977) epitomizes the student film maker turned professional—with a strong assist from Coppola.

THE ART OF FILM: PRODUCTION DESIGN

Pre-production sketches are often drawn as aids not only to the set designer, but to the director as well. Boris Leven's watercolor for *New York, New York* (1977) was precisely matched in the camera set-up.

been strongly influenced in their conception of dialogue by repeated exposure to the motion picture). Ideally, no screen character can be permitted the paragraphs of introspective speeches that the protagonist of a novel so often indulges in. And certainly the long, discursive passages in which the author explores the ramifications of his theme—always one of the primary attractions of the novel form—defy translation into film in terms of dialogue. When Budd Schulberg reversed the accepted procedure and expanded his screenplay for *On the Waterfront* (1954) into a novel, it was specifically in order to develop themes and ideas that he could not put into the mouths of the illiterate and half-articulate characters he had brought so vividly to life upon the screen.

Screen writers had to invent dialogue that was at once rich and colorful, pungent and amusing, but also stripped of inessentials. They had to learn not only what to say, but also how much could be left unsaid—how much could be left to the camera and the actor and the director to put on the screen through action and gesture or by implication. Here, for example, is a portion of the final scene from Dudley Nichols' splendid script for *The Informer* (1935), a model of terse cinematic writing:

"*The Vestibule of the Church*: Gypo comes in with the same slow, stiff walk [as in the previous shot], his arms limp at his sides. Dazedly he sees the font and reverently he dips his hand in and tries to cross himself. But that hand weighs a ton and he cannot do it. Stiffly he turns and staggers through the narrow Roman door, and we next see him inside the church, swaying in the dim, mysterious light. He tries to think where he is. Then he sees a kneeling figure in a black dress, alone in the church on the aisle, about halfway up, on the side, and he staggers on with that stiff, slow walk, finally reaching the kneeling figure. It is Mrs. McPhillip praying for her dead son. Gypo swallows the blood in his mouth and stands there weaving before her, and his voice is a thick whisper.

Gypo: 'Twas I informed on your son, Mrs. McPhillip. . . .Forgive me . . .

Mrs. McPhillip: (tears running down her worn, kindly face) I forgive you Gypo. You didn't know what you were doing."

Here is work for camera, director, actor, set designer *and* the sound recordist. The scenario provides the mood, the atmosphere, the dialogue and the main elements of the action in the scene. But it remained for John Ford, the director, to determine upon the diffused light from a street lamp as the key illumination behind Gypo when he stumbles into the church; to follow his leaden movements down the aisle with a camera placed to the rear, emphasizing at once his bulk and the emptiness of the room; to hold the camera in close on Mrs. McPhillip during the brief dialogue passage; and then, a moment later, to move the camera high behind the altar so that as the dying Gypo cries out, "Frankie! Frankie! Your mother forgives me!" he seems to be speaking directly to Christ on the altar cross. The script for a film, in short, is like an orchestral score. It is the conductor's interpretation of the music that finally brings it to life for the concert audience. It is the director's visualization of the script that creates the movie, blending dialogue with action to produce the most affecting combination of both.

The Informer demonstrated the advantages of a strong writer-director team, a collaboration that in Ford and Nichols produced such memorable films as *The Lost Patrol* (1934), *The Plough and the Stars* (1936), *Stagecoach* (1939) and *The Long Voyage Home* (1940). Another outstanding writer-director team of the thirties was Robert Riskin and Frank Capra. In such enormously popular comedies as *Lady for a Day* (1933), *It Happened One Night* (1934), *Mr. Deeds Goes to Town* (1936), *You Can't Take It With You* (1938) and *Mr. Smith Goes to Washington* (1939), Capra demonstrated his confidence in the ability of his colleague to write dialogue that held its own upon the screen by filming long passages without any change in camera position whatsoever. His special skill lay in recreating the speed and humor of silent comedy in the sound medium, feeling out the subtle relationship between dialogue and camera, sensing when cutting or camera movement was required and when words alone could carry the momentum of his scene. If the talk was good, he reasoned, why try to hide it? A favorite technique of his was to start an extended dialogue passage with the camera some distance away from his principals, then slowly, almost imperceptibly, track in to a large two-shot, as if irresistibly drawn by his interest in what the people were saying.

In *It Happened One Night*, with entire sequences played

within the confines of a bus or a small tourist cabin, Capra ingeniously contrived to keep his screen alive by scanning the faces of the passengers on the bus, or discovering his stars almost haphazardly among the people and the packages and seats that surrounded them. Only when the dialogue was important, when it bore significantly on the development of the story, did he move in for protracted close-ups. But these close-ups were completely functional: they emphasized the words. Capra sensed when he could count on Riskin's lines to carry a scene without additional visual pyrotechnics, when they could be shot with a static camera or when the full effectiveness of the scene required the extra mobility of the moving camera and staccato editing of silent days. A particularly delightful sequence illustrates his ability to blend the two: Clark Gable and Claudette Colbert are sitting on a fence by the side of the road holding an animated conversation on the best way to thumb a ride from the passing cars; Capra filmed this entire scene in a single shot without moving his camera. But when Gable walks out to the road to demonstrate his hitchhiking methods (capped by Colbert's conclusive evidence that the knee is mightier than the thumb), Capra builds the scene from short snatches of pantomimed action brilliantly edited together—climaxed with an adroit montage in which a glimpse of Miss Colbert's leg brings a car to a screeching halt.

Capra was also among the first to perceive that the use of dialogue on the screen involved not only the preparation of a taut, vivid, idiomatic prose, but also a more specialized handling of the actors delivering that dialogue. And here was perhaps the final adjustment that directors had to make to sound. In silent days the director could (and often did) build a star's performance out of bits and pieces—a close-up of the actor, a reaction shot, an insert of an object or an image that underscored the emotional content of the scene. With sound, much of this "synthetic" kind of acting was automatically eliminated. Not only did the actors now have to speak their lines, but—as Al Jolson in *The Jazz Singer* so clearly revealed—the sound track itself produced a far greater awareness of their essential personality than the silent camera ever had. Voice, face, mannerisms and temperament were fused together by the sound camera to create that elusive indefinable quality known as "box-office appeal." These were the elements that the actor brought to his part—along with whatever measure of talent he possessed. More important than acting ability, however, was the photogenic—plus now the microgenic—magnetism of the star, around which the director could create a characterization. It was a quality which, when properly used, added its own dynamism to the film. And directors like Capra, Ford, George Cukor and William Wyler who gained the reputation of being "good with actors" were good because they knew how to fit their stars to their roles, and how to utilize their personalities to sustain the momentum of a scene.

The Art of the Sound Film

For anyone who can remember seeing silent movies when *all* movies were silent, it comes as a distinct shock to realize that there are now far more years of sound film history than there were of silence. Sound films, the once despised "talkies," seem to have been here forever, while the silent film is almost lost in the mists of time—a museum piece, like Etruscan art. Within a year or two of their arrival, the talkies had ousted the silents. Their rapid acceptance soon dissipated the hostility with which critics, aestheticians and many of the film makers themselves first greeted the medium. The novelty of 1929 had come to stay, and whole generations have since grown up without ever having seen a silent picture—except, perhaps, at a museum, a film school or on an educational television program. But even these showings reveal the extent to which the sound film is beholden to the masters of silence. Griffith, Chaplin, Eisenstein, Pudovkin, Murnau—they provided the foundation stones on which the superstructure of sound continues to rise. Inevitably, however, the development of the sound film has produced new forms, new techniques. The quaint notion that the sound track merely replaced the convention of the printed title with the spoken word, while never literally true, now suggests an oversimplification that is almost demeaning. In the past half century, the sound film has become an art in its own right.

Considered as a whole, its development has been swifter, but less dramatic, less clear-cut, than the evolution of the silent film. There are fewer personalities of whom one can say, "He did this," or "He contributed that." After all, the big work of exploration had all been done in the silent era—the many functions of the cut, the interpretive powers of the camera, the evolution of a cinematic style of acting; these had been discovered long before the microphone took over. Not yet had sound produced a D. W. Griffith to take the raw materials of camera and microphone and forge from them a wholly new medium. Nor is it possible to speak of French symbolism, Russian cutting or German lighting and camera movement in the sound era. Instead, the same technical problems—and very much the same solutions—seem to have presented themselves almost simultaneously in every film-producing nation. First came the period of "canned theater" which vigorously exploited sound for its own sake and filled the screens of every nation with painfully static reproductions of stage plays and musicals. Then came the experimenters, the men who revolted against the rigid camera and theatrical dialogue, directors who sought to return to the screen some of the mobility of silent days, who sought to use the sound track itself for something more than the mere literal reproduction of dialogue. And, since the mid-thirties, there has been the slow, steady search for a balance, an integration of sound and visual—all leading to a new and universal film form that is, ideally, neither "canned theater" nor what Alfred Hitchcock once described as "silent talkies." Once that had been achieved, however imperfectly, there began the search for *style*.

What is style? Well, it's damned elusive, for one thing. The moment one becomes self-conscious about style, it becomes forced, mannered—like Victor Borge playing a popular tune "in the style of Mozart." Obviously, Mozart never said, "I think I'll write the Jupiter Symphony in the style of Mozart." The style is the man; there is no other possible way he could have written it. Or imagine if you will an art school to which have been invited half a dozen of the world's greatest painters—Leonardo, Rembrandt, Goya, Cezanne, Van Gogh, Picasso. They are led to a studio where there is a single model and told they must paint her. Can you imagine six more disparate portraits? It's not because Rembrandt said, "I'm going to paint like Rembrandt," and Van Gogh said, "I'm going to paint like Van Gogh." It's because they could paint in no other way. Each man has his *style*, which is the way his view of the world is filtered through his own consciousness, brain, nerves and muscles, and ultimately finds expression upon a piece of canvas.

Style in film is far more complex, since no movie is the work of any single individual. Actually, the sound film is not only the work of many individuals, but a composite of many arts, and the theater was only one of the contributors to the new medium. By the mid-thirties, music too was finding its place, not merely in the song-and-dance pictures but in the dramas as well. When Max Steiner's score for *A Symphony of Six Million* (1932) won unanticipated enthusiasm for a sentimental story of New York's East Side, music began to acquire a certain prestige—a prestige vastly enhanced by Steiner's thundering score for the perennially popular *King Kong* (1934). Soon music was being tossed into films indiscriminately, good or bad, necessary or not: it added "production value" to the picture. However, in such films as John Ford's *The Informer* (1935), there was a determined (if still rudimentary) effort to use music to strengthen dramatic values as well; and Steiner was joined in the studios by pioneers like Alfred Newman, Erich Wolfgang Korngold, Dimitri Tiomkin and Richard Hagemann. Toward the end of the thirties, serious composers like Aaron Copland, George Antheil, Hanns Eisler and Ernst Toch were making their way into American studios, while in Europe, Arthus Bliss, Arthur Honegger, Dmitri Shostakovich and Sergei Prokofieff were mastering the craft of scoring a film and helping to raise film music to an art. Today, it is no longer fashionable to look down the nose at a film score and dismiss it as mere "movie music"—not when composers like Elmer Bernstein, Leonard Bernstein, Alex North, David Raksin and Leonard Rosenman can feel every bit as much at home on a studio sound stage in Hollywood as on a concert stage anywhere in the world.

Similarly, the work of the cinematographer has come to be recognized as at least as much an art as it is a craft. Despite the early presence of such giants as "Billy" Bitzer, Lee Garmes, James Wong Howe, Arthur Miller and Gregg Toland, the cameraman was generally considered to be merely an adjunct of the director. "He puts the camera where I tell him," says Otto Preminger, in no uncertain terms. Yet René Clair recalls his first day of work in an American studio, on *And Then There Were None*. "I went over the set with my view-finder," he says, "and I found myself standing next to my cameraman. 'We'll put the camera here,' I said to him. 'Of course,' he said, 'What the hell do you think I'm standing here for?'" Certainly, one way of spotting the cameraman's contribution is by comparing the work of a director when teamed with different cinematographers. Daniel Mann, for example, made an extremely effective film debut with *Come Back, Little Sheba* (1952), but disappointed with *About Mrs. Leslie* (1954), then redeemed himself (to some extent) with *The Rose Tattoo* (1955). On *Sheba* and *Tattoo,* his cameraman just happened to be James Wong Howe.

And yet few cameramen seek personal glory. The very best will tell you that they see their function as interpreting the style and the will of the director to the best of their ability— provided, of course, that the director has something in mind to begin with. Again, comparisons would seem to be in order. It would be difficult to imagine two films more dissimilar than Martin Ritt's gentle, almost lyric *Sounder* (1972) and Roman Polanski's slick, hard-surfaced *Chinatown* (1974), yet both were photographed by John Alonzo, resourcefully re- sponding to the directors' wishes. Miraculously, the seventies have produced a sudden spate of these skilled and sensitive technicians—Alonzo, James Crabe, William Fraker, Conrad Hall, Owen Roizman, Vilmos Szigmond, Haskell Wexler, and their counterparts abroad. As many critics have noted, the seventies movie that doesn't look marvelous is really the ex- ception.

The editor's contribution is considerably more difficult to discern, partially because most directors demand—and many are getting—the "final cut" of their pictures, which means that they sit in with their editors until the film has been shaped entirely to their satisfaction. At that point, no one could possibly tell which editing effects had been the sugges- tions of the editor and which were directorial brainstorms. Beyond that, the general public, which sees only the final cut (by whomever), has no way of knowing how much footage the editor had to work with, or what its quality might have been, nor can the audience tell what ingenious devices the ed- itor may have hit upon, only to have them rejected by his director or producer. And sometimes the devices are so inge- nious that the audiences see them without realizing that an effect has been created. In *The Outsider* (1961), for example, editor Marjorie Fowler contributed a magnificent electrical storm simply by cutting in two frames of blank leader from time to time, yet who was to know that this pyrotechnic dis- play wasn't created by the studio electricians?

The Integration of Style: Orson Welles

Obviously, then, the addition of a sound track in no way eliminated the need for visual creativity, although in many ways it altered the nature of that creativity. Above all, it demanded a new perception of the tensions that can be created by dialogue, the spell that can be woven by the actor, the continuity that can be provided by music. Because of his early background in radio as well as in theater, Orson Welles brought to films a heightened awareness of the full potency of sound. His inventive staging of such classics as *Macbeth*, *Julius Caesar* and *Doctor Faustus* in the New York theater had set the pulses racing with their incantation-like drumbeats, trumpet flourishes and weird off-stage voices. His radio shows—not only the famous *War of the Worlds*, but his week-in, week-out mystery dramas and suspense pieces—were filled with echo chambers, filters and adroit musical bridges from one scene to the next, and in many cases they featured Welles himself as narrator. Narration—the voice of an all-knowing, all-seeing commentator who sets the scene, threads the story together and, from time to time, offers his special insights into the motivations and thoughts of the characters—was common enough in radio. Films, on the other hand, were still using long printed titles for prefaces and shorter ones for place names and dates, until Welles introduced the technique of narration in *Citizen Kane* (1941) and *The Magnificent Ambersons* (1942).

Of these two films, *Kane* has always received the greater attention, partly for its controversial treatment of an almost legendary figure in American publishing and politics, partly for its unique four-part story construction, and partly for the bold new look imparted by Gregg Toland's needle-sharp, deep focus photography—its style. Certainly, the film was experimental in the extreme, not only in its innovative uses of sound, but in its ingenious combination of camera and matte shots to create the illusion of vast spaces, and in its dramatic lighting that kept large portions of the screen in darkness while isolating a face, a hand, a lighted window or a crystal globe. Welles was equally entranced by extreme angles and extreme close-ups, with his actors—most of them veterans from his Mercury Theater—often playing directly into the camera. But while the close-ups invariably heightened the su-

perb performances, the angle shots tended to draw attention
to themselves in a disturbing manner. There is a scene, for
example, in *The Inquirer* office in which Jed Leland (Joseph
Cotten), slightly inebriated, asks Kane to transfer him to the
Chicago paper. It's very impressive, with Kane looming head
to foot off to one side of the frame while Leland weaves
toward him down the length of the room. The camera, fixed
within inches of Kane's heel, pivots with Leland as he approaches until both characters tower over us. And then you
ask, why? From whose point of view are we watching this
civilized parting of friends who will never be friends again—
Archie, the ubiquitous cockroach? This shot, and many like
it—such as the memorable traveling shot from the stage of
the Chicago Opera up, up, up into the flies where two stage-
hands solemnly hold their noses in criticism of the performance below—may be visually stimulating and extremely
clever; but lacking either physical or psychological motivation, the ultimate effect is shallow and pretentious.

However, if *Citizen Kane* suffered from an excess of experimentation, it also was strengthened by it, and its impact
has increased with the years. Pauline Kael has called it "a
freak of art"—and well it may be. Like *The Cabinet of Dr.
Caligari* of so many years ago, one can point to no films that
derived from it directly. Thanks to its unique plot structure, it
would have been a difficult film to emulate in any case—at
least, not without plagiarism suits in the offing. On the other
hand, its indirect effect upon the industry has been enormous.
Toland's photography, building on the extraordinary effects
that he had already created in *The Grapes of Wrath*, proved
the ultimate blow to the diffused, romantic style that Hollywood cameramen had inherited from the German invasion.
After *Kane*, unless they were working in the romantic tradition (i.e., *Casablanca* or *Now, Voyager*, both 1942),
cameramen gravitated toward the sharp, deep, wide-angled
photography of Toland, with its sense of a hard-edged realism. The editing, entrusted to youthful veteran Robert Wise
(long before his directorial debut), set new models of
economy. In one memorable transition, the banker Thatcher
(George Coulouris) says directly to young Charles Kane,
"Merry Christmas." There is a pause, then the voice continues, "and a happy New Year!"—only now it is a dozen years
later, and a very disgruntled Thatcher is dictating his rather
tart good wishes to a secretary. Another high point of the

film is the scene at the breakfast table, encapsulating in less
than three minutes the disintegrating relationship between
Kane and his socialite wife, Emily (Ruth Warwick). Years
are reduced to seconds as the camera swish-pans from one
end of the ever-lengthening table to the other, indicative of
their growing estrangement. In both instances, it should be
noted, writing, direction and editing all work together; for all
their precision, neither effect could have been accomplished
were they not the final link in a conceptual chain.

Similarly, one listens in amazement to the virtuosity of
Bernard Herrmann's score. Herrmann, who also had worked
with Welles in his radio days, opens the film with a series of
ominous chords that link together (and all but conceal the
transitions between) a long series of shots as the camera rises
from outside the gates of Kane's Xanadu castle and moves
across the grounds and up its walls to a single lighted window
in the highest turret. Music here serves as a kind of mucil-
lage, binding together the separate shots on the audio level
just as firmly as they are linked visually through lap dissolves.
A few moments later, it's "NEWS ON THE MARCH!", and
Herrmann launches into a zestful parody of the old *March of
Time* logo, heavy with brasses and drums. When Kane buys
out the staff of the rival *Chronicle*, he throws a big party,
complete with chorines who chant a lively ditty, "Oh, Mr.
Kane," which is heard in adroit variations throughout the
film—most notably in bitter mockery after Kane has been defeated in his bid for political office. The "Rosebud" theme,
first heard when young Charles is playing with his sled in the
snow while Thatcher is negotiating arrangements for his future, recurs during Kane's first encounter with Susan Alexander (he was on his way, he later explains, "in search of my
youth—a sort of sentimental journey"). And it is heard
again, of course, under the roaring fires of Xanadu's furnace
in the final sequence. As in radio, many of Herrmann's cues
are quite short, merely transitional phrases bridging the emotional temperature of one sequence to the climate of the next,
yet he also provided the opulent music for *Salambo*, the opera that was Susan Alexander's undoing.

Produced for about $750,000, *Citizen Kane* was a disap-
pointment to its studio. It broke even on its initial engagements, but no more than that. Despite critical raves and
several Academy nominations, Welles ended up with half an
Oscar for his share of the script (the other half went to co-

writer Herman J. Mankiewicz). Certainly, the Hearst press was no help; it refused to print ads, publicity or even reviews of the film. But more important, at a time when the big audience in America was still the small-town, grass-roots moviegoer, *Kane* proved a chill and forbidding experience, cold, objective and intellectual. Welles had so distanced all his characters that the kind of empathy most moviegoers then expected of a picture was totally lacking. They might be impressed, but they were rarely moved. Needless to say, *Citizen Kane* has gone on to have a second life unlike any film in motion picture history. But for Welles, it was too little and too late. For his second production, he was ordered by his studio to be less experimental. Accordingly, he scrapped the version of Joseph Conrad's *Heart of Darkness* he had been preparing (apparently with a first person singular, subjective camera), and went to work on an adaptation of Both Tarkington's moderately well-known novel, *The Magnificent Ambersons.*

Although *The Magnificent Ambersons* may look like a more conventional movie than *Citizen Kane,* actually it is no less inventive—but in subtler, more cinematic ways. Unfortunately, it is impossible to speak of *Ambersons* as a complete film. The Tarkington novel was a shrewd study of the disintegration of a Midwestern "first family" under the impact of the rising industrial aristocracy around 1910, and the original script—almost identical in length with *Kane*'s—indicates that Welles had filmed it with emphasis both on character and on social background. But bad relations between him and a new administration at RKO resulted in the picture's being taken away from his Mercury Productions unit soon after shooting was completed, while the film was still being edited. The studio reduced his footage to a shorter, "more commerical" picture than he had envisioned, and caused a new, more sentimental ending to be shot (for which Welles has never forgiven anyone involved). Cutting for story, RKO eliminated scenes calculated to prepare the audience for major changes in the characters, as well as much of the material showing the physical and social transformation of the town itself. What remains is there because it was essential for purposes of continuity. Still, it is enough to reveal much of Welles' intention and Welles' technique.

The picture opens with an adroit sequence designed to both establish the period and to introduce the leading characters of the film. Over Welles' witty narration we see, almost cartoon-fashion, the styles, the customs and the way of life in a small town at the turn of the century. He refers to "that prettiest of all vanished customs—the serenade," and we see a slightly intoxicated Eugene Morgan (Joseph Cotten) with a group of musicians courting Isabel Amberson (Dolores Costello)—awkwardly falling into his own bass viol. Next, Welles talks about the stovepipe hats then in fashion, and shows another suitor, Wilbur Miniffer, wearing one as he rows Isabel on a quiet lake. And a moment later we learn from the narration that Isabel is going to marry Wilbur even though she really loves Eugene. Thus, three minutes into the film, the background, the principals and the central situation have all been brought before the audience, presented with the unique economy made possible by Welles' voice-over narration. Welles uses it again at several points in the picture to give insight into character, and to comment upon the changing social scene or upon the action itself.

In radio, Welles had developed a special montage technique using a crescendo of voices, each speaking a sentence or sometimes merely a fragment of a sentence. This he carried over into film, photographing the various speakers in close-ups of one or two against a blank background. Spliced together in quick succession, the shots gave the impression of a whole town talking—and, no less important, what the whole town was talking about. Welles even altered traditional dialogue techniques to create a more vivid, more realistic sense of natural speech patterns. It has long been a stage—and now a movie—convention to permit one character to complete a speech before the next begins to reply. Actual conversations, of course, rarely progress in this orderly fashion. One person speaks and then, often before he has finished the sentence, the listener breaks in with his own reply. In a roomful of people, no one would dream of remaining silent until one person has completed his observations. Numerous conversations take place simultaneously, overlapping one another, often drowning out one another. Welles, after seeking to reproduce this effect in radio, found it even more suitable for films, where the source of the words is always visible. He had toyed with the device a bit in *Citizen Kane,* as in the sequence when Boss Gettys (Ray Collins) tells off Kane before his wife and his mistress. In *The Magnificent Ambersons* it became an important element in building the reality of his

scenes and his people. The farewells after the last great ball
at the Amberson mansion, the tired jumble of voices arguing,
questioning, nagging as the Ambersons prepare for bed, the
spontaneous gaiety of a family outing in the snow—all of
these came alive through Welles' naturalistic use of normal
speech patterns. In his drive to get this same kind of naturalism from his performers he sometimes went to extremes.
Thus he made Agnes Moorehead repeat and repeat her long
climactic scene of near hysteria until what the camera finally
captured was no longer an actress acting, but a woman literally on the verge of hysterics.

In camera techniques, Welles proved more eclectic than
original—understandably, since he put himself through an intensive series of viewing sessions of the classic films in New
York's Museum of Modern Art collection before leaving for
Hollywood in 1940, then actually stepped up the process
upon his arrival on the Coast. His sources were the best.
Welles himself has expressed his admiration for John Ford's
clean, lean economy in shooting, and Pauline Kael has
pointed out some startling stylistic similarities between Karl
Freund's *Mad Love* (1935) and *Kane* (both of them photographed by Gregg Toland). Von Stroheim seems to have
been peering over his shoulder as Welles conceived the long
carriage ride through the town's main street in *Ambersons,*
the camera catching the reflection of buildings and people on
the other side of the street in the polished shop windows, to
create an extraordinary sense of the three-dimensional reality
of the town itself. The many lingering lap dissolves are reminiscent of von Sternberg. There is even one long, slow iris-out
in *Ambersons* that reveals his familiarity with the work of
Griffith. Between Welles' highly original use of sound and
imaginative use of the camera, he established an exciting integration of the two—a cinematic style rooted in naturalism,
economy and theatrical flair. Seen today, *The Magnificent
Ambersons* seems, if anything, more impressive than when it
first appeared. The gradual absorption of the techniques that
it introduced has removed some of its strangeness, and time
itself the taint of intellectuality that repelled great sections of
the public back in 1942. Its artistry is clearer now, even
though—like von Stroheim's *Greed*—the film is an emascu-
lated version of what its director had intended.

Welles' subsequent film work has never lived up to his
early promise, and while he continues to find money on occa-

sion to direct a project of his own, he is far more familiar to-day as an actor and television personality than as the man behind the camera. Even so, much that he experimented with in the early forties—the voice-over narration, deep-focus photography, overlapping dialogue, sound perspectives, a functional use of music—has today become common practice, as the cameramen, editors, composers, even the producers who worked with Welles absorbed his techniques and ideas, and carried them along to their subsequent endeavors. Welles as a director may no longer be a major force, but his contributions to the medium continue through the men he trained and influenced.

One thing more: while the film makers of the thirties were diligently expanding the art of the film, the technicians were no less diligently developing the technology. Microphones were made more directional, more critical, less prone to pick up extraneous sounds. Recording very quickly became "noise-less," suppressing the background hiss that came from the grain of the film stock (which was also improved). Inconceivably, there was actually a time when editors had to work without Moviolas, or even sound readers, although this was soon rectified. But the greatest advances lay in the development of the mixing panel. Rouben Mamoulian recalls the reluctance of the early sound technicians to let him use two sources of sound for a certain scene in *Applause* (1929). The modern mixing panel can easily accommodate fifty such channels, with between thirty and forty the norm. Three men generally split the task of mixing the track between them— certain channels for dialogue, others for the dubbed dialogue, others for music, sound effects, background noise, whatever. With all of this at his command, the director can synthesize a sound track just as effectively as he synthesizes his picture out of innumerable short shots. Back in the twenties, we spoke of the subjective camera. By the late thirties, it became possible to speak of subjective sound.

For sound *is* a subjective thing, apprehended on the lowest threshold of consciousness. If one lives near a subway or a beach, the sounds of the trains or the waves may keep you awake for the first few nights, but gradually they become so much a part of the environment that their absence becomes far more disturbing than their presence. And have you ever really listened to a quiet room? There is the steady hum of the air conditioner or the occasional rattle of the radiator, the sound of distant traffic, a voice or footsteps heard in another part of the house. One focuses on what he wants to hear and eliminates the rest—until it forces itself upon him. Imagine that you are walking down a street, deeply engrossed in conversation with a friend. You aren't in the least aware of the street's traffic noises, the footfalls of other pedestrians or even the passing snatches of their conversations because you are concentrating on what your friend is saying. But suddenly, still in this conversation, you step from the curb and a cab screeches to a halt within inches of your ankle. You hear that screech—and no doubt the cabbie's immediate stream of abuse and the irate honk of his horn. If your friend was still trying to make his point, you probably missed it.

This is what the mixing panel can accomplish. It can suppress those background noises as the conversation continues. It can itensify the screech of the brakes, the honking, the driver's obscenities. And if your friend is still talking through all of this, it can make sure that the audience hears none of his words of wisdom—at least, no more than one would himself hear under the given circumstances. With total control over dozens of separate channels, the director can orchestrate his sound track to correspond to our psychological perception of sound. As with the visuals, sound becomes selective, manipulable, and hence has at least the potential of becoming a creative art. By the time Orson Welles appeared on the scene, most of the technical problems involved in this process had been worked out. (In this context, it's worth remembering that Walt Disney's *Fantasia,* with its multichanneled stereophonic sound, appeared in 1940—the year before *Citizen Kane.*) But it was Welles, with his background in radio, who first grasped the full capabilities of the sound track, and what it could add to a movie.

With the appearance of *Citizen Kane* and *The Magnificent Ambersons,* the incessant exploration of the resources of the camera and microphone that characterized the best films of the thirties came to a close. The pioneer days of sound were over. In little more than a decade directors everywhere had achieved a technical mastery that made them far less self-conscious in their search for "effect." Soon, in the work of men like Vittorio de Sica and David Lean, John Huston and Elia Kazan, one could discern the growing maturity of the medium. And because their films have won international acclaim, such directors have influenced the work and the think-

ing of film directors throughout the world. In their personal
styles and techniques are to be found the creative potentialities of the art of the sound film.

It is important to recognize that this absorption process is
constantly taking place, since it accounts for the steadily improving technical quality of the movies that we see. But it is
also necessary to realize that sheer technique does not produce inspired films. There must exist as well a love for the
medium, the urge to create, to communicate, and the talent
to do so with flair, discipline and imagination. In short, the
creative impulses behind all artistic endeavor are more important than technical facility in the production of a great
movie. There must be the single-minded vigor that once produced a *Birth of a Nation* or *Greed*, a *Modern Times* or *Citizen Kane*. Today, with hordes of specialists and experts each
anxious to contribute his own bit of technical perfection to a
picture, its identity is constantly in danger of being diluted,
watered down to a characterless average. And there lurks the
even greater danger that as film making grows more expensive and more departmentalized, the purely pragmatic interests of the box office will take precedence over all other
impulses behind film production. Certainly, in motion pictures the *vox populi* cannot safely be ignored; but neither can
the industry devote itself single-mindedly to the slavish repeti-
tion of proven box-office hits. Audiences soon tire of mere
technique, while the medium thrives and grows on the efforts
and accomplishments—even the box-office failures—of the
genuinely creative artist.

✦ 5 ✦

International Trends

American movies learned to talk with a sound that was heard around the world. To ensure their monopoly of the field, the great American electrical industries bought up the basic patents on existing, competing sound systems both here and abroad, and entered into trade agreements with those firms they could not buy out. With world-wide control assured, they lost no time in marketing their equipment to the European studios and theaters. As a result, sound on film soon became the standard system for talkies all over the world. And because the equipment everywhere was basically the same, the international exchange of films—and filmic ideas—could continue. Despite the language barrier, a French film could be run on German equipment, a Russian film on an American projector. Film makers could still learn from one another, profiting from advances in both the technique and the technology of the new medium. And a curious thing began to happen. The techniques of sound rapidly became standardized throughout the world. The stylistic differences that distinguished a French or Russian film from a Hollywood movie during the silent era virtually disappeared. National differences after sound are to be found less in style than in the emerging themes that, directly or indirectly, revealed each country's reactions to such world-wide crises as the depression, the Second World War and the difficult years of postwar reconstruction. The Cold War, Indonesia, Algeria and the emergence of the Third World nations provided the political backdrop for the new dramas as film became less a tool than a weapon.

France: Uncertainty and Despair

The arrival of sound in France had a disastrous effect upon its film industry. The new equipment was prohibitively expensive, but the studios had to have it if they were to stay in business. Wily investors seized upon this opportunity to gain control, buying into established companies solely to exploit them. With representatives of the banks, investment houses and equipment manufacturers sitting on their boards, the French studios quickly lost the spirit of independence and individuality that had distinguished their films during the twenties. The pictures that streamed from Gaumont, Pathé and French Paramount during the first years of sound were the cheapest kind of all-talking potboilers. To utilize the new equipment to the full, the same film was shot over and over again in different languages with different casts, but with the same settings and often the same director. Under such conditions, many of the better directors of the silent era simply withdrew from films, or left for studios in America and England. Only René Clair and a handful of others—Jean Benoît-Lévy, Julien Duvivier, Jean Renoir—had the combination of ability and tenacity to bring to the screen any truly distinguished works. And in 1934 even Clair departed, driven out by the cumulative clouds of the depression and political interference.

But all was not lost, for in the meantime two new figures emerged, men whose sharply contrasting viewpoints and techniques provided the main sources of inspiration for all subsequent French production. One was the youthful Jean Vigo, whose strong feeling for imagery, for atmosphere and milieu characterized the best French films during their brief period of optimism between 1935 and 1937, and through the long night of despair and tragedy as France fell under the shadow of World War II. Vigo's strange, almost surrealist approach to the medium found expression in only two pictures, *Zéro de Conduite* (1933) and *L'Atalante* (1934). He had a poet's instinct for the expressive symbol, for the beauty of the unexpected, for the intensity of an emotion captured in a single apt image. *Zéro de Conduite*, a nightmarish recollection of his youth in a boarding school, is filled with grotesques—the dwarfed school supervisor, the angular headmaster spying like a cat on the activities of his young charges, a pillow fight in the dormitories staged in slow motion. Similarly, in *L'Atalante*, a slight story woven around a riverbarge owner and his wife, Vigo derives a curiously nostalgic poetry from the drab industrial outskirts of Paris—the tangle of railway tracks and electric wires, its misty waterfront bars and boarding houses. In mood and atmosphere, in sensitivity to the nuances of milieu, his work clearly foreshadows Marcel Carné's sympathetic studies of haunted, tragic lives in the great era of the French sound film that lay just ahead. But Vigo was never to see that era; he died in poverty at the age of 29.

So completely did Vigo create his effects with the camera that one recalls his pictures almost as silent films. At the opposite extreme was the playwright Marcel Pagnol, first attracted to the medium by the successful filming of his satiric comedy *Topaze* (1932). Working for French Paramount, he wrote and supervised the filming of his famed trilogy *Marius* (1932), *Fanny* (1932) and *César* (1933), directing the last himself. Although strenuously attacked by critics of the day for what they termed a reversion to the theatrical style of the Film d'Art, Pagnol's witty and literate dialogue, the veracity of his Marseilles types and the heart-warming performances of his cast—Raimu, Pierre Fresnay, Orane Demazis and Charpin—immediately won for his pictures a wide popularity. Pagnol readily admitted that he used the camera primarily as a means of shifting the scene, but he introduced concepts of characterization and standards of filmic dialogue that soon exerted a strong influence upon the work of other French writers and directors. The best of the French sound films became, in fact, a fusion of Vigo's haunting imagery with Pagnol's pungent, thought-provoking dialogue and fully realized characters. But it took a second crisis in the French film industry to bring this about.

By the end of 1934, all the big studios in France had closed their doors, ruined by the depression and by the corruption and mismanagement of the people who had run the industry since sound. Prudently, Pagnol took the profits from his films and plays and opened his own studio near his beloved Marseilles, where he continued to function creatively until his death in 1974. For the less fortunate film workers, however, there was only panic, unemployment, possibly the end of all film production in France. Their salvation—indeed, the regeneration of the French film—came from the most unexpected source. In place of the few major studios, there suddenly appeared dozens of self-styled producers, promoters hoping to profit from the chaos by raising the capital to make independent productions. And by some miracle, they not only got production going again, but the films were more creative than ever before. Although from all accounts many of these promoters were shady fly-by-night operators, they differed in one important respect from their well-entrenched predecessors. They had no committees, no boards of directors to pass upon the merits of a script, to decide what was commercially safe. They were satisfied if a director came to them with a script he wanted to do, and perhaps the promise of a star name who would appear in it—these were enough to go out and raise money on. Certainly, many an honest man was cheated of his francs in this way, many an artist worked for a salary that he never saw. But under these unlikely auspices the individuality, the creative independence of the director was returned to the French cinema. At that darkest moment in the history of the French film, its artists stood unwittingly on the brink of their own brief "Golden Era."

Events on the entire European scene were helping to pave the way. The new republic in Spain, the Italian invasion of Ethiopia, the unmistakable threat of Hitler's Germany after the Saar plebiscite had the effect of stirring up a profound national consciousness among the French. During 1935, as crisis followed crisis, the traditional divisions of French politics and the French people began to disappear, the liberal and Leftist elements drawing together in that optimistic amalgam known as the "Popular Front." A new confidence pervaded vast sections of the country, the feeling that by working together, by uniting and solving small differences men of goodwill could together build a better world. For the next two years, between 1935 and 1937, this optimism dominated the French films—Jacques Feyder's *Carnival in Flanders (La Kermesse Héroique,* 1935), Duvivier's *They Were Five (La Belle Equipe,* 1936) were almost allegorical in their presentation of the theme that concerted action could overcome any calamity. Other pictures demonstrated a new concern and solicitude for the common man, expressing the need for understanding, for compassion—Renoir's *Toni* (1935), and *La*

Grande Illusion (1937), Marc Allegret's *Heart of Paris* (*Gribouille*, 1935).

But quickly the tide began to change. In 1937 the "Popular Front" saw its hopes dashed in Spain; while the fateful Munich pact clearly foreshadowed the imminence of war, causing a paralysis throughout all of France, a sense of doom that was quickly reflected in her films. Pagnol, in pictures like *Harvest* (*Régain*, 1937) and *The Baker's Wife* (*La Femme du Boulanger*, 1938), counseled a return to the soil, to the simple values of a pastoral existence. But most of the directors, looking at the contemporary scene, saw only despair. Their concern for people remained, but the cheerful image of Jean Gabin joining with his friends to build a new life in *They Were Five* gave way to a Gabin, sullen and alone, awaiting death in his besieged hotel room of *Le Jour Se Léve* (1939). Suffering, suicide, sudden death—these themes became virtually the obsession of French film makers as the thirties drew to a close. Symptomatically, *La Marseillaise* (1938), undertaken by Renoir as the "official film" of the "Popular Front," emerged as perhaps his weakest work. Planned during the period of optimism and realized when disillusion and fear were sitting in, it expressed the hope rather than the conviction that France would reunite and, with the strength of a united people, combat the forces of fascism on all sides. Far more significant, at least in retrospect, was his *La Règle du Jeu* (1939), a brilliant, mordant study of a society poised on the brink of disaster. Set in a magnificent château in the Sologne, it is part comedy, part melodrama as houseguests and servants play out their social games oblivious to the world around them. Understandably, the pitiless honesty of the film made it a total disaster in its initial release. As Renoir later explained it, "People who commit suicide do not care to do it in front of witnesses." Rediscovered after the war, *The Rules of the Game* is now recognized as one of the major artistic triumphs of the French cinema, if not indeed of the world cinema. But by that time, Renoir had fled his beloved country and launched a new career in Hollywood.

Throughout the five years of German occupation, the French studios continued to make films, although many of her best talents—Renoir, Duvivier, Benoît-Lévy, Feyder—had left the country. Those who remained held themselves notably aloof from contemporary themes, finding a kind of spiritual refuge in the past. Where Marcel Carné's *Port of Shadows* (*Quai des Brumes*, 1938) and *Le Jour Se Lève* reflected with grim reality the paralysis that gripped all of France as war drew near, his wartime *Visiteurs du Soir* (1942) and *Les Enfants du Paradis* (1945) were stylized allegories of death and despair set against the romantic backgrounds of bygone days. Scores of films used the old graceful châteaux, far from the realities of the occupation, as settings for medieval stories tinged with melancholy mysticism and somber fantasy—*Le Baron Fantôme* (1943), *La Fiancée des Ténèbres* (1944), *Sylvie et le Fantôme* (1945). Even Jean Cocteau, returning to the film medium more than a dozen years after his boldly experimental *Blood of a Poet* (*Sang d'un Poéte*, 1930), remained scrupulously in the past with his coldly handsome rendering of the Tristan legend, *L'Eternel Retour* (1943) and his sophisticated adaptation of *Beauty and the Beast* (1946). Lesser talents concerned themselves with pure trivia—a few comedies, a few musicals, many romances.

Of all the films from this period, only Henri-Georges Clouzot's *The Raven* (*Le Corbeau*, 1943) dealt in any way directly and searchingly with the contemporary scene. Devoid of all political reference, it was a melodrama based on the disintegrating effect of a series of poison-pen letters upon a small French town. But because he depicted the community in something less than ideal terms—at a time when national feeling was running particularly high—and because the Germans undertook to distribute the picture outside France under the unflattering title of *A Little French Town*, Clouzot was accused of being pro-German. Once the Nazis had left, his picture was banned and Clouzot himself barred from working for several years. Not until the tides of national feeling had somewhat abated could it be seen that Clouzot was neither pro-German nor anti-French, but anti-human. Such subsequent efforts as *The Wages of Fear* (*Salaire de la Peur*, 1935) and *Les Diaboliques* (1955) reveal that fundamentally his mastery lies in exploiting the basest instincts and most sordid elements to produce his brilliantly cinematic effects of shock, surprise and revulsion.

Throughout the decade following World War II, the French film industry became without question the most chaotic and disorganized in Europe. Suffering chronically from lack of funds, aided spasmodically by the constantly shifting governments, many of the producers then sought to stabilize their operations by turning out nothing but Eddie Constantine imitations of American gangster films, sex plays starring Martine Carol or Brigitte Bardot, and sordid, sensational melodramas patterned after the worst of the Italian neo-realist school. Still others found reassurance in a return to the earlier, literary style of film making based on popular or distinguished novels—*Symphonie Pastorale* (1946), *Devil in the Flesh* (*Le Diable au Corps*, 1947), *L'Idiot* (1947) and the movie versions of Colette's collected works. Nor did the image of the haunted, suffering individual altogether disappear from the French screen, as may be seen in such films as *The Walls of Malapaga* (1949), *Casque d'Or* (1952) and *The Proud and the Beautiful* (*Les Orgueilleux*, 1954). But these were holdovers from the past, a past that was already under attack by the vigorous young critics on the staff of *Les Cahiers du Cinéma*, a past that was soon to be buried by them as, toward the end of the fifties, they relinquished their typewriters in favor of the camera and formed a *"Nouvelle Vague"* for the French cinema.

What also survived, despite war and political chaos, is the strong individuality of the best French film makers. One finds it, for example, in the eccentric, highly personal comedies of Jacques Tati—*The Big Day* (*Jour de Fête*, 1949) *M. Hulot's Holiday* (1953) and *Mon Oncle* (1958)—done with the kind of pantomime humor once so distinctively Clair's. It is heartening too that such fresh and original talents as René Clément, Robert Bresson, Jacques Becker and Nicole Vedrès were also able to work, even though their output has been limited. Despite the extremely cautious financing behind most French films, they have still on occasion found the backing necessary for such daring and distinctive pictures as *Farrébique* (1946), *Life Begins Tomorrow* (*La Vie Commence Demain*, 1950), *Diary of a Country Priest* (*Journal d'un Curé du Campagne*, 1951) and *Forbidden Games* (*Jeux Interdits*, 1952). And then, of course, there are the remnants of the old guard, the men for whom individuality has always been a banner. Jean Cocteau continued to pursue his independent way right up to his death in 1963, turning chameleon-like from the rich brocades of *Beauty and the Beast* to the highly theatrical *Les Parents Terribles* (1948) and then the completely cinematic, elusive *Orpheus* (1950). Sacha Guitry, until his death in 1957, continued in the special style he had chosen for himself long before the fall of France—facile, witty, and more loquacious than ever. Above all, after a Hollywood hiatus René Clair returned to his native land as a personification of the continuity of the best in France's cinematic tradition. His *Beauty and the Devil* (1949), *Beauties of the Night* (1952) and *Gates of Paris (Porte des Lilas,* 1957) reveal a mellower talent, one that is as gay and inventive, as graceful and charming as before, but with a new seriousness and thoughtfulness in his themes. Such works remind us that the true greatness of French film making is still to be found in those directors who regard their medium as primarily a means of personal expression—and in those producers who can still think in terms of a single picture rather than an entire year's "product."

Germany: Films for Propaganda

Even while the German studios were converting to sound in 1929, the danger flags were flying. The National Socialists had already gained a considerable foothold in the Reichstag through the elections of 1928, while the dominant Social Democratic party had sunk into an apathy that was soon to prove disastrous. With the collapse of the stock market in America, the loans on which Germany had been subsisting since 1924 abruptly ceased and, as factory after factory closed its doors, the German people entered upon that period of unemployment and misery that paved the way for Hitler in 1933. The Social Democrats looked on with helpless neutrality while Communists sought to incite the masses to a Russian-style revolution or Nazis brought forward the mystic slogan of "blood and fatherland"—the promise of a better life for all who believed in Hitler and the glorious destiny of the German people. Those who refused to believe had a foretaste of things to come in the bitter street fighting between Communists and Nazis in the years 1930-1933. The Nazis, backed by some of Germany's biggest industrialists, had a program that knowingly exploited many of the deepest fears and dreams of the German people; the other parties wasted their strength by fighting within and between their ranks.

Throughout this period, with its forebodings, its sudden flareups of violence, its nightmare terrors of hunger and poverty, the German screen grimly mirrored the sequence of events. *The Blue Angel* (1930), for example, is virtually a tour de force of sustained sadism. Its schoolboys might be

Hitlerjugend in their heartless persecution of the professor, the professor himself a symbol of the old authority that had to be destroyed to make way for the new. More explicit reflections of the times were to be found in the many films in which unemployment served as either the background or the springboard for the central situation. The hero, frequently jobless or at best a sidewalk vendor, passes through a series of sordid adventures not unlike those in the "street films" of an earlier era—only this time there is no snug, safe parlor for him to go back to. In innumerable wishful romances and comedies, an impoverished or unemployed youth is transformed into a fabulously successful businessman through the touchstones of a little luck and the right girl. Even the musical comedies reflected the depression. In the popular *Three from the Filling Station* (*Drei von der Tankstelle*, 1930), a trio of bankrupt young men sell their car, buy a gas station, then blithely begin their melodious pursuit of Lillian Harvey. But the depression was not to be whistled away. As an antidote to the growing despair, contemporary dramas solemnly counseled submission and patience, while the incessant mountain films offered their Aryan heroes escape from the world's problems through an arduous climb high above the clouds.

As for quality, the German films of this era seem to have suffered less from the addition of sound than those of other lands. The best directors continued to put the emphasis on imagery rather than on dialogue, and the mobility of the camera was only temporarily impaired. Such men as Pabst, Fritz Lang and Max Ophuls all demonstrated a sustained interest in the emotional and symbolic content of the shot, never permitting their pictures to degenerate to the level of the "100% all-talkie" so prevalent elsewhere. In films like Pabst's *Westfront 1918* (1930) and *Die Dreigroschenoper* (1930), or Lang's *M* (1931), one finds already an impressive integration of sound with the visuals that was decidedly advanced for the time. Even Leontine Sagan's *Mädchen in Uniform* (1931), although adapted from a play, avoided the stigma of "canned theater" through sensitive use of the camera. There is a striking visual contrast between the innocence of Hertha Thiele, dressed always in white and photographed against light backgrounds, and the harsh, black-robed head of the school; while ominous, recurrent shots of the deep stair well in the institution dramatically foreshadow the film's final tragedy. In the early German

musicals as well, although scarcely scintillating when seen today, one still notes with considerable pleasure such inventions
as the flight of the two butterflies across a hundred years of
musical history at the opening of *Zwei Herzen im Dreiviertel
Takt* (1930), on the ballet of the chairs in Eric Charrell's
Congress Dances (1931).

As the depression deepened over Germany and the menace
of Nazism became more apparent, a few films were made
that seemed to take a positive stand against the growing reaction and rampant nationalism. Victor Trivas's *Hell on Earth
(Niemandsland,* 1931) was an ingeniously contrived anti-war
drama. Five soldiers—a German, a Frenchman, an Englishman, a Negro and a Jew—are trapped together in a bomb
crater between the two opposing armies of World War I. In
their enforced isolation, they learn to respect one another and
their common ambition for peace. But the war brings them
death instead, and the film ends with the shadow image of
the five marching together in double exposure across the bat-
tlefield—a vague assertion of internationalism somewhat ne-
gated by the fact that its protagonists are all dead. Slatan
Dudow's *Kühle Wampe* (1932) turned directly to the contemporary scene to study the effects of the depression on the
German working class, detailing with considerable vigor the
ceaseless search for jobs, the evictions, the suicides. Stronger
than any film of this era, it presented the Communist viewpoint, but its climax offered no solution to the multiple difficulties of its characters beyond the ambiguous statement that
"we must keep on fighting, ever advancing . . ."

Most impressive of all was G. W. Pabst's *Kameradschaft*
(1931), the story of a mine disaster on the frontier between
France and Germany, with German miners picking their way
to the entrapped Frenchmen through an underground tunnel
abandoned since the war. In it the theme of the international
solidarity of workers is underscored—"Miners are miners,"
the Germans say in explaining their willingness to risk their
lives to save their former enemies. Further, the workers must
persuade the mine owners to permit them to form their rescue parties and use the mine's equipment, a permission that is
granted with obvious reluctance. All of this Pabst detailed
with superb realism, particularly in his scenes of the subterranean terrors of a mine cave-in. But there is also a curious
coldness about the film, a remoteness suggesting that Pabst
was not above maneuvering scenes to fit Socialist theory. In

the finale there are speeches made in favor of international brotherhood by both the French and the German miners, but despite this the underground frontier barrier, torn down by the Germans to reach their French comrades, is gravely replaced by the officials of both nations. There is a special irony in the fact that the German working class, to which *Kameradschaft* was primarily addressed, stayed away from the film in droves.

Such films, with their combination of progressive sentiments and skilled use of the sound camera, were greeted in this country with considerable critical enthusiasm. At a time when the American film was still wrestling with the problem of sound, many of the pictures from Germany demonstrated that talk need not dominate the visual elements when the sound track is handled in a genuinely creative way. It can be seen today, however, that for all their skill with the medium, for all their apparent progressivism, these pictures and their makers had unwittingly been caught up in the storm that was sweeping across Germany. The gestures that seemed noble and brave, the sentiments that sounded boldly radical were in fact so vague, so remote from the realities of the situation— so intellectual at a time when Hitler was capturing the emotions and the imagination of the masses—that they proved pitifully inadequate as tools against the Nazis. Such were the films of dissent, the strongest outcries of protest. But they were not strong enough, nor were there enough of them, to turn the rising tide. The dissenters, taking their hint from the elections early in 1933, escaped whenever possible to other lands. There were concentration camps for the less fortunate.

No sooner had the Hitler régime come to power than it sought to force the German film industry to reflect the Nazi ideology in every way. It is said that one of Propaganda Minister Goebbels's first moves was to call together the heads of the various German studios and run off for them a print of Eisenstein's *Potemkin*. "Gentlemen," he announced when the lights came on, "that's an idea of what I want from you." What he got was a *Hans Westmar* 1934), so blatantly propagandistic that it had to be sent back for extensive revision before Goebbels could permit its release; or films like *Hitlerjunge Quex* (1933) and *SA-Mann Brand* (1934) which delivered their message so unsubtly that not even the most ardent Nazis were completely taken in. Goebbels changed his tack. After the first year or so of the Nazi rule, outright po-

litical propaganda became increasingly rare in the entertainment films. True, there were occasional "hate" films—hate
the British (*Oom Paul*, 1939), hate the Jews (*Jud Süss*,
1940)—but for the most part he was content to have the
studios turn out old-fashioned, sentimental "waltz dreams,"
the ever-popular stories of mountain climbers and military
comedies, and an occasional stiff, expensively mounted historical film recalling the pomp and splendor of Imperial Germany.

On the other hand, every theater was required to include in
its program an officially prepared newsreel and supplemen-
tary documentary shorts. It was through these ingeniously, in-
sidiously clever renderings of the "realities" of the Nazi
world that Goebbels sought, and held, the German mind and
soul. By 1939 his newsreels were often as much as forty
minutes long. But the crowning achievement of the Nazi film
makers was their documentaries. Repugnant as they are to
American eyes, it is impossible not to marvel at the technical
brilliance and subtle cunning that produced them. Made under the supervision of Leni Riefenstahl, who had progressed
from a mediocre actress in the pre-Hitler era to an able director and brilliant editor, they penetrated all aspects of Nazi
life—top echelon party meetings, Göring's new air force, the
land army, the Olympic Games. Perhaps best known and
most impressive is the massive three-hour spectacle *Triumph
of the Will* (1936), ordered by Hitler himself as a film
record of the first Party convention at Nuremberg. Every aspect of the historic meeting—the incessant parades, the impassioned oratory, the drilling of troops, their massed sports,
even their mass feedings—was captured by cameras that
seemed to be everywhere. Some thirty photographers covered
the event, and nothing was spared to ensure them strategic
positions. For ultimately, both Goebbels and Hitler realized,
the enthusiasm of the Party members at Nuremberg was less
important than the transmission of that enthusiasm to the
millions of ordinary Germans everywhere who would see the
film in their theaters. And there is no escaping the conclusion
that *Triumph of the Will* had an almost hysterical effect upon
its audiences with its endless torchlight parades, its close-ups
of speaker after speaker, its rank on rank of Brown Shirts
and Black Shirts listening transfixed before bursting out on
signal with a roaring *"Sieg Heil!"* To the jaundiced eye, all of
this may add up to a spectacle at once bewildering and

wearying. Not even the most prejudiced observer, however, can fail to respond to the almost mystic power of the first reel as Hitler flies in his airplane over the waiting city, an ancient god about to walk the earth among mere mortals; or the sequence in the stadium when Hitler and his top Party officials march down a lane of thousands on thousands of Nazi soldiers. One can only imagine the impact of such scenes upon a people who wanted fervently to believe in the godlike quality of their Führer, who had already elevated Nazism into a religion.

Nor were the Nazis satisfied simply to use the film to feed enthusiasm on the home front. Before long the German fact-film makers had become so adept at presenting their own version of reality that they could permit special editions of their pictures to go abroad. In this fashion, even the Olympic Games provided fodder for the Goebbels propaganda machine: the brilliantly photographed and assembled footage for *Olympia* (1938) was prepared in different "friendly" versions for distribution to each of the participating nations, with generous footage allotted to all their winners—and the Nazi officials ever present as their smiling, sportsmanlike hosts. Later, when Hitler's long-promised "just" war became a frightful reality, cameramen accompanied the Stuka bombers and Panzer divisions as they slashed into Poland. The film record of this brief campaign, *Baptism of Fire (Feldzug in Polen,* 1940), was rushed through to celebrate the victory in every German theater; then, as Hitler's armies prepared to move successively against Denmark, Norway, Holland, Belgium, Romania and Yugoslavia, special versions of the same film were shown to the high officials of each of those countries, emphasizing the futility of resistance. *Victory in the West (Sieg im Westen,* 1941), a similar report on the fall of France, was shown not only in Germany but in France as well, underscoring the weaknesses of the "decadent" French as opposed to the health and might of the new order. Throughout the war years the German people were frequently reminded by Goebbels that pictures don't lie; and they were constantly being shown newsreels, documentaries and information films in which their final victory was made to seem inevitable. But behind the pictorial realism of these films was a corps of technicians especially trained in distorting and transforming reality into the official version of the "truth." Through editing, commentary and the skillful use of

sound the Nazis manipulated the screen as thoroughly and in-
sidiously as they manipulated the minds and souls of their
people.

World War II ended with a partitioned Germany, its two
halves divided by an ideological Iron Curtain that became
palpable with the erection of the infamous Wall in 1961.
West Berlin emerged as both the bastion and the showcase
of the Western democracies. As luck would have it, though,
the great German studios of Neubabelsberg lay in East Berlin, while DEFA was in Dresden; and the occupying Russians
lost no time in taking them over—along with control of Germany's famed Agfacolor process. They rapidly restored the
studios to operation by granting quick amnesties to the best
German film makers. Ironically, the very men who just a
short while before had been making pro-German films for the
Nazis were now making anti-Nazi films for the Russians. The
first pictures to come from this Eastern zone, like *Murderers
Among Us* (1946) and *Marriage in the Shadows* (1947),
were somber stories probing into Germany's war guilt or condemning Nazi atrocities committed both before and during
the war. As might almost be expected, there was a considerable amount of soul-searching realism in the treatment of
these dramatic themes. As the Russians tightened their grip
on East German studios (and ideologies) in the fifties, however, the accent came to fall on films that glorified the German Communists and their battles against the Nazis in the
years before Hitler. Such pictures as *Mother Courage*
(1955), based on a story by Bertolt Brecht, and Slatan
Dudow's *Stronger Than the Night* (1955) are representative
of this new line—and as crudely propagandist and unconvincing as the earlier Nazi film versions of these same events.
The withering concept of socialist realism sapped the creative
vitality of directors who, having survived one form of dictatorship, found themselves swamped in the increasingly restrictive ideologies of yet another. As in the other satellite nations,
the film makers in the East German studios found themselves
endlessly re-fighting the battles of World War II and warily
avoiding the socialist realities that surrounded them.

Denazification proceeded far more slowly in the West German zone, and film production there until comparatively recently—the late sixties—has been both halting and timid.
Despite the presence of Erich Pommer, the great executive

producer at Ufa before the Hitler era, the films that emerged for about two decades after the cessation of hostilities were distinguished primarily by their absence of any point of view whatsoever. Unlike their countrymen in the Eastern zone, the directors were free of the pressure of party lines and propagandist directives. At the same time, they could not help being aware of the surveillance of the Allied powers. As if fearful of offending anyone, the film makers seem to have deliberately excluded from their pictures subjects that might be controversial or even merely timely. Helmut Käutner's skillfully directed and brilliantly acted film *The Devil's General* (1955), for example, was considered exceptional for West Germany because it actually dared to show the debauchery and disenchantment of top Nazi officials during the last years of the war! Far more of the pictures relied on the old, familiar *genres*. The bitter-sweet musicals, the military romances and the heavy, elaborate historical pageants were all back again, and showing no signs of improvement. Some few films, like Victor Vicas's *Master Over Life and Death* (1955) and Harald Braun's *As Long as You're Near Me* (1955), suggested a growing technical proficiency in the West German studios. For the most part, however, the film makers in the democratic zone seemed unwilling or unable to deal in any but the most superficial terms with either the past or the present-day life of their country. It is as if the tragic history of the sound film in Germany had bequeathed to them a legacy of fear, the fear of using the medium significantly in yet another era of crisis and change. It took a whole new generation, spearheaded by the likes of Alexander Kluge, Rainer Werner Fassbinder, Werner Herzog and Volker Schoelndorff, to break out of this morass with films of considerable social insight and cinematic vigor. Unlike their predecessors, they seized upon film as the ideal medium to challenge and criticize the existing order, both moral and political. In such essays as Schloendorff's *The Lost Honor of Katharina Blum* (1975) or Fassbinder's *Mother Kuster's Trip to Heaven* (1976), the West German cinema suddenly emerged as just possibly the most eloquent and most daring exponent of humanist values in all the world.

Russia and the Satellites

Sound came late in the Soviet Union. Although two systems had been in the laboratory stages since 1926, the first
Russian talking picture, Nikolai Ekk's *The Road to Life*, did
not appear until 1931. In the meantime critics in Europe and
in the United States, recalling the bold, experimental silent
films of the late twenties, looked hopefully to the Russian
directors to rescue the new medium from the stagnation of
"canned theater" and stereotyped musicals. Many were aware
that both Pudovkin and Eisenstein had written and lectured
extensively about the possibilities of sound long before any
practical work could begin. Could their teachings inspire a
type of sound film as vigorous and eloquent as their classics
of the silent era? Could they clear a truly cinematic path
through the new, uncharted areas of sound? For a short time
it seemed quite possible. *The Road to Life*, despite its naïve
story of the regeneration of a group of "wild boys," was en-
couragingly creative in its use of the sound track. Subsequent
films like Dovzhenko's *Ivan* (1932) and *Frontier* (1935),
Dziga Vertov's *Three Songs About Lenin* (1934), and Pudovkin's *Deserter* (1933) freely explored the new medium,
particularly in the use of music, mass chants, choruses and
the orchestration of noise into expressive sound. They created
effects of stunning if somewhat mystifying complexity, seeking always to intensify the visuals through the sound track,
not simply to verify with sound what the visuals had already
shown. Even where they failed, as in the climax of *Deserter*
or the incessant declamations of *Three Songs About Lenin*,
they were still provocative. Many advanced the theory that
because the film in Russia was not motivated by the profit-
seeking evaluations of hard-headed businessmen, its directors
had greater artistic freedom than directors in any other country.

But if film making in Russia was not tied to the profit motive, it was hedged with other restraints that came into sudden prominence at the dawn of the sound era. One of the
aims of the first Five-Year Plan was to increase the amount
of projection equipment throughout the country. Within little
more than four years, between 1929 and 1932, the number of
projectors had trebled to 27,000, drastically altering the status
of the film in the Soviet Union. Through this rapid "kinefica-

tion" of the country a vast new audience was created for the Russian film; and as this audience increased, so too did the responsibility of the film makers. Unquestionably, such works as *Ten Days That Shook the World, The New Babylon* and *Arsenal* were overly sophisticated fare for a nation that was still composed in the main of a backward peasantry and illiterate laborers. But because of the film's expanding sphere of influence, Soviet critics began to raise charges of "formalism" against the leading directors, accusing them of carrying on artistic experiment for its own sake without concern for the motion picture as a medium of propaganda and education in a socialist society. In 1932, with the start of the second Five-Year Plan, film makers were pointedly asked, "What kind of propaganda is this that appeals only to intellectuals, that fails to communicate with the broadest masses of the people?" They were urged to turn away from their aesthetic games, their tinkering with technique, and come to grips with what their critics termed "socialist realism." By this they meant the creation of a simple, straightforward, naturalistic kind of realism—and one that corresponded more closely to the Communist Party's aims and objectives at any given moment.

The immediate requirement of the Russian film at this time was for a hero with whom the masses could identify readily—not the "mass hero" of Eisenstein or the symbolic hero of Dovzhenko, but a man of the people who would be easily recognizable as such. Sound suddenly made it possible for the scenarists and directors to create heroes who quite literally spoke the common language. Eschewing experimental forms and simplifying their stories, they concentrated on realism of background, dialogue and character. When toward the end of 1934 two young directors, the brothers Sergei and Grigori Vassiliev, presented their *Chapayev*, it proved to be just what the Soviet propaganda chiefs had in mind. It dealt in clear, often humorous, somewhat romantic terms with a Red guerrilla leader during Russia's civil war, a man of the people who led his peasant partisans to victory and became in turn a well-disciplined Bolshevik. Its popularity within the Soviet Union was enormous; and abroad as well, where its tremendous gusto, its exciting battle scenes and the charm of its hero, as played by Boris Babotchkin, earned for it both critical acclaim and a wide following. *Chapayev* set the pattern for the big Russian films of the late thirties, almost down to the outbreak of war. Such films as *We Are from Kronstadt* (1936), *Baltic Deputy* (1937) and the *Maxim* trilogy (1938-1940) all dealt with the experiences of men who became heroes in the revolutionary events of 1917-1919—and often died for their heroism.

It is interesting to note that in preparing these ideological films the directors of the thirties continued to turn back to the Revolution for their characters and their themes, even as the directors of the silent era had done. Perhaps the present was too drab to be suitably inspiring. Certainly, the few pictures of this era that dealt with contemporary subjects chose the more remote aspects of the Soviet scene—a team of geologists working in the arctic, the creation of an air city at the far end of Siberia, or the difficulties of bringing education to a distant Russian village. The problems of urban life, the proletarian dramas of factory and mill that one might expect to find mirrored with "socialist realism" on the Soviet screen, were scrupulously avoided. It is as if the Soviet film makers suspected what Goebbels had already discovered, that the fiction film resists the outright propagandist treatment of contemporary material. Since the Nazis had no past to utilize for this purpose, Goebbels was forced to reject the fiction forms entirely, resorting to a skillful manipulation of actuality through the documentary film to impress the German people with the justice and invincibility of their cause. The Russians, on the other hand, had a highly serviceable past. By returning to the era of the Revolution, they were able to use the fiction film to dramatize and keep alive the ardor and enthusiasm of those early days when both enemies and issues were sharply defined.

As the sound era progressed, films were cut more and more closely to the needs of political dogma and expediency. Indeed, the history of the Russian film has become increasingly a reflection of the zigs and the zags of the Party line as it changed under one pressure after another. After the 1935 meeting of the Communist Internationale, for example, the line was drastically altered. As Germany emerged more clearly as a threat to the Soviet Union, Stalin openly abandoned the dream of world-wide revolution to build in Russia the fortress of world Communism. Directors, suddenly encouraged to make films that would strengthen national pride, now looked back not only to the period of the Revolution but on beyond to the Russia of the czars—back to Peter the

Great, Alexander Nevsky, Ivan the Terrible, back to the great
Russian leaders like Suvorov, Admiral Nakhimov, Minin and
Pozharsky, men who had contributed to the unification and
aggrandizement of Imperial Russia. One after another they
trooped across the screen, but no longer were they wicked oppressors or the warlike representatives of a hated régime. To
fan the latent fires of Russian nationalism they had been transformed into folk heroes, the saviors of their country in time
of crisis, the men who had made Russia great. For a brief
period the Soviet screen glittered with the pomp and glory,
the opulence and riches of a world that the Communists
themselves had banished.

With the growing tension between Germany and Russia,
there could be discerned an increasing hostility in the films of
this period. Eisenstein's *Alexander Nevsky* (1938) implied
that if the Russians had beaten the Teutonic Knights of the
thirteenth century with Prince Alexander as their leader,
they could certainly do it again under Stalin. At the same
time there were pictures more specifically anti-Nazi. *Professor
Manslock* (1938), *Soldiers of the Marshes* (1938), and *The
Oppenheim Family* (1939) presented vivid indictments of
Germany's treatment of the Jews and the inhumanity of its
concentration camps. The antagonism between the two nations kept mounting, both off screen and on. But when Russia
entered into the Nazi-Soviet Pact, all of these anti-German
films, including even *Alexander Nevsky*, were arbitrarily banished from distribution. The line had changed again.

The security promised by the mutual non-aggression pact
soon proved a delusion. In June of 1941 Hitler's legions
rolled across the frontiers of the Soviet Union to open the
bloodiest, bitterest campaign of World War II. And immediately the Russian film was fired by a vigor and passion that
recalled the finest of their silent classics. The wraps were off.
The enemy was clear. And the contemporary scene, with all
its blood and tragedy, had at last found the Russian screen. A
heightened nationalism inspired film after film recounting
Russian heroism in the face of the Nazis. German atrocities
provided the theme for many of these—*No Greater Love*
(1942), *Girl No. 217* (1944), *Zoya* (1944); resistance on
the home front was the subject of many more. Others dealt
with the sacrifices and daring of the men and women in the
services.

Even more important than the fiction films, however, was

the vast series of documentaries, features edited from footage that streamed in from every fighting front, from every guerrilla band operating perilously behind the German lines, from factory and farm, from city and village. These films literally poured upon the screen every aspect of the war in Russia. Many of the best directors and cameramen were assigned to this work, for it was quickly realized that no fiction could ever capture the full sense of the war's horror and destruction, the intensity of battle or the determination of the men and women in the armed forces to throw back the invading armies. During the war, feature production was halved, while the documentaries steadily increased in number. Of those seen in the United States, *A Day of War* (1942), compiled from reels of a hundred cameramen in all parts of the Soviet Union, created a magnificent cross-section of an entire nation united in its resistance to the enemy. Films describing a single campaign, such as *Moscow Strikes Back* (1942) and *The Siege of Leningrad* (1943), put the actuality of war on the screen with a vividness of detail and an awareness of the human element that has never been equaled anywhere. Unlike the Nazi war documentaries, they did not hesitate to show atrocities in all their horror, not did they shrink from revealing the toll in human lives that every victory cost them. Neither were they limited by the feelings of implacable hatred for the Nazis that characterized Russian fiction films of this period. There was instead a deep and terrible humanity about these pictures—a compassion that mourned the desolation of land and life and the human spirit everywhere.

Since the war the Russian film has steadily receded from the eloquence and vitality of those days. No sooner had peace been declared than the line on historical pictures was abruptly changed, relegating the czars, their generals and their admirals to their former disrepute. As a result, Pudovkin's *Admiral Nakhimov* (1946) had to be considerably revised before it could be released, the third part of Eisenstein's *Ivan the Terrible* was never filmed, and a number of other pictures either planned or in production were simply abandoned. The new line placed heavy emphasis on the scientific and cultural advances within the Soviet Union, and film makers obliged with a reverent series of dull biographies on scientists, composers and authors. In response to demands for pictures revealing "the honor and poetry of labor," shallow love stories featuring a girl, a boy and a tractor have become a commonplace of the Soviet screen. More recently, the emphasis has shifted to making the movies quite literally a "theater of the people," a medium for bringing great plays, ballets and operas to the masses living outside the few large cities where such presentations are normally given. Sometimes, as in *The Grand Concert* (1951), these appear as straightforward stage presentations with a slender thread of movie story woven in; and sometimes—as in the ballet film of Prokofieff's *Romeo and Juliet* (1954) or the grand-scale film version of Moussorgsky's *Boris Godounov* (1955)—the work is given a more cinematic adaptation. Needless to say, they still retain to a marked degree the theatrical flavor of the original. At the same time, the documentary techniques developed during the war have degenerated into interminable, full-color presentations of sports events, May Day parades, air shows over Red Square and similar topical displays. Those seen in this country have all shared a crude, perfunctory newsreel quality, naïvely gloating over the sheer abundance of planes, tanks and people that they put on the screen. Today more than ever the film in Russia functions as an ideological tool, a useful weapon in the Soviet's education and propaganda armory. It does a job. It fills a need. But somewhere in the process the idealism and imagination that made the films of the late twenties and early thirties so memorable have vanished without a trace. Or perhaps there is a trace, whenever the political skies are propitious. The death of Josef Stalin in 1953 opened the way, for a time, to what might be described as a more individual look at traditional themes, as in Grigori Chukrai's *The Forty-First* (1956), a remake of a Protazanov film of 1927 in which a Red partisan falls in love with her prisoner of war, a White officer. Both Kalatozov's *The Cranes Are Flying* (1957) and Chukrai's *Ballad of a Soldier* (1959) recalled the grim events of World War II with a warmth and humanism that won international acclaim. Nor can one deny the artistry of Joseph Heifits' tender and amusing adaptation of Chekhov's *The Lady With the Dog* (1960) or of the veteran Grigori Kozintzev's Shakesperian adaptations, *Hamlet* (1964) and *King Lear* (1970). There were still other aberrations in Serge Paradjonov's surreal *Shadows of Our Forgotten Ancestors* (1964), an outstanding success at New York's prestigious film festival that year, and in Andrei Tarkovski's *Andrei Rublov* (1967), an amazingly full-blooded re-creation of an artist and his period. But *Rublov* was denied distribution and Paradjonov was later sentenced to Siberia on homosexual charges. At this point, the occasional film experiment in the Soviet Union is occasional indeed, and undertaken at considerable risk. The entire history of the medium, however, suggests that there are always artists willing to take that risk—artists who can find openings for themselves even in the most Byzantine of political structures. Who ever claimed that art was easy?

Of the film work in other countries behind the Iron Curtain, one is granted only an occasional glimpse—just enough to suggest that it is largely an imitation of the pallid themes and styles currently ordained by the Soviet Union itself. In all of them the industry functions as an agency of the State; and in the years since the war these States have been listening with ever greater attention to the propaganda lines laid down by the Kremlin. Czechoslovakia, which inherited from the German occupation a large and well-equipped studio at Barandov, first attracted attention with her trick films—notably *The Emperor's Nightingale* (1949) and the many imaginative puppet shorts by Jiri Trnka. There have also been a number of bitterly anti-Nazi films recalling the years of German domination. Of these, Alfred Radok's *Distant Journey* (1950) is outstanding for the humanity with which its director re-created the Terezin ghetto in Czechoslovakia, a Nazi preconcentration-camp clearinghouse for Jews of all nations. On the other hand, such long and starchy film biographies as *Smetana* (1955) and *Jan Hus* (1955), both carefully researched and handsomely mounted, are strongly reminiscent of the nationalistic biographies coming from Russia since the war.

For a brief time, however, there was a breakthrough. As early as 1947, the Czech government had established in Prague a Film Academy, with an unusually well-stocked library of movies from around the world—including a considerable collection of little-known American films. Even pictures that were denied commercial distribution in Communist Czechoslovakia could still be studied by those enrolled in the Academy. Although hobbled by the necessity to conform to a party line that was, if anything, more erratic than that in the Soviet Union (if only because it was once removed), the nascent film makers nevertheless learned their craft so well that, once the political pressures were off, they were able to produce a veritable stream of minor masterpieces. Even under the repressive regime of the Communist leader Antonín Novotny, one began to see signs of what the Czechs themselves referred to as a "thaw" in the increasingly humanistic films of the mid-sixties—films like Milos Forman's *Black Peter* (1963) and *The Loves of a Blonde* (1965), Ivan Passer's shrewdly observed *Intimate Lighting* (1965) and *The Shop on Main Street* (1965) by Jan Kadar and Elmar Klos. By reason of its international success, the latter signaled to the world that something new and exciting was happening in the Czech cinema. For once, Germans in uniform were neither caricatured nor characterized as evil incarnate. Instead of stark black and white, there were shadings of gray that applied equally to the Czeck townspeople who watched helplessly as the Nazi occupation force insinuated itself into their community. Unlike previous films on a similar theme (including Kadar and Klos' earlier *Death Called Englechin,* 1963), there were no heroic partisans, only pathetic middle-class shopkeepers and blue-collar workers worried about making it from day to day under their new, uncomfortable circumstances. On the night of its first presentation at the New York Film Festival in 1967, the film—and Kadar—received a fifteen-minute standing ovation.

Kadar has subsequently stated that the American reception of *The Shop on Main Street* literally saved his career. The same elements that made it so attractive to an international audience were the very ones that made it—and Kadar—suspect in his native land. Indeed, the bureaucrats would have been quite happy to have shelved the picture entirely, and did in fact delay its release for many months. Typically, they bent all their efforts to forcing into the New York Festival instead a three-hour-long reconstruction of World War II as seen through the eyes of a small boy, *Long Live the Republic* (1965), an "official film" celebrating the twentieth anniversary of Czechoslovakia's "liberation."

In any case, thanks to the international film festivals, the world was not totally unprepared for the remarkable procession of films that came streaming out of the Czech studios between 1966 and 1968—films as varied as Jiri Menzel's *Closely Watched Trains* and Vera Chytilova's wildly experimental *Daisies* (both 1966), Forman's *Fireman's Ball* and Frantisek Vlacil's paganly erotic *Marketa Lazarova* (both

1967), or Jan Nemec's *Report on the Party and the Guests* (briefly and belatedly released in 1968).* There were whispered words about the greater freedom that would come with a new regime, when Novotny would be deposed and his bureaucrats removed from control of the film industry. Their whispers became fact in January of 1968, when the liberal and independent Alexander Dubček became the new secretary of the Slovak Communist Party, succeeding Novotny. Films like Nemec's *Report on the Party and the Guests*, held up on ideological grounds, went into release. Films like Jaraj Jakubisko's daringly surreal ode to nonconformism, *Birds, Orphans and Fools* (1969), went into production. The optimism that was so palpable in Karlovy-Vary in July, 1967, suddenly, gloriously had its confirmation. Then, on the night of August 20, 1968, Soviet tanks rolled into the streets of Prague, destroying the dreams of a nation and of a nation's film makers who are, after all, the keepers of the dream. Significantly, artists like Forman, Kadar and Passer left their homeland at the first possible moment. For those who remained behind, the glory days were clearly over. At last report, Jakubisko was the night gate attendant at the Barrandov studios where he once directed.

As in Czechoslovakia, the pall of the "official film" has hung heavy over the Polish film makers, with large-scale historicals, biographies and stories of the resistance by far the most popular—as well as the safest—choices for subject matter. As in Czechoslovakia, the young Polish film makers had a remarkable school at Lodz, where they could learn their trade through immediate reference to an enormous library of classic—and not so classic—movies from around the world.

---

* I had the good fortune to have been at the Karlovy-Vary Festival in the summer of 1967 at the moment that the dam burst, and the excitement that came from this creative outpouring is impossible to describe. I remember hauling myself out of bed one Sunday morning to catch a 10:00 A.M. screening at one of the more distant of the half dozen or so screening rooms that Karlovy-Vary had pressed into service. The picture had been described to me as a "masterpiece." No sooner did I arrive than the critic Susan Sontag burst into the hall exclaiming, "I've just seen a masterpiece!" She had been to an 8:00 A.M. screening of another picture. Typical too was the dilemma of Leo Dratfield, one of the more responsible American importers of European films. He was standing on a streetcorner, black notebook in hand, pondering which of six pictures to attend, all of which had been described to him as "masterpieces." It was a summer of masterpieces, and everyone looked forward to more to come.

"For me," Roman Polanski once said, "the greatest part of our learning experience at Lodz was to sit on the steps of our theatre, which had once been a church, and to dissect for hours the movie we had just seen with my fellow students." As in Czechoslovakia, the Polish film makers have always been constrained by a painful knowledge of when to hold back and when it was safe to let yourself go. In Alexander Ford, Poland had the advantages of a first-rate director. Each of his films to reach this country—*Border Street* (1949), *Young Chopin* (1952), *Five Boys from Barsky Street* (1954) and the astonishingly nonconformist *Eighth Day of the Week* (1958)—has been in a different style, but unified by a remarkable visual sense and an ability to create moving, believable characters. With his *Knights of the Teutonic Order* (1960), it was impossible to escape the suspicion that perhaps Ford was *too* adaptable, and one began to turn hopefully to such emerging talents as Andrej Munk, who impressed immediately with his unconventional treatment of a conventional theme in *Eroica* (1957) and again with the powerful *Passenger*, uncompleted at the time of his death in 1961. For a time it seemed as if Andrej Wajda would pursue Munk's singularly personal vision of World War II and its immediate aftermath, particularly since in the actor Zbigniew Cybulski he had found a protagonist who—very much like James Dean in our own country—seemed able to stand in for an entire generation of young people who had inherited a world they weren't quite prepared to cope with. In *Kanal* (1955) and *Ashes and Diamonds* (1958), Munk made this young man, caught in historic tension between past and present, wholly sympathetic and understandable. After Cybulski's untimely death in 1967, Wajda made an almost painfully autobiographical film, *Everything for Sale*, the story of a film director whose own values are submerged in the exigencies of a production on which everything is going wrong.

But perhaps the saddest commentary on the official Polish film has been its inability to provide a hospitable working environment for its more talented young people. Certainly, no new director has burst upon the scene with more promise than Roman Polanski, with such international prize-winning shorts as *Two Men and a Wardrobe* (1958) and *The Fat and the Thin* (1961), followed immediately by a feature that gained world-wide acclaim for Polish films, *A Knife in the Water* (1961). In all of them, Polanski revealed a very special talent for searching out the grotesque in the mundane, for finding the precise image to suggest sado-masochistic layers of meaning in seemingly the most innocent and superficial actions. Apparently the Poles were all too willing to let him go, and Polanski has pursued a highly successful, if erratic, career on the Continent and in the United States with such films as *Repulsion* (1965), *Cul de Sac* (1966) and *Rosemary's Baby* (1968)—pictures notable for their lack of anything resembling socialist realism! More sobering has been the career of Polanski's gifted compatriot, Jerzy Skolimowski, whose overwhelming interests have always been "social" without the erotic overlay that has helped to make Polanski's work commercially viable. In films like *Identifying Marks—None* (1964), *Walkover* (1965) and *Barrier* (1966), he created a kind of socialist surrealism which won him high marks on the film festival circuit if not in his own country. Unfortunately, the pictures that he was invited to direct abroad—*Le Départ* (1967) in Belgium, *The Adventures of Gerald* (1969) in Italy, *Deep End* (1971) in West Germany—were never sufficiently successful to permit him to break completely the ties with his homeland, nor to permit him to return there with the freedom from constraints a conquering hero is entitled to.

Yugoslavia, like Poland and Czechoslovakia, won many international brownie points by virtue of its superb animated cartoons (which invariably seemed to be inveighing against capitalist conformism, but could easily, by the slightest extension, be made to apply to socialist conformity as well). But Yugoslavia has for three decades been the no-man's-land between the East and West; and it would be unlikely that her films would not betray this uneasy position. Only two Yugoslavian directors have been able to establish their names abroad—Aleksander Petrovic and Dusan Makevejev—and their films demonstrate why. Although Petrovic works largely within the boundaries of socialist realism, his ultimate concerns are humanistic—not who won or who lost, but what was the effect of the struggle on the combatants. Almost unknown in the Western world is *Three* (1965), three stories from World War II with the common theme that war has no winners, that its only product is brutalization and death. *I Have Even Met Happy Gypsies* (1967) turned an amused but sympathetic eye on a downtrodden minority, the Gypsies who cling tenaciously to their own code of honor in a hostile society. He also directed a stylish adaptation of the Faust legend, *The Devil in Moscow* (1973), which daringly lampooned Soviet bureaucracy (and just possibly totalitarian bureaucracy in general). In tone, texture and outlook, Petrovic's work closely resembles the best of the Czech neorealists.

Far better known to the Western world, however, is Petrovic's gifted and audacious compatriot, Dusan Makevejev—no doubt because he has been responsible for two of the more outrageous and original cinematic explorations of sex in the past decade: *W. R.: Mysteries of the Organism* (1971) and *Sweet Movie* (1974). Makevejev's first feature, *A Man Is Not a Bird* (1966), however, was a relatively conventional film, a love story between a young girl and the older blue-collar worker with whom she lives. (Again, the feeling is very much like Forman's *Loves of a Blonde*, a warm and sympathetic capturing of the factory milieu, although lacking in Forman's wry humor.) Even so, there are foreshadowings of Makevejev's later style not only in the swift concision of his shots, but in the linkages created by editing—as when the girl, unfaithful to her mate, consummates an affair with a truck driver to the finale of Beethoven's Ninth Symphony; just as she achieves orgasm, he cuts to the concert audience in the factory applauding the performance. Through his editing, Makevejev contrives to imply that they are in fact applauding *both* performances. His next film, *The Tragedy of a Switchboard Operator* (1967), was essentially an expansion of the themes and techniques of the earlier work, although with livelier, freer intercutting, flash-forwards, and the arbitrary insertion of seemingly irrelevant material—a sex lecture that opens the film, and another on criminology that recurs from time to time as it progresses—all pointing in the direction of *W. R.* There are also details in both films to suggest that Makevejev was not wholly enchanted with the slogans and standardization of a socialist society.

W. R. (Wilhelm Reich) was a curious choice for any director in the Communist bloc, no matter how nonconformist. Reich was a disciple of both Sigmund Freud and Karl Marx, but he managed to fall from grace in both ideologies. For Makevejev, however, who was increasingly absorbed with sexuality as a function—even a determinant—of social behavior, the challenge was irresistible. (A heightening of the Cold War between Yugoslavia and the Soviet Union at the start of the seventies may also have encouraged the produc-

tion of this wholly nonconformist—and anti-Stalinist—
movie.) The result is a complex, complicated picture, a
collage of newsreel and documentary footage on Reich himself, additional footage on the treatment of mental patients in
both American and Soviet hospitals (often bizarrely used),
pieces from a Russian feature on Stalin (*The Vow*), sequences shot by Makevejev in the United States (most notably *Screw* editor Jim Buckley having his penis molded in red
plastic), and a lightly outlined story involving four young
people, filmed in Yugoslavia. All of these disparate pieces—
and more—are joined together to form the statement that
only through open, joyful sexuality can the fascisms of either
the left or the right be overcome. As John Russell Taylor
aptly observed, Makevejev managed this with "all the conscious virtuosity of a juggler keeping a twenty-four-piece dinner service flying through the air while he paints a nude with
a brush held between his teeth and picks out 'The Red Flag'
on a piano with his toes." Soon after its release, the film was
withdrawn from distribution in Yugoslavia, apparently at the
request of Soviet authorities; but because it was backed in
part by West German television, it went on to gain international attention. So did *Sweet Movie*, made with Franco-
Canadian financing. Technically every bit as exciting and
original as *W. R.*, and making (or attempting to make) very
much the same points as *W. R.*, *Sweet Movie* was created
under the compulsion to come up with a commercially viable
product. Makevejev's response was pure overkill—lovers
writhing in a bed of sugar, a girl being covered by a shower
of chocolate, a horrendous supper party in which the diners
vomit, urinate, defecate and otherwise relieve themselves. It
also offered the conceit that the richest man in the world, who
wanted to marry a virgin, was blessed with a phallus of pure
gold. Much of the film, which moves between Paris and Canada, has to do with the deflowering of the girls of his choice.
It became a cult film, the kind shown around midnight on Sat-
urdays. Makevejev, lacking the kind of commerical success
that would produce contracts for a new picture, has been lec-
turing at film schools in Canada and Yugoslavia. At the
present writing, neither Petrovic nor Makevejev has been
asked to make another picture in his country of origin.

Similar stories can be found in Albania, Bulgaria and Romania. Over all these countries at present hangs the heavy,
restrictive pall of the official film maker. Frequently their pic-

tures reveal intelligence and taste. But as long as questions of utility continue to take precedence over problems of artistry and personal expression, one must look elsewhere for the creative growth of the medium.

England and the Documentary Tradition

The British film, which had muddled through the silent era without distinction or success, reached its lowest ebb during the early years of sound. Production in the late twenties had been maintained primarily by the government's Quota Act of 1927 that granted distribution contracts for the profitable Hollywood films only to those studios that would make English pictures. As a result, the British producer became essentially a distributor, turning out cheap, artless "quota quickies" with his left hand in order to get his right hand on the popular, star-studded entertainments coming from America. In this way the studios survived, although their pictures reflected little credit either on the men or on the country that produced them. When in 1929 the studios were hit simultaneously by sound and the depression, the whole shaky structure collapsed. Sound equipment was too expensive for most of the companies to purchase outright, and the film business was hardly likely to attract investment capital at that moment. Many studios simply went bankrupt. Those that did survive immediately fell into the routine of filming stage plays.

Until the very end of the thirties, the British studios remained notoriously devoid of either inspiration or vitality. Disenchanted young men who might have contributed their vigor and talents to the entertainment film abandoned it in favor of the unexplored realms of documentary, while from the harried commercial studios came little more than shabby imitations of Hollywood's poorest offerings. And yet, behind the scenes, techniques and skills, courage and resourcefulness were growing steadily in both the documentary units and the studios. When the war finally brought together these two divergent groups, the result was not a clash but a fusion that marvelously transformed the entire British film.

While the English studios of the thirties continued to jog along in their quota-protected rut (and American television viewers are now well aware of what a rut that was), a few films did break away from the routine of cheap sets, excessive dialogue and hasty camera work. This dramatic departure was inspired by a single success that for a time intoxicated the entire industry and filled many with false hopes. It had always been the dream of the British to break into the rich American market. When Alexander Korda, a Hungarian director who had been only moderately successful in Hollywood and on the Continent, suddenly scored a hit in America with his relatively inexpensive production of *The Private Life of Henry VIII* (1933), the British thought they had their answer. The film starred Charles Laughton, an English actor who had already earned a considerable reputation through appearances in Hollywood films. With Laughton's name as a lever—and a highly salable title—it became the first British film to be booked into big American first-run houses and the major theater chains. Its profits were enormous. Obviously, the way to get British films into American theaters, the producers argued, was to bring over Hollywood stars and feature them in pictures as big and glossy as—and possibly slightly less vacuous than—the American spectaculars. After Korda's success, investors were suddenly willing to pour money into such grandiose plans.

Unfortunately, they were doomed to failure. Nobody can out-Hollywood Hollywood. It takes more than money, more than Hollywood stars. The flair, the exuberance, the showmanship that goes into the American super-production was something the British could neither buy nor reproduce. British pacing, British restraint, the clipped British accent made such star-studded films as *Catherine the Great* (1934), *Rembrandt* (1936) and *Things to Come* (1936) strange and unacceptable fare to the vast American public. Outside of the few sophisticated Eastern cities, their popularity was limited. And where *Henry VIII* had been able to show a profit because of its modest budget, the multi-million-dollar productions required a mass audience that simply was not available to British films in the American market. Despite the Hollywood stars and directors, despite the European technicians for whom they paid so bountifully, the British studios were unable to produce a type of film that could captivate a wide audience. By 1937 the speculators were reluctantly writing off their losses and once again turning a jaundiced eye upon the movie business.

But out of these costly extravaganzas, as well as from the welter of cheaply produced, indifferent little pictures, there began to appear in the studios for the first time a rising sense of professionalism and a corps of genuinely creative men. What finally liberated their talents was the revised Quota Act of 1938, designed by the government specifically to eliminate the "quota quickie." In order to qualify for quota benefits, the studios now had to spend on their films enough money to ensure a decent level of production.

The Act held out further benefits as an inducement for producers to exceed the £7,500 per reel minimum. While the amount of money spent on a picture is never in itself, of course, any guarantee of quality, the new budgets automatically provided more time for preparation and shooting, more leeway in the number of settings, more opportunity to work on location. At last the craftsmen in the British studios could take some pride in their work, and this new attitude was reflected immediately in their films. Such pictures as *South Riding* (1938), *Bank Holiday* (1938), *Owd Bob* (1938) and *The Stars Look Down* (1939) were all modest efforts by Hollywood standards, but they could stand on their own merits. And they did so in what was, for Britain, a new and important way. For the first time there were English pictures that seemed to be looking with some insight and appreciation at the life and spirit of the country itself. They spoke of the British character, British institutions—even of social problems such as unemployment and nationalization—with unprecedented frankness and awareness. Events on the Continent seemed to have startled the British into a reappraisal of their way of life. And where in France the film makers were already giving way to despair and resignation as the war clouds gathered over Europe, the British suddenly came forward with a sober affirmation of pride and confidence in their traditions and their future. By some rare good fortune, the British screen found its voice just at the moment that the nation needed it most.

In the short time that remained before the war broke out, the studios consolidated their gains. Each month their films seemed surer, more alive, more successful artistically—and, above all, more intensely British. New stars—Wendy Hiller, Deborah Kerr, Michael Redgrave, Ralph Richardson—were emerging with every new picture; while established players like George Arliss, Leslie Howard and Charles Laughton were returning home from Hollywood to lend their prestige to the reviving industry. New directors like David MacDonald, Michael Powell, Carol Reed and Robert Stevenson came forward to take their places beside such veterans as Anthony Asquith and Alfred Hitchcock. While behind the cameras, at the cutting benches, pounding the typewriters in the studio story departments, were many more of the men who were to mold the British film during the years ahead.

In the meantime, the independent documentary movement had also developed into a potent force, one that was to prove of inestimable value not only during the war years but also in shaping the intimate realism of the postwar British feature film. As a movement, documentary may be said to have had its official beginning in 1929 with the formation of the Empire Marketing Board Film Unit by John Grierson, a tough-minded Scot with a background in mass communications and a firm conviction that the motion picture could play a vital educational role in a democracy. Grierson persuaded Sir Stephen Tallents, head of the Marketing Board, to add film to the conventional media of books, pamphlets and posters already being used by that organization in its work of promoting and integrating the nation's food supply. As Grierson conceived it, the function of the E.M.B. Film Unit was to relate these activities in meaningful terms to the people of Britain—"to bring the Empire alive," he termed it. His ability to do so was evident from his very first film, *Drifters* (1929), revealing the drama behind the daily haul of the North Sea herring fishermen, enacted by the men themselves. Coming in the midst of the stilted, stagnant early all-talkies, its views of real people, real seas and storms had the additional impact of novelty. It remains one of the classics of the documentary form.

With the backing of Tallents, Grierson proceeded to gather around himself a group of men to study the techniques appropriate to putting actuality on the screen. In *Drifters* he had broken both with studio staging and with conventional story construction. Now the problem was to discover new ways to make fact exciting and provocative, to get information across without being dull or didactic. The unit spent long months in a critical reappraisal of earlier filmic treatments of reality—the masterworks of Robert Flaherty and von Stroheim, Eisenstein and Pudovkin, the American Westerns with their natural backgrounds, the "city symphonies" of the Continental avant-garde, as well as newsreels and scientific shorts from every nation. And from this study evolved the aesthetic base on which the documentary movement was founded. Grierson once described it as "the creative treatment of actuality," a phrase that indicates the equal stress placed upon artistry and subject matter. Its purpose was to project the facts of life under a democracy; its method, to show man in relation to his institutions.

It was this combination of social purpose and artistic experimentation that gave the British documentary its strength and its direction. As the movement matured, as its relation to government, to industry and to the general public became clearer, documentary was to undergo numerous changes in form and technique. From the early objective recording of fishermen, potters, miners and glass blowers going about their routine tasks, documentaries gradually came to include direct interviews and even dramatic recreations. As themes grew more complicated, it was sometimes necessary to introduce actors and studio settings into the films. Thus, it became increasingly apparent that documentary was less a technique than an approach. Reality was its theme, and the documentary director was properly concerned with the methods of capturing a sense of reality upon the screen. But whatever techniques he chose, his purpose remained the same—to inform and enlighten rather than simply to entertain. Indeed, Grierson himself preferred the stronger word, "propaganda." What he meant by this, of course, was not the calculated, cynical distortion of truth as practiced by the totalitarians, but its function of spreading information. "We can," he wrote, "by propaganda, widen the horizons of the schoolroom and give to every individual, each in his place and work, a living conception of the community which he has the privilege to serve."

In 1933 the Empire Marketing Board Film Unit was moved, virtually intact, to the General Post Office, where it remained until the early years of the war. With characteristic imagination, Grierson seized on the new affiliation as an opportunity to interpret communications in the widest sense of the word to the people of Britain—not just the pickup and delivery of mail but "the gale warning behind the Central Telegraph Office, the paradox of nationalism and internationalism behind the cable service, the choral beauty of the night mail, and the drama tucked away in the files of the ship-to-shore radio service." Now began the memorable series of films that, more than any others, have come to represent the highest and most characteristic achievements of British documentary—*Weather Forecast* (1934), *Song of Ceylon* (1934), *Coal Face* (1935), *Night Mail* (1936) and *North Sea* (1938). Within their framework of fact, they experimented with a wide variety of styles. Basil Wright's *Song of Ceylon* remains among the most lyric films of all time, with scenes of ageless native ritual juxtaposed against the jumbled voices of the tea traders, the shippers and the London Stock Exchange. Harry Watt's *Night Mail*, following the nightly run of the mail express from the south of England to Edinburgh, introduced a poetic commentary by W. H. Auden set to the music of Benjamin Britten. Auden's words conveyed not only the magnitude of this routine operation but brought it close to everyone when, over shots of the sleeping, smoky city the narrator's voice says, "Soon they will wake and listen for the postman's knock—for who can bear to feel himself forgot?" In *North Sea* Watt used a story line and actors to dramatize the work of the ship-to-shore radio service in bringing aid to the men of a trawler disabled by storm. It was also at this time that Len Lye began his delightful experiments in the synchronization of abstract animation and popular music, tied to postal messages like "mail early" or "ship via parcel post." In all, the G.P.O. Film Unit produced hundreds of documentaries in dozens of styles before being taken over as the Crown Film Unit to serve the Ministry of Information throughout the war years.

During its formative years, the British documentary movement owed its existence entirely to government support. As the thirties wore on, however, it began to attract an independent following. Although the movie houses paid them scant attention, a regular audience for fact films was growing in the universities, the film societies, in labor organizations and clubs of every kind. And with an established demand for the films, sponsorship by private industry began to appear. In England, it must be remembered, radio broadcasting had been totally non-commercial until the late fifties, a function of the government-operated B.B.C. Potential advertisers had to find other ways to reach their public. It was Grierson who persuaded them to invest in institutional advertising, in films that built goodwill for the company through documentaries on subjects of broad, general interest rather than in pictures that simply plugged their product. As a result of this farsighted policy, one finds films on nutrition sponsored by the Gas,

Light and Coke Company, on slum clearance by the British Commercial Gas Association, on housing by Cadbury's Chocolate, and brilliant instructional films for classroom use paid for by Shell Oil. By 1937, when Grierson withdrew from G.P.O. to form the London Film Centre, more documentaries were being produced for industry than for government; and the Film Centre acted as a clearing house to indicate those subjects on which films were needed, to assist in their planning, and to prevent wasteful duplication of effort. By the time the war broke out, the British documentary movement—headed by men like Paul Rotha, Stuart Legg, Basil Wright, Harry Watt, Alberto Cavalcanti, Arthur Elton and Edgar Anstey—had achieved a world-wide reputation and inspired scores of directors outside England to attempt documentary movements in their own countries.

The quality that made the British documentary so distinctive was the calmness of its presentation. Without resorting to flamboyant techniques or emotion-charged commentaries, it sustained interest and provoked thought. Even where the films took a stand—on the advantages of slum clearance, for example—the argument was generally given through unemphatic but revealing visuals. The facts were organized and presented; the viewer was left free to draw his own conclusions. As Britain prepared for war, the propriety of this approach was questioned for a time. Perhaps the line should become more forthright, more emotional, as in Alexander Korda's studio-made pastiche of documentary combat shots and jingoistic story, *The Lion Has Wings* (1939). Perhaps the documentary people could be used best in the creation of straight poster films, films urging the population to enlist, to buy war bonds, to save fuel and foodstuffs. While the government wavered, the documentary film makers clamored to be permitted to do what they knew best—to put on the screen, with characteristic understatement, the true face of Britain at war. After months of hesitation, the Ministry of Information acceded. The Crown Film Unit was formed, and soon began its extraordinary series of war-time documentaries. Pictures like *London Can Take It* (1940) showing London under the blitz; *Target for Tonight* (1941), an R.A.F. nightbombing mission over Germany; *Desert Victory* (1942), a stirring account of the North African campaign—all of these not only kept up morale on the home front but did much to win sympathy and support for England in the United States during the early years of World War II. As film became increasingly important to the war effort, literally hundreds of young people joined the documentary movement, working on subjects as various as recruiting pictures, training films and movies covering every aspect of the national emergency from *Wartime Factory* (1941) to *More Eggs from Your Hens* (c. 1943).

Soon after the outbreak of the war, the English studios were mobilized to turn out morale and training films in addition to their entertainment pictures. And here, for the first time, the documentary and fiction film makers of Britain joined forces. Some, like Alberto Cavalcanti and Harry Watt, moved from documentary to fiction; while fiction directors like John Boulting, Thorold Dickinson and Carol Reed became, at least for the time, documentalists. There was a distinct gain on either side. The documentary directors learned to make their pictures more dramatic, more immediate in their appeal to new audiences of tens of millions. The directors of entertainment films mastered the problems of creating a sense of realism on the screen. Dickinson, for example, was assigned to direct a training film for the armed forces that would dramatize the wartime slogan "the enemy is listening." Using an actual incident from official files, he produced in *Next of Kin* (1942) such an exciting spy story that it was shown not only to British and American troops but was also exhibited theatrically in both countries. Another outstanding wartime contribution by studio-trained talents was *The True Glory* (1945). Working with clips from the archives of the American and British Signal Corps, Carol Reed and the American director Garson Kanin supervised the editing and shaping of hundreds of thousands of feet of combat footage. Narrated by General Eisenhower and scores of anonymous soldiers' voices, the film became a vivid, authentic document of the allied campaign in Europe—and a fervent prayer for the peace.

It was the function of the British wartime documentaries to keep the nation informed on the progress of the war, to strengthen the morale and unity of purpose of the British people during those perilous years. Their appeal was to the intellect and the understanding—and their effectiveness was beyond question. But another force was needed to touch the emotions of the people, to provide them with a different kind of inspiration; and this became the task of the entertainment

film. Like the documentaries, many of them dealt with both
the effects of war on the home front and the direct encounters with the enemy on land, at sea and in the air. The primary difference—and in this lay their particular appeal—was
their concentration on the personal element.

How well these two film forms balanced each other during
the war years may be seen by comparing a documentary with
a fiction film on very much the same subject. In the
documentary *Target for Tonight,* dealing with a bombing
mission over Germany, it is the mission itself that concerns
us. We are shown in detail the intricate planning and
preparation behind the run, the timing and technical mastery
required to carry it through. One cannot watch this film without admiring the efficiency and skill of the operation, and the
dedicated spirit with which the men of the R.A.F. faced the
perils of what was for them just another routine assignment.
But there are no individual heroes, no thrills apart from those
intrinsic to such a mission. On the other hand, in Michael
Powell's fictional *One of Our Aircraft Is Missing* (1942),
also involving a bombing mission over Germany, the audience's sympathies and emotions are immediately engaged.
Where the documentary reported on the planes from base to
target and home again, in Powell's film the accent falls on the
men themselves. Each member of the crew seems to typify
some unique and positive aspect of the British character.
Their bravery, ingenuity and good cheer in the face of danger
became a source of pride and inspiration to the British
people. Identifying with them in their struggles and victories,
the audience renewed its own strength and in some measure
found the courage to carry on.

Other fiction directors followed much this same pattern,
producing pictures like *In Which We Serve* (1942), *Nine
Men* (1943), *Millions Like Us* (1943) and *We Dive at
Dawn* (1944). In each the hero is seen as a member of a
team whose sheer survival is often dependent upon concerted,
coordinated group action. By 1943 all the studios were releasing this type of film, but it was the Ealing Studio in particular that specialized in them. To heighten their realism
Michael Balcon, the head of Ealing, added to his staff a number of leading documentary directors, cameramen and editors—a fact that was to give his studio a distinct edge in the
postwar phase of British film making. For the vitality generated by this fusion of documentary and the fiction film was to

continue to shape and influence pictures coming out of the studios long after the war.

Once the war was over, other themes and other treatments began to emerge in both the fact and the fiction films. The documentalists quickly turned to the urgent problems of reconstruction—housing, food and health. And industry joined with government to sponsor films that would orient and encourage a war-weary people. Particularly pressing were the problems of the returning veterans, the paraplegics, the mounting numbers of mental cases directly or indirectly attributable to the war. Documentary rose to this challenge in dozens of films like *Out of True* (1950) and *The Undefeated* (1950), meeting each subject with a new flexibility of techniques. In *The Undefeated*, for example, Paul Dickson used reenactments to tell the story of an R.A.F. flier who had lost both legs at Arnhem but learned to walk again on artificial limbs. The flier himself acted out the painful stages of his rehabilitation in the same hospitals and rest homes where they had taken place. Filmed for the Ministry of Pensions, it held out the hope for a similar recovery to thousands of crippled veterans—and informed millions of Britons of one more aspect of their government's service. *Out of True*, on the other hand, like many of the mental health films, was studio-made and cast with professional actors in the main roles. The complexity of its problem virtually dictated the kind of control that, under the circumstances, could best be obtained with actors, sets and scenario. Indeed, dramatization either with actors or with non-professionals permeated great areas of the postwar British documentary. The techniques of fiction gave the documentary film makers new points of contact with the British people, as evidenced by films as varied as *Children on Trial* (1946), dealing with juvenile delinquency; *Highland Doctor* (1948), an account of medical services in the all but inaccessible Hebrides villages; and *David* (1951), a warm and gentle portrait of a Welsh school caretaker, his simplicity, his kindness and his love for the traditions of his country.

One important adjunct of these films of social welfare that attracted many documentalists after the war was the educational field, the production of pictures for classroom use sponsored both by government and by private industry. The Shell Oil films, made under the supervision of Sir Arthur Elton (one of the original Grierson group), attained a rare precision and lucidity in their exposition of the principles of physics, aerodynamics and the like. The Ministry of Health sponsored a notable series of pictures on child care—*Your Children's Eyes* (1945), *Your Children's Teeth* (1946), *Your Children's Sleep* (1947), and so on, that was both informative and witty; while instructionals like *Instruments of the Orchestra* (1947) and *Steps of the Ballet* (1949), produced by the Crown Film Unit, proved entertaining enough to win theatrical bookings both in England and in the United States. There was, in short, a pressing need for fact films on a wide variety of subjects in the years just after the war—and the documentary people came forward to fill this need with a versatility that produced hundreds of pictures combining a high level of artistry with maximum utility.

Less than ten years after the war, however, British documentary had passed its finest hour. As early as 1951 John Grierson had warned, "I think the time has come to say plainly that documentary as an art, documentary as a power of persuasion, documentary as a valuable instrument of national projection, is being allowed to go by default and a generation of film-makers ruined and lost to the State by a fumbling regime of sponsors unworthy of their predecessors and their origins." He was referring specifically to Britian's Labour government which, having gained power, strangely ignored the documentary film despite its long record of progressive sentiments and orientation. In the interest of economy, the Crown Film Unit, the direct descendant of Grierson's original Empire Marketing Board group, was dissolved. Grierson himself became increasingly identified with feature film production, and other leading documentalists were absorbed into the studios, government posts and television. In a concerted drive to build her tourist trade, the government put primary emphasis upon the production of travelogues, one- and two-reel visits to various points of interest in the British Isles. Handsomely photographed, often in Technicolor, they continued to reflect the high level of Britains fact-film technicians. Similarly, *The Conquest of Everest* (1954) revealed that the British documentarians were still able to organize and record the complexities of an extended operation in dramatic and meaningful images. But such films are a far cry from the high social purposes and ideals that had sustained the documentary movement through two decades. British documentary continues, but without the vigor, the prestige or the direction that marked its greatest years. As elsewhere, the immediacy of the television tube replaced the broader vision of Britain's pioneer documentary film makers.

Like the documentaries, the British feature films sustained a high level during the difficult period of postwar reconstruction. Still fired by the wartime spirit of "we're all in it together," British directors continued to explore with humor and affection the quirks and crannies of the British character already demonstrated in films like *The Life and Death of Colonel Blimp* (1943) and *Tawny Pipit* (1944), that amusing side glance at the Britisher's traditional devotion to bird watching. There was Roger Livesey's daft Scottish laird in the delightful *I Know Where I'm Going* (1945) and Rex Harrison's satiric portrait of a *Notorious Gentleman* (*The Rake's Progress*, 1945). There were the deftly-drawn vignettes from Somerset Maugham's *Quartet* (1948), *Trio* (1950) and *Encore* (1951), not to mention Alex Guinness's mild-mannered rogue in films like *The Lavender Hill Mob* (1950) and *The Promoter* (1952)—all delightful, and specifically British, eccentric types. Britain's cultural tradition was recalled in David Lean's exciting adaptations of *Great Expectations* (1946) and *Oliver Twist* (1947), and in Sir Laurence Olivier's memorable trilogy of Shakespearean plays, *King Henry V* (1944), *Hamlet* (1948) and *Richard III* (1956); his subsequent *Othello* (1965) was somewhat less than memorable.

The realist tradition that resulted from the wartime fusion of documentary and fiction techniques made possible what was perhaps the most notable group of postwar films. Dramas like *Brief Encounter* (1945), Carol Reed's *Odd Man Out* (1947) and *The Third Man* (1949), or the Boulting brothers' *Seven Days to Noon* (1950) all found their point of departure in the contemporary scene. It was in this field that the tiny Ealing Studio particularly excelled. The documentary people that Michael Balcon—now Sir Michael—had added to his staff during the war years were responsible for such successes as *Dead of Night* (1946), *The Cruel Sea* (1952) and *The Divided Heart* (1954), as well as that dizzying series of comedy hits, *Passport to Pimlico* (1949), *Tight Little Island* (1949), *The Lavender Hill Mob* and *The Man in the White Suit* (1951). But even as the documentaries had briefly flourished and declined after the first serious crises of reconstruction had passed, so too did an unfortunate lethargy settle over the British entertainment film. Part of the reason, to be sure, may be found in the waning of the strong sense of unity and purpose generated by the war and its aftermath; more of it lies in the postwar structure of the British film industry.

It had always been Balcon's contention that films should be produced to appeal primarily to the British market, and budgeted to show a profit within that market. Ealing's signal success had been based upon this policy. Oddly enough, it seems to have carried little weight with the other British studios. During the war J. Arthur Rank, the owner of Britain's largest theater chains, emerged as the strongest single figure on the motion-picture scene. He had bought into some studios, created others, financed independent producers on the grand scale. It was his dream to gain prestige for the British film—and for England—and ultimately to win over the vast American market for British movies. Costly films like *King Henry V* (1944), *Stairway to Heaven* (1945), *Red Shoes* (1948), and *The Tales of Hoffmann* (1951) became his "loss leaders," big films that he felt sure would edge their way into American theaters and, by their sheer opulence, create a demand for more British pictures. Hopefully, he named his American distribution organization Prestige Pictures. Certainly, it did much to enhance the prestige of British films—but at a cost to Rank of some $8,000,000. Popular in the art houses of the big cities, they failed to penetrate to the American mass audience. The motion-picture trade press on both sides of the Atlantic is still debating whether this failure has been due to public indifference or to the calculated sabotage of American distributors.

One thing is certain, however. In their second attempt to conquer America with big, lavish, costly productions, the British seriously overextended themselves. The government itself unwittingly fostered this extravagance. In 1948 it set up the National Film Finance Company to distribute £5,000,000 in an all-out effort to support and encourage domestic production. With this new source of capital, many of the smaller companies unhesitatingly followed Rank's lead. Less than six years later Sir Alexander Korda alone had lost about £2,000,000 of the £3,000,000 his British Lion Company had received. This seemed a bit excessive even for the movie business, and in June of 1954 the government abruptly withdrew what remained of its loan. The decision probably saved British taxpayers £1,000,000, but it threw the film industry into a panic from which it has not yet recovered. British Lion shut down, as did many smaller studios. And within a short time, the brightest luminaries in the British film world—men like Laurence Olivier, Alec Guinness, David Lean, Carol Reed—were either working in Hollywood or on co-productions financed jointly by English and American or Italian studios and intended for the international market. Early in 1956 even Balcon closed the Ealing Studio, selling it to television and finding an American affiliation for himself.

For a brief time, the British film enjoyed a renaissance, sparked by such "angry young men" of literature and the theater as John Braine and John Osborne—and, to some extent, by the government-financed British Free Cinema program. It was the Free Cinema that first proferred cinematic opportunities to Lindsay Anderson, Karel Reisz and Tony Richardson, who quickly assumed the leadership in this fascinating if short-lived British revival (even though Richardson was later to claim that the Free Cinema's influence on his own career was minimal). Nevertheless, when Richardson brought to the screen his adaptation of Osborne's tawdry play, *Look Back in Anger* (1958), he touched off what soon became known as the "kitchen sink" school of British naturalism—immediately augmented by Jack Clayton's far more penetrating and effective *Room at the Top* (1958) which, in tracing Joe Lampton's (Laurence Harvey) inexorable rise from factory hand to mill executive forthrightly attacked both Britain's ruling class and the dubious morality of the entire capitalistic system. (The fact that Joe was simultaneously enjoying the favors of his French mistress while impregnating the mill owner's daughter didn't hurt the film's box office appeal.)

During this period, Richardson scored repeatedly with films like *The Entertainer* (1960), *A Taste of Honey* (1961) and *The Loneliness of the Long Distance Runner* (1963), all of them impressively sensitive studies of a lower middle-class milieu that had seldom been explored upon the screen before, and hence found an enthusiastic reception not only in England but in the United States as well. (Educator John Culkin has called *Loneliness* "the *Silas Marner* of 16mm.") To these should be added the Boulting brothers' *I'm All Right, Jack* (1959), Karel Reisz's *Saturday Night and Sun-*

day Morning (1960), Brian Forbes' *The L-Shaped Room* (1962), Joseph Losey's *The Servant* (1963) and the Anderson-Reisz *This Sporting Life* (1963)—variations, perhaps, on a single theme, but persuasively handled, economically produced, and introducing such major new acting talents as Alan Bates, Albert Finney, Richard Harris and Rita Tushingham.

But the appeal of a kitchen sink can be fairly limited, and Richardson was the first to realize this. In 1963, he abandoned it for a funny, full-bodied adaptation of Henry Fielding's 19th Century classic, *Tom Jones*—and threw his contemporaries into an immediate panic. They simply didn't know which way to turn. Some plunked for anti-war themes—Kevin Brownlow with a sobering, documentary-like insistence on the grisly details in *It Happened Here* (1964) and Peter Watkins with more of the same in *The War Game* (1965). Richard Lester, an American expatriate who had been doing television commercials in London, adapted TV techniques to introduce the Beatles in his wildly imaginative and inventive *A Hard Day's Night* (1964). Carl Foreman, another expatriate, switched from the wide, costly canvas of *The Guns of Navarrone* (1961) to the more intimate, pastoral pleasures of *Born Free* (1966). Stanley Kubrick, in self-imposed exile since the early sixties, peered into our atomic future (like a Peter Watkins with a sense of humor) and came up with the black comedy of *Dr. Strangelove* (1964), drew on all the vast resources of Hollywood's technology for his sci-fi fantasy, *2001, A Space Odyssey* (1968), then in 1971 made the most British—and most pessimistic—of his movies, *A Clockwork Orange*. It was as if Britain's kitchen sink had stopped up and slopped over.

The sad thing is that, having found a very specific niche for itself in the world of cinema, the British industry has never been able to sustain it—not, at least, without generous infusions of foreign capital. But early in the seventies, this began slacking off. Rising costs, the declining value of the dollar, plus the notorious inflexibility of England's labor unions made production there just short of prohibitive. By the mid-seventies, it was once more panic time on the Thames. No longer able to underwrite production herself, Britain now offers to the film makers of the world some studios, many able technicians, and generous Eady Plan inducements to make pictures in England. While there have been many takers, production has reached a new low, with scripts and stars chosen with an ever greater concern for the presumed tastes of the American public. Co-productions like *Lawrence of Arabia* (1962) and *Ryan's Daughter* (1970), not to mention the innumerable James Bond thrillers, have further leveled off those unique essays on British character and manners that once gave the films from Britain their special distinction and appeal. It is unfortunate that, having raised up an entire generation of skilled, creative artists, England is no longer able to offer them full employment.

The Course of Italian Neo-realism

There had been signs of a new vitality in the Italian studios at the very end of the silent era, evidence that the film makers were beginning to catch up with the technical mastery that existed elsewhere. Under the leadership of Alessandro Blasetti, both as a director and as editor of the magazine *Cinematografo*, Italian films were breaking out of their moribund tradition of old-fashioned spectacles and cliché *romanzas*. Blasetti's first film *Sole* (1929) was a drama based on Mussolini's vast project of draining the Pontine marshes. Its immediate success suggested the possibility of turning to other positive aspects of the contemporary scene as sources for filmic material. But the established producers were hesitant; and as they waited, sound arrived to put an end for the moment to Blasetti's dream. The studios turned promptly to the stage for both themes and actors, and the sweet strains of Neapolitan love songs effectively drowned out any plea for greater realism or more imaginative techniques. The early years of sound in Italy were dominated by the musicals, and by romances and boudoir farces drawn from stage plays— "white telephone films" the Italians called them because so much of the action seemed to center about the white telephone in the heroine's bedchamber.

As noted earlier, the Fascist government at first took little interest in the motion-picture field. There was, of course, official encouragement for historical films celebrating the rise of the Fascist party or re-creating the life and times of such popular heroes as Garibaldi, Ettore Fieramosca and Salvator Rosa, but nothing more tangible. Fascist interests were, at that time, satisfactorily served by the flow of propaganda shorts and newsreels turned out by the government-owned LUCE. When the talkies arrived in 1930 this company promptly added three sound trucks to its equipment, with the result that impassioned harangues by Mussolini became part of all their newsreels. These, together with any other shorts turned out by LUCE, were shown by government decree in every motion-picture house throughout Italy. But aside from such minor inconveniences, Italian producers, distributors and exhibitors were left pretty much to their own devices until 1935. Between 1935 and 1940, however, things began to change. Mussolini was launching those wars and campaigns through which he hoped to extend the Italian empire and increase his own stature. National feeling, national pride had to be whipped up to a fever pitch. It was during this period that the government gradually gained control of the motion-picture industry, achieving this not by outright ownership but by a weird and complicated form of patronage that the State held out to the eighteen accredited producing studios. Producers now could easily borrow up to 60 per cent of the cost of a picture from the State-controlled banks; if they were able to show that their film was either popular, artistic, or propagandistically useful, they had only to repay a small portion of the loan. Under such conditions, it became virtually impossible for a studio to lose money no matter how unsuccessful its pictures might be. Before long the studios were offering top jobs to political favorites because of their ability to wangle even more profitable concessions from the venal officials directing the banks and the State credit agencies. When Mussolini's son Vittorio entered the industry as head of Europa Films, Italy's largest studio, the pattern of nepotism and patronage was complete.

The government further increased its influence over the industry when it decreed that all foreign films shown in Italy had to be dubbed, and that the dubbing had to be done by Italians. This not only created more film jobs, it also made it simple to eliminate from foreign imports any sentiments that were not fully in accord with Fascist ideology—a neat, unobtrusive form of censorship. At the same time, the State awarded the valuable licenses for dubbing and distributing these films to those studios that produced the most or the most expensive pictures each year—a form of patronage that proved completely demoralizing. Indeed, no system could have been more ideally designed to encourage wastefulness and to discourage creativity.

Considering the amount of control the government actually

held over the film industry both economically and by the appointment of political favorites to key positions, it is surprising how few of the pictures were made as outright Fascist propaganda. The Italians were satisfied, it would seem, with a primarily negative propaganda. They were content if their films simply ignored all ideas of democracy, civil rights, civil liberties or similarly "decadent" notions. Ettore Margadonna, one of the leadng historians of the Italian film, has estimated that "out of more than five hundred feature films [produced between 1930 and 1942], those which were one hundred per cent Fascist in content may be counted on the fingers of one hand." These exceptions would include *Black Shirt* (1933), Blasetti's *Old Guard* (1935), *The Siege of the Alcázar* (1940), proudly revealing Italy's part in the Spanish Civil War, and Carmine Gallone's soporific extravaganza *Scipio Africanus* (1937). Rumored to have been written by Benito Mussolini himself, it presumed to see in the ancient Italian victory in Africa the heroic counterpart of Mussolini's own campaign in Ethiopia. Filmed in Africa and on the giant stages of the new, State-financed Cinecittá, it was one of the most costly, most opulent productions of all time—and also one of the most overblown. Critics delighted in pointing to the telephone poles that sprouted from the hilltops of Imperial Rome, the wrist watches of the Roman legionnaires, and to the stupefying emptiness of the vast spectacle. Nevertheless, because it was an official film, the government made special efforts to have it shown abroad. Its reception did little to enhance the reputation of the Italian film makers. A few of the Italian opera films were also exported, notably Gallone's *The Dream of Butterfly* (1939), featuring long passages from Puccini's opera beautifully performed by Maria Cebotari, and a tear-stained story of a diva who, like Butterfly herself, loved not wisely but well. Aside from these—nothing.

But if the corrupt and corrupting Italian studios were unable to produce a masterpiece, at least they enabled talented people to gain a mastery of their art. Clearly, the neo-realist movement that burst forth with such vitality after the war could only have come from men whose artistic impulses had long been bottled up, from men who knew the techniques of film making but lacked the opportunity to use them significantly. Many had been trained at the government-operated Centro Sperimentale, the official film school in Rome. Many had worked under the dispiriting studio conditions that marked the final years of Fascism. Vittorio De Sica, for example, had alternated between stage and screen as a matinee idol throughout the thirties. He turned to directing in 1940, specializing in sentimental comedies which he handled with a good deal of superficial charm and, on occasion, sharp insights into the behavior of children. Roberto Rossellini worked on a number of documentaries before being assigned as assistant director on *The White Ship* (1941), a wartime propaganda film almost totally lacking in human feeling. Two more features, *The Return of the Pilot* (1942) and *The Man of the Cross* (1943), seem to have been equally devoid of any hint of his postwar style. Of the old guard, only Alessandro Blasetti gave any suggestion of the new themes and new techniques that lay ahead. His *Four Steps in the Clouds* (1943) for a moment took the Italian film out of the world of "white telephones" and official attitudes. It was a touching, warm-hearted comedy in which a kindly man from the city finds himself pretending to be the husband of a country girl he has met by chance—and the father of her unborn child. Though far from political, its picture of peasant life, its Italian peasant types and natural settings strongly foreshadowed the neo-realist films of the postwar era. Indeed, when *Four Steps* was first shown in New York, undated, critics assumed it had been made *after* the war, as part of the movement touched off by *Open City*.

For all its excellences, *Four Steps in the Clouds* remains a modest work, a harbinger. But late in 1942, when Mussolini's hold on his people was fast disintegrating, there appeared Luchino Visconti's *Ossessione*, a true masterpiece that contained all the seeds of the postwar neo-realist movement—the concern for people, the use of natural settings and types, the overwhelming sense of looking at life as it really is. An adaptation (although uncredited) of James M. Cain's *The Postman Always Rings Twice*, its sordid theme was played against the background of a small *trattoria* on the marshes of the Po and a fair at Ancona. And though Visconti used such familiar Italian actors as Massimo Girotti, Clara Calamai and Elio Marcuzzo, under his direction they performed with a naturalism that blended with the sweaty peasants who crowded the bar at the shabby inn and thronged the amusement booths of the *festa* The camera work was always arresting, using long traveling shots to keep the principals in screen center as they moved through the crowds, using concealed cameras for sequences in public parks and streets, mounting the camera on a crane to rise from a close-up of an actor to panoramas of an entire landscape within a single shot. Here were the faces of real Italians, the sights and sounds of everyday Italy mobilized upon the screen to tell a powerful and affecting story. It was a revelation, a film so far beyond anything produced in the twenty years of Fascism that its impression upon other Italian film makers could only have been profound. Unfortunately, it is a revelation that few Americans seem destined to share. Not only was Visconti's film a fairly flagrant violation of copyright, but the film rights to Cain's novel already belonged to M-G-M, which produced its own version of the story in 1946. M-G-M remained adamant in refusing to permit prints of *Ossessione* to enter the United States until as late as 1976.

As the war progressed, film making in Italy became increasingly chaotic (as did life itself). Loyalties were divided. Some favored the Allies—or thought the Axis a losing cause; some clung to their Fascist beliefs. After the fall of Mussolini, with war still ravaging the south and the Nazis occupying the remainder of the peninsula, film making came to a virtual standstill. In 1944 only sixteen pictures were produced in Italy, most of them coming from Scalera's studio in Venice, the last stronghold of the Fascist elements in the industry. Meanwhile, anti-Fascists went into hiding, awaiting the liberation of the Allied forces, awaiting the withdrawal of the Nazi army of occupation. Late in 1944, even before the Germans had completed their evacuation of Rome, Roberto Rossellini was already at work on *Open City*, the key film in the entire neo-realist Italian revival. In it he sought to re-create, as accurately as possible, the tensions, the trials and the heroic resistance of the common people of Rome during the years of the Nazi occupation. Aside from the principals, few in the cast were professional actors. Many, indeed, were simply citizens—or Nazi soldiers—photographed on the fly by cameras concealed on rooftops or hidden in cars. Little of the film was shot in a studio, partly for financial reasons, partly because Rossellini (and Cesare Zavattini, who wrote the script) sensed that the documentary value of actual streets, apartments and courtyards would heighten the authenticity of their story.

What emerged was a film strikingly unlike anything that

had been seen before. Technically, it was far from flawless. Rossellini had been forced to use whatever scraps of film stock he could lay his hands on, while the lighting—particularly in those interiors not taken in a studio—was often too weak for dramatic effects or even adequate modeling. Indeed, shooting had to be abandoned entirely several times while the director set about raising the necessary funds to continue. But the very passion that had inspired the production of *Open City* seemed to create the centrifugal force that held it all together. Its roughness, its lack of finish became a virtue. And the cumulative power of Rossellini's feeling for his subject was translated into a visual intensity that made the picture sometimes almost unbearable to watch. Here was true realism—the raw life of a tragic era. "This is the way things are," said Rosellini in presenting his film. It became the credo of the entire neo-realist movement.

Within the next five years there appeared in Italy a cycle of films in every way as remarkable and exciting as the great Russian pictures of the late twenties—and inspired, like them, by the sudden discovery of a national identity and the simultaneous liberation of creative talents. The complete breakdown of the Fascist régime removed all previous restraints. The years of repression under the Nazi occupation forces, the disenchantment under the Allies produced a social awareness that found its fullest expression in the neo-realist movement. At the outset, the mere ability to treat dispassionately the daily life of the ordinary Italian was inspiration enough for directors like Rossellini and De Sica. Rossellini's *Paisan* (1946) was an epic study of the last months of war in Italy. De Sica, the former matinee idol, revealed again his concern for children in *Shoeshine* (1946), but with a depth and passion unsuspected from his earlier films. It is a poignant, muted tale of an appealing group of Roman street urchins caught up in the black market that swept through Italy during the war years. The boys are jailed, then friend is set against friend so that their captors may gain a little more information on the gangsters who have been using them. De Sica makes it amply clear that the authorities are neither brutal nor stupid, merely hard pressed. But because they take the easy, obvious course, friends become enemies and murder is the final outcome. All of this is offered without either bitterness or cynicism as a dramatization of actual conditions. And if his revelations disturbed his audience it was, after all, up to them as citizens to do something about it. In such films can be detected the emergence of a truly democratic spirit—the objective presentation of social fact, with social action left to the conscience and the intelligence of the viewer.

With Rossellini and De Sica as its leaders, the neo-realist movement quickly gathered momentum and was confirmed in the work of a dozen or more directors in the period immediately after the war. Drawn irresistibly to social themes, they were united by a common philosophy that was perhaps most clearly expressed in Luigi Zampa's *To Live in Peace* (1946). Zampa selected an incident from the very end of the war to suggest that all men—even Nazis—could live together in friendship if they followed their instincts instead of their ideologies. An Italian farmer has given shelter to two American soldiers caught behind the German lines, one white and one black. During the night the German sentry from the village comes to the farm. In order to cover up the noises of the Negro drinking in the cellar, the farmer gets the German drunk. Suddenly the American bursts out of his hiding place, and there is a suspenseful moment as Nazi and Negro face each other. But all hate, all conflicting ideology has been drowned in the wine. The two wrap their arms around each other and go roaring through the village. "The war is over—Der Krieg ist kaput." In *Angelina* (1947), Zampa reiterated the same theme, that man's better instincts are subverted by his blind obedience to orders. In the title role, Anna Magnani gave a wonderfully funny and sympathetic performance as a working-class housewife who becomes the leader of all the women in her neighborhood against the local politicians and landlords.

Other directors took actual incidents from the postwar scene to create images of shocking or pitiable truth. In the first half of *Tragic Hunt* (1947), Giuseppe De Santis drew a remarkable picture of the chaos, the lawlessness that followed the end of hostilities in northern Italy, and although a taste for melodrama marred its second part, his scenes of peasants organizing and fighting for the right to return to their land were both moving and convincing. Also quite melodramatic (almost inevitably) was Alberto Lattuada's *Without Pity* (1947), centered on another serious postwar problem in Italy, the black G.I.'s who had deserted the Army and were living lawlessly in the Tombolo, north of Leghorn. There was sensitivity in this story of a Negro and his love for a white prostitute, but sensationalism as well. (The film was cut drastically for exhibition in the United States.) From Visconti, the director of *Ossessione*, came a ponderous but searching and indubitably sincere study of the lives of impoverished Sicilian fishermen, *The Earth Trembles* (1948), made documentary-fashion without actors or studio settings—and in a dialect so special that not even all Italians could follow it. Again it was a film that said, with sympathy: "This is the way things are. What are we going to do about it?"

Out of all these films—and many more—there emerged the image of the ordinary Italian. With a vividness and humanity unequaled by any other nation, the drama of commonplace joys and sorrows was projected from the screen. Curiously enough, such pictures were not at first too well received in Italy itself. Perhaps they reflected the ordinary too accurately. What the Italians wanted was the glitter, the glamour, the romance of the Hollywood movies after their years of misery and privation. In any case, it was the critical reception abroad of such pictures as *Open City, Shoeshine, Bicycle Thief* and *To Live in Peace* that opened the eyes of most Italians to what they really had. All of them proved far more successful on their subsequent runs in their native land than when first released.

As economic stability once more returned to Italy, the Italian producers began to consolidate their gains. In Cinecittà, just outside Rome, they had not only the largest and best equipped studios in all Europe but also, at the film school there, a well-trained corps of artists and technicians to draw upon. Furthermore, the new government took a healthy interest in film production, recognizing its value as a source both of goodwill and of revenue for the country. Outstanding pictures were rewarded with special tax rebates. As an additional aid to the home industry, acting on a plan put forward by the Italian producers themselves, the government permitted the American studios to take out of the country a portion of their war-frozen dollars provided that some of this money were allocated to the development of a market in the United States for Italian pictures. In 1950 the American producers agreed—and found themselves in the unprecedented position of actively encouraging the growth of a rival industry in their own country. Except for the British, no nation had ever before made such a concerted effort to break into the American market. To overcome the resistance of the average moviegoer to subtitled foreign films, they even set up their own dubbing studios in New York, matching the voices of Broadway actors to the lips of the Italian performers. The experiment failed. The contrast between Italian gesture and stage English all but destroyed the illusion of reality the directors sought to achieve; the pictures were neither good enough for the art-house circuits nor popular enough for the neighborhood chains. A few of the more spectacular exploitation items, like *Attila* (1958), were bought and adapted by American firms. Others—*Ulysses* (1955), *War and Peace* (1957), *Tempest* (1959)—have been costly co-productions with American firms, fusing the American box office with Hollywood's stars and budgets, and the Italian flair for elaborate pageantry.

Indeed, the Italians became so terribly anxious for wide box-office approval that the original tenets of neo-realism became increasingly distorted. While there was a concentrated effort to make everything as grim as possible—"this is the way things are"—there was also an increasing emphasis on such marketable aspects of reality as sex and sadism. And in place of the earthy, hearty Anna Magnani, the Italian screen abounded with cover girls like Gina Lollobrigida, Silvana Mangano, Silvana Pampanini, Sophia Loren and Eleanora Rossi-Drago—sleek, well-developed creatures, delightful to look at, but scarcely ideal as the heroines of neo-realistic dramas. In fact, as so often happens, the word itself had become little more than a catch-phrase. The Italian cinema continued to advertise its neo-realism, but what it actually provided was a series of melodramatic shockers photographed against natural exteriors.

In the meantime, several neo-neorealisms have emerged that hold new promise for the Italian screen—if ever the producers find the courage to follow them up. All of them are based firmly in the everyday life of ordinary Italians and motivated by a sympathy and affection for the common man. But a new dimension has been added, a new element of comedy, fantasy, even poetry. We can see now that De Sica's strange, fanciful *Miracle in Milan* (1951), with its hoboes soaring on broomsticks high above Milan's cathedral, was in fact the point of departure for this whole new genre. Renato Castellani's *Two Cents' Worth of Hope* (1952) and Luigi Comencini's *Bread, Love and Dreams* (1953), for example, created a fine sense of the reality of small-town life in the Italian hills, then used this as the background for broad comedy that also veered off into fantasy. Federico Fellini's *La Strada* (1954), a somber, tragic study of an itinerant side-show strong man and a simple-minded girl clown, explored a new blending of realism and poetry, a heightening of emotion through skillfully stylized performances juxtaposed against natural backgrounds. *Love in the City* (1954), a project conceived and organized by Cesare Zavattini and directed by half a dozen youthful enthusiasts, also seemed to mark a new direction. Here the emphasis is returned again to documentary realism, with people re-enacting their own tragedies or speaking urgently of their lives and problems directly in front of the cameras and microphones. But by skillful use of the camera, by dubbing and editing, Zavattini transformed simple documentation into genuinely artistic creation.

Here was fresh ore for the Italian film, new directions to be explored and developed with all the passion and enthusiasm that had marked the renaissance of the Italian film industry ten years earlier. And while, for commercial purposes, the Italians continued to produce such dim-witted spectaculars as *Hercules* (1956) and the ultra-violent "spaghetti Westerns" of Sergio Leone and his horde of less talented imitators, the true strength of the Italian cinema was to be found in the subsequent efforts of the progenitors of neo-realism and their direct descendants. Roberto Rossellini, after a disconcerting eclipse that lasted more than a decade, seemed to regain much of his former passion—and compassion—in *General Della Rovere* (1959), which starred his neo-realist compatriot, Vittorio De Sica, as the phony, ill-fated general; most of his subsequent work was for Italian television. De Sica himself alternated between acting and directing right up to the time of his death in 1974. A suave and facile comedian, he made frequent appearances in the films of others, but reaffirmed his directorial genius with the raw tragedy of *Two Women* (1960) and the more subtly-textured *Garden of the Finzi-Continis* (1970), both drawn from episodes of Italy's involvement in World War II. Luchino Visconti, whose *Ossessione* was a harbinger of neo-realism and whose *La Terra Trema* remains perhaps the least compromising example of the movement's ideology, returned to the contemporary scene with the powerful if melodramatic *Rocco and His Brothers* (1960), then slipped off into the past in such meticulous, if curiously de-energized, period pieces as *The Leopard* (1963), *The Damned* (1969) and the almost inanimate

Death in Venice (1971), all giving rise to the suspicion that Visconti had become more concerned with *décor* than with drama in his later years. He died in 1977.

Meanwhile, Federico Fellini, who had contributed to the scripts of the earlier Rossellini films, began to find his own direction as early as *I Vitelloni* (1953), a highly autobiographical account of the dreariness and near-hopelessness of young people growing up in a small Italian town. There was a warmth to his vision, an affection for people, and an extraordinary ability to penetrate surface appearances to convey inner feelings. *I Vitelloni* also established his mastery of finding the precise image to capture a mood or an atmosphere— the loneliness of a deserted square, the forced gaiety of a masked ball, the shabby glamor of a third-rate vaudeville house. All of these virtues achieved even fuller expression in *La Strada* (1954) and *The Nights of Cabiria* (1957), the two films that earned him a world-wide reception. They emphasized the individuality of his viewpoint, particularly when dealing with the poor and friendless in an urban setting. Above all, they demonstrated his ability to use the camera for revelation, not merely for exposition. Unforgettable is the moment when Cabiria's "gentleman" puts a cigarette in his mouth and immediately becomes a suspect, sinister character. This was carried further in his next two films, *La Dolce Vita* (1960) and *8½* (1963), both large-scale works and at the same time highly personal. As a working journalist, Fellini had come to know Rome well, and used the despair, the corruption and the decadence that he found there as an extended metaphor and microcosm of all the ills of modern society (as he was to do later, in 1969, in *Fellini-Satyricon*, in which the Rome of today is commented upon through themes drawn from Petronius). As a working director, Fellini had come to know not only the creative drain placed upon the film maker but also the commerical compromises demanded by venal or corrupt production heads. Part fantasy, part symbol, *8½* is clearly the work of an artist who knows he has reached a turning point in his career. With the sole exception of *The Clowns* (1970), made for Italian television, and the affectionate *Amarcord* (1974), which returns to the themes and times of *I Vitelloni*, Fellini has come up with ever grander— but emptier—historical creations, visually sumptuous but emotionally cold. By the time of *Casanova* (1976), one could well ask why he chose to make a picture about a character he so obviously detested. As with Visconti, the look had become more important than the feel.

Feeling, the pulsing emotions of flesh-and-blood people, was never the major concern of Michelangelo Antonioni, even though he too had his roots in the neo-realist movement (and had contributed one section, the semi-documentary *Attempted Suicide*, to Zavattini's *Love in the City*). Alienation was the pervasive theme of his pictures, the inability of people to relate to their society or to each other, a theme most masterfully stated in his trilogy, *L'Avventura* (1960), *La Notte* (1961) and *L'Eclisse* (1962). His tendency is to isolate a few people against backgrounds that are at best neutral and often hostile—the rocky island in *L'Avventura*, the threatening streets of Milan in *La Notte*, the blighted, barren wastes of *Red Desert* (1964) and *The Passenger* (1975). And generally he is more concerned with the end of an affair rather than its beginning or its consummation. His characters are wan, bloodless, remote. Even in *Blow-Up*, at once the most accessible and commercially successful of his works (made in England in 1966), the central character, a photographer who has stumbled upon a murder, seems totally unable to act upon his discovery. Stylistically, Antonioni has always been partial to protracted long shots, with the action situated far from the camera, or in even more protracted shots involving complicated camera movements. With *Red Desert* and *Blow-Up*, he began to experiment with color, controling his backgrounds by painting them to correspond to the psychological effects he hoped to produce. It is, therefore, not wholly coincidental that as Antonioni became more concerned with the formal aspects of his work, his characters became increasingly less interesting until, caught up in the virtuosity of his seven-minute pan around the room and through the window at the climax of *The Passenger*, we quite forget that the passenger himself, Jack Nicholson, lies dying in that room.

In the last decade, Italy has uncovered an astonishing number of first-rate talents—Bellocchio, Bertolucci, Olmi, Pasolini, Pontecorvo, Risi, Liliana Cavani—many of whom have already made their mark on the screens of the world. At the moment, however, none has excited greater international interest than the dynamic, prolific Lina Wertmuller. A former actress, she entered films in 1963 as an assistant to Fellini on *8½*—the chain continues—then immediately branched out on her own with a series of political satires that won only minor acclaim. Indeed, not until the enormous success of *Swept Away* (1975) and *Seven Beauties* (1976) did any distributor outside of Italy deem it worth the while to consider them, despite the fact that her earlier *Love and Anarchy* (1973) and *The Seduction of Mimi* (1974) had been well received both critically and on the art house circuits. The Wertmuller films are impudent and audacious, invariably centered upon her favorite working-class hero, Giancarlo Giannini. No words can fully convey the verve and vitality of her work, particularly since in synopsis her plots read like the gloomiest neo-realist tracts. No matter. Wertmuller has a tremendous insight into people—their strengths, their weaknesses, the things that make them human—and a rare ability to communicate those insights to her audiences. As a result, her films swirl with a sense of life and joyous celebration, even though, like a platinum blonde, they may be dark at the roots. Through her artistry, Wertmuller has given a new—and commerical—extension to the neo-realist approach. But after all, isn't it the artists in film—the directors and the writers—who tap the new and occasionally profitable veins of cinematic ore? The odd thing about the movies has always been that once the financial side moves in and tries to commercialize the operation, the outcome is generally disappointing to the audience, to the artists, and ultimately to the producers themselves. It may be pertinent to observe that as of the present writing, Dino de Laurentiis and Carlo Ponti, Italy's top producers, have long since quit the local scene, whereas Wertmuller (albeit with a Warner Brothers contract) is riding high.

The Classic Art of the Japanese Film

Until Akira Kurosawa's *Rashomon* won the Grand Prize at the Venice Film Festival in 1951, it was generally assumed that the industry in Japan—like the studios in India or Egypt—simply turned out great quantities of films of dubious merit and purely local interest. Although pictures had been made there since 1904, almost since the time that movies started, few had been seen by the Western world and none had roused any particular enthusiasm. In fact, not until the thirties, when Japan began her campaigns of conquest in the Orient, was there an industry of any size. As so often happens, the films followed the flag. Through wars and economic penetration, Japan had captured for herself a vast potential audience in China, Manchuria, Indochina and Korea, a market long dominated by the European and Hollywood studios. With their particular gift for cheap imitation, the Japanese were soon turning out between seven and eight hundred films a year—mostly pseudo-French romances or American-style crime and action pictures. Through this flood of films, they effectively ousted or undersold all competitors in the Far East, a market that Japan controls to this day.

At the same time, Japan's studios also began to produce specifically for home consumption films that were designed to inspire the maximum loyalty and enthusiasm of the Japanese people for the innumerable wars their country was waging. Incidents from the campaigns in China and Manchuria, the border clashes with the Soviet Union provided the basis for many of them. Also important for this purpose were the *jidai-geki*, the period dramas designed to give the Japanese a heightened awareness of their cultural and historical past, a pride in their strength and their traditions—all very useful in time of war. Less useful, apparently, were the *kindai-geki*, realistic studies of modern Japanese life which had been an outstanding film form of the late twenties. During the turbulent thirties, the tight military censorship saw to it that very few of these ever reached the screen. One of the rare exceptions was *Kimiko* (1936), a delicate and charming glimpse of Japanese domestic relations that received limited distribution in this country.

Soon after Pearl Harbor, the Japanese industry was nationalized and turned even more directly to propaganda purposes. Documentaries and fiction films combined to stress the duties, the honor of service to the Emperor—the privilege of dying gloriously for one's country. Such a film was *Volunteers of Death* (1942), the Japanese version of the Pearl Harbor attack. Despite the fate of its hero in the obviously staged battle scenes, it was considered to have a happy ending. The boy had died for his Emperor! The film, incidentally, was shown in Germany and distributed by the Nazis in occupied France as a demonstration of the might of the Eastern end of the Axis. At the same time, costume dramas were also being produced in great numbers—and apparently in very much the same style that has since won such recognition for the Japanese film makers. Hence the real liberation for Japanese talents, once the war was over, lay not in the field of period pictures but in their new freedom to comment upon the social conditions within the contemporary scene. Like the Italian directors under Fascism, the Japanese had acquired the skills and techniques of film making while producing the pictures demanded of them by their government. Now, with the war over and the old order swept away, with the Allied occupation forces everywhere and the devastation of the two atomic explosions that had shattered their cities still in evidence, they turned their creative energies to the world around them. And apparently, from the accounts of those who have been privileged to see any considerable number of these films, the Japanese directors have dealt with modern subjects in experimental forms as bold as the best of the Italian postwar films. Kurosawa's *Drunken Angel* (1948) and *Living* (1952), Imai's *Stained Image* (1953), Naruse's *The Echo* (1954), Toyoda's *Wheat Whistle* (1955), and innumerable pictures by the late Kenji Mizoguchi are only a few of the outstanding films on contemporary themes that were belatedly seen by the Western world.

In the meantime, most Americans had to judge Japanese film making largely on the basis of the half-dozen or so costume dramas that had been released here in the wake of *Rashomon.* It is, of course, a serious critical error to attempt to generalize from a handful of pictures. But when that handful includes such radically different yet authentic masterpieces as *Rashomon* (1951), *Ugetsu* (1953), *Gate of Hell* (1954), *The Magnificent Seven* (1954) and *The Golden Demon* (1955), one may safely conclude that they are the products of an already mature industry that has at its core film makers of extraordinary scope and creativity. Today it is clear that *Rashomon* was not the first masterpiece of Japanese film making but simply the first to gain world-wide recognition. Its physical beauty, the virtuosity of its cinematic techniques and above all the exoticism of its 8th century setting and story prepared Western audiences in some measure for what was to follow. While our Occidental films had leveled off at a plateau of technical perfection, these films from Japan explored psychological, physiological and aesthetic paths that were, in their implications, not merely different but revolutionary. They do not ask us to "identify" with the characters in them, nor is there any attempt to heighten psychological tensions through photographic trickery or editing techniques.

Our emotions are involved obliquely, through the mind rather than the nerves, while our eyes and senses are flooded by the unexpected beauties of a filmic art that derives from ancestral tradition. The camera frames each scene with the classic formalism of a Japanese print or painting. The performances of the actors are almost ritualistic, with attitudes and gestures drawn from the ancient Kabuki or No drama. Color, design, gradations of black and gray, the contrapuntal use of Oriental music add to an emotional tone that fortifies the sense of timeless tradition in these films. To the formalism of the past, however, has been added a new humanism, an interest in people that gives warmth and personality to their age-old themes, an intellectual and philosophic base to their art.

In *Rashomon*, for example, the center of the film is essentially an inquiry into the nature of truth. Its four principals have been involved in a murder and rape. Each recites his own version of the sequence of events. Each story, with its own protective colorations, is shown by the camera. The characters speak as to a tribunal, squatting directly before the camera, staring into its lens. It is the audience that must decide the relative truth of each one's testimony—if truth there be at all. The whole conception of *Rashomon*, both thematic and cinematic, was markedly different from Western conventions. Although Japanese critics spoke of its "European style," its closest relative is clearly Dovzhenko's daring and intense *Frontier* with its stylization and fluid movement of the camera. More important than its style or source, however, is the fact that *Rashomon* posed squarely a question that must have occurred to every thoughtful Japanese citizen during the years since the war. Their "divine" Emperor had been defeated, his myth of infallibility destroyed—and with it the entire elaborate structure of duties and obligations, the *chu* on which Japanese society was based. In place of the "truth" of unquestioning obedience, the Japanese were being force-fed the new "truth" of democratization. Through this story of the 8th century, Kurosawa sought some reassessment of the problems of today.

Similarly, *Ugetsu*, a legend of 16th century Japan, moved from the reality of the peasant wars onto a plane of supernatural fantasy as its hero, lured by the riches to be made in the cities, abandons his wife and farm and lives with a ghostly noblewoman in a mysterious castle. When eventually he returns to his home, he finds his dead wife waiting to receive him, to comfort him and give him rest. "What is truth?" asked *Rashomon*; "What is reality?" is the question posed by *Ugetsu*. *Gate of Hell*, based on a true story from the 12th century, is far more direct in its suggestion that, no matter what the form of a society may be, its basic strength derives from the code of personal honor that preserves the order, the moral fiber of a people. Its unhappy hero is a warrior, intoxicated by the beauty of a noblewoman whose life he has saved. He vows to have her even though she be married to another. When his rash persistence leads to her death, the man begs the husband to kill him. The husband refuses, and in a sudden, agonized gesture that is at once the mark of his repentance and an acknowledgment of the force of tradition, he crops his warrior's lock. The final shot shows him hurrying through the massive red temple gates of Kyoto to spend his remaining years as a monk.

Gate of Hell was the first Japanese film to use color, a carefully controlled color that not only enriched each beautifully composed shot but added immeasurably to the emotional values as well. Fiery red-oranges dominate the opening scenes of chaos in the Imperial palace, an icy blue bathes the scene in which the warrior, bent on assassination, approaches the home of his beloved. Japanese technicians spent three years in Hollywood mastering the technology of color. To these mechanical skills they added the age-old tradition of its use in Japanese art, an awareness of the psychology of color that made our own Technicolor films seem flat and one-dimensional by comparison. Shot on Eastman stock, its delicacy and subtlety so impressed the people in Rochester that they immediately requested a print for their own archives and research. Unquestionably, Japanese films became an important influence in refining the future use of color on the screen. Since the Japanese had no color process of their own, and paying for American raw stock in American dollars was prohibitively expensive, the studios at first prudently confined its use to themes that were not merely enchanced but psychologically intensified by color. Its development can readily be seen in such films as *The Golden Demon* and *Yang Kwei Fei* (1955). Ten years later, it was difficult to find a Japanese movie that was not in color; but while the artistry remained for those with taste and sensitivity, the color in most Japanese films now tends to be blatant, garish, postery. Indeed, as production has risen—with crude imitations of Hollywood gangster movies, action films and pornos—the traditional artistry of the Japanese cinema has been increasingly hard to come by.

After a sharp rise in production immediately after World War II (to more than 500 pictures in 1956), the Japanese industry has leveled off at about 300 pictures per year, most of them calculated to appeal to audiences in Japan's own 2,500 theaters or—more importantly—audiences in the 50,000 houses throughout the Far East. These audiences, to put it mildly, are not demanding. Godzilla and friends will more than do. And while Japanese producers, such as Masaichi Nagata of Daiei Studio, declared their intention to supply quality fare with a hopeful eye on the far richer Western market, few ever succeeded—Kurosawa's *Rashomon* and *The Seven Samurai*, Teshigahara's *Woman in the Dunes* (1964) and Oshima's *In the Realm of the Senses* (1976) being the rare exceptions. One can only hope that works of this quality will continue to find distribution here. No doubt it will take another European festival and another grand prize winner to insure it.

International Glimpses

It is not possible in a book of this size to touch on production in every country where films are made. Nor, in fact, is that the intention. In many lands production is far too limited or too specialized to be of interest to the outside world. In others, the industry is too derivative or inept to claim serious attention. India, for example, turns out hundreds of pictures every year—far more than Hollywood does today—yet these are rarely seen by international audiences. Their techniques are crude by western standards; their construction, their pace, their overemphatic acting are all alien to our tastes. Apart from the occasional film from Satyajit Ray and a scant handful of others, India's films are reminiscent of the most ordinary low-budget movie turned out by our own Republic studio back in the thirties. The same holds true of China, which also produces pictures in great numbers; while the few serious films from Egypt that have been shown in Europe or in the United States literally rocked their audiences with laughter. One can merely note that such industries do exist and await the day when, like the Japanese or the Italian, out of the quantities of pictures they produce there begins to emerge a quality, a strength that makes them of more than purely local interest.

The history of film confirms that no masterpiece has ever sprung suddenly from hitherto barren ground. It seems that there must always be a period of preparation, a period during which the strengths of native production are explored, tested and developed. When at last a work of true merit is produced, there are today the great European film festivals to help it win world-wide distribution. Such festivals as those at Cannes and Venice, Berlin, Edinburgh and San Sebastian are often lightly dismissed as tourist attractions for resort cities—which, of course, they are. But they have grown increasingly important in recent years as a kind of international merchandise mart where the films of the world are placed on display and prospective distributors from all nations gather to discover the latest and best. It was at the postwar festivals of Venice and Cannes that the rebirth of the Italian film received international recognition. There also the resurgence of a Scandinavian industry was discovered, and the sudden, dramatic emergence of the Japanese film. When India's Satyajit Ray won top honors at Cannes for his *Pather Panchali* (1956) and at Venice the following year for his *Aparajito*, it suddenly became impossible to ignore completely the Indian film industry any longer. At these festivals one can note a fresh enthusiasm turning into mastery, or a trend crystallizing into a national style.

In Sweden the first evidence of such stirrings was to be found in the experimental shorts of Gösta Werner and Arne Sucksdorff. Werner's *Midwinterblot* (1945) was an eerie evocation of a pagan ritual culminating in a human sacrifice. Imaginative sound and shadowy, deep-focus photography created the sense of an entire world in darkness. Sucksdorff, whose fascinating studies of wild life first attracted attention at the Cannes festival, spends months patiently waiting for his close-ups of birds on the wing or beasts on the prowl, then months more at the cutting bench. In such films as *A Divided World* (1948) and *Shadows on the Snow* (1948), he demonstrated his uncanny ability to capture and shape these moments of primeval life with a dispassionate hand. The killer kills, the captive waits, and elemental forces are neither sentimentalized nor transformed into moral fables. In *Symphony of a City* (1949) and *Summer Idyll* (1950), he applied the same objectivity to the people of Stockholm as they went about their daily tasks or made love at a nearby beach. Both Werner's and Sucksdorff's work was financed by Svensk Filmindustri, Sweden's leading studio. Even though Sucksdorff's shorts cost as much to make as an average feature film, Svensk had the feeling that the vitality of Swedish films depended upon such serious young craftsmen. They were not mistaken. The re-emergence of the Swedish feature film was heralded at Venice in 1947 with the screening of Alf Sjöberg's *Torment* (*Hets*), a suspenseful psychological study of a sadistic teacher given unbounded authority in his classroom. Since that time, despite severe financial restrictions, the Swedish directors have managed to maintain a high level of originality and integrity. Gone now are the Lagerlöf epics, the spectacular costume dramas; but the love of nature that once characterized the "Golden Era" of the Swedish film is still evident in such films as Sjöberg's *Miss Julie* (1950), Ingmar Bergman's *One Summer of Happiness* (1952) or Sucksdorff's first feature, *The Great Adventure* (1953). Bergman's films especially—*The Naked Night* (1954), *The Seventh Seal* (1956), *Wild Strawberries* (1958)—suggest that Swedish characters still feel the same guilt, the same need for expiation through suffering as their cinematic forebears of 25 years earlier. Bergman sets a very special example. No doubt little would be known of Sweden as a film producing nation were it not for the quality and quantity of his work. At first he seemed a mystic, his films almost impenetrable in their references to Biblical myths, pagan ballads, 19th-century legerdemain and arcane Freudianisms. Despite the (at the time) wanton nudity of *Naked Night*, *Illicit Interlude* (1950), *Summer with Monika* (1953) and the lush sexuality of *Smiles of a Summer Night* (1955), Bergman remained the ascetic, the intellectualizer of our baser emotions. This image persisted through his extraordinary trio of self-styled "chamber dramas"—*Through a Glass Darkly* (1961), *Winter Light* (1963), *The Silence* (1963)—in which human relationships are explored in what he terms "the absence of God." The private world of the artist was at the center of *Persona* (1966); while the social responsibilities of the artist provided the theme for both *The Hour of the Wolf* and *Shame* (both 1968). More recently, in *Cries and Whispers* (1972) and in two films edited down from six-hour television series, *Scenes from a Marriage* (1974) and *Face to Face* (1976), with minimal camera or editing pyrotechnics—but performances of unparalleled intensity—he plumbed psychological depths that not even most marriage counselors are willing to face. Bergman is an artist who has never ceased to grow, constantly searching out new themes, and also—no less important—the appropriate style and techniques with which to present them.

Denmark, too, is slowly edging back into the spotlight shared by film makers of the world. A leader before World War I, she gradually disappeared from view as her foremost artists left for other lands. Late in the thirties, however, her greatest director, Carl Dreyer, returned to Denmark to write and, occasionally, to make a short art or documentary film. (Because of limited finances, Danish production continues to be primarily in the documentary field.) But a kind of spiritual rebirth took place with the release of Dreyer's first feature in almost twelve years, *Day of Wrath* (1943). This extraordinary film created on the screen the living image of early 17th century Denmark. In that time of puritanical repression and superstition, the young wife of a kindly parson, suspected of being a witch, finally comes to believe the horrible accusation herself. Dreyer unfolded slowly and forcefully his theme of the power of evil to corrupt the good. While the film was immensely popular in Denmark, the critics complained of its tempo. But, as Archer Winsten of the *New York Post* wrote in his vehement defense of the film, "That any critic can suggest that its slow movement is a fault reveals a deep-rooted depreciation of taste. Far too many sensational films, the critics' daily poison, all action and no thought, create this sad hypnotism."

Soon after the war, the Danish film industry was further strengthened by the work of two young documentary film makers, Bjärne and Astrid Henning-Jensen. Their first feature, *Ditte, Child of Man*, based on a work by the outstanding Danish novelist Andersen Nexö, told the story of an unwanted, illegitimate child. Presented at the 1947 Venice Festival, its unaffected use of peasant types and natural exteriors, its simplicity and sincerity recalled the great days of the Scandinavian cinema. But while *Ditte* has everywhere ranked high in critical esteem, its theatrical distribution has been limited almost entirely to its own country. Like *Day of Wrath*, it was deemed too slow for popular tastes elsewhere. Today, with Dreyer gone, the Henning-Jensens have become his logical successors among Danish film makers. Their delightful short, *Palle Alone in the World* (1951), has been repeatedly shown on television programs; while their feature-length color film, *Where Islands Float*, a humane account of the difficulties of bringing medical care to the people of a small village in Greenland, won the top honors for documentary at the 1955 Venice Festival.

It is not too surprising that Denmark also won the Grand Prize in the feature-film category at the same festival with Dreyer's *The Word* (*Ordet*, 1955). For the Danes, in sustaining their tradition of limited, quality production, managed to resist for many years the commercial temptations of sex and violence so often exploited on the screens of the larger nations. Though they release but a handful of films annually, most of these are apparently made without concern for any market beyond their own four million inhabitants. Certainly, it was this individuality, this preoccupation with the Danish land and its people, that distinguished *The Word* at Venice. There were dozens of other pictures, many of them sensational, most of them swift-paced, polished and adroit. Yet it was Dreyer's slow-moving, gentle story, shrouded in an atmosphere of almost mystic dedication, that caused the only true sensation at the festival. It is perhaps Dreyer's most personal film, with its strange theme of a young farmer obsessed by the belief that he is Christ. Though pitied and ridiculed by his family, a little girl's faith finally enables him to work a miracle. Like all of Dreyer's pictures, *The Word* is unconventional, deeply felt and lovingly wrought. Each scene, each unhurried action creates an anticipation that reaches its summit in the moment of the miracle. The effect is impressive, even shocking; but its quiet, deliberate exposition—typical not only of Dreyer but of Danish film makers in general— made its commercial success outside Denmark debatable. A "smash hit" in its native land, it received only limited distribution in the United States, a source of prestige rather than profit. There is, then, a special—and distressing—irony in the fact that as we moved into the seventies, Denmark became a primary source for soft-core porno movies. Man, apparently, can not live on prestige alone.

The Word, like many another outstanding picture shown at the festivals, accentuates a problem for which there is no easy solution. Foreign films are generally purchased for distribution by people who believe that they can market them profitably in their own countries. Distributors coming to these festivals are aware of their public's taste and preferences, and they search for such qualities in the pictures exhibited there. For an obvious box-office attraction, like Clouzot's thriller *Les Diaboliques*, there were frantic bidding and high prices. But an uncompromising film like Luis Buñuel's *The Young and the Damned* (*Los Olvidados*, 1951) found few bidders, even though it had won festival honors. A harrowing study of Mexico's juvenile delinquents, this picture could not be considered "commercial" by any ordinary standards and only a true film enthusiast like the late Edward Kingsley would dare to buy it for American art houses. Few distributors, however, could afford to risk the thousands of dollars required to purchase the rights to a foreign film of such dubious box-office appeal.

Clearly, festival honors are not enough to ensure international success. A wide box-office acceptance of these products of varying cultures depends not so much on cinematic art as upon the sophistication and maturity of the audience—a situation over which the film maker exercises no control. But though the festivals may not appreciably affect public standards, they still provide an invaluable meeting place where film makers, film distributors and a fraction of the film audiences of many nations can gather together to exchange ideas and keep an eye on developments in other lands. Far more important than the big commerical movies and the occasional "smash hits" that turn up at these festivals is the opportunity to observe the artistic growth of films from every country around the world.

Changing Trends
in the American Film

Though American pictures are often casually dismissed as "escapist entertainment," the forms of that escape vary from era to era and have their own significance. Successive waves or cycles of films characteristic of any given period, charted against changes in the political and social climate of the country, reveal something of the temperament, the social attitudes of the people themselves. Thus the pictures of the early thirties reflected the national disaster. The drawing-room comedies, the sophisticated plays, even the "canned" musicals—the staples of the first years of sound—had begun to pall. As banks failed and lifelong savings were wiped out, as unemployment spread across the land, these artificial and outdated forms of entertainment became unacceptable. The public did not suddenly demand "realistic" pictures, but it could no longer be amused by high society exchanging bons mots at the cocktail hour nor stirred by the matinee idyls of pretty sopranos and impoverished young tenors. In the first unhappy years of the depression, audiences sought a more recognizable image of their own problems on the screen. Sound had made possible a new degree of realism in motion pictures and when, late in 1930, Warner Brothers' *Little Caesar* brought throngs to the box office once more, the course was clear. What the public obviously wanted was a hard-hitting, naturalistic form of drama that took its themes from the headlines of the day.

The studios quickly brought to the screen not only a staggering succession of gangster pictures (fifty in 1931 alone!)

but equally sensational exposés of rackets, political corruption, prison brutality, bank failures and newspaper scandal sheets. If there was any element of escapism in these films, it lay in their tendency to blame isolated individuals for what were in fact national problems. Audiences seemed to find some reassurance in the thought that everything could be solved by the jailing—or shooting—of a brutal warden, a hoodlum gangster or a power-hungry politician. In *The Big House* (1930), *Little Caesar* (1930), *The Front Page* (1931), *The Public Enemy* (1931), *The Secret Six* (1931) and many more, the public was given strong, unadulterated dramatizations of the stories behind the daily headlines. Often such films were cynical and cheap, but occasionally they proved to be sincere and perceptive investigations of evils and abuses aggravated by the depression. Indeed, the facts revealed by *I Am a Fugitive from a Chain Gang* (1932), based on an actual case, were so shocking that an aroused public forced a reformation of the chain-gang system.

Not only did the many topical films of this era reflect their times, but even the depression romances had a metallic twist. Their heroines—Constance Bennett, Tallulah Bankhead, Joan Crawford, Marlene Dietrich, Greta Garbo, Barbara Stanwyck—were frequently ladies who took to the streets or became rich men's mistresses in order to provide food for their babies, an education for their sisters or medicine for their husbands. Despite these sentimentalities, however, such films as *Susan Lenox* (1931), *Blonde Venus* (1932) and *Letty Lynton* (1932) were quite explicit in establishing the milieu of poverty that drove their heroines into a life of shame. Nor was it sheer coincidence that these virtuous prostitutes invariably encountered public enemies or crooked politicians in their rise from gutter to penthouse. In their own way, they were merely confirming the gangster theme that the only escape from depression-bred despair was to live outside the law. And the general public, if box-office returns are any index, not only condoned but applauded these fallen creatures, just as they were fascinated by the exploits of the gangsters and racketeers. The heroines may have sobbed a bit over their lost virginity, the Little Caesars may have ended up perforated by bullets, but while they lived there was a glamour and fascination to their lives that was in glaring contrast to the drab realities of 1931 and 1932.

Obviously, in making heroes of gangsters and heroines of

prostitutes, the movie companies departed far from both the letter and the spirit of the Production Code they had so virtuously agreed to in the halcyon year of 1927. The depression had produced a new world, a new morality—and the studios, in giving the public what it wanted, reflected the seamiest side of the picture with unprecedented accuracy. Far too accurately for some tastes. Letters of protest began to reach the studios and the Hays Office from all the more respectable elements in communities across the country. Church groups, women's clubs and patriotic associations passed resolutions condemning the industry. Editorials appeared in the newspapers and sermons were preached from pulpits denouncing the growing immorality of the movies, urging the film producers to assume a greater social responsibility for the pictures they were turning out, prodding local censorship boards to increased vigilance and more rigorous standards. *Scarface* (1932), for example, at once one of the best and most brutal of the gangster films, was held up for months until the producers inserted several placatory scenes showing an aroused citizenry demanding action against what the film's subtitle described as "the shame of a nation." Even with these additions, *Scarface* was severely censored in many communities, banned outright in others. As a result of such efforts the films became, if not more moral, at least more moralizing. Sermons on civic responsibility became the price one had to pay for pictures that dealt realistically with the more sensational aspects of the social scene. Under the sustained pressure of the protest groups, the wave of gangster films began to subside. During 1935 it gradually merged into another cycle, with the F.B.I. men and other law enforcers as the new heroes. Actually, the G-men were simply gangsters in disguise, acting with as little concern for "due process" as the gangsters they were hunting. But official morality was once more being served.

With the election of Franklin D. Roosevelt and the prompt introduction of N.R.A. relief measures and reforms early in 1933, a new note of optimism appeared both in the country and in its films. The musicals, which only a short time before had been singing *Brother, Can You Spare a Dime* and *Ten Cents a Dance*, were now shouting out that *Happy Days Are Here Again*, or *Stand Up and Cheer*—"good times are here!" Indeed, the musical comedies reflected this new optimism not only in their songs but in their themes as well. Typical of the era were the plots of *Footlight Parade* (1933) and *100 Men and a Girl* (1937), in which groups of starving musicians, singers and dancers were rounded up by Dick Powell or Deanna Durbin and prodded into putting on a show. Their success provided employment and happiness for all. In much the same way, King Vidor's *Our Daily Bread* (1934) showed a heterogeneous band of unemployed city people finding their salvation by working together on a farm cooperative. "Back to the soil" was reiterated as the solution to urban hard times in such films as *Stranger's Return* (1933), *State Fair* (1933) and *As the Earth Turns* (1934).

In keeping with the reformist trend of the N.R.A. period, the topical films, the exposés of rackets, corruption and abuses of power took a more positive stand. Prohibition and gangsterism, juvenile delinquency, strikebreaking and prison reform were problems that an enlightened citizenry could do something about, once the facts were brought to their attention. It was in this spirit that the studios—and especially Warner Brothers—put into production such frankly controversial pictures as *Wild Boys of the Road* (1933), *Massacre* (1933), *Black Fury* (1935) and *The Black Legion* (1936), such vigorously anti-lynch films as *Winterset* (1936), *Fury* (1936) and *They Won't Forget* (1937). While the predominantly affirmative and constructive outlook of these films was encouraged by the growing liberalism of the era, it is also true that a new sense of caution and constraint was forced upon the industry by the formation of the Legion of Decency during 1933, set up to implement a new Production Code. Drawn up by Catholic churchmen and lay members, the new Code was a thorough revision of the original strictures established by the Hays Office during the "flaming" twenties— but this time reinforced by the power of the Church to bring economic reprisals against any studio that violated its rulings. Sex and crime had become so prevalent on the screen that when at last the Legion of Decency made its official appearance, in April of 1934, many of the Protestant denominations were ready to support it in its announced campaign to clean up the movies. The Code, with but few minor revisions, remained in force until 1966—a mind-boggling 32 years, if one stops to consider the economic and political changes during that period. A Code drawn up during the depths of the depression was still being enforced while we were at war in Vietnam!

With the rise of the Legion, many of the crude excesses of the tough, realistic school of film making were quickly eliminated; but at the same time much of the forthright honesty of the period also disappeared from the screen as well. Mae West was an early victim. Her good-humored vulgarity and frank sexuality in films like *She Done Him Wrong* (1933) made her irresistible to the reformers. The biggest box-office draw of 1933-1934, she became a prime target for the outraged forces of decency. To conform to the new Production Code, her scripts were so bowdlerized that by 1936 the Mae West character had lost its sex and her films their appeal. Her few subsequent screen appearances consisted of innocuous parodies of her former roles in pictures like *My Little Chickadee* (1940) with W. C. Fields. To avoid a similar fate, James Cagney, Clark Gable and Edward G. Robinson, the movies' favorite gangsters of the early thirties, found it expedient to diversify their roles and lead more virtuous screen lives. The industry itself quite consciously began laying greater emphasis on purely escapist themes—big Westerns, costume dramas, historical films and adaptations of the classics—while treatment of the social scene was suffused with what Richard Griffith has aptly termed "the fantasy of good will," the feeling that if everyone were kind and generous to his fellow man, the depression could soon be overcome. This idea found its fullest and most popular expression in Frank Capra's *Mr. Deeds Goes to Town* (1936). Gary Cooper, a youthful millionaire, decides to give away his inherited fortune to the unemployed after discovering that his business associates are all parasites and cheats. The fact that no real-life millionaire has ever distributed his fortune with such openhearted innocence in no way diminished the attractiveness of the idea.

Mr. Deeds was one in a long cycle of films appearing during the mid-thirties that came to be called "screwball" comedies, pictures that did anything and everything for a laugh. But while the action in these films was always wildly at odds with any conventional response to a similar situation, most of them had as their point of departure the terrible realities of that period—unemployment, hunger and fear. In *My Man Godfrey* (1936), for example, William Powell plays one of the *"nouveaux* poor," a man ruined by the crash and reduced to living in the city dumps. Some scatterbrained socialites find him on a scavenger hunt and make him their butler. Because of his own experience with poverty, Godfrey is able to enlighten his employers and transform them into useful, social-minded citizens. In *Easy Living* (1937), Jean Arthur, an unemployed secretary, suddenly finds herself in possession of a priceless mink coat flung out the window by a millionaire in a moment of pique; her scathing denunciation of his thoughtlessness while others are starving was the high point of the picture. And yet both of these were presented—and taken—as comedies. As Lewis Jacobs has written, "If 'screwball' comedies successfully turned the world on its ear, that was perhaps the way it already looked to a depression generation which felt cheated of its birthright and apprehensively faced further loss in the steady approach of war."

As the thirties wore on, these growing tensions produced a notable series of films that rode the mounting wave of liberalism without recourse to either the "fantasy of good will" or "screwball" subterfuge. Labor unrest, slum housing, unemployment and dislocation aggravated by the dust storms of the mid-thirties—all of these were put on the screen with a directness that stressed the social and economic sources of such hardships. There were sympathy for the common man and new hope for a better tomorrow. In place of the contrived and improbable "happy endings" of the depression musicals and "back to the soil" films, there was now a forthright expression of belief in the inherent strength of democracy to bring about national recovery and a solution to these problems. Characteristically, when John Steinbeck's bitter novel *The Grapes of Wrath* was filmed by John Ford in 1939, the picture faithfully transmitted the shocking and desperate plight of California's migratory workers, but material in the book was freely transposed so that the film might end on a strong affirmation of faith in the ability of the American people to win through. By 1941, with war raging in Europe, Capra himself had deserted his "fantasy" of the best of all possible worlds. His *Meet John Doe,* a daring and angry exposé of American fascism, was directed specifically against those manipulators of public opinion who were using the slogans of democracy to sell their program of blind reaction to the masses. Significantly, Capra was later to admit that he never really knew how to end the movie. The optimistic answer didn't come so easily as the possibility of world fascism edged closer.

A belief in the democratic way of life was also implicit in

an impressive and highly popular series of biographies that appeared throughout the late thirties. Some of these films— such as John Ford's *Young Mr. Lincoln* (1939) or *Abe Lincoln in Illinois* (1940)—turned to American heroes whose lives and principles exemplified the democratic tradition. Others depicted great artists, scientists and political leaders in their battle with the bigots and reactionaries of their day. The careers of such international figures as Louis Pasteur, Dr. Ehrlich, Madame Curie, Emile Zola and Benito Juárez were presented as thinly-veiled sermons on behalf of democracy and enlightenment. *The Life of Emile Zola* (1937), for example, reached its climax in Zola's classic *"J'accuse"* defense of Captain Dreyfus, a scathing denunciation of anti-Semitism and intolerance in all its forms. Underlying all these films was the awareness that our cultural and intellectual freedom was a precious heritage that the growing forces of fascism both at home and abroad were threatening to destroy.

As World War II drew nearer, Hollywood films began increasingly to depict the joys, even the glamour of the military life. Though the government did not actually commission such pictures, the studios soon discovered that the War Department was willing to cooperate to the full in their production. A bomber, a battleship, even Annapolis itself was available to the producer of any film that might serve as a recruiting poster or simply as publicity for the various branches of the service. These films generally dealt with training rather than actual combat, using the Army, the Navy, the Marines or the Air Corps as a romantic background for a love story or a musical. Military preparedness was as far as the American people were willing to go at this time. They still clung desperately to the pacifism and isolationism of the thirties, echoing President Roosevelt's fervent declaration, "I hate war." But by the end of the thirties, with all of Europe in flames, American pictures began to take on a more ominous tone. In 1940 Alfred Hitchcock's spy thriller, *Foreign Correspondent*, chilled audiences across the nation when its hero, Joel McCrea, radioed the United States from bomb-torn London: "The lights are going out in Europe! Ring yourself around with steel, America!"

During this uneasy period of "lend-lease" and "bundles for Britain," the screen began a kind of orientation course, introducing the American people to their future allies, exposing the nature of their future enemies. From Hollywood came

such graphic expressions of sympathy and admiration for the
beleaguered British as *A Yank in the R.A.F.* (1941), *This
Above All* (1942), *Mrs. Miniver* (1942) and *Journey for
Margaret* (1942). The Nazis began to appear as villains—for
the first time—in such melodramas as *The Mortal Storm*
(1941) and *Man Hunt* (1941). The dangers of a Nazi "fifth
column" within the United States were exposed in the "pre-
maturely anti-fascist" *Confessions of a Nazi Spy* (1939),
while Chaplin in *The Great Dictator* (1940) spoke movingly
of the dangers of fascism to the human spirit everywhere.
And Russia, then linked to Germany by the Nazi-Soviet pact,
was lampooned in such films as *Ninotchka* (1939) and *Comrade X* (1940).

But until the fateful morning of Pearl Harbor, on December 7, 1941, the United States was technically a neutral nation. Whatever the sympathies of the American people,
whatever the implications of the government's "lend-lease"
policies, most of the studios walked a wary line between 1939
and 1942, conscious that any overt declaration of partiality in
their pictures could lead to economic reprisals on the part of
the offended nation and outright bans in those countries anxious to maintain their neutral status. Furthermore, America
itself was far from united. The strongly isolationist Midwest
was cold to any film that threatened to involve us in European affairs, while as late as 1940 Hollywood was being in-
vestigated by a House Un-American Activities Committee for
daring to incorporate anti-fascist sentiments into pictures like
Confessions of a Nazi Spy.

Once the United States was committed to the war, however, all such restraints vanished. Germans and Japanese immediately became the stock villains in film after film, while
Nazi and Nipponese brutality was exposed, denounced—and
exploited—in pictures like *Hitler's Children* (1943), *The Seventh Cross* (1944), *Behind the Rising Sun* (1944) and *Blood
on the Sun* (1945). At the same time, our newly acquired
Russian allies, who had been equally stock villains before
Pearl Harbor, were suddenly turned into brave, solid, somewhat picturesque characters and lauded in films like *North
Star* (1943), *Mission to Moscow* (1943) and *Days of Glory*
(1944). Sympathy for the people of the occupied countries
was expressed in an earnest and well-intended group of pictures—*The Moon Is Down* (1943), *Hangmen Also Die*
(1943), *This Land Is Mine* (1943)—that sought to put on

the screen some semblance of life under a Quisling dictatorship. Unfortunately, it was generally the Nazis who dominated these films while the people themselves remained shadowy and ill defined. Even more shadowy—although equally well intended—were their appearances as members of the anti-Nazi underground in the numerous war adventure films, where they smuggled American or R.A.F. fliers to safety beneath the very noses of the Gestapo. Certainly, these pictures served a useful propaganda function in depicting the French, the Poles, the Czechs and the Dutch as our friends and potential allies. But they also gave the quaint impression that all these people spoke an amusing pidgin English and led marvelously melodramatic lives in the underground when they weren't being tortured in Nazi prison camps. Needless to say, a sense of reality was not the strongest feature of these films.

When it came to showing American troops in action, however, Hollywood's directors became increasingly adept at creating a persuasive image of the war. They could scarcely have done otherwise, for as source material they had not only the weekly newsreels of actual combat but also a steady stream of magnificent documentaries from every theater of operations. These films were shown in theaters, factories, schools, union halls, clubs—wherever people gathered together for work or recreation. To make their own pictures properly convincing, the Hollywood directors were forced to match the realism of these documentaries in their studio-made versions of the fighting. By the end of the war, their vivid dramatizations of combat in films like *The Story of G.I. Joe* (1945), *A Walk in the Sun* (1945) and *Pride of the Marines* (1945) seemed to match frame for frame the footage sent back by the Signal Corps. Rarely did these films seek to glorify war, or attempt to make it seem a great adventure. On the contrary, most of them stressed the average American's distaste for killing and for regimentation—as well as his ability to rise to deeds of heroism when his country needed him. As in Britain, such films created a kind of group hero out of a platoon, a bomber crew or a patrol on a hazardous mission. The composition of these teams, however, was quite consciously—even self-consciously—American, with each group invariably composed of one Negro, one Jew, a Southern boy and a sprinkling of second-generation Italians, Irish, Scandinavians and Poles. America the melting pot was never more clearly in evidence.

This concern for the values of democracy was projected into the years immediately following the war in a series of films notable not only for their liberal sentiments but for their intelligent and courageous appraisal of the problems of the postwar world. The question of economic security for the hundreds of thousands of newly discharged veterans was squarely faced in a half-dozen or more films, and none more searching or honest than Samuel Goldwyn's *The Best Years of Our Lives* (1946). The emotional adjustments of returning veterans, the tragic loss of sons or fathers, the housing shortage, war profiteering and the black market were among the new themes that received serious consideration on the screen. Anti-Semitism was openly and thoughtfully discussed in *Crossfire* (1947) and *Gentleman's Agreement* (1947). In Capra's *It's a Wonderful Life* (1946) and *State of the Union* (1948), in Elia Kazan's *Boomerang* (1947), George Cukor's *Born Yesterday* (1950) and Robert Rossen's *All the King's Men* (1949) corruption in political life was admitted, but tempered by the honesty and sense of fair play of individual politicians. The wartime optimism, the belief in the American way kept all of these films from falling back upon the strident exposé techniques of the thirties.

On the other hand, the war had also familiarized movie audiences to the sight of blood and violence on the screen. In fact, it often seemed as if the stronger anti-Nazi and anti-Japanese films of the war period had used their themes as a pretext for sensational, even sadistic shots of torture, degradation and death. This suspicion was amply confirmed in the crime melodramas that took their place as the public tired of war themes. *Cornered*, appearing late in 1945, seemed to mark the transition. In it Dick Powell played an R.C.A.F. pilot who hunts down and wreaks personal—and violent—vengeance on the Nazis who murdered his wife. For a short while the heroes of these films continued to be ex-servicemen righting wrongs committed by Nazi spies or Gestapo agents. Very soon, however, this pose was dropped and they became simply rather shabby "private eyes" in the Dashiell Hammett–Raymond Chandler tradition, men who doggedly followed through on their sordid assignments despite knifings, druggings, beatings with whips and bludgeons, and fierce hand-to-hand encounters. There had been violence in the gangster films of the thirties, sensationalism in the numerous exposés. But this was qualitatively different, a psychopathic kind of violence that recalled nothing so much as the tortures in the concentration camps and the cellars of the Gestapo. In films like *The Dark Corner* (1945), *The Big Sleep* (1946) and *The Lady in the Lake* (1946), the sadisms of the earlier anti-Nazi films were visibly engrafted upon the time-honored strain of film melodrama—and there they have remained to this day.

Added to this physical violence was a new interest in the refinements of mental torture. During the war it had become fashionable to depict the omnipresent Nazis as psychological monsters, men who got a grim satisfaction out of the emotional anguish they inflicted on their victims. Even before the war was over this type of villain was appearing in a more everyday guise in such films as *The Brighton Strangler* (1945), *Hangover Square* (1945) or *The Strange Affair of Uncle Harry* (1945). In this new kind of thriller, the audience knew from the outset who the murderer was. The fascination lay in the revelation of his twisted mind and the torments he devised for his victims. This morbid interest in abnormal psychology quickly spread to other genres. Films that had all the outward appearance of tragic romance, like *Love Letters* (1945) and *Leave Her to Heaven* (1945), veered off into paths of insanity and paranoia. Never before had there been pictures with heroines as sinister as *Mildred Pierce* (1945) or as sodden as the hero of *The Lost Weekend* (1945). The killers in the crime films—like Richard Widmark's laughing hoodlum in *Kiss of Death* (1947)—were presented as psychopathic personalities. And the mad psychoanalyst took his place alongside the mad scientist and the mad artist in Hollywood's gallery of arch-criminals available for horror pictures. In the search for values and stability after World War II, psychology and psychoanalysis seemed to be the key. But whether for good or ill, few could say.

The Rise of Documentary

Documentary in the United States was a depression baby, born of hard times and the urge to influence public opinion toward one panacea or another. The pre-documentary pioneers of the twenties, men like Robert Flaherty and Merian C. Cooper, had already withdrawn from the field. Flaherty's lyric explorations of patterns of life in the remoter corners of the world were now alien to the harsh temper of the times; the early thirties found him in England working with John Grierson's new documentary unit there, while Cooper, who had skillfully combined ethnology with adventure in *Grass* (1925) and *Chang* (1927), moved to Hollywood to become a successful producer of studio films. These two men had sought to bring reality to the screen within the framework of the story-telling form. The new documentarians, however, were concerned with fact alone—the bitter fact of strikes, evictions, hunger marches and unemployment. Their techniques—and often their ideology as well—were derived from the Russian films of the late twenties, creating Left-tinged propaganda reels out of the violence and despair of the era. Inevitably, the theaters were closed to them. Shown primarily to the already convinced, their audience was limited, their influence slight. The development of a broader audience for documentary in this country resulted from the work of individuals and organizations quite apart from the scattered handful of dedicated souls who first introduced the form.

Clearly, the most important single step in this direction was the introduction of *The March of Time* early in 1935. Rightly called "a new kind of screen journalism," it stood midway between the ordinary newsreel and the probing social analysis of the British documentary school. It dramatized the news, getting behind the headlines to offer pertinent background information and editorial opinion. Not surprisingly, both its slant and its style bore striking resemblance to that of its successful parent, *Time* magazine. The voice of *Time*, Westbrook Van Voorhis, was the voice of authority—strident, implacable, decisive. There was no questioning his figures, his facts, his conclusions. Everything had been carefully researched, properly thought out and knowingly packaged. One could not say nay to "The March . . . of Time!"—although documentary people on both sides of the water tended to look down their noses at it. They claimed that it was superficial and that its editing was as slovenly and haphazard as the average newsreel. Actually, despite its aesthetic shortcomings, *The March of Time* had created a distinctive style that punched information across with a maximum of intensity and interest. The editing, functional if not artistic, was so closely tied to the commentary that transitions were often introduced simply by a "but" or a "however" on the sound track. Personalities, authorities on the topic under discussion spoke their views glibly into the camera in interviews especially arranged for the reel. Dramatic re-enactments became an increasingly important part of the technique. In their thirteen issues a year the editors managed to keep their material timely, lively and even, on occasion, controversial. Indeed, so successful was *The March of Time* during the late thirties that RKO-Radio Pictures was inspired to launch a rival reel, *This Is America*. For most Americans, these spelled documentary. They knew nothing else.

In the meantime, however, American film makers were beginning to see examples of European documentary styles that suggested the variety of ways in which fact could be handled creatively on the screen. Robert Flaherty's English-made *Man of Aran* (1934), a feature-length study of the primitive pattern of existence on a barren Irish island, emphasized the concept of a personal, dramatic shaping of reality. Continental documentary was represented by Joris Ivens, the distinguished Dutch director who in 1936 brought a group of his pictures to this country and remained to form an important independent documentary group, Contemporary Historians. His vivid, frankly partisan reporting of the wars in Spain and China, *Spanish Earth* (1937) and *The 400,000,000* (1938), were the first extended accounts of those tragic preludes to World War II to reach the American screen. Even more widespread and influential was the work of the Museum of Modern Art Film Library. Founded in 1935, it soon acquired a number of British documentary films and began circulating them to schools, universities and museums throughout the country. Under its sponsorship, Paul Rotha, the English documentary producer, director and historian, was brought to this country to tour with the films and introduce them to American film makers. The impact of all these films and personalities upon the Americans produced both a broadening and refinement of their own work. Documentary was no longer thought of as the crude presentation of fact through an assemblage of highly realistic shots. It was, they began to realize, a complex, artistic form with reality at its core and an infinite variety of techniques by which the documentarian could make his subject meaningful and affecting to his audience.

With the appearance of Pare Lorentz' *The Plow That Broke the Plains* (1936), American documentary may be said to have come of age, assimilating the best of the European tradition and adding to it a spacious lyricism that was peculiarly American. Produced for the United States Resettlement Administration, one of the New Deal agencies, it was a dramatic account of the tragic misuse of our Great Plains that led to the disastrous Dust Bowl of the mid-thirties. Like President Roosevelt's famous "fireside chats," this was a report to the nation on its government's efforts to meet the emergency—and the first to be made by film instead of by radio. It was followed by *The River* (1937), a broadly conceived history of the Mississippi basin and the changes being wrought by the T.V.A. soil-conservation and flood-control program. The style of these two films was poetic—Lorentz wrote his commentaries in free verse—the approach, humanistic. Implicit in each was the concern for people, for families blown off their land by the dust storms or forced to wrest a living from soil worn out by erosion and unscientific cultivation. There was a tragic grandeur in their evocation of the march of history, a thrill of pride as they recounted the government's efforts to combat the effects of generations of neglect, indolence and waste. These two films, not only pioneers but classics in American documentary, served as the recruiting ground of many of our leading documentary film makers. No less important, they began to focus public attention upon the form itself. Gradually foundations, public-service groups and even industry came forward in a very tentative way to sponsor production.

The real turning point for documentary in America, however, came with the New York World's Fair of 1939. Never before had such a variety of fact films been brought together in one place—sales films, promotion films, art films, travelogue and interest films as well as true documentaries. Never before had the many uses of the film medium been so graphically demonstrated. And what was quickly apparent was the popularity of the documentary with general audiences above all other forms except the outright entertainment feature. Crowds gathered throughout the day and night at the British Pavilion, where examples of the British documentary were on continuous display. Equally successful were the American documentaries, shown at the Little Theatre in the New York City Building. Outstanding, of course, were *The Plow That Broke the Plains* and *The River*. But the real hit of the show was *The City* (1939), a film made specifically for exhibition at the Fair by Willard Van Dyke and Ralph Steiner. Sponsored by the American Institute of Planners, it was a documentary on the need for city planning executed with great technical virtuosity and—what is even rarer in documentaries—considerable humor. By contrasting the peaceful New England scene against industrial slums and hectic glimpses of modern city life, it built a strong case for decentralized "green belt" communities—although ironically it never succeeded in making them seem quite as appealing as the ridiculously crowded and eminently human scenes of New York at its worst. The unmistakable popularity of documentaries at the Fair generated a greater interest in the form on the part of both the sponsors and the general audience, resulting in a sudden spurt in production during the years just before the war.

With more pictures being made, the problems of documentary distribution became more urgent than ever. For years the development of the field had been hobbled by its inability to make contact with the public. For the most part, theaters were closed to such films. They did not conform to the standard concepts of entertainment, and the educational channels through which they were available were unfamiliar to the average theater owner. When he wanted to play an informational short, he generally chose a *March of Time*, or perhaps an interest reel like Walter Futter's *Curiosities* or Lyman Howe's *Hodge-Podge*. Beginning in 1939, however, the documentary people instituted a vigorous program of publicity and information. Through the Rockefeller-financed American Film Center and their own Association of Documentary Film Producers they sought a wider public for their kind of film making. And to a degree they found it in the museums, the libraries, the clubs and schools—but rarely in motion-picture theaters.

This inability to break through to the mass audience proved doubly unfortunate. As the war drew nearer, the government needed hundreds of films to explain to the nation the reasons for a peace-time draft and lend-lease, the story behind America's increased production of tanks and bombers, the need for more women in industry and the necessity for closer cooperation with the Latin-American countries. But since the government wanted to reach the vast moviegoing public, it turned not to the documentarians but to Hollywood. Through 1940 and 1941 came short after short from Holly-

wood writers and directors. Some of these official films were
made by the studios, more of them by studio people who offered their services to the emergency organizations set up in
Washington. But however good their intentions, it was soon
apparent that their capacity to deal persuasively with factual
material was limited. Most of their reels were pseudo-*March
of Time* style, theoretically glamorized with narrations by
such stars as Ingrid Bergman, Katharine Hepburn, James
Stewart or Orson Welles. One recruiting film produced by
M-G-M actually sought to induce Navy enlistments by showing sailors strumming their guitars while native girls danced
on the beach at Waikiki. It was released only a few weeks
before Pearl Harbor!

These pseudo-documentaries, distributed by the industry's
efficient War Activities Committee, were shown in theaters all
over the country. The experienced documentary film makers,
on the other hand, were pointedly ignored by the government
at this time. Some indication of the official attitude may be
deduced from the fate of the Pare Lorentz unit. Organized
into the U.S. Film Service, it had continued to produce distinguished documentaries for various governmental agencies
throughout the late thirties—including Joris Ivens's *Power
and the Land* (1940), Robert Flaherty's *The Land* (1941)
and Lorentz's own feature-length *Fight for Life* (1940). But
to a Congress growing restive under the Roosevelt administration, these smacked too strongly of New Deal propaganda.
Early in 1941, at a time when the need for skilled documentarians had never been stronger, the Service was summarily
disbanded. Congressionals preferred the less controversial
style of the Hollywood people.

Once the war had started, however, film makers of every
description were sought for the various branches of the government's vast information and education program. Thousands of training films were needed on every conceivable
subject from military courtesy to the assembly of the M-1
rifle, from fighting venereal disease to spotting enemy aircraft. When the Army Signal Corps and the Navy could not
keep up with the demand, the production of such pictures
was parceled out under contract to the various Hollywood
studios. Of even greater importance to the development of
documentary, however, was the work of men like Frank
Capra, John Ford, John Huston and William Wyler, men
who left the studios completely to enter on wartime service in

the Army Signal Corps or the Navy or Air Force. For most of them it meant a wholly new orientation, a self-imposed course in acquiring the techniques of handling fact on the screen through much the same process that Grierson's group had trained itself in England a dozen years earlier. Two styles of films resulted. One was the edited documentary, perhaps best represented by Frank Capra's *Why We Fight* series (1943-1945). Capra and his skilled editors drew their clips from feature films, newsreel and combat footage to create a panoramic background of the events leading to World War II, and the issues at stake. Others, like Huston's *San Pietro* (1944), Wyler's *Memphis Belle* (1944) and John Ford's *Battle of Midway* (1944), were masterpieces of on-the-spot war reporting, a combination of powerful images and thoughtful commentary that reached through to every American in or out of uniform. These films spoke the language. They made facts significant, dramatic. And perhaps because they were created by civilian soldiers rather than by the military itself, they never suggested that war was a heroic, glamorous business. It was always a means—a nasty, sordid, murderous but necessary means to a vital end—the preservation of democracy. What was even more laudable, the democracy that they extolled was implicit in the films themselves, ingrained in the spirit of the men who made them.

All of these were widely shown, both at home and to the soldiers in their camps and bases in every theater of operations. But there was another notable series of documentaries that, originally, was never intended for American eyes. These were the films produced for the Overseas Branch of the Office of War Information, an organization set up to prepare pictures on life in the United States—our traditions, our customs, the way we live—against the day when our armies became victorious. The people of Europe had lived so long under Fascist and Nazi rule, had been fed so long on Fascist and Nazi propaganda, that our own counter-propaganda had to be ready. To O.W.I. Overseas flocked the men who had been the leaders in American documentary production before the war—Irving Lerner (who became its production chief), Willard Van Dyke, Henwar Rodakiewicz, Irving Jacoby, Alexander Hackenschmied, Jules Bucher, Joseph Krumgold and Sidney Meyers. They evolved a special style that was eminently adapted to the problem presented them. Because their pictures would be shown in many languages, direct dialogue obviously could not be used. They depended instead on a strong, clear narration, visually striking, indisputably authentic images and exceptionally skilled editing. A musical score, often prepared by such leading modern composers as Aaron Copland, Alex North or Virgil Thomson, completed the picture. For foreign distribution, the narration was simply translated into the appropriate language.

Quite apart from such stylistic considerations, the films of O.W.I. Overseas were differentiated from the productions of the War Department and O.W.I. Domestic in a far more basic way. The reels prepared for the troops and the home front were related to the progress of the war; their whole effectiveness lay in their timeliness. It was not, however, the passing moment that the Overseas unit sought to record. Its purpose was to discover typical and enduring elements in our culture that had grown from our European heritage, as well as those that might contribute to the postwar development of the liberated nations. The result was a series that included films like *Tuesday in November* (1945), a lucid explanation of the American electoral system; *A Better Tomorrow* (1945), examining the role of free education in the New York public schools in molding future citizens; *The Cummington Story* (1945), a true and touching incident in which a group of European refugees were welcomed and integrated into the life of a New England town. In anticipation of the liberation of Italy, there was a filmed performance by Arturo Toscanini and the N.B.C. Symphony of Verdi's *Hymn of the Nations* (1944). There were films on the public health services, the T.V.A. dam projects, the Library of Congress, the historic San Francisco Conference where the United Nations was born. It was a priceless collection, and one that might have been lost to the nation entirely had not the documentary people themselves urged distribution of these films in this country. Released at print cost through the U.S. Office of Education, they soon became the backbone of many of today's school and university film libraries.

After the war, both the Army and the State Department, through its Information Service, extended the policy of O.W.I. Overseas, commissioning films that continued to "bring alive" the American scene for the people of Europe and Japan. Again it was predominantly the documentary makers who created these pictures of our cultural, intellectual and regional life in films like *Journey into Medicine* (1947) or *Land of Enchantment* (1948), a portrait of New Mexico as seen through the eyes of the artist Georgia O'Keeffe. Meanwhile, the Hollywood people had returned to the studios, taking with them their new techniques for handling reality on the screen. Louis de Rochemont, creator of *The March of Time*, had already introduced the documentary approach into the entertainment field with his anti-Nazi spy film *The House on 92nd Street* (1945). A re-enactment of an authentic case out of the files of the F.B.I., it was photographed against the actual backgrounds of the original story. The success of this experiment, which for de Rochemont has since hardened into formula, led to an increased use of "location" shooting on what were essentially studio films. Directors of ordinary cops-and-robbers pictures like *Naked City* (1948) or *Union Station* (1950) found it definitely advantageous to take their cameras and crews to New York's lower East Side or the Los Angeles depot. The real backgrounds lent a note of authenticity to their melodramatic plots. Documentary—or at least semi-documentary—had entered into the ordinary parlance of Hollywood.

During the years immediately after the war, the outlook for documentary in this country was brighter than ever. The wartime use of films had removed any doubts as to the efficacy of the medium in influencing public opinion. In education, tests had proved that men could master a process at least one-third faster if they saw it demonstrated first through motion pictures. The estimated 400,000 16mm projectors used during the war to show training and morale films created an unprecedented market for non-theatrical pictures. The schools were setting up elaborate audio-visual programs, and even the libraries were investigating the possibilities of circulating films along with books. Government, private industry, textbook publishers, foundations all came forward as potential sponsors. John Grierson arrived in New York to prepare a documentary series, *The World Today*, for United Artists release. When Robert Flaherty's feature-length documentary *Louisiana Story* (1948) began playing the art-house circuits, it seemed to presage a whole new era. Financed by Standard Oil and produced with unprecedented freedom at a cost of a quarter of a million dollars, it was a model of institutional film making. Its sponsor neither asked for nor received credit or mention in the film—simply the goodwill that might accrue from its unaffected account of the discovery of oil in a Louisiana bayou and its effect upon a Cajun family. The picture's warm reception and the sponsor's expressed satisfaction added to the general optimism of the documentarians. They felt that the value of their kind of film making, their approach to reality, was at last receiving public recognition and support. They looked forward to the day when such enlightened public-relations programs would be the rule, not the exception. They envisaged a future in which the documentary would become as effective in peace as it had been in war. Unfortunately their hopes have yet to be realized.

Just what went wrong is difficult to say. Certainly, the rise of television drained off vast sums of money that might otherwise have been spent to sponsor institutional documentaries. TV's adverse effect on the movie box office also reached the documentarians: the market for shorts fell off so sharply that not only was the Grierson project scrapped but even the well-endowed *March of Time* was forced off the screen. Also since the war, in the interest of economy, both the Army and the State Department drastically curtailed their film production programs. Meanwhile, of course, documentaries were still being made. A few of them were privately financed, like Sidney Meyers' *The Quiet One* (1949), a moving and sensitive study of a disturbed Negro boy and the help he received at the Wiltwyck School. Some were created on foundation grants, like the challenging series produced by Alberta and Irving Jacoby for the Mental Health Film Board. Others have been made with public funds to serve a specific purpose, to meet an urgent need—films like George Stoney's *Feeling All Right* (1949), dramatically effective in the fight against syphilis in Mississippi, or his simple and touching *All My Babies* (1954), produced for the State of Georgia to help train Negro midwives.

At present, however, inspired production is both scattered and sporadic. Increasingly, the documentarians have had to support themselves by routine commercial assignments tailored to rigid sponsor specifications. In the sharp struggle for such contracts, they have lost sight of their original goal. At its best, during the depression and the war, the documentary movement was characterized by a dedication to social change and public enlightenment. With the return of peace and prosperity, that spirit seems gradually to have ebbed away.

Though there is still much to be learned, much to be said about the world and its people, the documentarians are no longer taking the lead in saying it. Without direction, lacking both leadership and enlightened sponsorship, they have become increasingly identified with technically proficient, uncreative industrial films whose main purpose is to promote a product or present a corporation's point of view. As we have noted earlier, a similar decline in vitality and purpose occurred in Britain after the war. Only in television has there been any significant use of documentary in recent years to inform, to stimulate and to challenge. It almost seems as if it takes a time of stress or crisis to crystallize the inherent strength of the documentary—its ability to build understanding in an increasingly complex world by revealing the relationship of man to his society, to his institutions and to his fellow men. This was Grierson's ideal, his concept of the mission of documentary film makers at all times. For true documentaries are concerned less with facts than with *meaning*. Mrs. Flaherty has called them "Films of Life," and in the deepest sense that is precisely what they are—life made meaningful by the creative artist. Their present eclipse can only be temporary. Documentary is too important a form to disappear entirely from the screen. The networks' carefully balanced "White Papers" or even the investigative journalism of the educational stations are not quite the answer. Documentary has always stood for commitment on the part of the film maker—the commitment to a specific project, cause, or view of life. Without this, documentary becomes merely reportage, and reportage can lay no valid claim to art. As we shall see, it is an issue that today's proponents of Cinema-verité have largely failed to take into account as yet.

Art Films and the New Avant-Garde

The willingness to experiment, to try out new forms, new techniques and ideas, is as vital to the arts as it is to science. Today, through an unfortunate limiting of the word, experiment in film has come to be associated almost exclusively with the efforts of small avant-garde coteries working quite apart from the main stream of motion-picture production. In the truest sense, however, Griffith was experimenting when he pushed his camera closer to the actors than the conventions of the day accepted, when he lit, photographed and edited his scenes in ways no other director had dreamed of. *The Cabinet of Dr. Caligari* was an experiment in a new form of storytelling as well as in scenic design. The moving camera of Murnau, the editing principles of Eisenstein and Pudovkin, the realism of von Stroheim's *Greed* and the lyricism of Flaherty's *Moana*—all were experiments on the then-existing borders of the medium. The additions of sound and, more recently, the wide screens are technological innovations that forced creative film makers to attempt still further experiments with film techniques.

It was during the twenties, when the avant-gardists were in full swing on the Continent, that the idea of experiment became identified exclusively with their peculiar kind of film making. If a picture were abstract, baffling or downright incomprehensible, it could always be described as "experimental." And since these films came from Europe they were also considered "artistic," an assumption based largely upon the naïve American tradition that anything European is necessarily more artistic than the native product. Thus experiment acquired a certain honorific connotation, a quality that has clung to it ever since. And because the men who were experimenting in the studios never claimed that they were doing anything but making pictures as best they could, a certain preciousness and "little cinema" aura gathered about the word as well. This was strengthened by the ardent espousal of avant-garde film making by the film aesthetes of the late twenties. A new phenomenon, these young men and women were members of the first generation that had grown up with the movies as their most familiar form of artistic expression. Toward the end of the silent era, they gathered in the few small art houses that had become the last-ditch stand of the silent film and watched with enthusiasm the European avant-garde works. They wrote about them in the little magazines of the period and met together to discuss them in their film forums and societies. Under the influence of the Europeans, they even began to try their own hand at making city symphonies, impressionist studies, film poems and abstractions.

Once made, however, where could such pictures be shown? The handful produced on theatrical 35mm stock—like James Sibley Watson's expressionist version of *The Fall of the House of Usher* (1928) or Ralph Steiner's semi-abstract H_2O (1929)—might be booked for an occasional showing in an art house. But more of them were being made with the relatively new, relatively inexpensive 16mm equipment—and 16mm at that time was considered entirely the province of the amateur. Outside of screenings for home movie clubs or possibly a local art group, the audience for such early experimentalists as Emlen Etting, Henwar Rodakiewicz or Herman G. Weinberg was limited indeed. The final sweeping victory of the talkies, followed almost immediately by the depression, brought this first American avant-garde period to an abrupt close. With sound now a necessity for theatrical distribution, a film like Robert Florey's *Life and Death of a Hollywood Extra* (1928) could no longer be made for a mere $97. As in Europe, a number of the experimentalists turned to documentary; others abandoned the field entirely.

When the form re-emerged, in the years immediately after the war, it found a new audience waiting for it in the suddenly important 16mm field. The troops had seen their training and orientation films on 16mm projectors by day, then 16mm prints of the latest Hollywood features on the same projectors by night. The magnificent wartime documentaries had been shown to millions of civilians on the 16mm "smokestack circuit." No longer could 16mm be thought of solely in terms of classroom films or pictures of baby in the garden. It had achieved a new stature, a new degree of professionalism. It had arrived. During the same period, the Museum of Modern Art Film Library was distributing 16mm versions of film classics to schools, universities and museums around the country. With its circulating programs of features, documentaries and early avant-garde works, it provided a basis for the development of undergraduate film societies and workshops, stimulated independent experimental film production and helped create a new awareness of the film as an art form.

It was to this audience, already exposed to avant-garde films, that the new avant-garde first turned for sympathy and support. The indefatigable Maya Deren pioneered the field in 1945, booking her three short film poems—*Meshes of the Afternoon* (1943), *At Land* (1944) and *Choreography for Camera* (1945)—at a number of leading universities. Everywhere she went, in everything she wrote, she proselytized for the new form, for film as a personal expression. And the warmth of the initial response was astounding, suggesting that at least in the cultural centers—the big cities and the college towns—there had emerged a new breed of moviegoer. Such was indeed the case, for the programs of the film societies, museums and community art centers had begun to attract a public that wanted something not available in the average movie. Its slogans were vague—it knew only that it wanted pictures that were "more mature," "more controversial," "more artistic." Eager to see the offbeat and the different, it made an ideal audience for the new avant-garde. Not surprisingly, many of the postwar experimentalists came out of this same audience. They were impressed by the early avant-garde works, by the films of Maya Deren and by the thought that the motion picture was the true art of the 20th century. Furthermore, they found that by using the relatively cheap, highly flexible 16mm camera they could turn out films for a few hundred dollars that were both individual and technically acceptable for public showing. Above all, they were stimulated by the realization that an audience for such pictures already existed.

Some estimate of the growth of this audience since the war years may be gathered from the history of Cinema 16, which was America's largest and most successful film society. Organized by Amos Vogel in the fall of 1947, it held its first sessions at the tiny Provincetown Playhouse. The programs consisted of "outstanding social documentaries, controversial adult screen fare, advanced experimental films, classics of the international cinema and medical-psychiatric studies." In a short time Vogel's screenings had attracted such a following that he had to find a larger auditorium. By 1955, to accommodate upward of 5,000 members, Cinema 16 had to run each of its eight programs five or six times in halls seating anywhere from 500 to 1,600. On a smaller scale, and for smaller audiences, Cinema 16's program pattern was soon being followed by some 450 film societies around the country, most of them affiliated with schools, universities, museums or similar cultural enterprises. Frequently such showings became the nucleus for still more experimental production. In 1946, for example, when the late Frank Stauffacher arranged his first Art in Cinema series for the San Francisco Museum of Art, his programs consisted in the main of Museum of Modern Art films—plus four by Maya Deren, Hans Richter's *Dreams That Money Can Buy* (1946) and a handful of new West Coast experimentals. Two years later, through the San Francisco Museum's active encouragement of experimental work—and Stauffacher's own monumental enthusiasm—the

West Coast avant-garde movement had grown to such proportions that Art in Cinema was able to present ten programs built entirely from contemporary works.

And what are these experimental films? What do they look like? How do they differ from ordinary movies? Actually, no single word, no simple explanation can quite answer those questions. Despite a multiplicity of styles and intentions, however, experimental work falls into two main categories—the abstract film and what might best be called the subjective film. The abstract film, concerned with color, form, texture, movement and spatial relationships, continues the line of inquiry set up in the twenties by Hans Richter, Fernand Léger, Oskar Fischinger and others. In most of them the primary concern is with the discovery and development of animation techniques that will impart movement to abstract or non-objective forms and designs. Fischinger, for example, who worked briefly in Hollywood, drew a separate picture for each of the thousands of frames in every film he made—an extension of the principle of the primitive thumb-books that existed years before the camera was invented. Francis Lee, a painter and photographer, combines cutouts that he moves from frame to frame with pastel backgrounds that shift and change as new colors are added under the camera. Douglass Crockwell, whose folksy paintings for beer ads have adorned the pages of most national magazines, worked out a fascinating technique in which thick, manipulative paints or molded wax forms are made to change their shape from moment to moment. In Mary Ellen Bute's "visual symphonies," commonplace objects—pins, buttons, collars—are photographed through distort lenses and animated to the music of the *Danse Macabre* or a Bach Toccata and Fugue. While in Canada, the witty and inventive Norman McLaren paints abstract designs directly upon strips of clear 35mm motion-picture film. In his *Begone Dull Care* (1950), fine wire-like lines move across a velvety dark screen to the accompaniment of a dreamy blues played by Oscar Peterson. Spots of light dart about, holding on the screen until a note fades away, appearing again elsewhere with the next note. Then, as the music turns into a frantic boogie-woogie finale, the whole screen seems to burst into a riot of swift, explosive color forms.

In all of these—and there are many more—the camera is used simply as a recording machine, an instrument that reproduces whatever material the artist has painstakingly prepared for it and in the course of that reproduction creates the illusion of motion. Others have devised ways to bring the camera itself more fully into the creative process. James Davis, for example, an artist who has gained a considerable reputation for his mobiles of plastic, used film at the outset merely to record his compositions, building colorful, rhythmic patterns from the shifting flashes of light reflected or refracted from them. Later, in films like *Through the Looking Glass* (1955) and *Analogies* (1955), he played with the distorted images mirrored on irregular gold and silver surfaces. His most ambitious, complex work, *Becoming* (1956), is a study in evolution expressed entirely in abstract visuals. Jordan Belson, perhaps the most talented and inventive of the numerous West Coast abstract film makers, has devised a form of in-camera animation, building jazzy rhythms through swift glimpses of objects that fly by before the eye can fully identify them. In *Dime Store* (1949) Dorsey Alexander created a *ballet mécanique* through stop-motion photography, moving colorful spools of thread, marbles and toothpicks in sprightly designs to the music of Offenbach's *Gaîté Parisienne*. Leonard Tregillus and Ralph Luce also used stop-motion to animate modeling clay in their amusing, semi-abstract telling of Lewis Carroll's *Proem* (1950). Frank Stauffacher composed his *Zigzag* (1950) from shots of the night patterns of neon signs cut rhythmically to Stravinsky's *Ebony Concerto*. And for more than two decades John Whitney and his talented sons have been feeding computers with the information to produce their lacy, infinitely detailed abstractions, often shown on triple-screens and to the accompaniment of exotic Indian or African scores.

Few of these films are intended to convey a message or even a mood, although the free association of forms may suggest meanings and symbols of which their creators are quite unaware. Primarily, however, they are made to give a sensual pleasure. When they succeed—as James Davis and Norman McLaren have so many times—they create moments of delight impossible to describe, a gratification that springs from the unexpected congruencies of line, form, color and sound. When they fail—which is not infrequent—there still remains quite often the fascination of techniques, materials and visual effects found in no other kind of movie.

If the abstract film is concerned with technique, the subjective film is the story form of the avant-garde—stories told through the dream symbols and Freudian trappings first introduced on the screen by the surrealists of the twenties. Here is a field where anything goes, where the imagination is boggled and the sensibilities often chafed by the persistently personal imagery and deliberately sensational themes pursued by their makers. Often their objective is quite frankly to shock or, at the very least, to disturb the spectator with visuals and connotations of an unpleasant or downright perverse nature. Even when the film maker avoids sensationalism, his work will still seem strange to the uninitiated. The normal story—the mystery, the comedy, the romance—can be handled on the screen with ordinary, straightforward techniques. But dreams, the drives and hungers of the subconscious, the performance of an occult ritual or the visualization of a surrealist poem—these require new forms, a feeling for symbol, for overtone, for the special rhythms of the world of unreality. Because such themes are generally avoided in the commercial movie, they offer a special challenge to the experimental film maker. In a sense, the subjective film bears much the same relation to ordinary pictures as poetry does to prose. Its successful realization depends entirely upon the sensitivity of the artist, his ability to project affectingly his own private vision. Unfortunately, simply because such films are so very personal, the field is quite inviting to pretentious frauds and precocious charlatans. So rarely does one have the opportunity to mask exhibitionism under the guise of art.

To this caveat it is necessary to add that many of the film makers of the new avant-garde are serious, honest and genuinely talented. As in any art form, only through repeated exposure can one begin to separate the sincere from the phony, the talented from the merely pretentious. The films of Maya Deren, for example, not only have a strong visual impact through her bold and unconventional use of the camera, but they create and sustain moods of dreamlike revelation with startling consistency. James Broughton, a San Franciscan poet and playwright, is less concerned with camera trickery than effects within the frame—adults playing children's games, incongruous juxtapositions of symbol-laden objects, the invention of absurd yet nostalgic business for his players and an overall textural richness that recalls the paintings of Ivan Albright. By contrast, Curtis Harrington, a leading experimental film maker before graduating to the Hollywood studios, is almost abstemious in the amount of detail he includes in his scenes. His characters play against broad, unbroken backgrounds where every object shown—a large knitting needle, a white dress blowing against a sandy dune—acquires an added significance. It was a training that stood him in good stead in his subsequent career as a studio-based director of such Gothic horror tales as *Games* (1967), *What's the Matter with Helen?* (1971), and *Ruby* (1977). Ian Hugo's *Bells of Atlantis* (1954) with its glimpses of a subaqueous world seen through layers of masking, lattice-like designs—and set to the cool, bell-like poetry of Anaïs Nin—delights through the complexity of its textures and shifting, elusive forms.

Throughout the fifties and well into the sixties, this movement continued to expand, attracting gifted young artists like Bruce Conner, Stan Brakhage, Kenneth Anger, Gregory Markopoulis, the Kuchar brothers, and hosts of others, for most of whom Jonas Mekas, editor of *Film Culture* and critic for the New York-based *Village Voice,* was both guru and booking agent. And Mekas gave his approval without stint. If it was experimental, it was good. Overnight, with his laying on of the hands, one could become an instant artist. And these instant artists received instant exposure. Universities, art museums, film societies, even art houses (which began special showings of experimental film programs around midnight on Friday and Saturday nights) booked, generally sight unseen, out of Mekas' New York Film Co-op. Inevitably, the field invited charlatans of every stripe and description—young men and women who made a virtue of being out of focus, underexposed and with inaudible sound. Pop artist Andy Warhol created an entire "factory" for this purpose alone, with monumental non-stop bores like *Sleep* (1963), *Empire* (1964), and *The Chelsea Girls* (1966) to show for it. Films like Jack Smith's *Flaming Creatures* (1969) ventured boldly—and crudely—into areas of transvestism and sexual perversion. But the raunch from the Co-op's amateurs was nothing compared to the professional porn being purveyed toward the end of the sixties by the likes of Russ Meyer, Bill Osco and Louis Sher. Despite the presence of many gifted and sincere experimentalists, the movement—as a movement—began to go down the tubes.

And yet, the impulse for this kind of creativity persists in the work of Hollis Frampton, Ron Rice, Harry Smith, the now veteran Brakhage, and many more. In each instance, the film maker presents a highly personal vision of the world, filling it with highly subjective imagery. If there is narrative content, it generally evades literal interpretation. Meanings emerge through the sensations they create in their audience, through a continuity of mood and feeling rather than any formal story line. Frequently they are shocking—sometimes merely by their strangeness, more often in a deliberate attempt to jolt the audience. It is impossible to view these pictures passively. They demand that the spectator participate both emotionally and intellectually in their presentation. It is this extraordinary sense of involvement that has won a special audience for these films—and perhaps also alienated those who were either unwilling or unprepared to make the effort required to appreciate this unconventional, challenging film form.

The Twilight of the Major Studios

For Hollywood, the years of World War II proved an era of unprecedented prosperity. The war itself created a tremendous need for entertainment, a need to escape from the daily headlines of battles fought on distant fronts and from the daily anxieties about friends and loved ones who might be fighting those battles. And, apart from radio (with its disconcerting propensity for broadcasting bad news every hour on the hour), movies provided the cheapest and most readily available escape route. Actually, since gas rationing virtually eliminated any form of pleasure driving, your friendly neighborhood movie house became just about the only place that one could go to forget about war for a few hours—except, perhaps, your friendly neighborhood tavern. Also, after ten years of the depression, people suddenly had money again. War plants, munitions factories and shipyards operated on a round-the-clock schedule, and wages rose as industries competed in a labor market depleted by the hundreds of thousands of young men and women in uniform overseas. The farmers were selling everything they could grow, and at good prices. The only hitch was that there was nothing to buy. The government had restricted the production of commodities to the bare essentials and had eliminated certain critical items from the consumer market altogether, such as the metals and electronic parts required for television receivers. And so, on their way to or from the factory, Swing Shift Maisie and Rosie the Riveter dropped off at the movies. What else was there?

These same restrictions, of course, applied to the movie studios as well. As the war went on, the government placed a $5000 limit per picture on new construction. With lumber at a premium, old sets were simply redecorated and used again in film after film, while new sets were held to a minimum. With a few judicious alterations, the costume worn by the star in one picture would encase the second lead of another. But if on occasion the pictures betrayed their penny-pinching budgets, no one seemed to mind. Since Hollywood had the only candy store in town, it was almost impossible to lose money on a movie.

Of far greater consequence to the studios than the loss of their precious right to squander money on sets and costumes, however, was their loss to the armed services of their most precious commodity, their stars. Top actors like Clark Gable, Robert Montgomery and James Stewart, top directors like Frank Capra, John Ford, John Huston and William Wyler quit the studios to contribute their mite to the war effort. Others, like Bing Crosby and Bob Hope, lent their talents to the USO and made innumerable personal appearances in the combat zones of literally every theater of operations around the world. Hollywood's all-out dedication to the cause is perhaps epitomized by the tragic death of the popular comedienne, Carole Lombard, killed in a plane crash while returning home from a War Bonds-selling swing around the country. Despite these losses, however, the studios whistled up their second line of defense and went right on grinding out their profitable entertainments for soldiers and civilians alike.

During the war years, it must have seemed to the industry that it could do no wrong. Between 1941 (which culminated in Pearl Harbor) and 1946 (the last year before the impact of television made itself felt), the studios' income more than doubled, rising from $809,000,000 to $1,692,000,000. By the industry's own estimate, about 95,000,000 Americans were going to the movies every week. When the war ended, studio executives faced the future with a rosy glow, confident that the bonanza would continue. They looked forward not only to the return to the fold of their most profitable stars and directors, but also to the return of their profitable foreign markets which, prior to the war, had been responsible for almost 50 percent of their total income. How wrong they were!

And how wrong they continued to be! Indeed, for the next several years it began to seem that they could do nothing right.

As early as July, 1938, the United States had filed suit against Paramount Pictures, *et al.*, charging the major studios with a long series of monopolistic practices. The case ground through the courts for several years, was set aside during the war, then surfaced again in 1946. It had been initiated by independent theater owners, disgruntled because, as they charged, the studios that owned theaters were discriminating against them, booking their pictures into their own houses rather than opening them to public bidding. (They also protested such long-standing industry practices as block-booking—selling pictures in packages of a dozen or more—and blind-booking—selling pictures before the exhibitor had a chance to look at what he was buying. Obviously, both of these charges related to the monopolistic position of the eight major movie companies, five of which had extensive theater holdings.)

Through the late forties and early fifties, the Supreme Court handed down a series of "consent decrees," all to a single effect—those movie companies that owned their own studios, distribution offices and theater chains constituted a monopoly operating in restraint of trade. They were ordered by the government to divest themselves of one of their branches. Reluctantly, studio after studio relinquished its theater holdings. ("Divorced" was the official terminology.) For the independent theater owners, however, it proved a Pyrrhic victory. Once separated from their theater chains, the studio heads quickly realized that they no longer had to supply a new movie each week for their own houses. They cut back on their production schedules. And as the amount of product diminished, the competition for the best ones increased in open bidding. So did the prices. Trapped between rising prices and a diminishing audience, many of the proud independent theater owners of the late thirties were out of business by the early fifties.

On the production side, even though they must have known that divorce was inevitable, the studio heads clung to the notion that theatrical distribution was their sole concern. They blinded themselves to the threat of television. "As long as we have theaters," said Howard Dietz, MGM's vice president in charge of advertising, in 1949, "it's our duty to fight off television if it takes the next twenty years." And he said this to someone trying to persuade him to use TV in advertising his wares! How could he know that in only three years his firm would be out of the theater business entirely? But this blindness typified the relationship of the entire motion picture industry to television in those early post-war years. In 1946, television was no more than a small dark cloud on the movies' bright horizon. Although there had been some experimental telecasting in the late thirties and early forties, the wartime ban on the manufacture of receivers soon brought this to a halt. Why put on shows if no one can see them?

However, no sooner did the government relax its restrictions on the crucial raw materials than the manufacture of TV sets was resumed with a vengeance—better than 40,000 a month. And TV programs returned to the air in force, this time with major sponsors and big budgets. New stations sprang up all around the country. "Uncle Miltie" and dozens of other personalities held audiences glued to their tiny seven-inch screens. By 1948, most movie makers were forced to recognize television as a major threat to their very existence. The odd thing is that they did nothing about it, except pretend to ignore it. They refused to sell their vast libraries of old movies to the networks or to advertise their upcoming features on the rival medium. Most studios wrote clauses into their player contracts forbidding them to make any television appearances whatsoever within six months before or after the release of the picture for which they had been signed—not even to plug the film itself! As a result, the stations began buying up packages of old British movies, dubbed foreign films, and whatever independent product—like the *Hopalong Cassidys*—they could lay their hands on. This artificial barrier was broken in 1952 when Republic, a very minor major, chose to sell its collection of Gene Autry and Roy Rogers Westerns to TV. The price was right; but the exhibitors wrathfully refused to book Republic's one claim to distinction for the year, John Ford's *The Quiet Man,* in retribution. A year later, Republic was out of business.

While most of the film companies looked upon Republic's demise as a justification of their own position that the theater owner must come first, it also meant that they had missed their opportunity to play a dominant role in the emerging television field. For television went to the networks almost by default. Both CBS and NBC (and, for a time, Dumont) were in the television business because they were primarily in the business of manufacturing television sets. Since no one would purchase a receiver unless there was something to receive, they were reluctantly placed in the position of manufacturing programs as well—a position that they gratefully relinquished to the big advertising agencies once TV's potency as an advertising medium had been established. By the mid-fifties, the airlanes were agency-dominated. But they could just as easily have been dominated by the movie studios, as the handiest and most logical creators of mass entertainment, had the studios themselves not been cowed by their theater outlets. Belatedly, in the late fifties, the Hollywood studios not only began to sell off their pre-1948 libraries to television, but began to produce for the networks series like *Bonanza* and *Cheyenne*—a practice pioneered by Walt Disney and hastily latched onto by Jack L. Warner. By the sixties, the success or failure of every major studio was being measured in terms of the number of series it had managed to sell to television. But, unlike the feature films, the ultimate control of these series lay not with the studios but with the networks. The studios were merely the suppliers. They had let the control slip by default.

What the studios had also let slip by default in those crucial years of the late forties were their blue-chip lists of contract players, directors, cameramen and writers. As they cut back on their production schedules subsequent to the protracted divorce proceedings, it seemed to make a good deal of sense to terminate those long-term contracts that had for so many years been the backbone of studio operations. If you had Clark Gable on a $500,000-a-year contract, and could use him in perhaps five or six pictures a year, fine. But if the level of studio production was being cut to less than half, why not forget the contract and bring him in on a weekly basis for maybe two or three pictures a year? Fine again—except that a change in the income tax laws suddenly made it far more profitable for a star to operate as a corporation than as an individual. From their agents, lawyers and business managers they learned the not insignificant difference between taxes on personal income in the higher brackets and taxes on corporate profits, and promptly began forming their own companies—often with those same agents, lawyers or business managers as partners. "LOOK, MA, I'M A CORPORA-

TION!" was the way *Variety* headlined this new trend. As a result, now when a studio wanted to use one of its former contract players in a picture, it found it was no longer dealing with an individual, but with a corporate entity—an entity with its own corporate ideas on how to participate in that picture's profits.

It was a process that continued—and continues—to snowball, particularly as the ranks of guaranteed box-office personalities continue to thin out. During the fifties, star salaries soared astronomically, from $500,000 to $1,000,000 for whoever was hottest at the moment—this plus a percentage of the gross. Not atypical of the new order of business was the financing of Universal-International's *Operation Petticoat* (1959), starring Cary Grant and Tony Curtis. Budgeted at about $3,250,000, it was made as a Granart production (Cary Grant's personal corporation). Yet it was wholly financed by Universal, used Universal's equipment and facilities, and Tony Curtis (still under contract to Universal at the time) was added to the package at his contract salary—which meant that he got about $55,000 as opposed to Grant's $350,000. But it doesn't stop there. For the privilege of releasing this little comedy that it had already paid for, Universal was contractually entitled to receive 10 percent of the gross. And after seven years, ownership of the negative reverted to Granart. As Grant explained it at the time, "The studios let go of their star players because they felt it would save them money, then failed to develop new ones. Besides," he added, "if the studio didn't think they could make out all right with this kind of an arrangement, they would never go for it. Nobody held a gun on them." But veteran Samuel Goldwyn had another view. At a meeting of the Screen Producers Guild that same year he demanded, "How long do you think this will continue when actors demand and get a half-million, three-quarters of a million dollars a picture—and a huge share of the gross or of the profits in addition?"

Since it is now almost twenty years later, and movies are still being made, obviously the industry has been able to make some accommodation with the new order of things; but to do so meant abandoning almost entirely the studio system that had proven so profitable for almost three decades. No longer could studio heads like Harry Cohn, Louis Mayer, Jack Warner or Darryl Zanuck rule their concrete fiefdoms as absolute monarchs; even before they had disappeared from the scene, their policies, pictures and deals were being dictated by the distribution arm, which held the purse strings. For these one-time moguls, the fifties marked a particularly difficult era of transition. Whereas they started the decade holding the power of life and death over every person and every project on their lot, by the end of the fifties those who had managed to stay in office found themselves surrounded by a new breed of independent producer, each with his own autonomous unit. What must have made it especially galling was the realization that most of these independents were the same people that they had cut loose from their contracts at the first pinch of television.

The authorship of this singular change in the production picture can be traced to a single firm: United Artists. Essentially a distribution company, U.A. owns no studio and has no theater chain; its facilities are devoted to the advertising, promotion and selling of those independently-made productions that it has taken for distribution. In a sense, it is still carrying out the functions for which it was created back in 1919. At that time, the leading film makers of the day—Griffith, Chaplin, Fairbanks and Mary Pickford—formed United Artists as an outlet for their own pictures. They wanted complete autonomy of production, the freedom to make what they wished as they wished—and to share in the profits rather than work for a salary, no matter how lucrative. To do so, they realized that they had to break with the established studios. Their ideal was quality, the custom-made film. During the twenties, they were joined by such leading independents as Samuel Goldwyn and Joseph M. Schenck, and later by David O. Selznick, Alexander Korda and Walt Disney. But there was a hard lesson in economics to be learned. By concentrating exclusively on independent quality production, United Artists lacked sufficient product to sustain the expense of a costly distribution apparatus. By the late forties, the company's position had become desperate.

When United Artists were reorganized in 1951 by two young lawyers, Arthur Krim and Robert Benjamin, they immediately substituted a new policy of taking virtually anything they could get, low budget or high budget, domestic or foreign, good or impossible, simply to build up the volume of their business. And they soon discovered that quality does not always correspond to budget, that an inexpensive picture can be a gold mine while a multimillion-dollar all-star attraction can lay a multimillion-dollar egg. By carefully nursing the better small ones that came their way, like *High Noon* (1952), and boldly exploiting such big ones as *The African Queen* (1951) and *Moulin Rouge* (1952), Krim and Benjamin gradually wiped away the tarnish that had gathered on the U.A. escutcheon. As the new owners gathered strength, they made a shrewd assessment of the industry. They saw talented writers and directors, not to mention high-priced stars, who no longer were tied to the studios, but had their own producing firms. All they lacked were two things—finance and distribution. Now U.A. was in a position to offer both. The plan was quite simple. Would-be producers (preferably with some sort of track record) were invited to submit their scripts, plus whatever other elements they had assembled in terms of stars or directors to help make up the "package." If the United Artists top brass approved the script, they might offer some casting suggestions or present a list of directors in whom they had confidence; but once they had agreed to accept a project, the producer was on his own. He could make the picture wherever he chose and, so long as he kept within a stipulated budget, however he chose. Nor was U.A. interested in supervising the picture on a day-to-day basis; what its executives were concerned with was the completed film—the commodity that they would then market. For film makers accustomed to the tight-fisted controls of the old studio system, it was the next thing to nirvana, a freedom they never dared hope for. Not surprisingly, the leading independents—producers like Sam Spiegel, Otto Preminger and Stanley Kramer, actor-producers like Burt Lancaster and Kirk Douglas—were soon beating on the U.A. doors; and pictures as varied and off-beat as *The Barefoot Contessa* and *Beat the Devil* (both 1954), the intimate, low-keyed *Marty* and Otto Preminger's daringly controversial *Man With the Golden Arm* (both 1955), star-studded spectaculars like *Alexander the Great* and *Trapeze* (both 1956), and such intensely personal dramas as *Paths of Glory* and *12 Angry Men* (both 1957), were the direct result of the new policy. Most of these were projects that would never have been touched by a major studio.

Within a single year, the new management at United Artists had taken the company out of the red (where it had been languishing since 1948) and brought it into the black.

By the end of the fifties, it was consistently among the leading money-makers in the entire industry. Its success could hardly be ignored. By 1955, every major studio was beginning to welcome—however grudgingly—these independent units to their lots, holding out as bait not only the promise of finance and distribution, but access to the studios' prized production facilities—the sound stages, back lots, recording rooms, props, sets, wardrobes, all the paraphernalia and specialized know-how that had always been their main stock in trade, their most precious and private possessions. They weren't precisely up for grabs; the studios were still in the position of being able to choose which independents they might be willing to work with. But the tide was beginning to turn. Perhaps the most significant sign of this change was the 1956 resignation of Darryl F. Zanuck as the top executive in charge of production on the 20th Century-Fox lot, a position he had held for more than twenty years, in order to form his own autonomous unit. Instead of supervising anywhere from thirty to fifty pictures each year, he declared his intention to make perhaps two or three a year—each personally chosen, each personally produced. Many years before, Samuel Goldwyn had said, "I make my pictures to please myself." The oldest and most conspicuously successful of all the independents, he lived long enough to see his private tenets become the watchword of whole new generations of film makers in Hollywood.

The Blacklist Years

If freedom was advancing on the production level, however, on the ideological level there were frightening, even nightmarish, developments. The movies, from their very inception, have always been subject to censorship in one form or another. As early as 1907, Chicago instituted a municipal review board with the power to cut pictures or to reject them in their entirety. Throughout the next decade, other cities—and then the states—grabbed a piece of the action. During the twenties, under the increasingly stern surveillance of Will Hays and the M.P.P.D.A., the studios began to censor themselves (although they always sought to draw a distinction between censorship and *self*-censorship). In 1934, it was the clergy's turn to take over, with the Legion of Decency—abetted by the Hays Office and its Production Code—imposing

standards of morality that were to stand almost without mod-
ification for the next 32 years.

But at least, these were all out in the open. The Chicago
censors, the censors in Pennsylvania, the administrators of the
Production Code (with their painstakingly spelled-out "thou
shalt nots" and "be carefuls") supplied fairly explicit guide-
lines governing what could pass and what might be excised.
With the advent of the House Un-American Activities investigations, and the subsequent rise of Senator Joseph McCarthy,
these overt censorships were superseded by a censorship of
fear—the fear of speaking one's mind, the fear of losing one's
job. "Un-American" ideas or ideologies were forced off the
screen by the simple expedient of denying employment to
anyone accused or suspected of harboring them. Although always vigorously denied by industry spokesmen, an industry-
wide blacklist went into effect immediately after the HUAC
1947 hearings of the Hollywood Ten and remained in effect
right through to the end of the fifties.

In point of fact, 1947 was not the first time that Hollywood had been scrutinized by the House committee. As early
as 1940, under the chairmanship of Martin Dies, HUAC had
launched an investigation into what was later termed the industry's "premature anti-fascism," as evidenced by such films
as *Confessions of a Nazi Spy* (1939). There can be no
doubt that Dies, a Texan, was more interested in seeking
headlines than subversives. In 1940, on the very brink of our
entry into World War II, great sections of the country—
particularly in the Midwest—were still strongly isolationist
and cold to any film that threatened to involve us in European affairs. This was the gallery that Dies was playing to;
and some forty top film personalities, from little Shirley
Temple to big Jack L. Warner, were called upon to testify
on Communist (meaning anti-fascist or anti-Nazi) influences
on our movies. When it became evident that the fascists and
the Nazis were indeed our national enemies, the investigations ground to an abrupt and inconclusive halt.

Without question, once the United States had been forced
into the global conflict on that fateful morning of December
7, 1941, the motion picture industry served the nation faithfully and well. Quite apart from the numerous documentaries
that the studios turned out virtually as recruiting posters for
the various armed services, or to induce women on the home
front to enter the labor force, Hollywood's features examined

the war—and often its issues—with an unbridled enthusiasm. There may have been more than an iota of self-justification here, since the liberals' anti-fascist positions of the thirties, so often linked to Communism, were proven to have been correct all along; and the Russians, the dread menace of the thirties, had inexplicably become our allies! Suddenly, it was not only safe but patriotic to champion the Soviet Union and to denounce fascism. Whatever their own personal politics may have been up to that time, during the war years the American film makers were united in their determination to use their medium as effectively as possible to present not merely the image of a strong and unified America, but of an even stronger and more unified Free World. By an ugly irony, within a few short years this access of patriotic fervor was to be used against many of them in a series of politically motivated investigations that thundered through Hollywood during the next decade.

For by 1947 the liberalism of the Roosevelt years was fast running out. Russia had emerged from the war as a strong, militant and increasingly hostile power. In the growing hysteria of the "cold war," radicalism was almost instinctively linked with all shades of liberal thought. Conformity became the new order of the day, and congressional committees again began to institute investigations into "un-American" activities in every sphere of American life. No investigations were more persistent—nor more publicized—than those into the motion picture industry.

The hearings of the House Un-American Activities Committee, begun in Hollywood in October of 1947 under the aegis of Rep. J. Parnell Thomas, sent a chill of fear through the studios. Pictures like *Mission to Moscow* and *Song of Russia*, made during the years when the Soviet Union was an American ally in the war against Germany, were suddenly brought forward as evidence that the screen was being used to win converts to Communism. A committeeman claimed that he had detected Communist ideology in *The Best Years of Our Lives* and *Margie,* an innocuous comedy based on the postwar housing shortage. But while the Committee's charge that known Communists were using the screen for purposes of propaganda was never substantiated, ten members of the Hollywood community—nine writers and one director—were jailed as "unfriendly witnesses" for six months or a year. As an immediate result, Hollywood's enthusiasm for controversial subjects was effectively dampened. Jack L. Warner, after an uncomfortable probe into the details surrounding the production of *Mission to Moscow* (which he claimed was made at the specific prompting of both President Roosevelt and the State Department), flatly stated that, so far as he was concerned, his studio would make no more pictures dealing with "the little man." Other producers were perhaps less forthright but no less decided. As William Wyler observed early in 1948, "I wouldn't be allowed to make *The Best Years of Our Lives* in Hollywood today. That is directly the result of the activities of the Un-American Activities Committee."

The fear and uncertainty created by those investigations were augmented when, on March 8, 1951, Rep. John S. Wood chaired yet another House investigation aimed at removing known subversives from the motion picture industry and the Broadway theater. By this time, McCarthyism was at its height; and Wood was further aided in his investigations by the publication of *Red Channels*, a booklet that purported to give the television industry inside information on the Communist affiliations of actors, writers and directors (and anyone else) working in the studios. Since these included people employed by both the Hollywood studios and the Broadway stage, the net was flung wide. The investigation lasted for almost two years. What it proved, if anything, was that the New York theater was impregnable to such attacks, but television and the movies were not. Wood called dozens of witnesses, who named literally hundreds of names. Those who made their livelihood primarily in the theater found little difficulty in continuing their careers—such as Abe Burrows or Lillian Hellman. "Friendly witnesses"—witnesses who named names, such as Elia Kazan and Budd Schulberg—were able to resume their careers almost as if nothing had happened. But while no jail sentences came out of the 1951-52 investigations, there were some—like Carl Foreman—who fled the country, and hundreds more who were forced off the screen (at least, under their own names) for the next decade. It is a story that director Martin Ritt and writer Walter Bernstein (both backlisted) were ultimately able to document in their movie, *The Front* (1976). It tells of a blacklisted writer for television who persuades Woody Allen to front for him in selling scripts to the networks. During the fifties, the practice was no less widespread in Hollywood—as was ironically pointed up when the Academy's Oscar for Best Screenplay in

1956 went to one Robert Rich for *The Brave One*. No one claimed the statuette, but it was subsequently revealed that Robert Rich was a pseudonym for Dalton Trumbo, perhaps the most prominent of the blacklisted writers.

Like successive combat waves in a battle that has already been lost, the Committee continued its activities until well into 1958, calling in new names, making new allegations. The Wood investigations of 1951-52 summoned approximately 85 witnesses, more than half of whom were labeled "unfriendly." They were promptly enrolled on the industry's "nonexistent" blacklist. The attacks were resumed in 1953, this time under the leadership of Harold H. Velde and Francis S. Walter, and during the next three years, no less than 650 witnesses were interrogated (most of whom took either the Fifth Amendment or what came to be called the "diminished Fifth"—declaring that they were not now members of the Communist Party, but refusing to state whether or not they had been members in the past on grounds of possible self-incrimination). Although the Committee compiled hundreds of new names for its lists, and had more than its share of "unfriendly" or "uncooperative" witnesses, it never resorted to the Parnell Thomas device of contempt citations and prison sentences for the recalcitrants. Perhaps the knowledge that the blacklist was in good working order provided an adequate alternative.

Even so, enthusiasm for these witch hunts was beginning to wane. By 1954, the bloom was pretty much off the peach. The list of actors, actresses and directors who had the stature to grab headlines merely by being summoned to appear was rapidly diminishing (and there can be little doubt that both Velde and Walter were well aware of the publicity potential in every name they called to the stand). Also, the Roman circus atmosphere of the hearings was beginning to pall on great sections of the public, and to appall even more. Witness after prominent witness would be introduced as if he or she had personally organized a Communist conspiracy in the United States (which, of course, made all the evening headlines) only to have it revealed in court the next day that the guilt consisted of attending some meetings or signing their names to some documents of organizations that had subsequently been identified by the Attorney General's office as "subversive." Not atypical was the case of Lucille Ball, in 1953 at the peak of her popularity as television's Lucy. Headlines screamed the fact that in the 1936 elections she had registered to vote Communist. In private session she admitted that she had so registered "to please her grandfather," but stated that she never actually voted Communist. Her television sponsor, Philip Morris (unlike too many sponsors at that time), indicated that they were going to stand by her. The matter was quietly dropped.

Since these were all House hearings, the feared and fearsome Joseph McCarthy, the junior Senator from Wisconsin, was never directly involved; he was busy frying other, bigger fish in the glare of bigger, brighter spotlights. But HUAC battened on—and contributed significantly to—the national *malaise* summed up in the word McCarthyism. So much so that when, on December 2, 1954, the U.S. Senate voted to condemn McCarthy for his own acts in contempt of Congress, thus effectively bringing to an end his years of unbridled power, the end of HUAC was also in sight. In August of 1955, the Committee's new chairman, Francis E. Walter, began a new, rather half-hearted probe of Communist infiltration of the Broadway theater (again) involving perhaps two dozen of Broadway's lesser lights. In 1956, Walter found richer pickings in two highly publicized hearings to deny U.S. passports to actor-singer Paul Robeson and to playwright Arthur Miller (on the eve, as everyone in America knew, of his impending nuptials with Marilyn Monroe, then in England); both were issued contempt citations which were later dropped. There was one lone hearing in 1957 (actress Lee Grant); and a last scraping of the barrel in June, 1958, when a dozen minor Broadway figures were brought into court. Although all were unfriendly, none was charged with contempt. And then the Committee quietly, all but unnoticed, passed out of existence. Actor-writer Robert Vaughn delivered its epitaph in his scrupulously researched study, *Only Victims:* "Through thousands of investigations over a twenty-two-year period, in and out of the entertainment world," he concluded, "no law or laws remotely essential to the security of the nation ever resulted from the committee's work."

Even without laws, however, it can be argued that the House Un-American Activities Committee achieved its goals, as related to the motion picture industry. For better than a decade, all shades of liberal thought were stifled. Film material that might in any way be labeled controversial was shunned—along with those controversial individuals best qualified to bring them to the screen. Simply in human terms, in terms of the hundreds of careers that it destroyed and the hundreds of lives that it wrecked, the history of HUAC is as shameful as anything that ever happened in this country. But when to that is added its effect upon film content during the fifties, the story is even more degrading. As if to prove how very patriotic they were, the studios launched a series of anti-Communist movies—*The Red Danube* (1949), *The Red Menace* (1949), *I Married a Communist* (1951), *I Was a Communist for the F.B.I.* (1951), *Big Jim McLain* (1952), *My Son, John* (1952), *Blood Alley* (1955). Significantly, most of them were low-budget affairs, at once halfhearted and hysterical, made as if their producers knew they were doomed from the start. They were right.

In the atmosphere of uncertainty and fear that pervaded the movie colony as an aftermath of these investigations, it was inevitable that the studios concentrated on presumably safe and purely escapist entertainments. In 1949, after Stanley Kramer and Louis de Rochemont, two independent producers, released *Home of the Brave* and *Lost Boundaries,* several of the major studios also made pictures that vigorously attacked racism—*Intruder in the Dust* (MGM, 1949), *The Lawless* (Paramount, 1950) and *No Way Out* (Fox, 1950). But the paucity of these attacks during the subsequent decade was emphasized by the fact that when Kramer returned to the subject in *The Defiant Ones* (1958), the material still seemed fresh, controversial and daring. The anti-war fervor of the forties was absent from the screen until late in 1957, when it was affirmed again in Stanley Kubrick's *Paths of Glory* and David Lean's *Bridge on the River Kwai.* Significantly, both were independent productions. The fifties became the era of the movie musicals—escapism *sans pareil*—as represented by such glittering specimens as *An American in Paris* (1951), *Singin' in the Rain* (1952), *The Band Wagon* (1953), *Carmen Jones* (1954), *Guys and Dolls* (1955), *High Society* (1956), *Funny Face* (1957) and *Gigi* (1958). They came from all studios, and in all sizes and shapes (including the then-new CinemaScope, Todd-AO and VistaVision processes); but none were more elaborate and glittering than those from MGM. As even this partial listing reveals, however, the musicals were either drawn from established Broadway hits or relied on the nostalgic appeal of the assorted song books of Cole Porter, the Gershwins and

Dietz & Schwartz. "Original" musicals of the period tended to
be smaller, more intimate, and were frequently based on
studio-owned properties that had originally been filmed
straight. A good example of what could happen to such
material during the McCarthy years is Warners' *She's Working Her Way Through College* (1952), a musical adaptation
of the James Thurber-Elliott Nugent comedy, *The Male Animal*. In both the play and Warners' 1942 film version, the
central issue was whether or not an English teacher could
read to his college class from the letters of Sacco and Van-
zetti. By 1952 the issue had become whether or not Virginia
Mayo should be permitted to pay her college tuition with
money earned by working as a burlesque queen!

This careful skirting of possibly controversial material also
extended to movies deemed controversial at the time. While
From Here to Eternity (1953), based on James Jones' best-
seller, could hardly be called an Army recruiting poster, it effectively whitewashed the service (which Jones never did) by
focusing upon a self-seeking officer and a particularly sadistic
sergeant. When the Inspector General learns of the Captain's
activities, the man is promptly discharged from the service,
while the brutal non-com (Ernest Borgnine) is slain in a
knife fight with Montgomery Clift. Where Jones was indicting
a system that encouraged and rewarded brutality, the film
narrowed the charge to two particular individuals. The same
approach, Stanley Kramer later admitted, was the only way
he could secure the cooperation of the Navy for the filming
of Herman Wouk's bitter novel, *The Caine Mutiny* (1954),
which Wouk had written as a scathing exposé of the Navy's
propensity for protecting its own. Even *On the Waterfront*
(1954), widely regarded as the most daring and forthright
film of the period, managed to fudge when it came to revealing who were the "higher ups" who were manipulating
corrupt unions and waterfront dissension to their own advantage. Typical was the case of *Storm Center* (1956), a film
depicting the effects of a book's banning upon an entire community. Daniel Taradash, its author and director (and previously the author of the screenplay for the enormously
profitable *From Here to Eternity*), has stated that he had
sought to make the picture for five whole years before the
front office reluctantly gave its consent. (And Mary Pickford,
who had professed interest in playing the central character, a

staunchly liberal librarian, withdrew as the property became increasingly "hot"; Bette Davis ultimately played the role.)

Such were the rare "message" movies from an industry that was almost ostentatiously avoiding messages during the fifties. Writers withdrew to the safer grounds of individual maladjustments—snipers who hated their mothers, slashers who loathed their wives, alcoholics, drug addicts, juvenile delinquents and assorted psychotics of every hue and description.*

Symptomatically, comedy was in particularly short supply during the fifties, especially the topical comedy that ridicules or satirizes the world around us—the kind of comedy epitomized by the Marx Brothers on the one hand and by Preston Sturges on the other. Time has lent sufficient perspective to the HUAC investigations to reveal their inherent inanity—the scrutiny of scripts for nonexistent evidence of Communist ideology, the insistence on the naming of names that the Committee already knew, the search for a Communist conspiracy by men who had only the vaguest notion of what Communism was all about. But during the McCarthy years, nobody felt like laughing.

---

* But if these films were often starkly factual in describing their heroes' problems, they were also strikingly diffident about ascribing their anti-social acts to any social causes.

✦ 7 ✦

The Auteur Theory,
and a Few Others

In Europe far more than in the United States, films are generally identified by the director—not by the star, not by the studio. To be sure, Hollywood could always boast a few directors who were stars in their own right, like Cecil B. De Mille and Alfred Hitchcock (especially after his rubicund features were made familiar through his television series), possibly John Ford, possibly Elia Kazan, possibly John Huston. But if anyone knew by name many more directors than that, he was probably either a film student, a film buff, or a member of the Directors Guild. Until well into the fifties, American pictures were identified by the studios that produced them, and were sold by the stars who appeared in them. Who directed was about as important to the ticket buyers as which lab made the prints.

While the average European moviegoer was probably every bit as devoted to superstars as any American fan (as evidenced by the avid press coverage of Brigitte Bardot's every move for at least a decade, or the national mourning on the death of Anna Magnani), a fundamental difference in the *mode* of production automatically threw greater emphasis on the European directors. In France, all studios had closed their doors as early as 1934, forced out of business in part by a national depression, in part by scandalous revelations of swindles and corruption on the highest levels of management. By default, production passed into the hands of entrepreneurs who became self-styled producers, putting together the elements of a "package" in ways strikingly similar to those fol-

306

lowed in latter-day Hollywood. They would assemble a script, a star and a director, then go off in search of the financing, after which they would rent space as needed in the idle studios. Since the key to getting both the script and the star—and hence the money—was generally the director, his name was featured prominently in subsequent advertising of the film itself. The producer was essentially a money man, uninvolved in the creative aspects of the completed work.

This was even more evident in Italy after World War II. During the long reign of Mussolini, the studios were not only state controlled, but were handed over to personal favorites (and relatives) of Il Duce. Even before his regime had fallen, these studios were virtually out of business; and before the German occupation forces had withdrawn, the new style of Italian film making known as neo-realism had begun to emerge. It centered completely about such directors as Roberto Rossellini, Vittorio De Sica, Luchino Visconti and their favorite scenarists, Federico Fellini, Sergio Amidei, Suso Cecchi d'Amico and Cesare Zavattini. (It is especially worth noting that the neo-realist directors frequently originated their own stories, and invariably worked on their own screenplays in collaboration with the writers.) By the early fifties, cinema *cognoscenti* were also becoming familiar with the work of Sweden's Ingmar Bergman, the exiled Luis Buñuel, the rediscovered Carl Dreyer, and even Japan's Akira Kurosawa after his *Rashomon* won the top prize at the 1951 Venice Film Festival. The stage was being set for the *"auteur"* theory.

Ironically, while the concept of the director as *auteur*—the individual who gives a film its style, its shape, its "signature"—erupted in France in the mid-fifties, it was touched off by a new generation of critics, writing for the influential *Cahiers du Cinéma,* who had suddenly discovered and fallen in love with American movies. All during the war years, during the years of the Nazi occupation, they had been deprived of these; and France's post-war monetary difficulties delayed their arrival even longer. The war over, American films began to trickle in, supplemented by intensive screenings of older pictures valiantly preserved throughout the German occupation by Henri Langlois and the *Cinémathèque Française* at considerable risk to himself and his cohorts. François Truffaut, who first enunciated the *"politique des auteurs,"* was not the only critic (and later film maker) who made the *Cinémathèque* his academy. Jean-Luc Godard, it has been said, knew the collection so well that if he wanted to see a particular scene or sequence, he could time his arrival at the projection room precisely to the minute. The irony lies in the fact that the American movies that they saw there were all products of the despised Hollywood studio system. They had far less to do with *"auteurism"* than the contemporary works then being produced on the Continent!

Yet another circumstance existed in France to favor the emergence of the theory in 1954, as Truffaut himself has been frank enough to admit. His *"politique des auteurs"* did indeed reflect a political struggle, but it was less a struggle between writers and directors over who was really the *"auteur"* than it was the struggle of a new generation of would-be film makers to bash down the doors of the Establishment by hammering away at the "well-made film" and its dependence on well-paid writers, such as Bost and Auvrenche, guardians of what was derisively termed the "Tradition of French Quality." "Primarily," according to Truffaut, "the idea was that the man who has the ideas must be the same as the man who makes the picture." For examples in the French cinema, he pointed to highly personal directors like Jacques Becker, Robert Bresson, Jean Renoir and Jacques Tati. But when the *"auteurists"* turned to the American film, they seemed almost perverse by naming to their Pantheon primarily directors of "B" movies (like Robert Aldrich, Joseph Losey, Nicholas Ray and Edgar G. Ulmer—plus, of course, Alfred Hitchcock, always one of Truffaut's idols). They claimed that they could trace in his collected works the personality of the director, and that this was more important than whether any given film was good or bad. To put it in its most extreme form, Truffaut once declared that "the best film of Jean Delannoy would never equal the worst film of Jean Renoir."

Since these were the utterances of a generation of film critics who were about to launch themselves as a "new wave" of film directors, it is difficult to avoid the suspicion that there was something supremely self-serving in their critical stance. They were exalting the position of the director, no matter what he happened to be directing. André Bazin, the veteran French critic and editor of *Cahiers du Cinéma*, fully recognized the importance of personality in every work of art, but, in one of his last articles before his death in 1958, added perceptively, "The *politique des auteurs* seems to me to harbor and to defend an essential critical truth, of which the cinema has need more than all the other arts, precisely in the measure to which the act of veritable artistic creation finds itself more uncertain and menaced there than elsewhere. But its exclusive use would lead to another peril: the negation of the work to the profit of the exaltation of its *auteur*. . . . This is not at all to deny the role of the *auteur*, but to restore to it the preposition without which the noun is only a lame concept. 'Auteur,' without doubt, but *of* what?"

Bazin died before most of his brood of larval critics could spread their wings and flit like butterflies from one directorial triumph to another. The crucial year was 1959, when Truffaut's *The 400 Blows* and Alain Resnais's *Hiroshima, Mon Amour* (along with Marcel Camus's *Black Orpheus*) emerged as top winners at the Cannes Film Festival; both had served as major critics on Bazin's *Cahiers du Cinéma*. Added to these in short order were films by fellow-staffers Claude Chabrol (*Les Cousins*, 1959) and Jean-Luc Godard (*Breathless*, 1960), Louis Malle's daringly sexual *Les Amants* (1959) and Roger Vadim's daringly sensual *And God Created Woman* (1958). The French cinema was about to be inundated by the New Wave.

It would be less than accurate, however, to suggest that all of these changes were wrought solely by the lucubrations of the *Cahiers* crowd. For one thing, a modest American film by Morris Engle and Ruth Orkin, *Little Fugitive* (1952), shot with a hand-held camera on Coney Island's beach and boardwalk, made a profound impression on these youthful critics. No less important, yet another crisis on the French production scene had suddenly made extremely costly studio pictures, such as René Clair's *Portes des Lilas* (1957), extremely risky propositions. Veteran producers like Pierre Braunberger were not looking around for something new so much as they were looking for something cheaper. They found what they wanted in the young dissidents who had either written for or had been influenced by the *Cahiers du Cinéma*. Some, including Malle and Truffaut, were actually able to supply part of the financing for their first features; Vadim, with his propensity for marrying his leading ladies, had Brigitte Bardot as security. Between 1959 and 1964, close to 175 new directors became identified with the New Wave—most of them young, all of them daring, some of them talented.

As a unifying tag, however, "New Wave" was hardly useful. The talents (and non-talents) who marched under its banners were far too disparate ever to make a single wave; they made instead currents and counter-currents, riptides and deep, quiet pools. Once Vadim and Malle had shown the way, many (including Bazin's successor on *Cahiers,* Jacques Daniol-Valcroze) plunged promptly into what can only be called sexploitation features, films that took advantage of the relaxed French attitude toward sex in the movies and were made with both eyes on the rich American market. At the other extreme was the complete intellectuality of Alain Resnais, whose pictures after *Hiroshima, Mon Amour—Last Year at Marienbad* (1961); *Muriel* (1963); *La Guerre Est Finie* (1966); *Je T'Aime, Je T'Aime* (1968); and *Stavisky* (1976)—resembled nothing so much as cinematic double-crostics. His themes were always engrossing (the toll of the Algerian war on French civilians in *Muriel,* the tired responses of a dedicated worker to a lost cause in *La Guerre Est Finie*); but the flash-backs and flash-forwards, the voice-over inner monologues, the tricky juggling with time always managed to place greater emphasis on the how than the why, on the technique rather than the content. In this purely formalistic approach, Resnais was soon joined by Marguerite Duras (who had written *Hiroshima, Mon Amour*) and Alain Robbe-Grillet (who had written *Last Year at Marienbad*); both were representative of another "new wave"—one that had swept over French literature in the late fifties and early sixties, the so-called "new novel"—and both discovered the ultimate expression of their imagist ambiguities as directors of film, as *auteurs.*

Certainly the most prolific—and most exasperating—of this protean group was Jean-Luc Godard, who worked briefly as an actor in films before turning to film criticism. Even while writing, however, he was also experimenting with both documentary and fiction shorts, testing many of the techniques that seemed so totally revolutionary in his first feature, *Breathless.* Made on an extremely limited budget ($80,000) from an idea by Truffaut, it was essentially little more than the story of a petty thief (Jean-Paul Belmondo) who shoots a cop and is ultimately turned in by his existential girlfriend (Jean Seberg). But Godard made it the occasion for a *tour de force* in reverse, a picture that deliberately broke all the rules for a well-made film. He eliminated establishing shots, plunging directly into action, often seemingly in midscene. Also gone were the carefully planned series of shots that ordinarily would bring a character from a cafe, through the streets, up the stairs, to the door, and into the girl's apartment; Godard cut ruthlessly from Belmondo rising from his cafe table to Belmondo closing the door behind him in the girl's boudoir. In the early sequence in which Belmondo drives to Paris in a stolen car, Godard seems wholly oblivious to the mismatches of the passing landscape as he cuts back and forth on a conversation. Shooting, whether on the streets of Paris or in the film's few interiors, was accomplished (by Raoul Coutard) largely with hand-held cameras and in short, machine-gun bursts. Since the very nature of this kind of camerawork eliminated the possibility of stringing microphones, the entire film was post-synchronized (as, of course, were the earlier Italian neo-realist pictures).

With such deliberate flaunting of the conventions, *Breathless* became a subject of controversy the instant it appeared. Many critics ascribed its technique to sheer ineptitude or—more charitably—to an inadequate budget. Some simply called it an abomination. But there were also those who saw what Godard was up to, who admired his energy and daring, who even (as Godard had hoped) began to question the necessity of showing close-ups of hands turning doorknobs and people eternally walking up flights of stairs. They spoke of the tremendous compression that was possible in film once one had stripped away the niceties and got down to the essentials of character and plot. They welcomed the ambivalence of the film's finale, leaving the audience to rationalize the reasons for Seberg's willful destruction of her lover. Only his harshest critics failed to be impressed by the freshness and liveliness (or lifelikeness) of his Paris street scenes. And for the film buffs, there were amusing little "in" jokes, like Belmondo ruminatively running his thumb over his lower lip *à la* Humphrey Bogart. (Such references to favorite stars, movies, directors and publications—including the *Cahiers*—crop up frequently in the work of New Wave directors. Indeed, it might be the *only* tie that binds them all together.)

Actually, what Godard had done was to put a new, raw edge on films, rejecting the smoothness and slickness of standard studio fare. His picture was jagged, but it was alive—it moved! Many of the techniques that Godard introduced in *Breathless,* particularly the hand-held camera and the jump cut, have long since been incorporated into the standard vocabulary of cinemas. As time went by, however, it became increasingly clear that Godard was less interested in filmic devices than in political statements. He could still, when he wished, create incredible *tours de force*—as in the seemingly endless, relentless tracking shot that opens *Week-end* (1967), revealing car after car after car that has been smashed or set afire while the wounded stagger about in agony among the corpses lining the roadway; or, in the same film, a virtuoso combination of a 360° pan and tracking shot in a barnyard, the camera discovering and then rediscovering a series of actions at various stages of their unfolding. Both would have earned nods of approval from his *Cahiers* master, André Bazin, who felt that editing interfered with the reality of a scene.

But as early as *Masculin Féminin* (1966), it began to appear that Godard might be using the camera as almost an extension of the tape recorder, photographing in single takes scenes that played upwards of five minutes (in some of which two actresses were simply photographed straight on while talking into a tape recorder). In *Le Gai Savôir* (1968), which was shown at the New York Film Festival but—understandably—had no other distribution in the United States, Godard staged long passages of political conversation between Jean-Pierre Léaud and Juliette Berto in the semi-darkness of a television studio; at times, the screen was completely black, as if to suggest that words now had become more important than images to the film maker. At least, to the ideologically committed film maker. In his more recent pictures, many of them made for television, Godard has introduced elements drawn from pop art, comic strips and TV news coverage to popularize his Maoist sentiments; at the same time, being an intense intellectual, he managed to intellectualize these popular elements until they become no longer acceptable to the average audience—or even, for that matter, to the television networks for which they were created. In a strange way, Godard's career parallels Orson Welles's (of whom he once said, "All of us will always owe him everything"). In the same piece he also wrote, "It isn't easy for a wonder kid to grow old gracefully." Both of these observations, written of Welles in 1963, might equally apply to Godard himself perhaps a dozen years later. If his earlier works turned up much that was right, his later films were filled with pitfalls that could just as profitably be spurned.

François Truffaut, his close friend from the *Cahiers* days

and collaborator on several of Godard's early works, has traveled an alternate route. Actually, apart from its freeze-frame finale, it is a bit difficult to see why *The 400 Blows* was considered particularly innovative in 1959. Bosley Crowther, writing in *The New York Times*, hailed it as a French film that "brilliantly and strikingly reveals the explosion of a fresh creative talent in the directorial field." Essentially, however, the talent revealed in *The 400 Blows* was a marked ability to handle delicate material realistically, yet with compassion—no mean accomplishment for a young man of 27. Especially when one realizes that, without bitterness or rancor, Truffaut drew upon incidents from his own wretched childhood for his scenario. Like Antoine Doinel, his cinematic *alter ego*, the young Truffaut was something of a hell-raiser, a source of irritation and mortification to his otherwise insensitive parents. Like Doinel, he was frequently in trouble at school, played hookey, and ultimately was sent to a reformatory (although not for supposedly stealing a typewriter, as in the film, but for actually stealing brass doorknobs, which he then sold to buy food after he had run away from home). Apparently, the reformatory was every bit as cheerless as the one he depicted; Truffaut once described it as "half an insane asylum and half a house of correction."

Truffaut's own future might well have been as bleak and hopeless as Antoine's at the end of *The 400 Blows*, the authorities closing in from behind and nothing but the vast, unfriendly sea ahead, were it not for his tremendous love of the movies. Lotte Eisner, of the *Cinémathèque Française*, recalls letting "little Truffaut" slip in free of charge to the tiny screening room on the Avenue des Messines where, hunched off to the side, he would sit through endless hours of films from around the world. While still in his teens, he attempted to form his own film society, which led to a chance acquaintance with Bazin, which in turn led to his subsequent career. There were still scrapes with the law, including a brief imprisonment after going AWOL on the eve of his regiment's departure for combat duty in Indochina (much as recounted in the third Doinel adventure, *Stolen Kisses*, 1968); but now he had Bazin as both mentor and protector. After a number of odd, menial jobs (again spelled out in *Stolen Kisses*), he was invited by Bazin to become a regular contributor to the *Cahiers du Cinema*, and was soon writing his acid-dipped film reviews for other publications as well. In 1955 he tried his hand at film making for the first time—a 16mm short (with Alain Resnais and Jacques Rivette, both of the *Cáers*) titled *Une Visite*. His next film, *Les Mistons* (1958), was almost a sketch for *The 400 Blows*, a 25-minute study of adolescent love and loyalties, jealousy and mischief-making. It was clearly the work of a young director to be watched. Truffaut not only loved and understood the kids in his movie; he also loved and understood the medium he was working in.

It may be an oversimplification to describe Truffaut as the humanist of the New Wave and Godard as the idealogue, but the fact is that while Godard was turning increasingly to "head" movies, Truffaut—at his best—always aimed for the heart. In *Shoot the Piano Player* (1960), an affectionate takeoff on American gangster films, he may have been a bit too much the cinematic wise-guy: a tough says, "If I'm lying, may my mother drop dead," and Truffaut promptly cuts to a shot of mother dropping dead. But with his next film, *Jules and Jim* (1961), the youthful director asserted for all time his mastery of certain aspects of his chosen medium—an ability to project period and *milieu* seemingly without effort, certainly without strain; an ability to extract breathtakingly accurate performances from both adults and children (in *Jules and Jim*, Jeanne Moreau was never better. Oskar Werner never more appealing, and Sabine Haudepin epitomized every wondering, vulnerable child); and a bittersweet lyricism that makes one ache for the what might have been. And if the film's climax, Catherine's suicidal ride with Jim, seems both forced and arbitrary, at least Truffaut can claim the virtue of having been true to a literary source that he esteemed highly.

All of these qualities are visible in the best of his subsequent films—*Bed and Board* (1970), the last of the Doinel series; *The Wild Child* (1970), in which Truffaut himself essayed the role of an 18th-century doctor who attempted to civilize a savage foundling; in *Small Change* (1976), a sunnier, more mature return to the children's world he first explored in *Les Mistons* and *The 400 Blows;* and in *Day for Night* (1973), a wondrously affectionate tribute to the big studios, the big stars, and to a style of movie making that had all but passed even as he made the film. *The Bride Wore Black* (1968) was also, at least in spirit, cast in the form of a tribute—to Alfred Hitchcock, the director that he most ad-

mires; but Truffaut is far too much the committed humanist
to build real sympathy for a woman (Jeanne Moreau) who
sets out on a cold-blooded campaign to murder the men she
holds responsible for the death of her husband. For that sort
of thing, one turns instinctively to Truffaut's fellow *Cahiers*
critic, Claude Chabrol.

Chabrol, whose *Le Beau Serge* (1959) was probably the
first authentically New Wave feature, has been unjustly
neglected or dismissed because, after the success of his second picture, *Les Cousins* (1959), he plunged into a career
that many critics decried as "too commercial." His major
crime, it seemed, was that he wanted to keep working, even if
that meant turning out a routine mystery film for Universal
like *The Champagne Murders* (1968). Chabrol found it a
challenge primarily because he had to shoot English and
French versions simultaneously—and his English wasn't that
good. Indeed, no film was ever merely routine to him, and
out of his persistence came a technique that grew sharp as a
scalpel, and a way of looking at bourgeois relationships that
was every bit as scathing as the later-day Buñuel's, but with a
pinch of Hitchcock on the side. (In 1957, with Eric Rohmer,
he wrote an admiring monograph on Hitchcock, and that
same admiration is evident in all of his subsequent pictures.)
As with Hitchcock, most of his movies center about a murder, beginning with his cool, almost existential study of the
mass-murderer *Landru* (1963), from a script by Françoise
Sagan—and made memorable by his felicitous use of Truffaut's still fresh device of the freeze-frame to signal rather
than to show the demise of the suave seducer's starry-eyed
victims. In *La Femme Infidèle* (1968), Michael Bouquet por-
trays a quiet, upper-middle-class gentleman who, in a sudden
and unaccustomed access of rage, kills the seducer of his wife
(Stephane Audran)—and, ironically, gains a new respect
from her in the process. In *Just Before Nightfall* (1971), the
order is reversed; the husband (Bouquet again) accidentally
kills his mistress when she threatens to disrupt his otherwise
conventional, complacent married life (again his wife is the
svelte Audran, who in private life is Mme. Chabrol). In *The
Butcher* (1969), when Audran as a prissy but pretty school
teacher rejects the amorous advances of the village butcher
(Jean Yanne), she unwittingly touches off a series of grisly
sex murders. In a scene that is typical of Chabrol's obesiance
to Hitchcock, one of the corpses is discovered by children on

a picnic. A little girl sits under a rocky ledge and prepares to open her sandwich just as a trickle of blood oozes down the ledge and a drop falls on her head. She looks up to see if it's raining. She looks down again, and the next drop falls on the white bread, staining it crimson. She screams.

But where Hitchcock relishes the fact of murder for its sheer shock value and the subsequent twistings and turnings of the murderer to escape his fate, Chabrol's interest lies less in the murder itself than in its effect upon the relationships of those involved in the crime. Many critics have complained of Chabrol's films, along with Rainer Werner Fassbinder, that "there are no people there, only shadows. Shadows with an elusive glamour whose tale will be well told." For others, the art of the telling is enough—Chabrol's impeccable camera positions and moves, his spare but telling use of close-ups, and his ever-present concern for *milieu*. It is also worth noting that the *milieu* which apparently concerns him most is that of the French *haute bourgeoisie;* and no one, with the possible exception of Luis Buñuel, has been more ardent in discrediting its values and life style. Why else did the French censors seek to ban his *Wedding in Blood* (1973), yet another murder story set against a background of the wealthy and well-born? Unless perhaps because this time the underlying political implications of his pictures were apparent even to the French censors.

Chabrol, Truffaut, Godard and Resnais have all been concerned primarily with the visual aspects of the sound film. Not that content is irrelevant to them, but they have always wanted to find cinematic, as opposed to literary or theatrical, ways to express themselves. Even when Godard chose to black out the image completely in *Le Gai Savôir*, it was his *cinematic* way of throwing the emphasis on the words. Indeed, ever since the birth of the "talkies," there has been the underlying assumption that dialogue is essentially uncinematic, that talk in and of itself undermines what is properly the dominant role of the camera. No one in film has done more to counter this impression than Eric Rohmer, the fifth major *Cahiers* critic to turn film maker (and also, after Bazin's death, his successor as editor-in-chief of that publication). A full decade older than his youthful fellow critics, Rohmer also anteceded them as a film maker; his first picture was *Le Journal d'un Scélérat* (1950), and he made half a dozen more shorts before attempting his first feature, *Le*

Signe du Lion, in 1959. But it was not until 1968, with *My Night at Maud's,* that his particular genius made itself evident. Not to everyone, of course. The dialogues between Marxist Antoine Vitez and the Pascalian Jean-Louis Trintignant were hardly calculated to ensnare the average moviegoer (even though they were brilliantly translated and condensed into English subtitles by Rohmer's producer, Pierre Cottrell). But one could sense, however dimly, that here was a major breakthrough, that the director had so artfully balanced words against images, the personalities of the performers against backgrounds, *milieu,* even the weather (a snowstorm forces Trintignant to reluctantly accept Maud's hospitality overnight), that the esthetics of the talking film would never again be quite the same. In her perceptive *New Yorker* review, Penelope Gilliatt wrote, "And oh, the pleasure of a film that looks at people for long takes instead of going chop-chop-chop, like television; that so often finds a listener's face more interesting than a speaker's; that lets people *talk,* instead of yielding to the cant that talk isn't 'visual'. . . . The word is one of the more inanely used elements in the cinema. You imagine that one day, off camera, your truly filmic hero is going to have to leap out of his chair and say to his girl friend, 'Let's go out and do something visual.' "

Few American directors have attempted to do this sort of thing. One thinks of Joseph L. Mankiewicz (who was essentially a writer) in *All About Eve* (1950) and *The Barefoot Contessa* (1954), Billy Wilder in *Sunset Boulevard* (1950) and *Ace in the Hole* (1951), of Preston Sturges in *Sullivan's Travels* (1941) and, of course, Orson Welles (with Herman Mankiewicz) in *Citizen Kane.* Perhaps the list could be extended, but not very far, because there is always the danger of breaching that fine line between true cinema and "canned theater." Properly, the wide critical acceptance of *My Night at Maud's* should have prompted an extended reevaluation of André Bazin's classic inquiry, "What Is Cinema?" Instead, critics had grown so accustomed to the all-talking picture that they commended *Maud* on its high literary quality (Trintignant and Vitez spend much of their night at Maud's discussing Pascal, Jensenism, Marxism and the law of probabilities), failing to see that in fact Rohmer had found a valid solution—possibly the *only* valid solution—to cinematizing such literary dialogues. By espousing the Bazin approach of long takes and deep-focus photography, Rohmer was able at once to sustain unbroken the long train of philosophical argument while also sustaining a sense of the reality of his scenes by his emphasis on background details—the movement of people at a bookstore, a restaurant or beach, always oblivious to the words or actions of the principals, a maid tiptoeing unobtrusively out of Maud's salon. It is a style that enables us, as Miss Gilliatt pointed out, to observe the faces of people talking (and listening) while preserving the integrity of *mise en scène*, which was always Bazin's greatest concern.

Far from prolific, Rohmer continued his "moral tales" with *Claire's Knee* (1970) and *Chloe in the Afternoon* (1972), both made with the same painstaking artistry that no doubt prompted Pauline Kael to call him "a superb lapidary craftsman"—an appellation all the more appropriate since the films were photographed (impeccably, of course) in glowing, gemlike colors. But it was impossible not to wonder just what the morality consisted of. In each of the films, the hero is sorely tempted by a woman (even if, in *Claire's Knee*, the temptation is nothing more carnal than a caress of the girl's knee). When Trintignant finally is lured into bed by Françoise Fabian in *Maud*, he carefully wraps himself in a blanket and stretches out on top of the fur throw under which she lies naked. The alluring Zouzou as Chloe may coax Bernard Verley to dry her off after a shower, but when she invites him into her bed, he promptly runs home to his wife. Surely, these are the thinnest pretexts of morality, lacking not only in sophistication but in any awareness that contemporary morality consists of a bit more than who is sleeping with whom. Perhaps Rohmer himself was conscious of this, for in 1976 he retreated to more decorous times, the 19th century, and an adaptation of Heinrich von Kleist's *The Marquise of O*, which dealt with the delicate question of whether the Marquise's life had been saved or destroyed by the gallant officer who snatched her from rape but then impregnated her himself. As always, critics praised the perfection of his *mise en scène*, the superb performances (by a German cast), and the sense of the director's intellect shaping and controlling every scene; but many questioned his choice of von Kleist's remote and fragile story as a showcase for his technical skill.

While still speaking of Rohmer and the *auteurs*, mention should also be made of a member of an older generation whose work was frequently cited with approbation by the critics of the *Cahiers du Cinéma*, no doubt because his highly personal style of film making notably reflected their own early ideals. Robert Bresson, born in 1907, could hardly be identified with the young Turks of 1959; but two of his earlier films, *Les Anges du Péché* (1943) and *Les Dames du Bois de Boulogne* (1945), and even more, his *Diary of a Country Priest* (1951), were ardently championed by André Bazin while he was still refining his own esthetic of cinema; they became, in effect, the *Battleship Potemkin* of his anti-montage formulations. The fact that Bresson wrote his own screenplay for *Diary* (based on a novel by Georges Bernanos) and used non-actors effectively against natural settings—and also perhaps the fact that none of his films ever found a wide following—contributed significantly to his appeal to the *Cahiers* crowd. The comparisons to Rohmer are many. Although never as sensual in his use of the camera as Rohmer, there is the same control and precision, the same deep-focused placement of heads against their proper environment—the grim, gray countryside of *Diary*, the even grimmer and grayer French prison of *A Man Escaped* (1956), the cold stone cell and courtroom of *The Trial of Joan of Arc* (1962). Apart from Joan, however, Bresson's characters are rarely as loquacious as Rohmer's: their dialogues are mostly in the head. But the two share the same concern for right and wrong, the same concern for moral values, the same concern for people rather than plot—except that where Rohmer's people are inherently graceful, Bresson's are searching for a state of grace.

From France, riding the crest of the New Wave, the "*auteur* theory" spread to England in the early sixties, where it was earnestly taken up by youthful film enthusiasts (centered mostly at Oxford), but was always held at arm's length by such established publications as *Sight and Sound* and *Films & Filming*. They recognized that it existed (in fact, thanks to the bear-baiting tactics of the editors of *Movie*, they could hardly have done otherwise); but while both publications were strongly director-oriented, they were unwilling to accept the limiting strictures of *auteurism* or the concept of a directorial pantheon. Not so Andrew Sarris, an editor of the avant-garde *Film Culture*, whose rather tentative *Notes on the Auteur Theory in 1962*, followed by a full issue of the magazine devoted to his "pantheon" of American directors, heralded the arrival of *auteurism* in the United States. The cudgels were promptly seized by Pauline Kael, who used them to flail away at both the theory and its proponent in the pages of *Film Quarterly*. The Sarris-Kael controversy, which raged on in the *Quarterly* for more than a year (until a wearied editor cried "Hold, hold, enough!"), served to focus attention not only on the theory, but also on Miss Kael herself.

Despite its ardent advocates, primarily on the college campuses where film was even then being discovered with a vengeance, the *"auteur* theory" had no considerable impact on American criticism. It had little appeal for those critics who came to film from a literary background, and made no sense whatsoever to those aware of the realities that shape Hollywood productions—the uncredited writers, the unheralded editors, the producer who might be a frustrated director at heart, and the ultimate decision-making powers of the front office. Even Sarris, reexamining the *"auteur* theory" in 1970, seems to have retreated from his original position, declaring that it was "never a theory at all, but rather a collection of facts, a reminder of movies to be resurrected, of genres to be redeemed, of directors to be rediscovered." Which is all to the good if one can forget the "pantheonism" that accompanied his original exposition—a terrifyingly rigid ranking of who was great, who was "second line," "third line," or "fallen idol." Significantly, in citing Otto Preminger as one of the directors of the "second line," he speaks of *Laura* as "Preminger's *Citizen Kane*," while actually parts of it were directed by Rouben Mamoulian, listed by Sarris as a "fallen idol." By their credits, not necessarily shall ye know them.

Just possibly, the immediate appeal of *auteurism* to the college crowd was the ability that it afforded them to become, without excessive study, instant authorities. If Sarris inexplicably placed Howard Hawks in his "pantheon," Raoul Walsh in his "third line," and William Wellman among his "fallen idols"—and listed Stanley Kubrick as a "minor disappointment"—then, obviously, you didn't have to see all those movies. You saved both time and money by being able to assess them in advance. But this isn't entirely fair. Because of Sarris's early espousal of the *"auteur* theory," major universities are now offering in-depth studies of the films not only of D. W. Griffith and Sergei Eisenstein, but of Vincente Minnelli and Don Siegel, and are regularly "redeeming" genres like the gangsters, the musicals and the Westerns. And 16mm distributors, who service this market, have regrouped their entries (once arranged simply under country of origin) to emphasize directors, genres and thematic content.

But the newest approach to film analysis is "structural," and demands not a familiarity with *all* films, but simply with a good many of the movies produced within a certain period or genre—horror movies, war movies, the depression musicals, sci-fi pictures, gangsters, the *"film noir,"* the decline and fall of the Western. This approach is less critical than surgical, an analysis based on what *is*, rather than on what is good or bad. Or, for that matter, an analysis based on what *is*, without reference to historical importance, historical context, or audience acceptance. For the structuralists, the public doesn't exist; the film is all—and let's slip it into its proper slot. Let's analyze it thematically, taking note of its congruencies with films in the same genre and where it departs from them. If societies find the myths they need, we can learn about our society from the myths embodied in our movies—and who cares if the film itself is good or bad?

The answer is that the critic cares—and so does the public. There is something marvelous about the way the audiences smell out the right film at the right time. Far better than critics, who are concerned with long-range concepts called "art." Notoriously, critics have derided and shunned popular successes from *Gone With the Wind* to *The Towering Inferno*. But the critic cares about the artistry of the occasion, not the thematics. Art arises out of fitting appropriate esthetic means to the appropriate pragmatic end, whether you are painting the Sistine Chapel or filling a Cinerama screen. The critic is concerned with the esthetics of the work itself, the audience with its own gut reaction of the moment. And neither is to be denied. What can be questioned, however, is the structuralist who comes in well after the fact and, ignoring either critical or audience responses at the time of release, attempts to force a whole series of movies into thematic pigeon holes of his own devising. Not coincidentally, there is a strong relation to *auteurism* here. We have had structural analyses of the films of Howard Hawks, Alfred Hitchcock, Buster Keaton and, in graduate schools throughout the land, God knows who all. The *"auteur"* theory posits a unifying will or intelligence behind each *auteur* movie; the structuralists set out to document it in the myth-related patterns that they find in these films, and the dialectic that either unifies or seemingly contradicts their basic thesis.

Narrowing analysis still further are the semiologists, who seek less to interpret than to describe. Semiology derives from the study of linguistics, and more particularly from the linguistic studies of Christian Metz (who only recently has himself attempted to apply his own discipline to film). It places its reliance on words, on language, to recreate not only what we see, but what we feel as we are seeing. It looks on the film medium as primarily an iconography of images and signs that demand interpretation with scientific precision. Or, as Peter Wollen explains it from his advocacy position, "Unless we understand the code or mode of expression which permits meaning to exist in the cinema, we are condemned to massive imprecision and nebulosity in film criticism, an unfounded reliance on intuition and momentary impressions." Which is all very well except for the fact that, to combat the "imprecision and nebulosity" of film criticism, the semiologists have developed their own *lingua franca* that is understandable only by other semiologists. Describing a scene from Dziga Vertov's *The Man With a Movie Camera* (1929), semiologist Vlada Petric, Luce Professor of Film Studies at Harvard, observed that "The camera's panning continues the previously abstracted montage tempo on a spatial ground, which is also kinesthetic in its own way, thus shifting the viewer's perceptual experience from the stroboscopic montage rhythm to the ontological authenticity of the film image whose cinematic sensation generates from the notion that it represents 'life as it is.' " The higher criticism?

Unfortunately, on too many campuses this pretentious gobbledygook has found a home. Linguistics is an established and respected discipline, while the motion picture is still a somewhat raffish and disreputable art form. Many academics still regard teaching film as just a half-step removed from operating a trade school. In universities that offer not only courses in the performing arts but also law schools, medical schools, business schools and dental schools! The line of distinction is difficult to discern for anyone except the confirmed academic. But the confirmed academic can understand another class in linguistics that is film-related, or a structuralist approach in the Philosophy Department, or even a course on the Egyptian film that can be tied in with African studies. Without question, the motion picture is finding a place on American campuses—but through how many back doors? Why must it be spayed before it can become acceptable?

One last esthetic movement must be mentioned, even though its esthetics have a tendency to vary with just about every practitioner who espouses it. Cinema-verité may be said to have established its validity in 1961 with Jean Rouch and Edgar Morin's *Chronique d'un Été*, in which they asked a random selection of Parisians if they were happy, then later played back the footage to them and recorded their reactions to seeing themselves on film. Rouch, an anthropologist and ethnographer with the Musée de L'Homme in Paris, had made a number of exploratory films before—films on burial rites in Egypt and a fascinating study of a primitive African tribe that had made an idol of a ditched airplane and gave its local dignitaries such oddly urban titles as Pilot, Mailman, and Streetcar Conductor. Although the films themselves were technically inferior (Rouch wouldn't burden himself with a tripod!), they introduced us to remote cultures with all the immediacy—although none of the poetry—of Robert Flaherty at his best. But where Flaherty would have tried to develop a story built around and explicating the life styles of these exotic peoples, Rouch simply documented his findings, convinced that their strangeness would make them interesting.

Cinema-verité translates readily into "film truth," and has ites ideological origins in Dziga-Vertov's *Kino-Pravda* a kind of agit-prop newsreel introduced in the Soviet Union back around 1922. The original *Kino-Pravda* often bent reality to correspond to an ideology; Rouch had the scientist's interest in ferreting out not only facts, but the larger sociological phenomena that confirmed them. In *Chronique d'un Été*, he achieved this more fully than ever before or since.

Once again, however, it was a matter of technology supplying the impetus for a new esthetic. The development of the light, portable, but thoroughly professional 16mm Arriflex camera, the equally portable quartz lights and sun guns and (perhaps above all) the portable Nagra tape recorders with their plug-in capability of reproducing sync sound, gave the documentarians just about everything they needed to go out into the field and come back with footage of acceptable theatrical quality. The labs helped as well, providing a process for blowing up 16mm to 35mm so that it became virtually on a par with the theatrical standard. Others, like the Maysles brothers in the United States, contributed shoulder mounts and gyroscope balances that made the operation of a hand-held camera almost as smooth and steady as a Mitchell on its dolly. Also, the zoomar lens allowed the camera operator to go from long shot to close-up without changing his position (which turned out to be something less than a blessing).

It had to be more than sheer coincidence that even as all of these technological improvements were under way, and even as Rouch, the Maysles, Richard Leacock and many others were taking their first faltering steps toward this new form of documentary, Siegfried Kracauer was working out his *Theory of Film* (published in 1960), significantly subtitled "The Redemption of Physical Reality." Kracauer emphasizes the realistic vs. the "formative" (i.e., staged) tendencies of film, the "found" story vs. the invented plot, because, as he put it, the motion picture "gravitates toward unstaged reality." Ironically, he was writing off most of the movies that had been made up to that point, and ideologically favoring a form of cinema that was just about to be discovered. Actually, as Kracauer pointed out, the movies began with "unstaged reality"—the Lumières' 50-second shot of workmen felling a wall, or the uncredited cameraman who photographed the swans in Central Park for the Edison Company. But the "formative tendency" asserted itself almost immediately when Fatima performed her belly dance before a painted curtain at Edison's New Jersey studio, or Annie Oakley took potshots at clay pigeons. Even before the turn of the century, Georges Méliès had begun to photograph brief *tableaux* in his Théatre Robert Houdin—episodes which he then strung together to form a primitive narrative. Indeed, Kracauer traces the dual "tendencies" of film back to these two sources, Lumière and Méliès. Because the film is essentially a photographic medium, however, and much of the charm of photography is its ability to capture the unexpected or to freeze the fleeting moment in mid-flight, Kracauer argues—far too didactically—that this is the true mission of pure cinema. "Films come into their own," he wrote, "when they record and reveal physical reality. . . . And since any medium is partial to the things it is uniquely equipped to render, the cinema is conceivably animated by a desire to picture transient material life, life at its most ephemeral. Street crowds, involuntary gestures, and other fleeting impressions are its very meat."

Curiously, despite the abundance of documentaries that might have illustrated this thesis, Kracauer preferred to find most of his examples in studio films that embraced some measure of reality, such as Pabst's early *Kameradschaft* (1931) or John Ford's *Grapes of Wrath* (1939). "Staging is aesthetically legitimate to the extent that it evokes the illusion of actuality," he argued. But he favors the "found story," as in Flaherty's *Nanook of the North* (1922) and the "open-endedness" of the Chaplin films, or of De Sica's *The Bicycle Thief* (1949). Above all, what Kracauer cherishes in movies is the sense of a "flow of life"—the moment that was of necessity frozen in time by the still photographer but released by the man with the movie camera. Kracauer was naïve enough to believe that he was providing a useful, pragmatic esthetic to a new generation of studio film makers. Actually, he was supplying a *raison d'être* for a generation of film makers who were to have nothing to do with the studios whatsoever. One wonders how many of them ever read his book.

Consciously or not, the Cinema-verité documentarians have been observing Kracauer's precepts in ways that the good doctor would surely have approved. (He died in 1966.) For them, every picture is a "found story"; ideally, like Flaherty before them, they go into the field without a script, without an outline, without even so much as a preconception. They chose their subject—a person, a tribal custom, an event that is about to take place—and then life writes the scenario. Their function, again ideally, is to capture each moment as it unfolds, using their own perceptions to let us know what is important, to find the revealing gesture or the look that says more than words. The "flow of life" is what their films are all about; and since they are invariably dealing with some very specific segment of time—Jane Fonda rehearsing for a Broadway play, the events at a rock concert or the tour of a rock group, a bunch of Army recruits receiving basic training—they are also perforce "open-ended." We know that, one way or another, life will go on even though there no longer are any cameras around to record it.

While there is a basic consensus that the aims of Cinema-verité (or "direct cinema," as some prefer to call it) are to capture the moment and make it meaningful to the viewer, there is by no means a consensus as to how this can be best accomplished. The argument has divided the movement into two camps. On the one hand, there are the film makers who believe that the camera should be as unobtrusive as in any studio-made story film, that the awareness of cameras and microphones destroys the sense of reality for the audience. No one has been more scrupulous in keeping the paraphernalia of film off the screen than Frederick Wiseman, a lawyer who turned documentary director with the shocking and controversial *Titicut Follies* (1967); he has subsequently scrutinized with his customary noncommittal compassion such samplings of American institutionalism as our police departments (*Law and Order,* 1969), our high schools (*High School,* 1969), our sorely burdened hospitals (*Hospital,* 1970), the Army (*Basic Training,* 1971), and a religious community (*Essene,* 1972). When someone chances to look into the camera in his movies (as happens, momentarily, in *Hospital*), it almost shatters the fabric he has so carefully woven. "The way I try to make a documentary," he once said, "is that there's no separation between the audience watching the film and the events in the film." Such a separation, he feels, would result from any audience awareness of the camera's presence.

At the other end of the stick are such purists as the Maysles brothers, Albert and David, who maintain with no less vehemence that once the camera is actually on the scene, it becomes part of that scene, and to deny its presence is to falsify reality. They make the point (as do many Cinema-verité directors) that they stay with a subject so long that they gradually fade from view, becoming as familiar and unnoticed as the wallpaper or a piece of furniture. "To establish this relationship," says David Maysles, "we have perfected a camera that doesn't make any noise. It helps us get that type of spontaneity, or rapport, without someone being self-conscious because of the equipment." In some of their films, such as *Salesman* (1969), this is astonishingly true; the Bible salesman who has lost confidence in himself and in his work seems to fall apart before our very eyes, and without any show of self-consciousness. (It is also worth noting that lights, microphones and photographic equipment are less in evidence here than in any other of the Maysles films.) In *Showman* (1962), on the other hand, where the showman under observation is the indomitable Joseph E. Levine, it is impossible not to believe that at least part of his flamboyance came from the awareness that he was being photographed from moment to moment. Or, in *Gray Gardens* (1975), that Edith Bouvier Beale, Jr., a failed fashion model and cabaret singer, isn't overcompensating for her years of obscurity by strutting her pathetic stuff for the Maysles cameras. The lights are always in evidence, the microphone is constantly being thrust in her face, she talks through the camera directly to the Maysles. But how much is truth, how much is *film* truth? It's a question that the film poses, then lets each viewer work out for himself.

Obviously, there are deeper concerns here than whether a pitiable ex-socialite thinks she can make some kind of come-back through a feature-length documentary. On a broader scale, doesn't the presence of the media at a tense encounter, like the Watts riots in Los Angeles or the grim confrontations at the 1968 Democratic convention in Chicago, add its own dynamic to the situation? Isn't the reality of the moment altered by the very presence of the Cinema-verité camera? To pursue this a step further, in filming *Gimme Shelter* (1970), which follows the Rolling Stones' cross-country tour that climaxed so tragically at Altamont, the Maysles' cameras quite by accident caught the moment of the fatal stabbing that put a period to the whole era of happy hippiedom in the United States. In preparing their film, the stabbing—not the tour—became the central event. An entire sequence was added in which the fracas was reprised, this time in slow motion, for the benefit of Mick Jagger, lead singer of the Rolling Stones, who was in turn photographed while watching the footage on the Maysles' Steenbeck. While this is an extreme case, it underlines the fact that the nature of the filmed reality can be significantly altered in the editing stage long after the event itself.

And what about sound? Thanks to the portability of the Nagra recorder, sound can now be recorded just about any-where—in rooms, the streets, a moving car, the open country-side. Indeed, probably the most ubiquitous image of our time, thanks to television, is the man with the microphone soliciting a "spontaneous" man-in-the-street reaction to the daily head-lines, or the headline-maker himself pausing in the midst of his busy day to deliver a 30-second profundity for the benefit of your roving reporter. It's the camera as tape recorder, of course, with the image merely confirming that the words we are hearing were actually spoken by Jimmy Carter, or verify-ing (to a certain extent) that the man-in-the-street is really a man in the street and not an actor hired for the occasion by the television station. What these clips cannot do is to assure us that we have heard *all* of Carter's words on the given subject, or that the random sampling of street opinion is quite as random as it seems. In fact, the effect is often just the opposite. We know that no politician has ever limited his remarks to 30 seconds, and we can also sense that if the street interviews produced, say, 8 pros and 3 cons on any given subject, television will "balance" the news by giving us 2 of each. In other words, sound is every bit as manipulable as the image. Without the slightest alteration of the original statement, the film maker can select only those sentences that he thinks are important or that he wants his audience to hear.

But this kind of editing, which is every bit as common in Cinema-verité as on television's six o'clock news, is only one aspect of the problems raised by the sound track. Happily, the time-honored device of the voice-over narrator has largely disappeared from the documentary scene, an uncherished hold-over from a time when direct dialogue recording in the field was both cumbersome and costly. And although there were always a few who could write imaginative, poetic narrations (one thinks of Pare Lorentz and Archibald MacLeish in this country, W. H. Auden and Dylan Thomas in England), too often the voice-overs turned the films into illustrated lectures, the words serving as crutches for the limping visuals. But what has taken its place? Just as television has accustomed us to the man-in-the-street type of interview, it has also accustomed us to the *Face the Nation* sort of thing where a panel of "experts" are quizzed on a specific topic by one or more presumably knowledgeable newsmen (or Barbara Walters). There are also programs, considerably rarer, where the interviewer and his questions have been edited out, and what we are left with are simply the responses of the interviewee, spliced together into what one hopes is coherence.

All of these devices are available to, and have been used by, the Cinema-verité documentarians. Which is hardly surprising since, for many, television is their main outlet, and public service TV their main source of income. Since generally their films are aired first and then marketed in 16mm, it would probably be more surprising if they *didn't* incorporate television techniques. For verification, one need only look to Canada, England, France and West Germany, all of which have flourishing Cinema-verité movements, and all of which have state-operated television networks that are hospitable to this kind of film making. In Canada, there is Allan King, whose *Warrendale* (1966) boldly championed a new and still-controversial treatment for the mentally disturbed, and whose *A Married Couple* (1969) documents with shattering honesty the not-so-private lives of a young couple on the verge of breaking up. Many of the National Film Board of Canada's documentaries are either produced for or eventually are seen over the Canadian Broadcasting Corporation's network, and the CBC has its own documentary production unit. England's BBC has long backed Denis Mitchell's documentaries, heavily dependent upon the direct interview approach—and has tended to shy away from Peter Watkins's brilliant adaptation of the Cinema-verité style in such artful, if controversial, works as *Culloden* (1964), the re-creation of an eighteenth-century battle in Scotland, and his profoundly disturbing projections of the world of tomorrow today, *The War Game* (1966) and *Punishment Park* (1971). Where Wiseman observes reality and turns it into drama, Watkins creates drama and makes it seem like observed reality. No small part of his success, however, is his skillful simulation of the techniques of the realist film makers, the techniques of Cinema-verité. In West Germany, practically all of the younger film makers—Fassbinder, Kluge, Herzog, Straub, Wenders—have consolidated their positions by working extensively in the television medium, and more often than not in some very personal variation on the Cinema-verité approach.

For film makers working in this area, the basic question would seem to go considerably beyond Kracauer's "realist" vs. "formative" formulations. It is really a matter of goals. As a film maker, do you want to inform or amuse? People buy their tickets to a movie house because they want to be entertained—which is only a cliché if one thinks of entertainment solely in terms of movie musicals, light comedies and brainless Westerns. But people have also been entertained by such films as *The Grapes of Wrath*, *The Pawnbroker*, and *All the President's Men*, all of which addressed themselves to fairly serious subjects. They learned to hate war in *All Quiet on the Western Front*, to fear native fascism in *The Black Legion* and *All the King's Men;* while a whole series of notably successful films—*Pride of the Marines, Gentleman's Agreement, Pinky, The Defiant Ones, Guess Who's Coming to Dinner, Voyage of the Damned*—have spoken out against racism and anti-Semitism. But it has always been the entertainment values that attracted the audiences. The same issues treated

straight, without the added lures of stars and story, have
never been able to draw more than a fraction of the already-
convinced to the box office.

On the other hand, television reaches literally millions of
viewers every night, at least some of whom are eager to
switch away from *Kojak* and *Starsky and Hutch*. The various
NBC White Papers and CBS Reports may not be the most
creative forms of documentary, but they have stimulated a
taste for factual reportage that today is being fed not only by
the Maysles brothers, Ricky Leacock's Cinema-verité films
for Drew Associates, and the continuingly astonishing camera
explorations of Frederick Wiseman, but by such masterful
European efforts as Marcel Ophul's *The Sorrow and the Pity*
(1970) and *The Memory of Justice* (1976)—four-hour com-
pilations of film clips and direct interviews that manage to be
at once objective and humanistic, suffused with the
resonances of history absorbed and understood. With an
added 16mm life in schools and colleges, in museums and so-
cially oriented organizations, this is a field that has only begun to realize its potential.

New Directors, New Directions

Back in 1951, director Mervyn LeRoy wrote a book on
"how to get a job in the movie industry—told in specific,
practical and detailed terms." He called it *It Takes More
Than Talent*, and his thesis seemed to be that if you want a
top job in a studio, you must first make it big somewhere
else. Traditionally, the motion picture industry, unlike any
other major industry in the United States, has been indifferent
to any kind of apprenticeship programs or scholarships that
might enable studio technicians to enhance their skills
through outside learning, the theory being that they could always afford to buy the best whenever they needed anything
or anyone. With the pinch of television, this snug theory lost
some of its appeal. On one occasion, toward the end of the
fifties, a number of key executives in New York met with
some university people to explore the possibility of subsi-
dizing university film departments in the hope of developing
fresh talents—but it soon became evident that the fresh talents they were talking about were suitable replacements (at
considerably less cost) for such superstars as Marlon Brando
and Elizabeth Taylor. The negotiations were abruptly termi-

nated when the university people pointed out that they offer training in just about every aspect of film making *but* acting.

Back in the thirties, MGM had what it called a "junior writers program," ostensibly to train young writers. Actually, it meant that the studio was getting feature scripts from young professionals who were being paid a mere $50 or $75 a week. The program disappeared once the newly formed Screen Writers Guild established a $150 per week minimum wage. Similarly, several of the studios have set up "talent schools" from time to time where promising young actors and actresses, under contract to the studio at minimum salaries, receive not only acting lessons but lessons in speech, manners, dress, deportment, etc., and are on occasion called upon to perform bit roles in features or, more often, in the television series being produced on the lot. Clint Eastwood recalls that after a year in Universal's "Golden Circle," he withdrew because the studio refused to advance him from $100 to $125 a week, as stipulated in his contract, but offered to keep him on for another six months without a raise. Some measure of the status of these training programs may be deduced from a 20th Century-Fox executive's description of the school on his own lot (which has since passed out of existence). He referred to it as "the deer park."

So far as the technicians go, however, it has always been strictly a matter of on-the-job training, with no schools or special classes to hasten the process. If a young man (or, more recently, young woman) is accepted into one of the craft unions, he can count on two years of the most menial labor—carrying cans, loading film, lugging cameras—before even beginning to approach the more technical aspects of his chosen profession, and usually no less than eight before he reaches the status of a full cinematographer, editor or sound recordist. Actually, unless one is extremely fortunate—or better yet, extremely well connected—the process of moving up the ladder in the craft unions is apt to take considerably longer than the stipulated eight years thanks to such considerations as seniority rosters, number of consecutive days worked, and similar rulings designed by the unions (with the complicity of the studios) to protect their senior citizens. Just getting into these unions is itself a major feat, more often achieved by nepotism or family friendships than by merit. And once in, everything seems designed to discourage the person of talent, not to mention the person of genius. When the power of the industry was concentrated in eight major studios, there was ample reason for the formation of the craft unions. Hours were often unreasonably long, wages unreasonably low—with no time-and-a-half for overtime. The unions were formed to correct these abuses, and over the years they have succeeded. At this point, however, it seems fair to say that they are mindlessly strangling the goose that lays their golden eggs.

So long as on-the-job training was the only form of preparation that was available, this system—for all its regrettable inadequacies and inequities—was acceptable. But beginning with the sixties, as in journalism during the thirties, there has been a mushrooming of film schools and film courses. By 1978, over 1,000 colleges and universities were offering more than 9,000 courses in film and television to about 40,500 students; more than 300 of these are graduate programs leading to advanced degrees in film, television, or a related field, such as journalism; while the number of students studying film as non-majors has been estimated by the American Film Institute as over 200,000. In other words, many schools were graduating students who were qualified—often more than qualified—to move directly into the technical areas dominated by the unions and guilds. The guilds governing directors, writers and actors have remained relatively open; anyone getting a job in one of these fields is not only eligible to join, but required to. Not so the craft unions. Despite programs offering generous benefits for early retirement, they remain difficult to get into and persist in ignoring academic credits that might enable a young person to move ahead more rapidly than the eight years specified by union regulations. As a result, while there are thousands of film school graduates plying their trade, the majority are doing so far from the major studios—making commercials, documentaries, educationals and nuts-and-bolts informationals in smaller shops not covered by union contracts. Talented young people who might have gone into feature production, and often wanted to, have been denied access by labor unions intent on protecting the jobs of their older members and the good old-fashioned way of doing business. Many of the older cameramen, for example, have balked at using the newer, more mobile cameras and lighting equipment, while their union has insisted on "featherbedding" whenever these technological innovations are utilized, thus substantially reducing the economies that might be realized. In an industry that for more than a decade has been in the throes of change, the unions act as a sheet-anchor to hold it to the past.

All this might have passed unnoticed had not the industry discovered, late in the sixties, that the pattern of movie attendance had altered. In 1968, an industry-sponsored survey by the Donald Sindlinger organization turned up the startling statistic that some 48 percent of the domestic box-office receipts was accounted for by the 16-to-24 age bracket. The movies had what was thereafter referred to as a "youth market"—and the immediate problem became how best to serve it. To studio executives and independent producers alike, the answer was obvious: hire young people. And almost overnight, the walls that traditionally surrounded the studios—walls that often seemed to have been constructed specifically to keep the novice out—began to crumble. For new directors and writers, the producers turned instinctively to the proliferating film schools. MPAA President Jack Valenti made repeated appearances on college campuses, occasionally accompanied by seasoned film makers such as Stanley Kramer, to stress the industry's interest in the "now" generation. Through such activities as the sponsorship of student film competitions and support for the newly established American Film Institute, Valenti made every effort to lend substance to his words.

And the movies began to change. Fresh out of UCLA, with a masters degree in Cinema (and one sexploitation film under his belt), came Francis Ford Coppola, whose *You're a Big Boy Now* (1967) proved precedental in reaching and developing this new audience. At American-International, which hitherto had specialized in such youth-oriented fare as *Beach Blanket Bingo* (1965), the youthful Roger Corman led the way with such films as *The Wild Angels* (1966) and *Wild in the Streets* (1968)—and, not coincidentally, gave employment to a whole new generation of young film makers. Among them was Peter Bogdanovich, an actor who had also done some off-Broadway directing, but who was beginning to build a reputation as a film critic and historian. Corman entrusted him with the second unit work on *Wild Angels*, then backed him on a low-budgeted action movie, *Targets* (1968), on which much of his subsequent fame has rested. The first of the sniper-in-the-tower pictures, it not only incorporated moments of technical brilliance recalling Hitchcock, but also money-saving minutes from an earlier Corman movie (*The Terror*, 1963) starring Boris Karloff and Jack Nicholson. But the runaway success of 1968 was Mike Nichols' *The Graduate*, with Dustin Hoffman as the youthful nonconformist whose attentions are almost equally divided between his girl friend (Katharine Ross) and her mother (Anne Bancroft). It encapsulated to perfection the disillusion and disaffection of the Vietnam generation with the materialistic values and hypocritical morality of their elders. The following year, Hoffman was starred again in *Midnight Cowboy*, this time as the streetwise mentor of a blond, blue-eyed stud from Texas (Jon Voight). As directed by John Schlesinger, it became one of the biggest and most talked-about hits of 1969. Both films served to reveal to studio executives that the "youth market" was indeed a profitable reality, and for the next few years "youth must be served" became the industry's watchword.

But with what? Apart from the obvious youth-orientation of their themes, both *The Graduate* and *Midnight Cowboy* were wholly conventional in their treatment, with none of the stunning visual impact and originality of Michelangelo Antonioni's earlier *Blow-Up*. Filmed in London in 1966, the picture spoke in an oddly oblique way of contemporary man's detachment from life and reality (for which the protagonist's occupation and array of photographic equipment served as a particularly apt metaphor). Its style, its symbols, its deliberate imprecision may have mystified the more stolid industry types—and irked many of the American critics as well; nevertheless, *Blow-Up* promptly became the "in" film for the college crowd, which returned to it repeatedly in order to analyze and interpret its challenging layers of meaning. Obviously, this was a real "youth" movie. The lightning failed to strike twice, however. When MGM brought Antonioni to the United States to film *Zabriskie Point* (1970), which viewed American materialism with a decidedly bilious eye, it was clearly hoping for a movie that would be even more appealing and prestigious than its predecessor. Instead, they got a pretentious bore—one that very quickly disappeared amidst the plethora of youth-oriented movies in 1970. The critics also attacked Antonioni's presumption in taking on a film so derogatory of a life style that he barely knew.

On the other hand, there was *Easy Rider* (1969), which had actually begun as a 16mm exploration of the American scene. Columbia executives saw the early footage (the New

Orleans sequence), and gave the go-ahead to Dennis Hopper to complete the film. Hopper, an alumnus of Roger Corman's innumerable "bike" movies (as were Peter Fonda and Jack Nicholson, who made the film with him), turned it into the ultimate "trip"—a trip from Los Angeles into the heart of the redneck Southland, a trip through the cultures and counter-cultures of late-sixties America, a trip into doing "your own thing in your own time." The trip included the drug scene and alcoholism, idealistic communes and venal cops, fun-loving prostitutes and fun-hating rurals. Largely improvised, the script captured the "now" feeling—the restless search for freedom, the deep-felt need for meaningful relationships—like no other film before and few since. And if, in the end, the hopes and dreams were shattered by the mindless blasts of a couple of crackers ridding the land of two long-haired "hippies," this too bespoke the prevailing defensive attitude of a generation that had learned to distrust and fear its elders, and what Joseph Morgenstern has termed their "wanton destruction of harmlessness."

Above all, what *Easy Rider* demonstrated, to the consternation of the studios, was that a movie could be produced for less than $500,000 and gross more than $40,000,000. These were statistics that they were neither familiar with nor able to cope with—as evidenced by the fact that Universal, possibly the most conservative studio remaining in Hollywood, promptly offered an almost unlimited purse to Dennis Hopper to film *The Last Movie* (1971), and to Peter Fonda (the producer as well as co-star of *Easy Rider*) for a pseudo-Western titled *The Hired Hand* (1971). Both proved impossibly pretentious; both lost a great deal of money. Obviously, the youth audience was not to be seduced on the same terms that had served Hollywood so well in the past. Indeed, 1970 and 1971 provided a virtual litany of youth-oriented movies that, for one reason or another, fell wide of the mark—*Getting Straight, The Magic Garden of Stanley Sweetheart, R.P.M., The Strawberry Statement, Zabriskie Point* (all 1970), *Drive, He Said, Making It* and *Taking Off* (all 1971). It wasn't so much a matter of audience satiation as of the films themselves, almost all of them backed by major studios, being designed after the fact, not following the intuitions of film makers who were really "with it." Without question, Donald Cammell and Nicholas Roeg's *Performance* (starring Mick Jagger, 1970) alienated vast sections of the American moviegoing public; but there were also vast sections of American youth (not necessarily habitual moviegoers) who were with Mick Jagger and bought the camp of his king-sized bathtubs and harem-sized beds. *Joe*, low-budgeted and independently produced, also alienated many—some for its vivid depiction of drug-oriented youth, others for its seeming indictment of white- (and blue-) collar prejudices. In the long view, neither was correct; the picture happened to touch a particularly sensitive nerve—and possibly simply because it waffled any special point of view, it became one of the surprise hits of 1970. So was *Little Fauss and Big Halsey*, with a motorcycle background and Robert Redford as the existential (meaning without conscience) hero. Again a youth-oriented movie, it established Redford as a major star and his co-star, Michael J. Pollard, as a kind of cult hero. In all of these films, the real excitement lay in the fact that they were *discovered*, not *sold*.

Perhaps the biggest discovery of 1970 was *Five Easy Pieces*, which reunited many of the talented behind-the-scenes people of *Easy Rider* in another picture that quite clearly had its finger on the pulse of alienated young Americans. Here was yet another alienated youth, Robert Eroica Dupea (Jack Nicholson), an accomplished pianist working in an oil field. With Rayette (Karen Black), his mistress of the moment, he returns to the family seat in Washington, there to achieve an uneasy peace with his aged father—and to seduce his brother's intended. It's the story of a young man for whom everything is much too easy, and at the same time far too hard. An intriguingly ambiguous finale in which Dupea deserts Rayette raises the question of whether he was doing it for his sake or hers. It's a picture that never answers questions, merely poses them, and forces us to search our own hearts to understand the tangled motivations of everyone in the film. Like *Blow-Up*, it invited interpretation and avoided easy answers. Like *Blow-Up*, it was quickly assimilated, and cherished, by the youth audience.

The same was true of *Carnal Knowledge* (1971), Mike Nichols's superbly disenchanted view of the relationship between the sexes, arguing in effect that without love, sex becomes first a game, and ultimately merely a commercial arrangement. Never has Nichols been more precise in spelling out the *modus vivendi* of his characters, their starry-eyed early hopes, their middle-aged willingness to settle for considerably less. Again, the youth audience subscribed whole-heartedly to his theory. The picture, which starred Nicholson, Ann-Margret, Candice Bergen and one of the top recording stars, Art Garfunkle, became a solid commercial hit despite—or perhaps because of—the utter detachment of Nichols's (and Jules Feiffer's) all-too-human comedy. It was, in the contemporary argot, "cool," an appellation that was also frequently used to describe Stanley Kubrick's nightmare version of future shock, *A Clockwork Orange* (1971)—in contrast to the "trip" involvement of his earlier *2001: A Space Odyssey* (1968).

What these films—and others—had in common to win them their youthful following was their articulation of con-temporary attitudes and emotions, in a language that had its own modern rhythms and nuances. Just as rock carried popu-lar music beyond the conventional patterns of ballads and blues, creating a sound and a beat that often conveyed more emotion and meaning than the words themselves, so too did these "now" movies break away from conventional story structure, classic camera techniques and editing. As Godard put it, these movies had a beginning, a middle and an end—but not necessarily in that order. For the first time, pictures were being shown to a generation that had not grown up in a movie house, a generation that had spent a staggering total of hours looking at moving images on a television tube. During the sixties, Marshall McLuhan repeatedly referred to it as an "eye-minded" generation, and noted that its perceptions were no longer "linear," which comes from reading books, but in-stantaneous assimilations of the whole of a scene. One has only to view an old movie with a young audience to realize that the kids have gotten the message of a shot almost at the first flash; when it remains on the screen, they giggle because the protraction seems to underline what is, for them, the ob-vious. As a result, editing tempos have had to be stepped up. Indeed, thanks to this "eye-minded" generation, the whole syntax of the screen has undergone a change. The slam-bam cutaways of live or taped television have virtually eliminated all taste for the discreet cutting on movement that Pabst in-troduced so many years ago. Similarly, the constrictive close-ups of television have become so common that Ingmar Bergman could blow up from 16mm two of his TV series in Sweden, *Scenes from a Marriage* (1974) and *Face to Face* (1976), and have them accepted as completely suitable cinematic fare. (Conversely, it should also be noted that many of the American *Movies of the Week*, produced in this country specifically for television, are released abroad as feature pictures for theatrical distribution.) Thanks to rock concerts and recordings, even sound has undergone a change. In *McCabe and Mrs. Miller* (1971) and again in *Nashville* (1975), Robert Altman suggested that the ambience of the sound track might be more important than the information it conveys.

Obviously, all of this posits a marked change in the sensibilities behind the camera. Altman, like many others, moved up from industrials and TV series. Richard Lester, whose *A Hard Day's Night* (1964) and *Petulia* (1968) were frontrunners of the new style, came out of television commercials. But more than anything else, it was the success of George Lucas's *American Graffiti* (1973) that convinced the studios to look to the film schools for their "now" talent, for the young people who could handle the "newspeak" of that crucial 16-to-24 age bracket. *Graffiti* recalled the early sixties, when John Kennedy was in office and all seemed right with the world. Mel's neon-lit diner was the social center for the high school crowd, and tomorrow was another year. The film's sound track, a composite of the Top 40's from the fifties and early sixties, laid down a wall-to-wall carpet of instant nostalgia. The picture jolted (especially in its rollcall of the dead just before the final credits); but it also reminded us of the bright promise of a world that was abruptly terminated by an assassin's bullet in Dallas. Essentially, for all its youthful high spirits, the film was a *billet-doux* to a generation cheated of its birthright, a memoir contrasting what was with what might have been.

Lucas, a graduate of the film school at the University of Southern California, first demonstrated his remarkable talent in a dramatic short that he had written and directed as a student project, *THX 1138* (which he subsequently developed into a feature for Warner Brothers). The short, depicting a man's frenzied attempts to escape from a computer-regulated society of the future, not only won dozens of international awards, but earned Lucas a six-month scholarship at the Warner studio "to observe." There he had the good fortune to come under the expansive wing of Francis Ford Coppola, who was then working on *Finian's Rainbow* (1968). Coppola took him on as an assistant on his next film, *The Rain People* (1969), and suggested that Lucas film a behind-the-scenes documentary on the making of that movie. When his 40-minute *Filmmaker* (1969) was better received than the feature, Warner permitted him to expand *THX 1138* (1971) to feature length. Because this film was less than successful at the box office, however, the studio lost interest in him and Lucas encountered considerable difficulty in getting his next project, which was *American Graffiti,* off the ground. In fact, not until Coppola, fresh from his triumph as director of *The Godfather* (1972), agreed to serve as producer and in effect guarantee the film despite its low budget, would Universal agree to put it into production. The rest, as they say, is history—but that history would be incomplete without noting that Lucas brought onto the film many of his former classmates from USC, including Gary Kurtz (co-producer), Walter Murch (sound recordist) and Willard Huyck (screenplay—with Lucas and Gloria Katz, formerly a student at UCLA Cinema). For all of them, it marked the real jump-off point for important careers.

Actually, the number of film school graduates who had established themselves among the mainstream film makers by the mid-seventies (often with Francis Ford Coppola's or Roger Corman's aid) is decidedly impressive. For many, writing provided the key to the kingdom; by first establishing a reputation with a series of successful scripts, they were able to move on to the ultimate dream of all film students: directing. Others—like Brian de Palma, John Hancock, Martin Scorsese and, of course, George Lucas—based their reputations on their student films and worked their way to their present eminence by proving that these were no mere flukes. Ironically, they have become the new establishment, keeping in close contact with each other and offering jobs to those they knew, and liked to work with, in their student days. Above all, they are film buffs, who love their medium and know it well.

In the Hollywood of the mid-seventies, de Palma, the Huycks, Lucas, John Milius, Paul Schrader, Scorsese, David Ward, possibly Peter Bogdanovich, certainly Steven Spielberg (who, although not a film student, made a half-hour movie that unlocked the doors for him at Universal)—these are the "in" group, and presumably will go on to greater fame and considerably more fortune. But the sad fact is that they represent but a fraction, important a fraction as it may be, of the students being graduated from colleges and universities every year. What happens to the rest of them? Some, inevitably, go back into the colleges and universities as teachers. Others move into television, industrials, commercials, educationals, documentaries, sales films, travel films, experimental and underground films—the list is endless.

But it is only just beginning. The era of videotape and the cassette is already upon us. There is cable TV, and closed circuit television for both theaters and schools. Experts have announced that within a few short years it will be possible to bounce at least 300 channels via satellite directly into the home. MCA has already displayed its Discovision, a phonograph disc that plays the movie of your choice through your own television receiver. Hotels now make it possible to phone the front desk and select the picture you want to see in your room that night. With the spread of cable systems, satellite channels, discs and cassettes, the vast amounts of program material required will have to come from somewhere. Where? From the generation of film students in colleges and universities at this very moment. The past decade has seen an enormous growth in regional theater. Why not a similar growth in regional films? The land mass of the United States, after all, is roughly equivalent to the land mass of Europe. And yet we can differentiate between Italian films and French, English and German, Swedish and Polish, Spanish and Czechoslovakian. At the moment, however, American films are polarized; they are made in either Los Angeles or New York, with perhaps a brief stop-over in Chicago. Given the multiplicity of technological choices that lie before us, this need no longer be the case. A story indigenous to Texas, made by Texans, can be shown and understood in northern Michigan. A story rooted in northern Michigan, such as *Anatomy of a Murder* (1959), might possibly be made better by indigenous Michiganders than by a team from Hollywood that moves into the area with its pre-formed script and preconceptions.

What I'm arguing is a film that recognizes the multiplicity of this vast country, a film that places differences above similarities. Each year, our colleges and universities are turning out thousands of students technically equipped to handle this challenge. And each year we come closer to the moment when their special expertise will be demanded. Critics have written about the imminent demise of film, which may well be the case. But film is simply a chemically coated acetate base. The images, which are our prime concern, can be as well presented on discs, video-tape or cassettes, and made at costs that are a mere fraction of today's studio budgets. In other words, the liveliest art is still lively, still evolving. The new forms of what Robert Gessner once called "the moving image" will certainly require new techniques to cope with the new technology. Can anyone today presume to discuss the esthetics of three-dimensional laser images free-floating in space? And what about the esthetics of Aldous Huxley's long-awaited "feelies," which even now may be on somebody's drawing board? But regardless of new inventions and new techniques, the impulses that inspired the first film makers remain the same—to inform, to instruct, to entertain. Out of these have come a potent educational tool and a powerful art form. It seems unlikely that this medium will ever just disappear. We need it too badly. And many of us love it too well.

General Index

Index to Film Titles